Azure Databricks Cookbook

D1607048

Accelerate and scale real-time analytics solutions
using the Apache Spark-based analytics service

Phani Raj

Vinod Jaiswal

BIRMINGHAM—MUMBAI

Azure Databricks Cookbook

Copyright © 2021 Packt Publishing

Group Product Manager: Kunal Parikh
Publishing Product Manager: Aditi Gour
Senior Editor: Mohammed Yusuf Imaratwale
Content Development Editor: Sean Lobo
Technical Editor: Devanshi Ayare
Copy Editor: Safis Editing
Project Coordinator: Aparna Ravikumar Nair
Proofreader: Safis Editing
Indexer: Manju Arasan
Production Designer: Jyoti Chauhan

First published: September 2021

Production reference: 2150921

Published by Packt Publishing Ltd.
Livery Place
35 Livery Street
Birmingham
B3 2PB, UK.

ISBN 978-1-78980-971-8

www.packt.com

Contributors

About the authors

Phani Raj is an Azure data architect at Microsoft. He has more than 12 years of IT experience and works primarily on the architecture, design, and development of complex data warehouses, OLTP, and big data solutions on Azure for customers across the globe.

Vinod Jaiswal is a data engineer at Microsoft. He has more than 13 years of IT experience and works primarily on the architecture, design, and development of complex data warehouses, OLTP, and big data solutions on Azure using Azure data services for a variety of customers. He has also worked on designing and developing real-time data processing and analytics reports from the data ingested from streaming systems using Azure Databricks.

About the reviewers

Ankur Nayyar is an architect who builds and deploys advanced, customer-specific big data analytics solutions using his advanced knowledge of data architecture, data mining, machine learning, computer programming, and emerging open source technologies such as Apache Spark. He stays up to date with the recent advancements in the machine learning/AI industry, such as TensorFlow, and actively prototypes with these open source frameworks. He has participated in internal and external technology and data science forums, competitions, conferences, and discussions.

Alan Bernardo Palacio is a data scientist and an engineer with vast experience in different engineering fields. His focus has been the development and application of state-of-the-art data products and algorithms in several industries. He has worked for companies such as Ernst and Young, Globant, and now holds a data engineer position at Ebiquity Media helping the company to create a scalable data pipeline. Alan graduated with a mechanical engineering degree from the National University of Tucuman in 2015, participated as the founder in startups, and later on earned a master's degree from the Faculty of Mathematics in the Autonomous University of Barcelona in 2017. Originally from Argentina, he now works and resides in the Netherlands.

Table of Contents

Preface

1

Creating an Azure Databricks Service

2

Reading and Writing Data from and to Various Azure Services and File Formats

3

Understanding Spark Query Execution

4
Working with Streaming Data

5

Integrating with Azure Key Vault, App Configuration, and Log Analytics

6
Exploring Delta Lake in Azure Databricks

7
Implementing Near-Real-Time Analytics and Building a Modern Data Warehouse

8
Databricks SQL

9
DevOps Integrations and Implementing CI/CD for Azure Databricks

10

Understanding Security and Monitoring in Azure Databricks

Preface

Azure Databricks provides the latest and older versions of Apache Spark and allows you to integrate with various Azure resources for orchestrating, deploying, and monitoring your big data solution. This book shows you how you can ingest and transform data coming from various sources and formats and build a modern data warehouse solution that meets the demands of near real-time data requirements in the data warehouse.

You will begin with how to spin up an Azure Databricks service and what cluster options are available. You will gain knowledge of how to process data from various files formats and sources, including Kafka, Event Hub, Azure SQL Databases, Azure Synapse Analytics, and Cosmos DB. Once you know how to read and write data from and to various sources, you will be building end-to-end big data solutions using large datasets and streaming data.

Once the big data solution has been built, you will learn how to deploy notebooks to various environments such as UAT and production. Later on, you will learn security aspects associated with data isolation, where you will learn how to restrict access to the data in ADLS that AAD users can see while reading the data from Azure Databricks. Finally, you will learn how to monitor your Azure Databricks cluster utilization by learning about Ganglia reports.

Who this book is for

This book is for anyone who wants to learn how to ingest and process data from various Azure sources using Azure Databricks and build a modern data warehouse. This book takes a recipe-based approach to help you learn how to ingest, process, secure, deploy, and monitor the big data solution you have built on Azure Databricks. Working knowledge of Spark and a familiarity with the basics of Azure should be sufficient to get started on this book.

What this book covers

Chapter 1, Creating an Azure Databricks Service, explains how to create an Azure Databricks service from the Azure portal, Azure CLI, and ARM templates. You will get to understand the different types of clusters in Azure Databricks, while also learning how to add users and groups and how to authenticate to Azure Databricks using a personal access token.

Chapter 2, Reading and Writing Data from and to Various Azure Services and File Formats, explains how to read and write data from and to various data sources, including Azure SQL DB, Azure Synapse Analytics, ADLS Gen2, Storage Blob, Azure Cosmos, CSV, JSON, and Parquet formats. You will be using native connectors for Azure SQL and an Azure Synapse dedicated pool to read and write the data for improved performance.

Chapter 3, Understanding Spark Query Execution, dives deep into query execution and explains how to check the Spark execution plan and learn more about input, shuffle, and output partitions. You will get to understand the different types of joins while working with data frames. Also, you will learn about a few commonly used session-level configurations for changing partitions.

Chapter 4, Working with Streaming Data, explains how to ingest streaming data from HDInsight Kafka clusters, Event Hub, and Event Hub for Kafka, and how to perform certain transformations and write the output to Spark tables and Delta tables for downstream consumers. You will get to know the various options to use while ingesting data from streaming sources.

Chapter 5, Integrating with Azure Key Vault, App Configuration, and Log Analytics, integrates Azure Databricks with Azure resources such as Azure Key Vault and App Configuration to store credentials and secrets that will be read from Azure Databricks notebooks and explains how to integrate Azure Databricks with Log Analytics for telemetry.

Chapter 6, Exploring Delta Lake in Azure Databricks, explains how to use Delta for batch and streaming data in Azure Databricks. You will also understand how Delta Engine will assist in making your queries run faster.

Chapter 7, Implementing Near-Real-Time Analytics and Building a Modern Data Warehouse, explains how to implement an end-to-end big data solution where you read data from streaming sources such as Event Hub for Kafka, as well as from batch sources such as ADLS Gen-2, and perform various data transformations on data and later store the data in destinations such as Azure Cosmos DB, Azure Synapse Analytics, and Delta Lake. You will build a modern data warehouse and orchestrate the end-to-end pipeline using Azure Data Factory. You will be performing near real-time analytics using notebook visualizations and Power BI.

Chapter 8, Databricks SQL, explains how to run ad hoc SQL queries on the data in your data lake. You will get to know how to create SQL endpoints with multi clusters, write queries, create various visualizations in Data Lake, and create dashboards.

Chapter 9, DevOps Integrations and Implementing CI/CD for Azure Databricks, details how to integrate Azure DevOps Repo and GitHub with Databricks notebooks. You will learn how to implement Azure DevOps CI/CD for deploying notebooks across various environments (UAT and production) as well as how to deploy Azure Databricks resources using ARM templates and automate deployment using the Azure DevOps release pipeline.

Chapter 10, Understanding Security and Monitoring in Azure Databricks, covers pass-through authentication in Azure Databricks and how to restrict access to ADLS Gen-2 using RBAC and ACLs so that users can read data to which they have access from Azure Databricks. You will learn how to deploy Azure Databricks in a VNet as well as how to securely access the data in an ADLS Gen-2 storage account.

To get the most out of this book

This book is for data engineers, data analysts, and data scientists who are familiar with Spark and have some knowledge of Azure. If you understand the basics of Spark and want to learn how to build an end-to-end data pipeline in Azure Databricks and productionize it, then this book is for you. Data scientists and business analysts with some knowledge of SQL who want to run ad hoc queries on large volumes of data using Databricks SQL will also find this book useful.

Basic knowledge of Python and PySpark is all you need to understand and execute the code:

Software/hardware covered in the book	OS requirements
Python 3.6 +	Windows, macOS, and Linux (any)
Latest Az PowerShell module	Windows

If you are using the digital version of this book, we advise you to type the code yourself or access the code via the GitHub repository (link available in the next section). Doing so will help you avoid any potential errors related to the copying and pasting of code.

Download the example code files

You can download the example code files for this book from GitHub at `https://github.com/PacktPublishing/Azure-Databricks-Cookbook`. In case there's an update to the code, it will be updated on the existing GitHub repository.

We also have other code bundles from our rich catalog of books and videos available at `https://github.com/PacktPublishing/`. Check them out!

Download the color images

We also provide a PDF file that has color images of the screenshots/diagrams used in this book. You can download it here: `https://static.packt-cdn.com/downloads/9781789809718_ColorImages.pdf`.

Conventions used

There are a number of text conventions used throughout this book.

`Code in text`: Indicates code words in text, database table names, folder names, filenames, file extensions, pathnames, dummy URLs, user input, and Twitter handles. Here is an example: "`--location -l`: The Azure region where the workspace will be created."

A block of code is set as follows:

```
$appId="sdasdasdsdfsa7-xxx-xxx-xx-xx"
$appSecret="xxxxxxx~.xxxxxxjgx"
$tenantId="xxxxx-xxx-xx-xxxx-xxxcdxxxxxx"
$subscriptionName="Pay As You Go"
$resourceGroup = "CookbookRG
```

Any command-line input or output is written as follows:

```
az databricks workspace update
```

Bold: Indicates a new term, an important word, or words that you see on screen. For example, words in menus or dialog boxes appear in the text like this. Here is an example: "We will select **New Job Cluster** here, select **Edit** option and provide the cluster configuration for the new cluster."

> **Tips or important notes**
> Appear like this.

Sections

In this book, you will find several headings that appear frequently (*Getting ready*, *How to do it...*, *How it works...*, *There's more...*, and *See also*).

To give clear instructions on how to complete a recipe, use these sections as follows:

Getting ready

This section tells you what to expect in the recipe and describes how to set up any software or any preliminary settings required for the recipe.

How to do it...

This section contains the steps required to follow the recipe.

How it works...

This section usually consists of a detailed explanation of what happened in the previous section.

There's more...

This section consists of additional information about the recipe in order to make you more knowledgeable about the recipe.

See also

This section provides helpful links to other useful information for the recipe.

Get in touch

Feedback from our readers is always welcome.

General feedback: If you have questions about any aspect of this book, mention the book title in the subject of your message and email us at customercare@packtpub.com.

Errata: Although we have taken every care to ensure the accuracy of our content, mistakes do happen. If you have found a mistake in this book, we would be grateful if you would report this to us. Please visit www.packtpub.com/support/errata, selecting your book, clicking on the Errata Submission Form link, and entering the details.

Piracy: If you come across any illegal copies of our works in any form on the internet, we would be grateful if you would provide us with the location address or website name. Please contact us at copyright@packt.com with a link to the material.

If you are interested in becoming an author: If there is a topic that you have expertise in and you are interested in either writing or contributing to a book, please visit authors.packtpub.com.

Share Your Thoughts

Once you've read *Azure Databricks Cookbook*, we'd love to hear your thoughts! Scan the QR code below to go straight to the Amazon review page for this book and share your feedback.

https://packt.link/r/1-789-80971-1

Your review is important to us and the tech community and will help us make sure we're delivering excellent quality content.

1
Creating an Azure Databricks Service

Azure Databricks is a high-performance Apache Spark-based platform that has been optimized for the Microsoft Azure cloud.

It offers three environments for building and developing data applications:

- **Databricks Data Science and Engineering**: This provides an interactive workspace that enables collaboration between data engineers, data scientists, machine learning engineers, and business analysts and allows you to build big data pipelines.

- **Databricks SQL**: This allows you to run ad hoc SQL queries on your data lake and supports multiple visualization types to explore your query results.

- **Databricks Machine Learning**: Provides end-to-end machine learning environment for feature development, model training , experiment tracking along with model serving and management.

In this chapter, we will cover how to create an Azure Databricks service using the **Azure portal**, **Azure CLI**, and **ARM templates**. We will learn about different types of clusters available in Azure Databricks, how to create jobs, and how to use a **personal access token (PAT)** to authenticate Databricks.

By the end of this chapter, you will have learned how to create a Databricks service using the Azure portal, Azure CLI, and ARM templates and how to create different types of clusters. You will also start working with Notebooks and scheduling them as Databricks jobs. Finally, you will understand how to authenticate to Azure Databricks using a PAT.

We're going to cover the following recipes:

- Creating a Databricks service in the Azure portal
- Creating a Databricks service using the Azure **CLI** (**Command-Line Interface**)
- Creating a Databricks Service using **Azure Resource Manager** (**ARM**) templates
- Adding users and groups to the workspace
- Creating a cluster from the **user interface** (**UI**)
- Getting started with Notebooks and jobs in Azure Databricks
- Authenticating to Databricks using a **personal access token** (**PAT**)

Technical requirements

To follow along with the examples in this chapter, you will need to have the following:

- An Azure subscription
- The Azure CLI installed on one of the following platforms:

  (a) For Windows (install the Azure CLI for Windows | Microsoft Docs `https://docs.microsoft.com/en-us/cli/azure/install-azure-cli-windows?tabs=azure-cli`)

  (b) For Mac (install the Azure CLI for macOS | Microsoft Docs `https://docs.microsoft.com/en-us/cli/azure/install-azure-cli-macos`)

  (c) For Linux (install the Azure CLI for Linux manually | Microsoft Docs `https://docs.microsoft.com/en-us/cli/azure/install-azure-cli-linux?pivots=apt`)

- You can find the scripts for this chapter at `https://github.com/PacktPublishing/Azure-Databricks-Cookbook/tree/main/Chapter01`. The `Chapter-01` folder contains the script for this chapter.

- As an Azure AD user, you will need the Contributor role in your subscription and create the Azure Databricks service via the Azure portal. You must also be the admin of the Azure Databricks workspace.

- The latest version of Power BI Desktop (`https://www.microsoft.com/en-in/download/details.aspx?id=58494`). We will use this to access Spark tables using PAT authentication.

Creating a Databricks workspace in the Azure portal

There are multiple ways we can create an Azure Databricks service. This recipe will focus on creating the service in the Azure portal. This method is usually used for learning purposes or ad hoc requests. The preferred methods for creating services are using the **Azure PowerShell**, **Azure CLI** and **ARM templates**.

By the end of this recipe, you will have learned how to create an Azure Databricks service instance using the Azure portal.

Getting ready

You will need access via a subscription to the service and have a **Contributor** role available in it.

How to do it...

Follow these steps to create a Databricks service using the Azure portal:

1. Log into the Azure portal (`https://portal.azure.com`) and click on **Create a resource**. Then, search for `Azure Databricks` and click on **Create**:

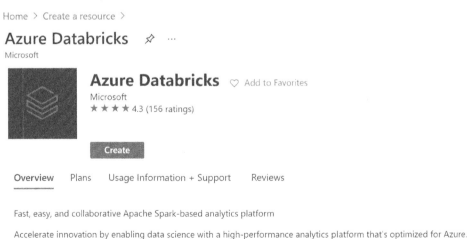

Figure 1.1 – Azure Databricks – Create button

2.   Create a new **resource group** (CookbookRG) or pick any existing resource group:

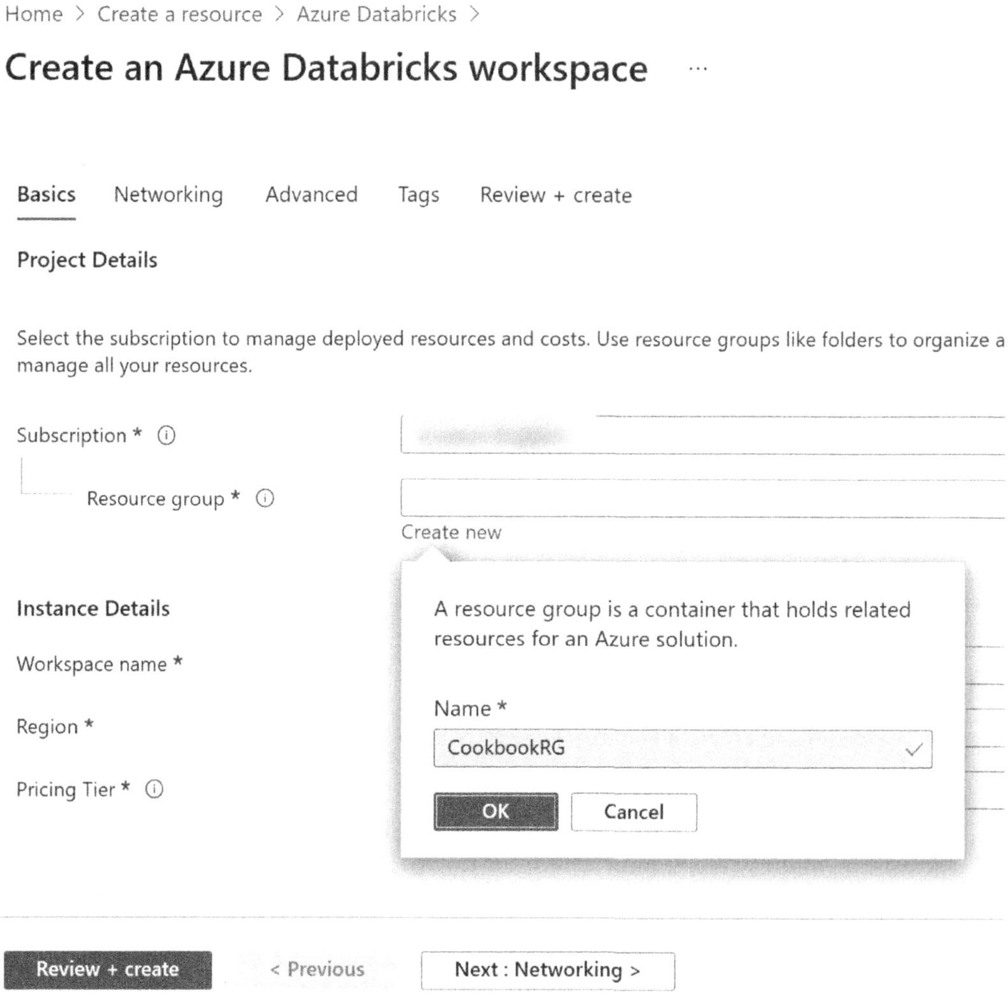

Home > Create a resource > Azure Databricks >

Create an Azure Databricks workspace   ⋯

Basics   Networking   Advanced   Tags   Review + create

Project Details

Select the subscription to manage deployed resources and costs. Use resource groups like folders to organize a manage all your resources.

Subscription * ⓘ

Resource group * ⓘ

Create new

Instance Details

Workspace name *

Region *

Pricing Tier * ⓘ

A resource group is a container that holds related resources for an Azure solution.

Name *

CookbookRG   ✓

OK   Cancel

Review + create   < Previous   Next : Networking >

Figure 1.2 – Create an Azure Databricks workspace page

3. Provide a name for the workspace. Alternatively, you can use
    `BigDataWorkspace`, as shown in the following screenshot. For **Pricing Tier**,
    select **Trial tier**. By doing this, you can get **Databricks Units (DBUs)** for free for
    14 days:

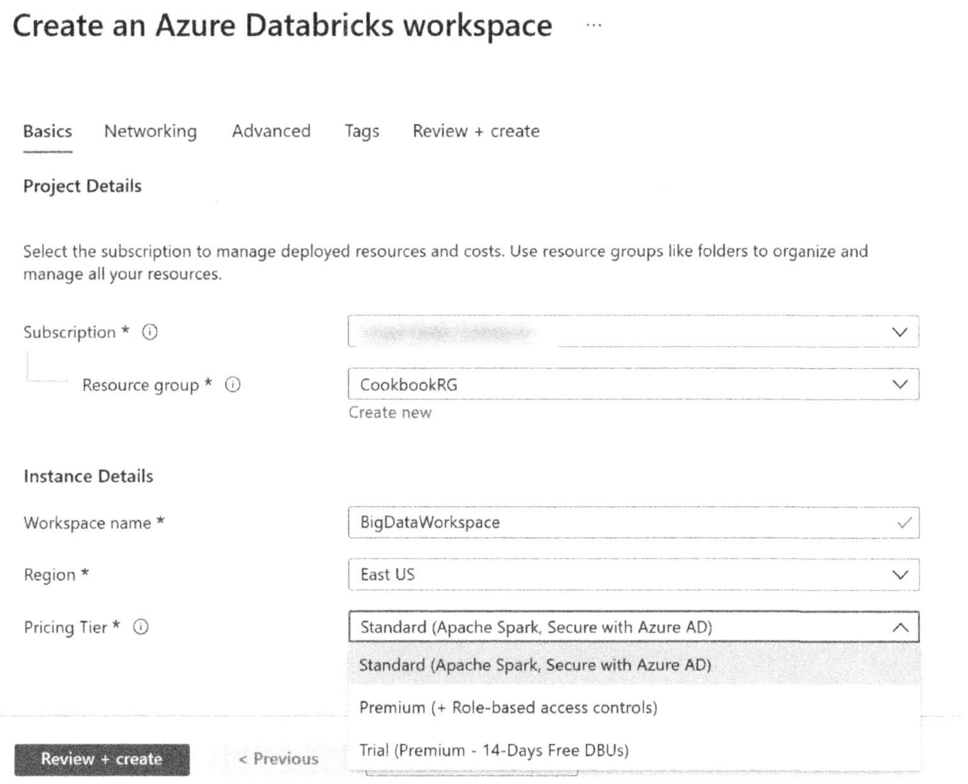

Create an Azure Databricks workspace   ...

Basics   Networking   Advanced   Tags   Review + create

Project Details

Select the subscription to manage deployed resources and costs. Use resource groups like folders to organize and
manage all your resources.

Subscription * ⓘ	_____ ⌄
Resource group * ⓘ	CookbookRG ⌄
	Create new

Instance Details

Workspace name *	BigDataWorkspace ✓
Region *	East US ⌄
Pricing Tier * ⓘ	Standard (Apache Spark, Secure with Azure AD) ⌃

Standard (Apache Spark, Secure with Azure AD)

Premium (+ Role-based access controls)

Trial (Premium - 14-Days Free DBUs)

Review + create   < Previous

Figure 1.3 – Create an Azure Databricks workspace page – continued

4. You need to select **No** on the following screenshot. This will ensure the Databricks service is not deployed in a VNet:

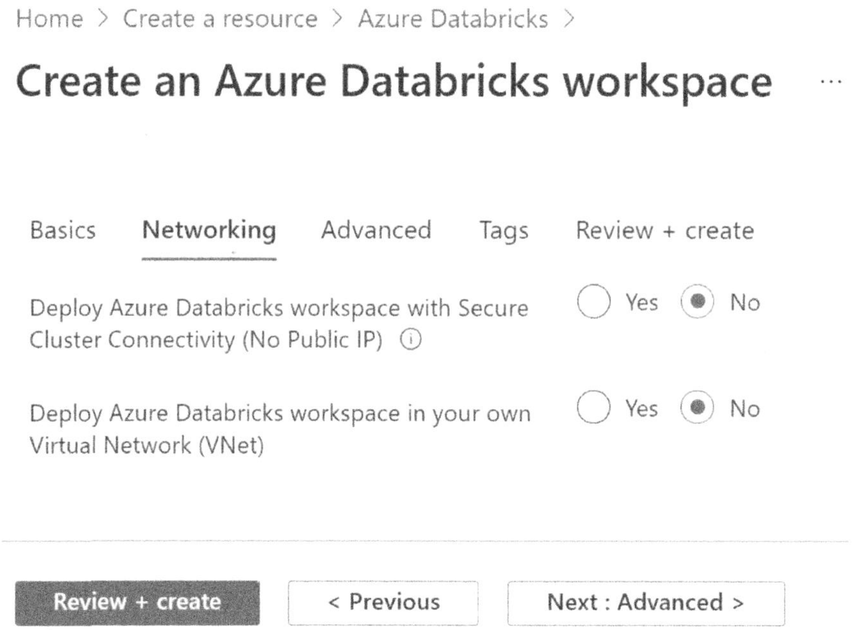

Home > Create a resource > Azure Databricks >

Create an Azure Databricks workspace ...

| Basics | **Networking** | Advanced | Tags | Review + create |

Deploy Azure Databricks workspace with Secure
Cluster Connectivity (No Public IP) ⓘ   ◯ Yes ⦿ No

Deploy Azure Databricks workspace in your own
Virtual Network (VNet)   ◯ Yes ⦿ No

Review + create   < Previous   Next : Advanced >

Figure 1.4 – Create an Azure Databricks workspace page – continued

5. Click on **Review + create**:

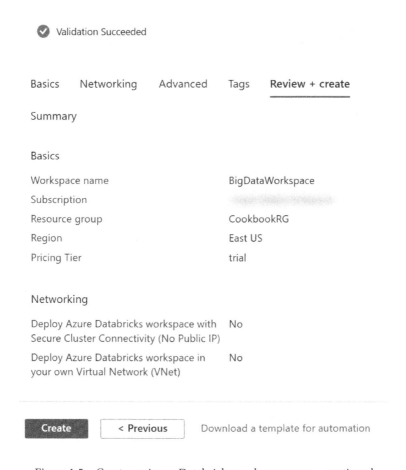

Create an Azure Databricks workspace   ...

Validation Succeeded

Basics   Networking   Advanced   Tags   **Review + create**

Summary

Basics

Workspace name	BigDataWorkspace
Subscription	
Resource group	CookbookRG
Region	East US
Pricing Tier	trial

Networking

Deploy Azure Databricks workspace with Secure Cluster Connectivity (No Public IP)	No
Deploy Azure Databricks workspace in your own Virtual Network (VNet)	No

Create   < Previous   Download a template for automation

Figure 1.5 – Create an Azure Databricks workspace page – continued

6. You can check the Azure Databricks service you've created in the **CookbookRG** resource group:

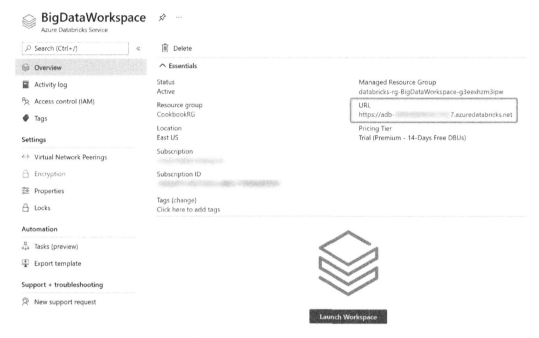

Figure 1.6 – Launch Workspace

This completes creating the service using the Azure portal.

How it works...

Let's deep dive into how the Databricks service operates in Azure:

- When we create an Azure Databricks service, it operates in the **control plane** and the **data plane**:

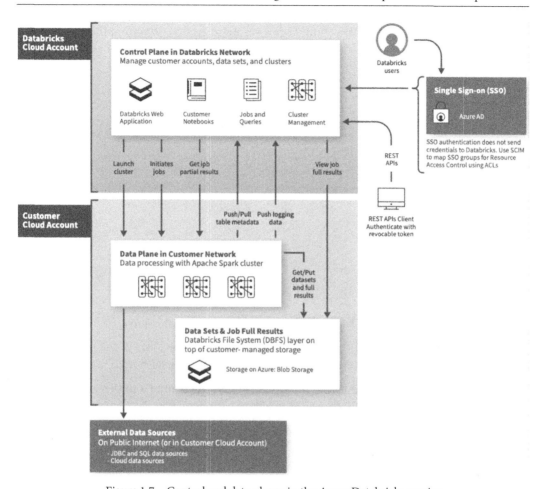

Figure 1.7 – Control and data planes in the Azure Databricks service

- The **control plane** contains all the services that are managed by Azure Databricks in its own Azure account. All the commands we run will be in the control plane fully encrypted. The customer never resides in the control plane.

- The **data plane** is managed in the customer's Azure account and is where the data resides.

- From the Azure portal, you should see a resource group containing the name of your workspace, as shown in the following screenshot. This is called as Managed Resource Group.

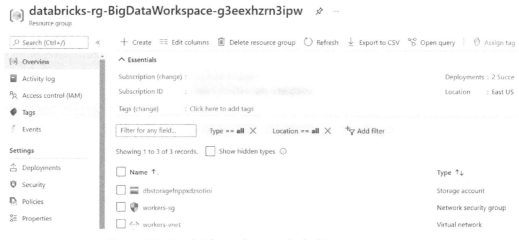

Figure 1.8 – Databricks workspace – locked in resource group

- Since we haven't created the cluster yet, you won't see the VMs in the managed resource group that was created by the Azure Databricks service.

- We won't be able to remove the resources or read the contents in the storage account in the managed resource group that was created by the service.

- These resources and the respective resource group will be deleted when the Azure Databricks service is deleted.

Creating a Databricks service using the Azure CLI (command-line interface)

In this recipe, we will look at an automated way of creating and managing a Databricks workspace using the Azure CLI.

By the end of this recipe, you will know how to use the Azure CLI and deploy Azure Databricks. Knowing how to deploy resources using the CLI will help you automate the task of deploying from your DevOps pipeline or running the task from a PowerShell terminal.

Getting ready

Azure hosts the **Azure Cloud Shell**, which can be used to work with Azure services. Azure Cloud Shell uses preinstalled commands that can be executed without us needing to install it in our local environment.

This recipe will use a **service principal** (**SP**) to authenticate to Azure so that we can deploy the Azure Databricks workspace. Before we start running the SP script, we must create one.

You can find out how to create an Azure AD app and a SP in the Azure portal by going to **Microsoft identity platform | Microsoft Docs** (`https://docs.microsoft.com/en-us/azure/active-directory/develop/howto-create-service-principal-portal#:~:text=Option%201:%20Upload%20a%20certificate.%201%20Select%20Run,key,%20and%20export%20to%20a%20.CER%20file`).

In the local cloned GitHub repository, you will find a PowerShell file called `AzureCloudShell.ps1` or you can directly get it from the GIT URL `https://github.com/PacktPublishing/Azure-Databricks-Cookbook/tree/main/Chapter02/Code`.

How to do it...

Let's learn how to execute a PowerShell script which has the Azure CLI commands to create an Azure Databricks resource group and Azure Databricks service:

1. Azure Cloud Shell can be accessed from `https://shell.azure.com` or by selecting the **Launch Cloud Shell** button from the top right of the Azure portal:

Figure 1.9 – Azure Cloud Shell

2. After launching **Azure Cloud Shell**, select **PowerShell** as your environment:

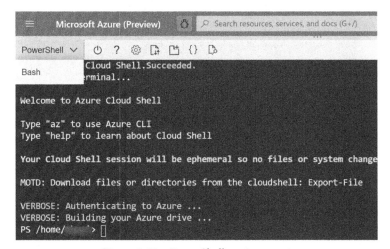

Figure 1.10 – PowerShell environment

3. Now, change the variable values that are used in the `AzureCloudShell.ps1` script and assign them based on the service principal and resource group name you have created, as shown in the following code:

```
$appId="sdasdasdsdfsa7-xxx-xxx-xx-xx"
$appSecret="xxxxxxx~.xxxxxxjgx"
$tenantId="xxxxx-xxx-xx-xxxx-xxxcdxxxxxx"
$subscriptionName="Pay As You Go"
$resourceGroup = "CookbookRG"
```

4. Upload the `AzureCloudShell.ps1` script to the Cloud Shell using the **Upload** button from the **Cloud Shell** menu. When the upload is complete, you will see a message confirming this, along with the destination folder where the file has been uploaded:

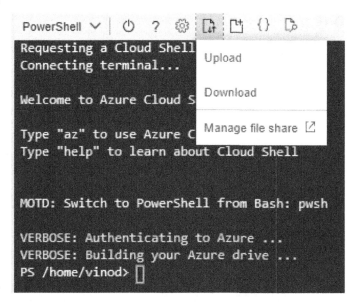

Figure 1.11 – PowerShell script – Upload

5. From the **PowerShell** terminal, run the PowerShell script using the following command:

```
PS /home/vinod> ./AzureCloudShell.ps1
```

6. Now, you will see a new Azure Databricks workspace called **BigDataWorkspace** in the **CookbookRG** resource group.

How it works...

The Azure CLI provides a set of commands. It is very powerful tool and can be used to automate the process of creating and managing Azure resources. In real-world scenarios, and in most cases, developers won't have access in the higher environments. Azure CLI commands can be used to create resources using predeveloped scripts.

There's more...

The Azure CLI provides lots of other options for managing workspaces. A few of them, as well as their purposes, are as follows:

- Use the following command to update the workspace:

```
az databricks workspace update
```

- Use the following command to manage workspace vnet peering:

```
az databricks workspace vnet-peering
```

- Use the following command to create vnet peering:

```
az databricks workspace vnet-peering create
```

- Use the following command to list all the Databricks workspaces:

```
az databricks workspace list
```

The required parameters for creating an Azure Databricks workspace are as follows:

- --location -l: The Azure region where the workspace will be created
- --name -n: The name of the workspace
- --resource-group -g: The name of the resource group
- --sku: The SKU tier's name (premium, standard, or trial)

Creating a Databricks service using Azure Resource Manager (ARM) templates

Using ARM templates for deployment is a well known method to deploy resource in Azure.

By the end of this recipe, you will have learned how to deploy an Azure Databricks workspace using ARM templates. ARM templates can be deployed from an Azure DevOps pipeline, as well as by using PowerShell or CLI commands.

Getting ready

In this recipe, we will use a service principal to authenticate to Azure so that we can deploy the Azure Databricks workspace. Before we start running the SP script, you must create one.

You can find out how to create an Azure AD app and service principal by going to the Azure portal and selecting **Microsoft identity platform | Microsoft Docs** (https://docs.microsoft.com/en-us/azure/active-directory/develop/howto-create-service-principal-portal#:~:text=Option%20 1:%20Upload%20a%20certificate.%201%20Select%20Run,key,%20 and%20export%20to%20a%20.CER%20file).

For service principal authentication, we will use password-based authentication, as mentioned in **Option 2** in the preceding link.

In your locally cloned GitHub repository, you will find a PowerShell file called CreateDatabricksWorkspace.ps1 and two JSON files called azuredeploy. json and azuredeploy.paramters.json. These two JSON files contain the ARM templates we will be using to deploy an Azure Databricks workspace.

How to do it...

Follow these steps before running the PowerShell script:

1. First, change the variable values in the script and assign new values based on the service principal and resource group name you have created, as shown in the following code:

    ```
    $appId="dfsdfdxx-xxxx-xx-xx-xxxxx"
    $appSecret="xxxxx~.xxxx"
    $tenantId="xxxxx-xxx-xx-xxxx-xcdxxxxxx"
    $subscriptionName="Pay As You Go"
    $resourceGroup = "CookbookRG"
    ```

2. AzureDeploy.json is the main template file. It contains the details that are required to deploy a Databricks workspace. We will update the name of the workspace and **Stock Keeping Unit (SKU)** in the parameter file (azuredeploy. parameters.json).

3. Update the `azuredeploy.parameters.json` file by changing the name of the workspace, if required. Alternatively, you can use the default name and SKU value provided in the parameter file. We are using a `premium` SKU in the parameter file:

```
{
    "$schema": "https://schema.management.azure.com/
schemas/2019-04-01/deploymentParameters.json#",
    "contentVersion": "1.0.0.0",
    "parameters": {
      "workspaceName": {
        "value": "BigDataClustersWS"
      },
      "pricingTier" : {
        "value": "premium"
      }
    }
}
```

4. From a PowerShell terminal, go to the folder that contains the PS file, along with the JSON files, and run the PS script:

```
PS C:\CreateWorkspace> .\CreateDatabricksWorkspace.ps1
```

5. Now, you will see that a new Azure Databricks workspace has been created in the **CookbookRG** resource group.

How it works...

ARM helps you implement Infrastructure as Code for your Azure solutions. Templates help you define your infrastructure, as well as all the configuration for the project and the resource you are deploying. A **SKU** represents a purchasable **Stock Keeping Unit** for a product. Refer to the following link to find out more about SKU properties:

https://docs.microsoft.com/en-us/partner-center/develop/
product-resources#sku.

In this recipe, we used an ARM template, along with a command line, to deploy the resource. In the `az login` script, we have a service principal, which is used to authenticate to Azure. This is used instead of a username and password as it is the preferred method.

Adding users and groups to the workspace

In this recipe, we will learn how to add users and groups to the workspace so that they can collaborate when creating data applications. This exercise will provide you with a detailed understanding of how users are created in a workspace. You will also learn about the different permissions that can be granted to users.

Getting ready

Log into the Databricks workspace as an Azure Databricks admin. Before you add a user to the workspace, ensure that the user exists in Azure Active Directory.

How to do it...

Follow these steps to create users and groups from the Admin Console:

1. From the Azure Databricks service, click on the **Launch workspace** option.

2. After launching the workspace, click the user icon at the top right and click on **Admin Console**, as shown in the following screenshot:

Figure 1.12 – Azure Databricks workspace

3. You can click on **Add User** and invite users who are part of your **Azure Active Directory (AAD)**. Here, we have added **demouser1@gmail.com**:

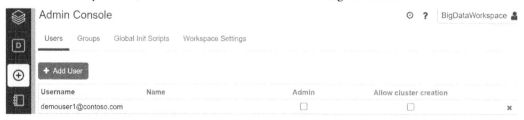

Figure 1.13 – Adding a user from the admin console

4. You can grant admin privileges or allow cluster creation permissions based on your requirements while adding users.

5. You can create a group from the admin console and add users to that group. You can do this to classify groups such as data engineers and data scientists and then provide access accordingly:

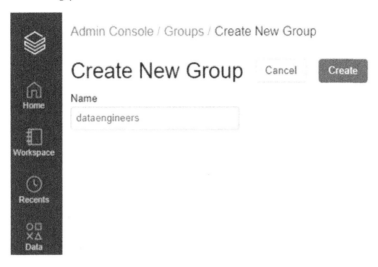

Figure 1.14 – Creating a group from the admin console

6. Once we've created a group, we can add users to it, or we can add an ADD group to it. Here, we are adding **the ADD user** to the group that we have created:

Figure 1.15 – Adding users to the group

How it works...

Using the admin console, we can perform many activities, such as add groups, delete groups, add users to groups, and grant and revoke permissions to groups. If we want multiple users to be admins, which means they would be responsible for managing clusters and users, then we can add the required users to the **admins** group. We can also add and remove users from the group, which would simplify the management overhead of managing users. Finally, we can grant and revoke permissions to the group based on which role and responsibility the user has.

There's more...

You can enable and disable table access and other access control options from the **Admin Console** page, as shown in the following screenshot:

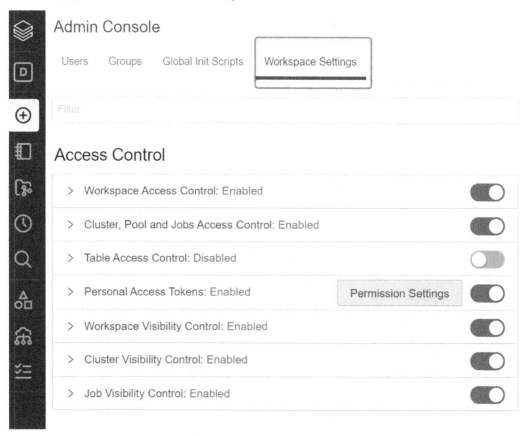

Figure 1.16 – Admin Console page – access control

These options can be enabled and disabled based on your project's requirements. Users who can enable and disable these options are admin users.

Creating a cluster from the user interface (UI)

In this recipe, we will look at the different types of clusters and cluster modes in Azure Databricks and how to create them. Understanding cluster types will help you determine the right type of cluster you should use for your workload and usage pattern.

Getting ready

Before you get started, ensure you have created an Azure Databricks workspace, as shown in the preceding recipes.

How to do it...

Follow these steps to create a cluster via the UI:

1. After launching your workspace, click on the **Cluster** option from the left-hand pane:

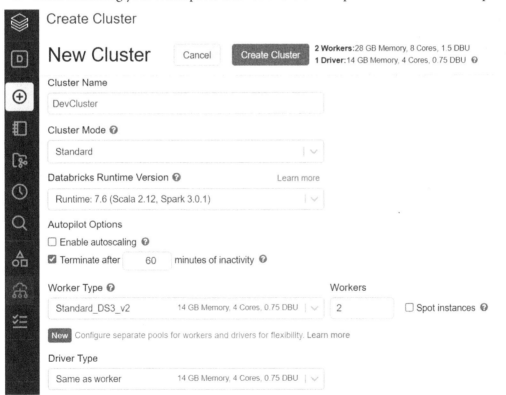

Figure 1.17 – Create Cluster page

2. Provide a name for your cluster and select a cluster mode based on your scenario. Here, we are selecting **Standard**.

3. We are not selecting a pool here. Let's go with the latest version of Spark (3.0.1) and the latest version of the Databricks runtime (7.4) that's available at the time of writing this book.

4. The possibility to terminate has been set to 60 mins (120 mins is the default value). Deselect the **Enable autoscaling** option here.

5. Here, we have selected two workers. **Worker Type** has been set to **Standard_DS3_v2**. The same configuration is required for **Driver Type** and based on how many cores and memory you need you can change the **Worker Type** and **Driver Type** configuration:

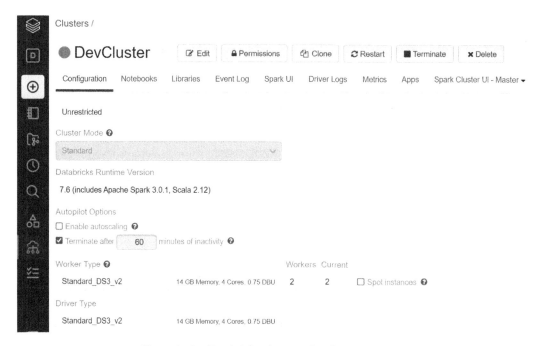

Figure 1.18 – Databricks cluster – Configuration page

6. The preceding screenshot shows the status and properties of the cluster once it has been created.

How it works...

There are three cluster modes that are supported in Azure Databricks:

- **Standard clusters**

  This mode is recommended for single users and data applications that can be developed using **Python**, **Scale**, **SQL**, and **R**. Clusters are set to terminate after 120 minutes of inactivity, and **Standard cluster** is the default cluster mode. We can use this type of cluster to, for example, execute a Notebook through a Databricks job or via ADF as a scheduled activity.

- **High Concurrency clusters**

  This mode is ideal when multiple users are trying to use the same cluster. It can be used to provide maximum resource utilization and has lower query latency requirements in multiuser scenarios. Data applications can be developed using Python, SQL, and R. These clusters are configured not to terminate by default.

- **Single-Node clusters**

  Single-Node clusters do not have worker nodes, and all the Spark jobs run on the driver node. This cluster mode be used for building and testing small data pipelines and to do lightweight **Exploratory Data Analysis (EDA)**. The driver node acts as both a master and a worker. These clusters are configured to terminate after 120 minutes of inactivity by default. Data applications can be developed using Python, Scale, SQL, and R.

The Databricks runtime includes Apache Spark, along with many other components, to improve performance, security, and ease of use. It comes with Python, Scala, and Java libraries installed for building pipelines in any language. It also provides **Delta Lake**, an open source storage layer that provides **ACID** transactions and metadata handling. It also unifies batch data and streaming data for building near-real-time analytics.

To learn how to size your cluster, you can refer the following link.

```
https://docs.microsoft.com/en-us/azure/databricks/clusters/
cluster-config-best-practices#cluster-sizing-considerations
```

There's more...

Once we have a cluster created and running, we will see that multiple VMs have been created in the control pane, which is managed by Azure Databricks in its own Azure account, as we discussed in the *Creating a Databricks service in the Azure portal* recipe. Here, we have created a cluster with two worker nodes and one driver node, which is why we see three VMs in the Databricks managed resource group, as shown in the following screenshot:

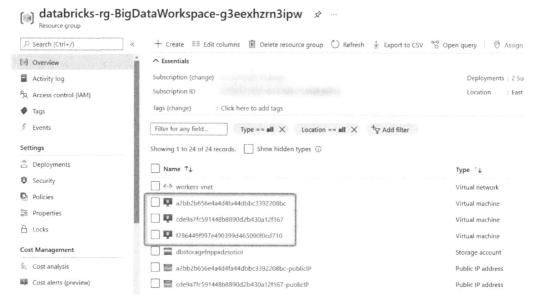

Figure 1.19 – Databricks locked-in resource group resources when the cluster is running

The preceding screenshot is of the Databricks managed resource group. You can navigate to this resource group from the **Databricks Service** launch page. The name of the managed resource group can be found above the **Pricing Tier** option.

Getting started with notebooks and jobs in Azure Databricks

In this recipe, we will import a notebook into our workspace and learn how to execute and schedule it using jobs. By the end of this recipe, you will know how to import, create, execute, and schedule Notebooks in Azure Databricks.

Getting ready

Ensure the Databricks cluster is up and running. Clone the cookbook repository from `https://github.com/PacktPublishing/Azure-Databricks-Cookbook` to any location on your laptop/PC. You will find the required demo files in the `chapter-01` folder.

How to do it...

Let's dive into importing the Notebook into our workspace:

1. First, let's create a simple Notebook that will be used to create a new job and schedule it.

2. In the cloned repository, go to **chapter-01**. You will find a file called **DemoRun. dbc**. You can import the **dbc** file into your workspace by right-clicking the Shared workspace and selecting the **Import** option:

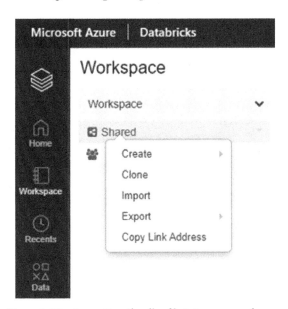

Figure 1.20 – Importing the dbc file into your workspace

3. By selecting **Import**, you will get the option to browse the file you want to import:

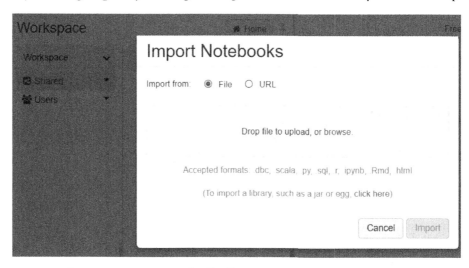

Figure 1.21 – Importing the dbc file into your workspace – continued

4. Browse for the **DemoRun.dbc** file and click on **Import**:

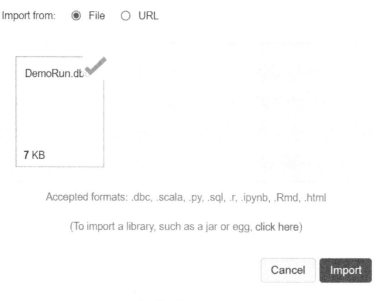

Figure 1.22 – Importing the dbc file into your workspace – continued

5.   Once you've done this, you should see a Notebook called **DemoRun** in the shared workspace:

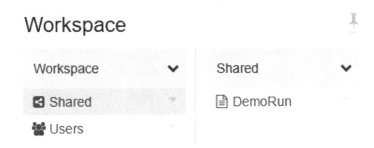

Figure 1.23 – Status after uploading the dbc file

6.   This Notebook is using **PySpark APIs** to perform the following steps:

(a) List the default Databricks datasets in the cluster.

(b) Read the Mnm csv file.

(c) Write the data that's been read from the Mnm csv file to a Spark managed table.

7.   When you open the Notebook, you will see that the Notebook starts with a comments section, stating what the Notebook is doing.

8.   You can execute each cell by hitting *Shift + Enter*. Alternatively, you can click on the **Run All** option, which can be found at the top of the Notebook, to execute all the cells in the Notebook.

9.   You can schedule the Notebook by creating a job in Azure Databricks. Go to the **Jobs** option via the left-hand pane of the workspace.

Name the job something like **DailyJob**, assuming that this job has been scheduled to run every day. Under the **Task** option, select the notebook that we uploaded in the preceding step:

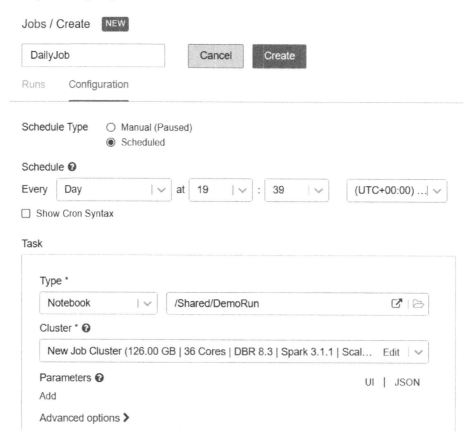

Figure 1.24 – Databricks job configuration

10. You can create a new cluster for the job or use an existing cluster, such as the one we created earlier. Here, we are creating a new cluster to learn how to an create on-demand cluster. This will be used to run the job.

11. Click on cluster drop down list for the job you are creating. You will see two options under the cluster type: **New Job Cluster** and **Existing DevCluster** that you have created. We will select **New Job Cluster** here, select Edit option and provide the cluster configuration for the new cluster. Click on **Confirm** as shown in the following screenshot:

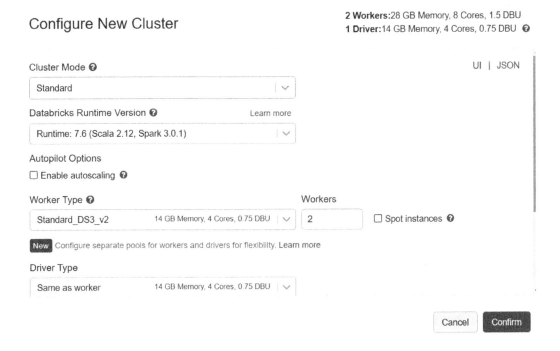

Figure 1.25 – Cluster type details for the Databricks job

12. You can run the job now or you can schedule it to run every minute, hour, day, week, or month. When you run the job, you will see the status of all your **Active runs** and all the jobs that have been completed in the past 60 days:

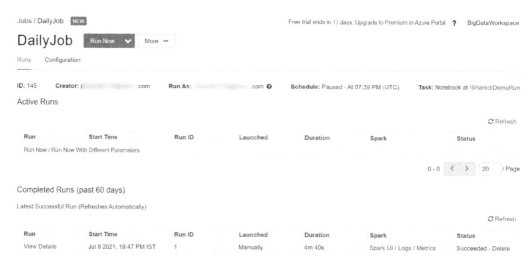

Figure 1.26 – Databricks job – details and history

13. As soon as the job completes, the cluster will be deleted automatically.

How it works...

There are also two types of clusters in Azure Databricks:

- **Interactive** (Existing All-Purpose Cluster): This type of cluster is used for all interactive queries in the Databricks Notebook and when we want various tools to create various visualizations.

- **On Demand** (New Job Cluster): This type of cluster is used when we want to spin up a cluster just to execute a job. It is deleted once the job completes.

When you run the Notebook, we will see a Spark managed table being created. You can find that table via the workspace UI. Go to the **Data** option in the workspace; you will see a table called **mnmdata** that was created in the default database:

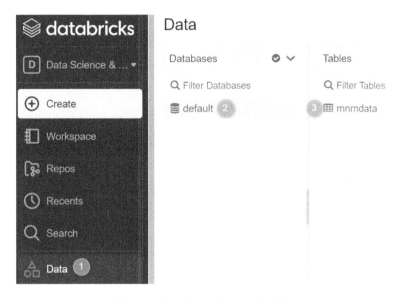

Figure 1.27 – Databricks Spark tables

You can select the table that shows the schema of the table and view **sample data**.

Authenticating to Databricks using a PAT

To authenticate and access Databricks REST APIs, we can use two types of tokens:

- **PATs**

- **Azure Active Directory tokens**

A PAT is used as an alternative password to authenticate and access Databricks REST APIs. By the end of this recipe, you will have learned how to use PATs to access the Spark managed tables that we created in the preceding recipes using Power BI Desktop and create basic visualizations.

Getting ready

PATs are enabled by default for all Databricks workspaces created on or after 2018. If this is not enabled, an administrator can enable or disable tokens, irrespective of their creation date.

Users can create PATs and use them in REST API requests. Tokens have optional expiration dates and can be revoked.

How to do it...

This section will show you how to generate PATs using the Azure Databricks UI. Also, apart from the UI, you can use the Token API to generate and revoke tokens. However, there is a limitation of 600 tokens per user, per workspace. Let's go through the steps for creating tokens using the Databricks UI:

1. Click on the **profile** icon in the top-right corner of the Databricks workspace.
2. Click on **User Settings**.
3. Click on the **Access Tokens** tab:

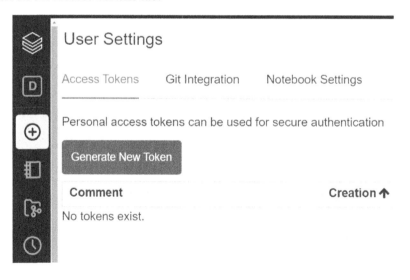

Figure 1.28 – User Settings page

4.   Click on the **Generate New Token** button.

5.   Enter a description (**Comment**) and expiration period (**Lifetime (days)**). These are just an optional, but it's good practice to have a lifetime for a token and comment on where it is being used:

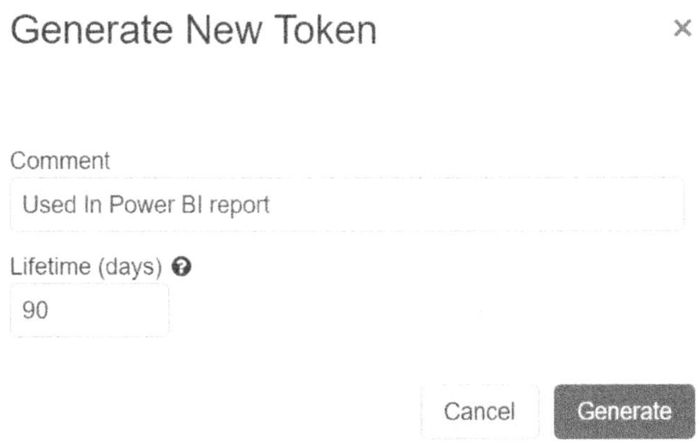

Generate New Token   ✕

Comment

Used In Power BI report

Lifetime (days) ❷

90

Cancel   Generate

Figure 1.29 – Generate New Token

6.   Click the **Generate** button.

7.   Copy the generated token and store it in a secure location.

Now that the access token has been created, we will learn how to connect a Databricks cluster to Power BI using a PAT:

1.   Click on the cluster icon in the left sidebar of your Azure Databricks workspace.

2.   Click on the **Advanced Options** toggle.

3.   Click on the **JDBC/ODBC** tab.

4. Copy the hostname, port, and HTTP path provided:

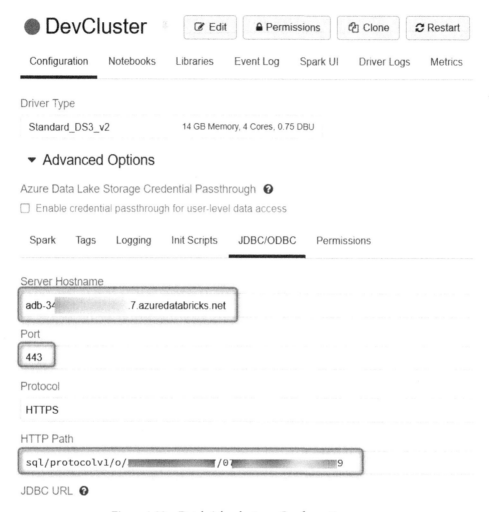

Figure 1.30 – Databricks cluster – Configuration page

5. Open Power BI Desktop, go to **Get Data** > **Azure**, and select the **Azure Databricks** connector:

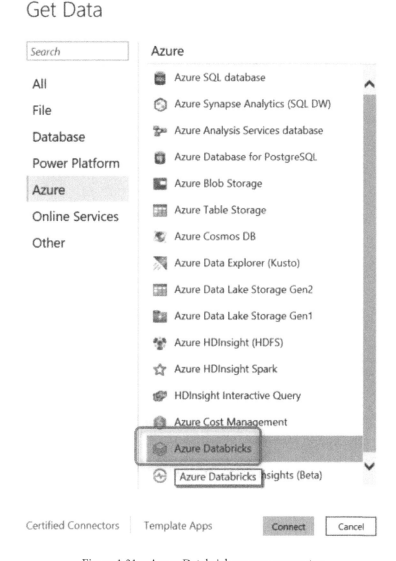

Figure 1.31 – Azure Databricks source connector

6. Click **Connect**.

7. Paste the **Server Hostname** and **HTTP Path** details you retrieved in the previous step:

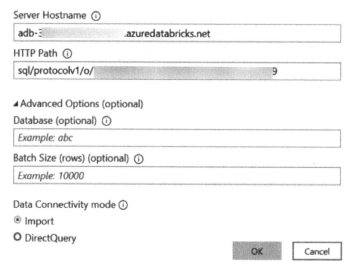

Figure 1.32 – Databricks cluster details

8. Select a **Data Connectivity mode**.

9. Click **OK**.

10. At the authentication prompt, select how you wish to authenticate to Azure Databricks:

    (a) Azure Active Directory: Use your Azure account credentials.

    (b) PAT: Use the PAT you retrieved earlier.

11. Click **Connect**.

12. Create a Power BI report about the mnmdata dataset, which is available in Azure Databricks:

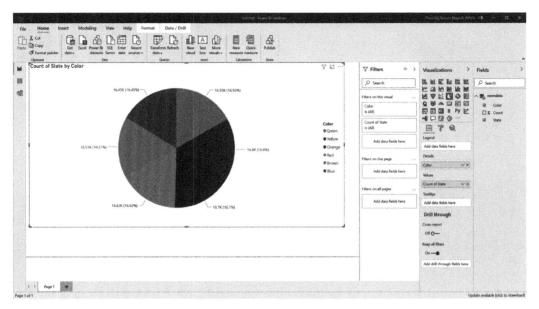

Figure 1.33 – Power BI report

Now, you can explore and visualize this data, as you would with any other data in Power BI Desktop.

How it works...

Azure Databricks admins can use the Token Management API and Permissions API to control token usage. These APIs are published on each workspace instance. Users with the right permissions can create and use tokens to authenticate with the REST API.

There's more...

PATs can be used with the REST API to complete multiple automation tasks. Some of them are as follows:

- Creating clusters in an Azure Databricks workspace
- Creating jobs
- Creating folder structures
- Deleting folder structures
- Importing Notebooks or directories

You can learn more about the REST API 2.0 for Azure Databricks from following link. `https://docs.microsoft.com/en-us/azure/databricks/dev-tools/api/latest/`

2
Reading and Writing Data from and to Various Azure Services and File Formats

Azure Databricks provides options for data engineers, data scientists, and data analysts to read and write data from and to various sources such as different file formats, databases, NoSQL databases, Azure Storage, and so on. Users get a lot of flexibility in ingesting and storing data in various formats as per business requirements, using Databricks. It also provides libraries to ingest data from streaming systems such as Events Hub and Kafka.

In this chapter, we will learn how we can read data from different file formats, such as **comma-separated values (CSV)**, Parquet, and **JavaScript Object Notation (JSON)**, and how to use native connectors to read and write data from and to **Azure SQL Database** and **Azure Synapse Analytics**. We will also learn how to read and store data in **Azure Cosmos DB**.

By the end of this chapter, you will have built a foundation for reading data from various sources that are required to work on the **end-to-end** (**E2E**) scenarios of a data ingestion pipeline. You will learn how and when to use **JavaScript Database Connectivity** (**JDBC**) drivers and Apache Spark connectors to ingest into the Azure SQL Database.

We're going to cover the following recipes in this chapter:

- Mounting **Azure Data Lake Storage Gen2** (**ADLS Gen2**) and Azure Blob storage to Azure **Databricks File System** (**DBFS**)
- Reading and writing data from and to Azure Blob storage
- Reading and writing data from and to ADLS Gen2
- Reading and writing data from and to an Azure SQL database using native connectors
- Reading and writing data from and to Azure Synapse Dedicated **Structured Query Language** (**SQL**) Pool using native connectors
- Reading and writing data from and to the Azure Cosmos DB
- Reading and writing data from and to CSV and Parquet
- Reading and writing data from and to JSON, including nested JSON

Technical requirements

To follow along with the examples shown in the recipe, you will need to have the following:

- An Azure subscription and required permissions on the subscription, as mentioned in the *Technical requirements* section of *Chapter 1, Creating an Azure Databricks Service*.
- ADLS Gen2 and Blob storage accounts. You can use the following links to create the required resources:

  ```
  https://docs.microsoft.com/en-us/azure/storage/common/
  storage-account-create?tabs=azure-portal
  https://docs.microsoft.com/en-us/azure/storage/common/
  storage-account-create?tabs=azure-portal
  ```

- Azure SQL DB and Azure Synapse Dedicated SQL Pool

  ```
  https://docs.microsoft.com/en-us/azure/azure-sql/database/
  single-database-create-quickstart?tabs=azure-portal
  https://docs.microsoft.com/en-us/azure/synapse-analytics/
  sql-data-warehouse/create-data-warehouse-portal
  ```

- For creating Azure Synapse Analytics and Dedicated SQL Pool you can go through the steps mentioned in the following link.

  `https://docs.microsoft.com/en-us/azure/synapse-analytics/ quickstart-create-sql-pool-studio`

- An Azure Cosmos DB account. You can find out more information about this here: `https://docs.microsoft.com/en-us/azure/cosmos-db/create- cosmosdb-resources-portal`.

- You can find the scripts for this chapter in the GitHub repository at `https:// github.com/PacktPublishing/Azure-Databricks-Cookbook/tree/ main/Chapter02/Code`. The `Chapter02` folder contains all the notebooks for this chapter.

> **Important note**
>
> You can create resources based on the recipe you are working on—for example, if you are on the first recipe, then you need to create Azure Blob storage and ADLS Gen2 resources only.

Mounting ADLS Gen2 and Azure Blob storage to Azure DBFS

Azure Databricks uses DBFS, which is a distributed file system that is mounted into an Azure Databricks workspace and that can be made available on **Azure Databricks clusters**. DBFS is an abstraction that is built on top of Azure Blob storage and ADLS Gen2. It mainly offers the following benefits:

- It allows you to mount the Azure Blob and ADLS Gen2 storage objects so that you can access files and folders without requiring any storage credentials.

- You can read files directly from the mount point without needing to provide a full storage **Uniform Resource Locator (URL)**.

- You can create folders and write files directly to the mount point.

- Data written to the mount point gets persisted after a cluster is terminated.

By the end of this recipe, you will have learned how to mount Azure Blob and ADLS Gen2 storage to Azure DBFS. You will learn how to access files and folders in Blob storage and ADLS Gen2 by doing the following:

- Directly accessing the storage URL

- Mounting the storage account to DBFS

Getting ready

Create ADLS Gen2 and Azure Blob storage resources by following the links provided in the *Technical requirements* section. In this recipe, the names of the storage resources we are using will be the following:

- `cookbookadlsgen2storage` for ADLS Gen2 storage

- `cookbookblobstorage` for Azure Blob storage

You can see the **Storage Accounts** we created in the following screenshot:

	Name ↑↓	Type ↑↓	Location ↑↓
☐	cookbookadlsgen2storage	Storage account	East US
☐	cookbookblobstorage	Storage account	East US

Figure 2.1 – Storage accounts created in the CookbookRG resource group

Before you get started, you will need to create a **service principal** that will be used to mount the ADLS Gen2 account to DBFS. Here are the steps that need to be followed to create a service principal from the Azure portal:

1. **Application registration**: You will need to register an **Azure Active Directory (AAD)** application. On the Azure portal home page, search for **Azure Active Directory** and select it. On the **Azure Active Directory** page, in the left pane, select **App registrations** and click on **New registration**:

Home > demo

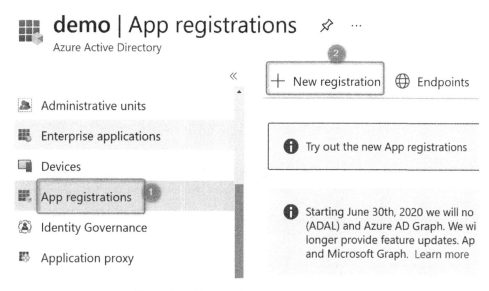

Figure 2.2 – New application registration page

2. On the **Register an application** page, give any name to the application you are creating, leave the other options at their default values, and click **Register**:

Register an application   ⋯

* Name

The user-facing display name for this application (this can be changed later).

ADLSGen2App|

Supported account types

Who can use this application or access this API?

◉ Accounts in this organizational directory only (demo only - Single tenant)

○ Accounts in any organizational directory (Any Azure AD directory - Multitenant)

○ Accounts in any organizational directory (Any Azure AD directory - Multitenant)

○ Personal Microsoft accounts only

By proceeding, you agree to the Microsoft Platform Policies 🗗

Register

Figure 2.3 – New application registration page (continued)

3. Once an application is created, you will see it listed on the **App registrations** page in AAD, as seen in the following screenshot:

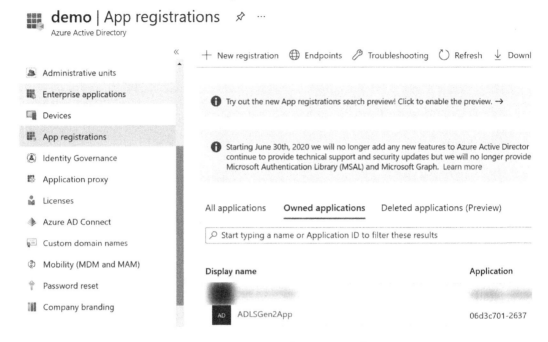

Figure 2.4 – New application created

4. Select the new application you have created and get the application **identifier** (**ID**), and the tenant ID for the application that will be used for mounting the ADLS Gen2 account to DBFS:

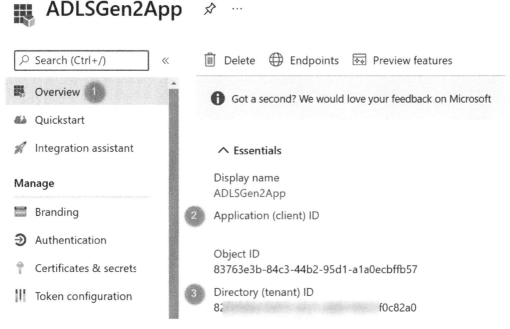

Figure 2.5 – Getting application ID and tenant ID

5. To create a secret, click on **Certificates & secrets** under the **Manage** heading and click on the **+ New client secret** option listed under **Client secrets**. You can provide any description for the secret and provide expiry as **1 year** for this exercise:

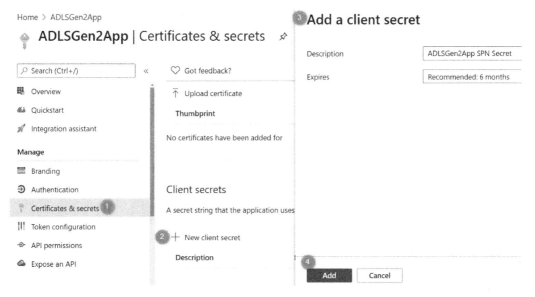

Figure 2.6 – Adding client secret for the application

6. As soon as you create a secret, ensure you copy the value of the secret, else you cannot get the value of the existing secret later. You will have to create a new secret if the secret value is not copied immediately after it is created:

Client secrets

A secret string that the application uses to prove its identity when requesting a token. Also can be referred to as application password.

+ New client secret

Description	Expires	Value		Secret ID	
ADLSGen2App SPN Secret	1/12/2022	H...	⧉	63e4d48d-cbb2-4a86-b52d-...	⧉ 🗑

Figure 2.7 – Client secret value page

7. You now have an application ID, a tenant ID, and a secret—these are required to mount an ADLS Gen2 account to DBFS.

Once the application is created, we need to provide Blob storage contributor access to ADLSGen2App on the ADLS Gen2 storage account. The following steps demonstrate how to provide access to the ADLS Gen2 storage account:

1. From the Azure portal home page, go to the CookbookRG resource group and select the cookbookadlsgenstorage (ADLS Gen2 storage) account you have created. Click **Access Control (IAM)** then click on **+ Add**, and select the **Add role assignment** option. On the **Add role assignment** blade, assign the **Storage Blob Data Contributor** role to our service principal (that is, ADLSAccess):

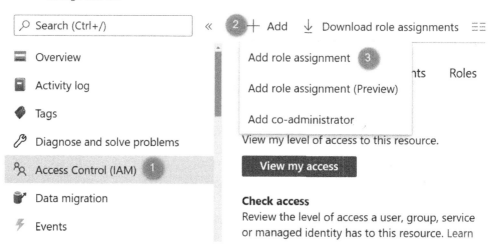

Figure 2.8 – Adding permissions to ADLS Gen2 for service principal

2. Under **Add role assignment**, select a role and access for ADLSGen2App, as shown in the following screenshot, and click on the **Save** button:

Add role assignment   ×

Role ⓘ

| Storage Blob Data Contributor ⓘ   ∨ |

Assign access to ⓘ

| User, group, or service principal   ∨ |

Select ⓘ

| adls |

| ADLSGen2App |

Figure 2.9 – Adding permissions to ADLS Gen2 for service principal

We require a storage key so that we can mount the Azure Blob storage account to DBFS. The following steps show how to get a storage key for the Azure Blob storage account (cookbookblobstorage) we have already created.

3. From the Azure portal home page, go to the CookbookRG resource group and select the cookbookblobstorage (ADLS Blob storage) account you have created. Click on **Access keys** under **Settings** and click on the **Show keys** button. The value you see for the key1 key is the storage key we will use to mount the Azure Blob storage account to DBFS:

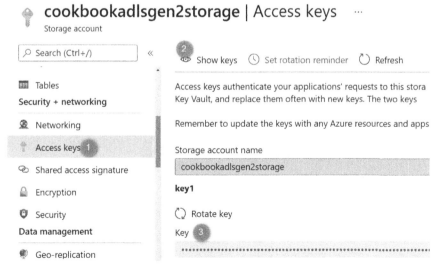

Figure 2.10 – Azure Blob storage account access key

4. Copy the value of `key1`, which you will see when you click on **Show keys**. The process of getting a storage key is the same for an Azure Blob storage account and an ADLS Gen2 storage account.

5. You can find the notebook that we will be using to mount Azure Blob storage and ADLS Gen2 in the `Chapter02` folder of your local cloned Git repository.

6. After you import the following two notebooks, you can follow along with the code in the two notebooks for this recipe:

    (a) `2-1.1.Mounting ADLS Gen-2 Storage FileSystem to DBFS.ipynb`

    (b) `2-1.2.Mounting Azure Blob Storage Container to DBFS.ipynb`

7. Create a container named `rawdata` in both the `cookbookadlsgen2storage` and `cookbookblobstorage` accounts you have already created, and upload the `Orders.csv` file, which you will find in the `Chapter02` folder of your cloned Git repository.

> **Note**
>
> We have tested the steps mentioned in this recipe on Azure Databricks Runtime version 6.4 which includes Spark 2.4.5 and on Runtime version 7.3 LTS which includes Spark 3.0.1.

How to do it...

The following steps show how to mount an ADLS Gen2 storage account to DBFS and view the files and folders in the `rawdata` folder:

1. Launch a Databricks workspace, open the `2_1.1.Mounting ADLS Gen-2 Storage FileSystem to DBFS.ipynb` notebook, and execute the first cell in the notebook, which contains the code shown next. Follow the steps mentioned in the *Getting ready* section to get the application ID, tenant ID, and secret, and replace the values for the variables used in the following code snippet for `clientID`, `tenantID`, and `clientSecret`:

```
#ClientId, TenantId and Secret is for the
Application(ADLSGen2App) was have created as part of this
recipe
clientID =" XXXXXb3dd-4f6e-4XXXX-b6fa-aXXXXXXX00db"
tenantID ="xxx-xxx-XXXc-xx-eXXXXXXXXXX"
```

```
clientSecret ="xxxxxx-xxxxxxxxxx-XXXXXX"
oauth2Endpoint = "https://login.microsoftonline.com/{}/
oauth2/token".format(tenantID)


configs = {"fs.azure.account.auth.type": "OAuth",
          "fs.azure.account.oauth.provider.
type": "org.apache.hadoop.fs.azurebfs.oauth2.
ClientCredsTokenProvider",
          "fs.azure.account.oauth2.client.id": clientID,
          "fs.azure.account.oauth2.client.secret":
clientSecret,
          "fs.azure.account.oauth2.client.endpoint":
oauth2Endpoint}

try:
   dbutils.fs.mount(
   source = storageEndPoint,
   mount_point = mountpoint,
   extra_configs = configs)
except:
    print("Already mounted...."+mountpoint)
```

2. After the preceding steps are executed, the ADLS Gen2 storage account will be mounted to /mnt/Gen2 in DBFS. We can check the folders and files in the storage account by executing the following code:

```
%fs ls /mnt/Gen2
```

3. You can also check the files and folders using the dbutils command, as shown in the following code snippet:

```
display(dbutils.fs.ls("/mnt/Gen2"))
```

4. Upon executing the preceding command, you should see all the folders and files you have created in the storage account.

5. To ensure we can read the orders.csv file from the mounted path, we will execute the following code:

```
df_ord= spark.read.format("csv").option("header",True).
load("dbfs:/mnt/Gen2/Orders.csv")
```

6. The following code will display the DataFrame's contents:

```
display(df_ord)
```

Up to now, we have learned how to mount ADLS Gen2 to DBFS. Now, the following steps show us how to mount an **Azure Blob storage** account to DBFS and list all files and folders created in the Blob storage account:

1. Launch a Databricks workspace, open the 2-1.2.Mounting Azure Blob Storage Container to DBFS.ipynb notebook, and execute the first cell in the notebook, which contains the following code:

```
#Storage account and key you will get it from the portal
as shown in the Cookbook Recipe.
storageAccount="cookbookblobstorage"
storageKey ="xxxxxxxxxxxxxxxxxxxxxxxxxxxxxxxxxxxxxxxx=="
mountpoint = "/mnt/Blob"
storageEndpoint =    "wasbs://rawdata@{}.blob.core.
windows.net".format(storageAccount)
storageConnSting = "fs.azure.account.key.{}.blob.core.
windows.net".format(storageAccount)


try:
    dbutils.fs.mount(
    source = storageEndpoint,
    mount_point = mountpoint,
    extra_configs = {storageConnSting:storageKey})
except:
        print("Already mounted...."+mountpoint)
```

2. After the preceding steps are executed, the ADLS Gen2 storage account will be mounted to /mnt/Gen2 in DBFS. We can check the folders and files available in the storage account by executing the following code:

```
%fs ls /mnt/Blob
```

3. You can also check the files and folders using dbutils, as shown in the following code snippet:

```
display(dbutils.fs.ls("/mnt/Blob"))
```

4. You should see all the folders and files you have created in the storage account as the output of the preceding code.

5. Run the following code to read the CSV file from the mount point:

```
df_ord= spark.read.format("csv").option("header",True).
load("dbfs:/mnt/Blob/Orders.csv")
```

6. The following code will display the DataFrame's contents:

```
display(df_ord.limit(10))
```

The preceding code will display 10 records from the DataFrame.

How it works...

The preferred way of accessing an ADLS Gen2 storage account is by mounting the storage account file system using a service principal and **Open Authentication 2.0 (OAuth 2.0)**. There are other ways of accessing a storage account from a Databricks notebook. These are listed here:

• Using a service principal directly without mounting the file system

• Using a storage key to access the Gen2 storage account directly without mounting

• Using a **shared access signature (SAS)** token

We will learn about the preceding options in the next recipes. For Azure Blob storage, you have learned how to mount a storage account by using a storage key, but there are other options as well to access an Azure Blob storage account from a Databricks notebook. These are listed here:

• Using the **Spark Dataframe application programming interface (API)**. We will learn about this option in the next recipe.

• Using a **Resilient Distributed Dataset (RDD)** API. We will not talk about this option as all our examples are using DataFrames, which is the preferred method for loading data in Databricks.

To view files in the mount points, Databricks has provided utilities to interact with the file system, called dbutils. You can perform file system operations such as listing files/folders, copying files, creating directories, and so on. You can find an entire list of operations you can perform by running the following command:

```
dbutils.fs.help()
```

The preceding command will list all the operations that can be performed on a file system in Databricks.

There's more...

You can also authenticate to ADLS Gen-2 storage accounts using storage account access key as well, but it is less secure and only preferred in non-production environments. You can get the storage account access key using the same method you have learnt for Azure Blob storage account in the *Getting ready* section of this recipe. You can run the following steps to Authenticate ADLS Gen-2 using access keys and read `Orders.csv` data.

Run the following to set the storage account and access key details in variables.

```
#This is ADLS Gen-2 accountname and access key details
storageaccount="demostoragegen2"
acct_info=f"fs.azure.account.key.{storageaccount}.dfs.core.
windows.net"
accesskey="xxx-xxx-xxx-xxx"
print(acct_info)
```

To authenticate using access key we need to set the notebook session configs by running the following code.

```
#Setting account credentials in notebook session configs
spark.conf.set(
    acct_info,
  accesskey)
```

Run the following code to verify we can authenticate using `access` key and list the `Orders.csv` file information.

```
dbutils.fs.ls("abfss://rawdata@demostoragegen2.dfs.core.
windows.net/Orders.csv")
```

Let's read the `Orders.csv` file by running through the following code.

```
ordersDF =spark.read.format("csv").option("header",True).
load("abfss://rawdata@demostoragegen2.dfs.core.windows.net/
Orders.csv")
```

In this section you have learnt how to authenticate and read data from ADLS Gen-2 using Storage Account access keys.

Reading and writing data from and to Azure Blob storage

In this recipe, you will learn how to read and write data from and to Azure Blob storage from Azure Databricks. You will learn how to access an Azure Blob storage account by doing the following:

- **Mounting storage**: Covered in the *Mounting ADLS Gen2 and Azure Blob storage to Azure DBFS* recipe of this chapter.

- **Directly accessing the Blob storage account**: In this scenario, we will not mount the Blob storage account, but we will directly access the storage endpoint to read and write files.

By the end of this recipe, you will know multiple ways to read/write files from and to an Azure Blob storage account.

Getting ready

You will need to ensure that the Azure Blob storage account is mounted by following the steps mentioned in the previous recipe. Get the storage key by following the steps mentioned in the *Mounting ADLS Gen2 and Azure Blob storage to Azure DBFS* recipe of this chapter. You can follow along by running the steps in the `2-2.Reading and Writing Data from and to Azure Blob Storage.ipynb` notebook in your local cloned repository in the `Chapter02` folder.

Upload the `csvFiles` folder in the `Chapter02/Customer` folder to the Azure Blob storage account in the `rawdata` container.

> Note
>
> We have tested the steps mentioned in this recipe on Azure Databricks Runtime version 6.4 which includes Spark 2.4.5 and on Runtime version 7.3 LTS which includes Spark 3.0.1

How to do it...

We will learn how to read the csv files under the Customer folder from the mount point and the Blob storage account directly. We will also learn how to save the DataFrame results as Parquet files in the mount point and directly to the Azure Blob storage without using the mount point:

1. Let's list the csv files we are trying to read by using the following code:

```
display(dbutils.fs.ls("/mnt/Blob/Customer/csvFiles/"))
```

2. Now, we will read the csv files in a DataFrame directly from the mount point without specifying any schema options:

```
df_cust= spark.read.format("csv").option("header",True).
load("/mnt/Blob/Customer/csvFiles/")
```

3. When you run df_cust.printSchema(), you will find that the datatypes for all columns are strings.

4. Here, we are asking Spark to infer the schema from the csv files by using option("header","true"):

```
df_cust= spark.read.format("csv").option("header",True).
option("inferSchema", True).load("/mnt/Blob/Customer/
csvFiles/")
```

5. Run the df_cust.printSchema() code, and you will find the datatype has changed for a few columns, such as CustKey, where the datatype is now being shown as an integer instead of a String.

6. We will create a schema and explicitly assign the schema while reading the CSV files:

```
cust_schema = StructType([
    StructField("C_CUSTKEY", IntegerType()),
    StructField("C_NAME", StringType()),
    StructField("C_ADDRESS", StringType()),
    StructField("C_NATIONKEY", ShortType()),
    StructField("C_PHONE", StringType()),
    StructField("C_ACCTBAL", DoubleType()),
    StructField("C_MKTSEGMENT", StringType()),
    StructField("C_COMMENT", StringType())
])
```

7. We will now create a DataFrame with the schema created in the preceding step. In this step, we are further controlling datatypes, such as for `NationKey`, where we are using `ShortType` as the datatype instead of `IntegerType`:

```
df_cust= spark.read.format("csv").option("header",True).
schema(cust_schema).load("/mnt/Blob/Customer/csvFiles/")
```

8. In this step, we will write the DataFrame that we have created in the preceding step to a mount point as a Parquet file. We will repartition the DataFrame to 10 so that we are sure 10 Parquet files are created in the mount point:

```
Mountpoint= "/mnt/Blob"
```
```
parquetCustomerDestMount = "{}/Customer/parquetFiles".
format(mountpoint)"{}/Customer/parquetFiles".
format(mountpoint)
```
```
df_cust_partitioned=df_cust.repartition(10)
```
```
df_cust_partitioned.write.mode("overwrite").
option("header", "true").parquet(parquetCustomerDestMount)
```

9. We are creating a `storageEndpoint` variable that stores the full URL for the storage account; this is used to write the data directly to Azure Blob storage without using the mount point and is declared in the second cell of the notebook:

```
storageEndpoint ="wasbs://rawdata@{}.blob.core.windows.
net".format(storageAccount)
```

10. Set up a storage access key so that we can directly read and write data from and to Azure Blob storage:

```
spark.conf.set(storageConnSting,storageKey)
```

11. After the preceding step is executed, you can directly read the CSV files from Azure Blob storage without mounting to a mount point:

```
df_cust= spark.read.format("csv").option("header",True).
schema(cust_schema).load("wasbs://rawdata@
cookbookblobstorage.blob.core.windows.net/Customer/
csvFiles/")
```

12. You can view a few records of the DataFrame by executing the following code:

```
display(df_cust.limit(10))
```

13. Let's save the `csv` data in Parquet format in Azure Blob storage directly without using the mount point. We can do this by executing the following code. We are repartitioning the DataFrame to ensure we are creating 10 Parquet files:

```
parquetCustomerDestDirect = "wasbs://rawdata@
cookbookblobstorage.blob.core.windows.net/Customer/
csvFiles/parquetFilesDirect"

df_cust_partitioned_direct=df_cust.repartition(10)

df_cust_partitioned_direct.write.
mode("overwrite").option("header", "true").
parquet(parquetCustomerDestDirect)
```

14. You can view the Parquet files created in the preceding step by executing the following code:

```
display(dbutils.fs.ls(parquetCustomerDestDirect))
```

How it works...

We have seen both ways to read and write data from and to Azure Blob storage, but in most scenarios, the preferred method is to mount the storage. This way, users don't have to worry about the source or destination storage account names and URLs.

The following code is used to directly access the Blob storage **without mounting it to DBFS**. Without running the following code, you will not be able to access the storage account and will encounter access errors while attempting to access the data:

```
spark.conf.set(storageConnSting,storageKey)
```

You can only mount block blobs to DBFS, and there are other blob types that Azure Blob storage supports—these are `page` and `append`. Once the blob storage is mounted, all users would have read and write access to the blob that is mounted to DBFS.

There's more...

Instead of a storage key, we can also access the Blob storage directly using the SAS of a container. You first need to create a SAS from the Azure portal:

1. Go to the Azure portal home page, and then, in the `CookBookRG` resource group, open the `cookbookblobstorage` Azure Blob storage account. Select the **Shared access signature** option under **Settings**:

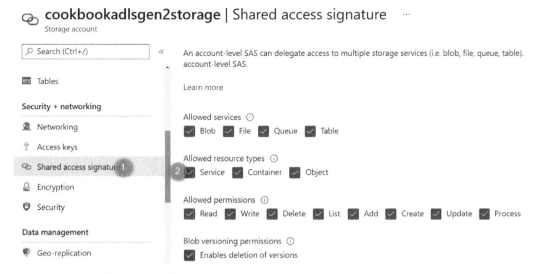

Figure 2.11 – Generating a SAS token for Azure Blob storage account

2. Once you click on **Generate SAS and connection string**, it will list the SAS token, URL, and other details, as shown in the following screenshot:

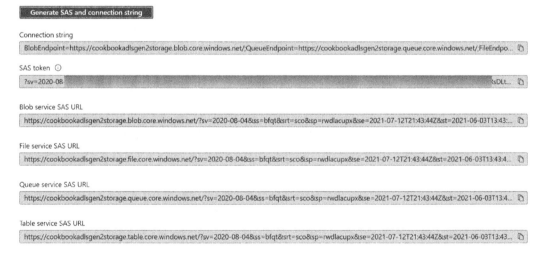

Figure 2.12 – Getting SAS token keys

3. We will be using a SAS token, as seen in the preceding screenshot, to authenticate and use it in our `spark.conf.set` code.

4. You can execute the following code to set up a SAS for a container. You will find this code in the second-to-last cell of the notebook:

```
storageConnSting = "fs.azure.sas.rawdata.{}.blob.core.
windows.net".format(storageAccount)
spark.conf.set(
  storageConnSting,
  "?sv=2019-12-12&ss=bfqt&srt=sco&sp=rwdlacupx&se=2021-
02-01T02:33:49Z&st=2021-01-31T18:33:49Z&spr=https&sig=zzz
zzzzzzzzzz")
```

5. `rawdata` in the preceding code snippet is the name of the container we created in the Azure Blob storage account. After executing the preceding code, we are authenticating to the Azure blob using a SAS token.

6. You can read the files and folders after authenticating by running `display(dbutils.fs.ls(storageEndpointFolders))`.

Reading and writing data from and to ADLS Gen2

In this recipe, you will learn how to read and write data to ADLS Gen2 from Databricks. We can do this by following these two methods:

-   **Mounting storage**: Covered in the *Mounting ADLS Gen2 and Azure Blob storage to Azure DBFS* recipe of this chapter.

-   **Directly accessing the ADLS Gen2 storage using a SAS token and a service principal**: In this scenario, we will not mount the storage, but we will directly access the storage endpoint to read and write files using storage keys, service principals, and OAuth 2.0.

ADLS Gen2 provides file system semantics, which provides security to folders and files, and the hierarchical directory structure provides efficient access to the data in the storage.

By the end of this recipe, you will know multiple ways to read/write files from and to an ADLS Gen2 account.

Getting ready

You will need to ensure you have the following items before starting to work on this recipe:

- An ADLS Gen2 account, mounted by following the steps in the first recipe of this chapter, *Mounting ADLS Gen2 and Azure Blob to Azure Databricks File System*.

- Storage keys—you can get these by following the steps mentioned in the first recipe of this chapter, *Mounting ADLS Gen2 and Azure Blob to Azure Databricks File System*.

You can follow along by running the steps in the 2-3.Reading and Writing Data from and to ADLS Gen-2.ipynb notebook in your local cloned repository in the Chapter02 folder.

Upload the csvFiles folder in the Chapter02/Customer folder to the ADLS Gen2 account in the rawdata file system.

> **Note**
> We have tested the steps mentioned in this recipe on Azure Databricks Runtime version 6.4 which includes Spark 2.4.5 and on Runtime version 7.3 LTS which includes Spark 3.0.1

How to do it...

We will learn how to read CSV files from the mount point and the ADLS Gen2 storage directly. We will perform basic aggregation on the DataFrame, such as counting and storing the result in another csv file.

Working with the mount point, we'll proceed as follows:

1. Let's list the CSV files we are trying to read from the mount point:

    ```
    display(dbutils.fs.ls("/mnt/Gen2/Customer/csvFiles/"))
    ```

2. We will read the csv files directly from the mount point without specifying any schema options:

    ```
    df_cust= spark.read.format("csv").option("header",True).
    load("/mnt/Gen2/Customer/csvFiles/")
    ```

3. When you run df_cust.printSchema(), you will find that the datatypes for all columns are strings.

4. Next, we will run the same code as in the preceding step, but this time asking Spark to infer the schema from csv files by using option("header","true"):

```
df_cust= spark.read.format("csv").option("header",True).
option("inferSchema", True).load("/mnt/Gen2/Customer/
csvFiles/")
```

5. Run df_cust.printSchema(), and you will find the datatype has changed for a few columns such as CustKey, where the datatype now being shown is an integer instead of a string.

6. We will now create a schema and explicitly provide it while reading the csv files using a DataFrame:

```
cust_schema = StructType([
    StructField("C_CUSTKEY", IntegerType()),
    StructField("C_NAME", StringType()),
    StructField("C_ADDRESS", StringType()),
    StructField("C_NATIONKEY", ShortType()),
    StructField("C_PHONE", StringType()),
    StructField("C_ACCTBAL", DoubleType()),
    StructField("C_MKTSEGMENT", StringType()),
    StructField("C_COMMENT", StringType())
])
```

7. Create a DataFrame by using the schema created in the preceding step:

```
df_cust= spark.read.format("csv").option("header",True).
schema(cust_schema).load("/mnt/Gen2/Customer/csvFiles/")
```

8. In the following step, we will be performing basic aggregation on the DataFrame:

```
df_cust_agg = df_cust.groupBy("C_MKTSEGMENT")
.agg(sum("C_ACCTBAL").cast('decimal(20,3)').alias("sum_
acctbal"), avg("C_ACCTBAL").alias("avg_acctbal"),
max("C_ACCTBAL").alias("max_bonus")).orderBy("avg_
acctbal",ascending=False)
```

9. We will write the DataFrame we created in the preceding step to the mount point and save it in CSV format:

```
df_cust_agg.write.mode("overwrite").option("header",
"true").csv("/mnt/Gen-2/CustMarketSegmentAgg/"))
```

10. To list the CSV file created, run the following code:

```
(dbutils.fs.ls("/mnt/Gen-2/CustMarketSegmentAgg/"))
```

We'll now work with an ADLS Gen2 storage account without mounting it to DBFS:

1. You can access an ADLS Gen2 storage account directly without mounting to DBFS using OAuth 2.0 and a service principal. You can access any ADLS Gen2 storage account that the service principal has permissions on. We need to set the credentials first in our notebook before we can directly access the file system. `clientID` and `clientSecret` are the variables defined in the notebook:

```
spark.conf.set("fs.azure.account.auth.type.
cookbookadlsgen2storage.dfs.core.windows.net", "OAuth")

spark.conf.set("fs.azure.account.oauth.provider.
type.cookobookadlsgen2storage.dfs.core.windows.
net", "org.apache.hadoop.fs.azurebfs.oauth2.
ClientCredsTokenProvider")

spark.conf.set("fs.azure.account.oauth2.client.
id.cookbookadlsgen2storage.dfs.core.windows.net",
clientID)

spark.conf.set("fs.azure.account.oauth2.client.
secret.cookbookadlsgen2storage.dfs.core.windows.net",
clientSecret)

spark.conf.set("fs.azure.account.oauth2.client.
endpoint.cookbookadlsgen2storage.dfs.core.windows.net",
oauth2Endpoint)
```

2. After the preceding step is executed, you can directly read the `csv` files from the ADLS Gen2 storage account without mounting it:

```
df_direct = spark.read.format("csv").
option("header",True).schema(cust_schema).load("abfss://
rawdata@cookbookadlsgen2storage.dfs.core.windows.net/
Customer/csvFiles")
```

3. You can view a few records of the DataFrame by executing the following code:

```
display(df_direct.limit(10))
```

4. We will now write a DataFrame in Parquet format in the ADLS Gen2 storage account directly, without using the mount point, by executing the following code. We are repartitioning the DataFrame to ensure we are creating 10 Parquet files:

```
parquetCustomerDestDirect = "abfss://rawdata@
cookbookadlsgen2storage.dfs.core.windows.net/Customer/
parquetFiles"

df_direct_repart=df_direct.repartition(10)

df_direct_repart.write.mode("overwrite").option("header",
"true").parquet(parquetCustomerDestDirect)
```

5. You can create a DataFrame on the Parquet files created in the preceding step to ensure we are able to read the data:

```
df_parquet = spark.read.format("parquet").
option("header",True).schema(cust_schema).load("abfss://
rawdata@cookbookadlsgen2storage.dfs.core.windows.net/
Customer/parquetFiles")
```

6. You can view the Parquet files created in the preceding step by executing the following code:

```
display(dbutils.fs.ls(parquetCustomerDestDirect))
```

How it works...

The following code is set to directly access the ADL Gen2 storage account without mounting to DBFS. These settings are applicable when we are using DataFrame or dataset APIs:

```
spark.conf.set("fs.azure.account.auth.type.
cookbookadlsgen2storage.dfs.core.windows.net", "OAuth")

spark.conf.set("fs.azure.account.oauth.provider.type.
cookbookadlsgen2storage.dfs.core.windows.net", "org.apache.
hadoop.fs.azurebfs.oauth2.ClientCredsTokenProvider")

spark.conf.set("fs.azure.account.oauth2.client.
id.cookbookadlsgen2storage.dfs.core.windows.net", clientID)

spark.conf.set("fs.azure.account.oauth2.client.secret.
cookbookadlsgen2storage.dfs.core.windows.net", clientSecret)

spark.conf.set("fs.azure.account.oauth2.client.endpoint.
cookbookadlsgen2storage.dfs.core.windows.net", oauth2Endpoint)
```

You should set the preceding values in your notebook session if you want the users to directly access the ADLS Gen2 storage account without mounting to DBFS. This method is useful when you are doing some ad hoc analysis and don't want users to create multiple mount points when you are trying to access data from various ADLS Gen2 storage accounts.

Reading and writing data from and to an Azure SQL database using native connectors

Reading and writing data from and to an Azure SQL database is the most important step in most data ingestion pipelines. You will have a step in your data ingestion pipeline where you will load the transformed data into Azure SQL or read raw data from Azure SQL to perform some transformations.

In this recipe, you will learn how to read and write data using SQL Server JDBC Driver and the Apache Spark connector for Azure SQL.

Getting ready

The Apache Spark connector for Azure SQL only supports Spark 2.4.x and 3.0.x clusters as of now and might change in future. SQL Server JDBC Driver supports both Spark 2.4.x and 3.0.x clusters. Before we start working on the recipe, we need to create a Spark 2.4.x or 3.0.x cluster. You can follow the steps mentioned in the *Creating a cluster from the UI to create 2.x clusters* recipe from *Chapter 1, Creating an Azure Databricks Service*.

We have used Databricks Runtime Version 7.3 LTS with Spark 3.0.1 having Scala version as 2.12 for this recipe. The code is tested with Databricks Runtime Version 6.4 that includes Spark 2.4.5 and Scala 2.11 as well

You need to create an Azure SQL database—to do so, follow the steps at this link:

```
https://docs.microsoft.com/en-us/azure/azure-sql/database/
single-database-create-quickstart?tabs=azure-portal
```

After your Azure SQL database is created, connect to the database and create the following table in the newly created database:

```
CREATE TABLE [dbo].[CUSTOMER] (
    [C_CUSTKEY] [int] NULL,
    [C_NAME] [varchar](25) NULL,
    [C_ADDRESS] [varchar](40) NULL,
    [C_NATIONKEY] [smallint] NULL,
```

```
        [C_PHONE] [char](15) NULL,
        [C_ACCTBAL] [decimal](18, 0) NULL,
        [C_MKTSEGMENT] [char](10) NULL,
        [C_COMMENT] [varchar](117) NULL
) ON [PRIMARY]
GO
```

Once the table is created, you can proceed with the steps mentioned in the *How to do it...* section. You can follow along the steps mentioned in the notebook *2_4.Reading and Writing from and to Azure SQL Database.ipynb*.

How to do it...

You will learn how to use SQL Server JDBC Driver and the Apache Spark connector for Azure SQL to read and write data to and from an Azure SQL database. You will learn how to install the Spark connector for Azure SQL in a Databricks cluster.

Here are the steps to read data from an Azure SQL database using SQL Server JDBC Driver:

1. First, create a variable for the connection string and the table from which we will be reading and writing the data. We will load the csv files from ADLS Gen2 that we saw in the *Reading and writing data from and to ADLS Gen2* recipe:

    ```
    # Details about connection string
    logicalServername = "demologicalserver.database.windows.
    net"
    databaseName = "demoDB"
    tableName = "CUSTOMER"
    userName = "sqladmin"
    password = "Password@Strong12345" # Please specify
    password here
    jdbcUrl = "jdbc:sqlserver://{0}:{1};database={2}".
    format(logicalServername, 1433, databaseName)
    connectionProperties = {
       "user" : userName,
       "password" : password,
        "driver" : "com.microsoft.sqlserver.jdbc.
    SQLServerDriver"
    }
    ```

2. As you can see from the preceding step, the driver we are using is called SQLServerDriver, which comes installed as part of Databricks Runtime.

3. Create a schema for the csv files, store this in ADLS Gen-2, and mount the storage to DBFS. Follow the steps mentioned in the third recipe, *Reading and writing data from and to ADLS Gen2*, to learn how to mount storage to DBFS:

```
#Creating a schema which can be passed while creating the
DataFrame
cust_schema = StructType([
    StructField("C_CUSTKEY", IntegerType()),
    StructField("C_NAME", StringType()),
    StructField("C_ADDRESS", StringType()),
    StructField("C_NATIONKEY", ShortType()),
    StructField("C_PHONE", StringType()),
    StructField("C_ACCTBAL", DecimalType(18,2)),
    StructField("C_MKTSEGMENT", StringType()),
    StructField("C_COMMENT", StringType())
])
```

4. Once a schema is created, we will read the csv files in a DataFrame:

```
# Reading customer csv files in a DataFrame. This
Dataframe will be written to Customer table in Azure SQL
DB
df_cust= spark.read.format("csv").option("header",True).
schema(cust_schema).load("dbfs:/mnt/Gen2/Customer/
csvFiles")
```

5. After the preceding step is executed, we will write the DataFrame to the dbo. CUSTOMER table that we have already created as part of the *Getting ready* section:

```
df_cust.write.jdbc(jdbcUrl,
                   mode ="append",
                   table=tableName,
                   properties=connectionProperties)
```

6. After loading the data, we will read the table to count the number of records inserted in the table:

```
df_jdbcRead= spark.read.jdbc(jdbcUrl,
                   table=tableName,
```

```
                          properties=connectionProperties)
# Counting number of rows
df_jdbcRead.count()
```

Here are the steps to read data from an Azure SQL database using **Apache Spark Connector** for Azure SQL Database.

Connector	Maven Coordinate	Scala Version
Spark 2.4.x compatible connnector	com.microsoft.azure:spark-mssql-connector:1.0.2	2.11
Spark 3.0.x compatible connnector	com.microsoft.azure:spark-mssql-connector_2.12:1.1.0	2.12

Table 2.1 - Compatible connectors for Spark 2.4.x and Spark 3.0.x clusters

You can also download the connector from `https://search.maven.org/search?q=spark-mssql-connector`.

1. After a Spark 2.4.x or 3.0.x cluster is created, you need to install Spark connector for Azure SQL DB from Maven. Make sure you use the coordinates as mentioned in the preceding table. Go to the Databricks **Clusters** page and click on **Libraries**. Then, click on **Install New** and select the library source as **Maven**. Now, click on **Search Packages** and search for `spark-mssql-connector`:

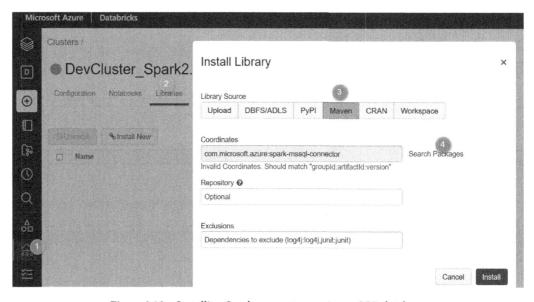

Figure 2.13 – Installing Spark connector on Azure SQL database

2. Under **Search Packages**, select **Maven Central** and search for `spark-mssql-connector` and select the version with artifact id `spark-mssql-connector_2.12` with **Releases** as 1.1.0 as we are using Spark 3.0.1 cluster and click on **Select**. You can use any latest version which is available when you are going through the recipe. If you are using Spark 2.4.x cluster then you must use the version with Artifact Id as `spark-mssql-connector` with **Releases** version 1.0.2.

← Search Packages   ×

Maven Central ∨	Q spark-mssql-connector		
Group Id	**Artifact Id**	**Releases**	**Options**
com.microsoft.azure	spark-mssql-connector	1.0.2 ∨	Select
com.microsoft.azure	spark-mssql-connector_2.12	1.1.0 ∨	Select
com.microsoft.azure	spark-mssql-connector_2.11_2.4	1.0.2 ∨	Select
com.microsoft.azure	spark-mssql-connector_2.12_3.0	1.0.0-alpha ∨	Select

Figure 2.14 – Installing Spark connector on Azure SQL database (continued)

3. After selecting the package, it gets installed and you will see the status as **Installed**:

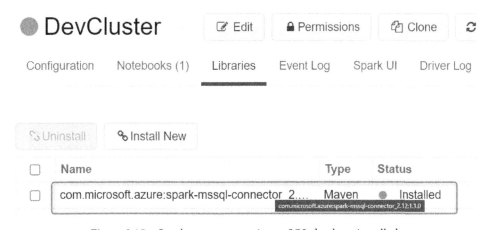

Figure 2.15 – Spark connector to Azure SQL database installed

4. After the Spark connector for Azure SQL is installed then you can run the follow code for setting the connection string for Azure SQL

```
server_name = f"jdbc:sqlserver://{logicalServername}"
database_name = "demoDB"
url = server_name + ";" + "databaseName=" + database_name
+ ";"
table_name = "dbo.Customer"
username = "sqladmin"
password = "xxxxxx" # Please specify password here
```

5. After the Spark connector is installed, we will read the records from the dbo. CUSTOMER table using the newly installed Spark connector for Azure SQL:

```
sparkconnectorDF = spark.read \
        .format("com.microsoft.sqlserver.jdbc.spark") \
        .option("url", url) \
        .option("dbtable", table_name) \
        .option("user", username) \
        .option("password", password).load()
```

6. Run the following code to check the schema of the DataFrame created as part of the preceding step:

```
display(sparkconnectorDF.printSchema())
```

7. To view a few records from the DataFrame, run the following code:

```
display(sparkconnectorDF.limit(10))
```

8. Create a schema for the csv files, store this in ADLS Gen-2, and mount it to DBFS. Follow the steps mentioned in the *Reading and writing data from and to ADLS Gen2* recipe to learn how to mount ADLS Gen-2 Storage Account to DBFS:

```
#Creating a schema which can be passed while creating the
DataFrame
cust_schema = StructType([
    StructField("C_CUSTKEY", IntegerType()),
    StructField("C_NAME", StringType()),
    StructField("C_ADDRESS", StringType()),
    StructField("C_NATIONKEY", ShortType()),
    StructField("C_PHONE", StringType()),
```

```
        StructField("C_ACCTBAL", DecimalType(18,2)),
        StructField("C_MKTSEGMENT", StringType()),
        StructField("C_COMMENT", StringType())
    ])
```

9. Once a schema is created, we will load the csv files in a DataFrame by running the following code:

```
df_cust= spark.read.format("csv").option("header",True).
schema(cust_schema).load("dbfs:/mnt/Gen2/Customer/
csvFiles")
```

10. In the following step, we will learn how we can write the DataFrame to an Azure SQL database table using the append method:

```
#Appending records to the existing table
try:
  df_cust.write \
    .format("com.microsoft.sqlserver.jdbc.spark") \
    .mode("append") \
    .option("url", url) \
    .option("dbtable", tableName) \
    .option("user", userName) \
    .option("password", password) \
    .save()
except ValueError as error :
    print("Connector write failed", error)
```

11. The preceding code will append the data in the existing table; if no table exists, then it will throw an error. The following code will overwrite the existing data in the table:

```
try:
  df_cust.write \
    .format("com.microsoft.sqlserver.jdbc.spark") \
    .mode("overwrite") \
    .option("truncate",True) \
    .option("url", url) \
    .option("dbtable", tableName) \
    .option("user", userName) \
    .option("password", password) \
```

```
        .save()
except ValueError as error :
        print("Connector write failed", error)
```

12. As the last step, we will read the data loaded in the customer table to ensure the data is loaded properly:

```
#Read the data from the table
sparkconnectorDF = spark.read \
        .format("com.microsoft.sqlserver.jdbc.spark") \
        .option("url", url) \
        .option("dbtable", table_name) \
        .option("user", username) \
        .option("password", password).load()
```

How it works...

The Apache Spark connector works the latest version of Spark 2.4.x and Spark 3.0.x. It can be used for both SQL Server and Azure SQL Database and is customized for SQL Server and Azure SQL Database for performing big data analytics efficiently. The following document outlines the benefits of using the Spark connector and provides a performance comparison between the JDBC connector and the Spark connector:

https://docs.microsoft.com/en-us/sql/connect/spark/connector?view=sql-server-ver15

To overwrite the data using the Spark connector, we are in overwrite mode, which will drop and recreate the table with the scheme based on the source DataFrame schema, and none of the indexes that were present on that table will be added after the table is recreated. If we want to recreate the indexes with overwrite mode, then we need to include the True option (truncate). This option will ensure that after a table is dropped and created, the required index will be created as well.

Just to append data to an existing table, we will use append mode, whereby the existing table will not be dropped or recreated. If the table is not found, it throws an error. This option is used when we are just inserting data into a raw table. If it's a staging table where we want to truncate before load, then we need to use overwrite mode with the truncate option.

Reading and writing data from and to Azure Synapse SQL (dedicated SQL pool) using native connectors

In this recipe, you will learn how to read and write data to Azure Synapse Analytics using Azure Databricks.

Azure Synapse Analytics is a data warehouse hosted in the cloud that leverages **massively parallel processing** (**MPP**) to run complex queries across large volumes of data.

Azure Synapse can be accessed from Databricks using the Azure Synapse connector. DataFrames can be directly loaded as a table in a Synapse Spark pool. Azure Blob storage is used as temporary storage to upload data between Azure Databricks and Azure Synapse with the Azure Synapse connector.

Getting ready

You will need to ensure you have the following items before starting to work on this recipe:

- An Azure Synapse Analytics workspace. You can follow the steps mentioned in the following link to create Synapse Workspace and SQL Pool.

  https://docs.microsoft.com/en-in/azure/synapse-analytics/ get-started-create-workspace

- We are using Azure Databrick Runtime 7.3 LTS with Spark Cluster 3.0.1

- A database master key for Azure Synapse Dedicated SQL Pool. Run the following command in the SQL Pool to create the Master Key.

```
CREATE MASTER KEY
```

- Account Name and Storage keys for Azure Storage Blob —get these by following the steps mentioned in the *Mounting ADLS Gen-2 and Azure Blob storage to Azure DBFS* recipe of this chapter

- Service principal details—get these by following the steps mentioned in the *Mounting ADLS Gen-2 and Azure Blob storage to Azure DBFS* recipe of this chapter

- A mounted ADLS Gen-2 storage account—get this by following the steps mentioned in the *Mounting ADLS Gen-2 and Azure Blob storage to Azure DBFS* recipe of this chapter

- Use the same Customer `csvFiles` that was used in the *Reading and writing data from and to Azure Blob* recipe.

- Get the JDBC connection string of Synapse Workspace. Go to the **Dedicated SQL Pool** that you have created in the Synapse Workspace and in the **Overview** tab click on **Show database connection strings**. Under the **Connection strings** tab, click on **JDBC** and copy the connection string under **JDBC (SQL authentication)**

You can follow the steps by running the steps in the `2_5.Reading and Writing Data from and to Azure Synapse.ipynb` notebook in your local cloned repository in the `Chapter02` folder.

Upload the `csvFiles` folder in the `Chapter02/Customer` folder to the ADLS Gen2 account in the `rawdata` file system. We have mounted the `rawdata` container as `/mnt/Gen2Source`.

How to do it...

In this section, you will see the steps for reading data from an ADLS Gen2 storage account and writing data to Azure Synapse Analytics using the Azure Synapse connector:

1. You need to mount the storage location for accessing the data files from the storage account. You can find detailed steps on how to mount ADLS Gen-2 in the *Mounting ADLS Gen-2 and Azure Blob Storage to Azure Databricks File System* recipe. Run the following to mount ADLS Gen-2 Storage Account.

```
storageAccount="teststoragegen2"

mountpoint = "/mnt/Gen2Source"

storageEndPoint ="abfss://rawdata@{}.dfs.core.windows.
net/".format(storageAccount)

print ('Mount Point ='+mountpoint)


#ClientId, TenantId and Secret is for the
Application(ADLSGen2App) was have created as part of this
recipe
clientID ="xxx-xxx-xx-xxx"

tenantID ="xx-xxx-xxx-xxx"

clientSecret ="xx-xxx-xxx-xxx"

oauth2Endpoint = "https://login.microsoftonline.com/{}/
oauth2/token".format(tenantID)


configs = {"fs.azure.account.auth.type": "OAuth",
```

```
"fs.azure.account.oauth.provider.type": "org.apache.
hadoop.fs.azurebfs.oauth2.ClientCredsTokenProvider",

"fs.azure.account.oauth2.client.id": clientID,

"fs.azure.account.oauth2.client.secret": clientSecret,

"fs.azure.account.oauth2.client.endpoint":
oauth2Endpoint}
```

```
dbutils.fs.mount(

source = storageEndPoint,

mount_point = mountpoint,

extra_configs = configs)
```

2. Copy and run the following code to see the csv files in the ADLS Gen-2 account:

```
display(dbutils.fs.ls("/mnt/Gen2Source/Customer/csvFiles
"))
```

3. Provide the Azure Storage account configuration like Storage Account name and Storage Key. This is used by both the Azure Databricks cluster and Azure Synapse Dedicated SQL Pool to access a common Blob Storage Account for exchanging data between them. Azure Synapse connector triggers the Spark job in Azure Databricks cluster to read and write data from and to the common Blob Storage Account.

```
blobStorage = "stgcccookbook.blob.core.windows.net"
blobContainer = "synapse"
blobAccessKey = "xxxxxxxxxxxxxxxxxxxxxxxxx"
```

4. The following code will be used for specifying an intermediate temporary folder required for moving data between Azure Databricks and Azure Synapse:

```
tempDir = "wasbs://" + blobContainer + "@" + blobStorage
+"/tempDirs"
```

5. Execute the following code to store the Azure Blob storage access keys in the Notebook session configuration. This configuration will not impact other Notebooks attached to the same cluster.

```
acntInfo = "fs.azure.account.key."+ blobStorage
spark.conf.set(
  acntInfo,
  blobAccessKey)
```

6. Run the following code to load the DataFrame from the `csv` files in the ADLS Gen-2 Storage Account:

```
customerDF =
spark.read.format("csv").option("header",True).
option("inferSchema", True).load("dbfs:/mnt/Gen2Source/
Customer/csvFiles")
```

7. Run the following command to store the JDBC URL for the Synapse Dedicated SQL Pool in a variable.

```
# We have changed trustServerCertificate=true from
trustServerCertificate=false. In certain cases, you might
get errors like
'''
The driver could not establish a secure connection
to SQL Server by using Secure Sockets Layer (SSL)
encryption. Error: "Failed to validate the server name
in a certificate during Secure Sockets Layer (SSL)
initialization.". ClientConnectionId:sadasd-asds-asdasd
[ErrorCode = 0] [SQLState = 08S '''

sqlDwUrl="jdbc:sqlserver://
synapsetestdemoworkspace.sql.azuresynapse.
net:1433;database=sqldwpool1;user=sqladminuser@
synapsetestdemoworkspace;password=xxxxxxx;encrypt=true;
trustServerCertificate=true;hostNameInCertificate=*.sql.
azuresynapse.net;loginTimeout=30;"
db_table = "dbo.customer"
```

8. Execute the following code to load the `customerDF` DataFrame as a table into Azure Synapse Dedicated SQL Pool. This creates a table named `CustomerTable` in the SQL database. You can query the table using **SQL Server Management Studio (SSMS)** or from Synapse Studio. This is the default save mode where when writing a DataFrame to Dedicated SQL Pool, if table already exists then an exception is thrown else it will create a table and populated the data in the table:

```
customerDF.write \
    .format("com.databricks.spark.sqldw")\
    .option("url", sqlDwUrl)\
    .option("forwardSparkAzureStorageCredentials", "true")\
```

```
.option("dbTable", db_table)\
.option("tempDir", tempDir)\
.save()
```

9. Connect to the SQL database using SSMS, and you can query data from the CustomerTable table:

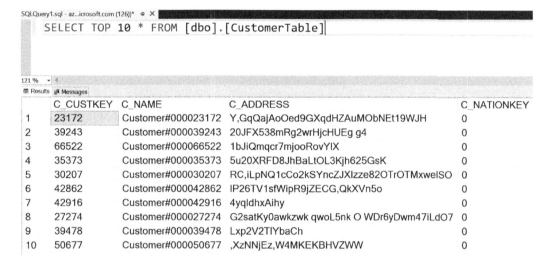

Figure 2.16 – Azure Synapse table verification

10. Run the following code which will append the data to an existing dbo.Customer table.

```
# This code is writing to data into SQL Pool with append
save option. In append save option data is appended to
existing table.
customerDF.write \
    .format("com.databricks.spark.sqldw")\
    .option("url", sqlDwUrl)\
    .option("forwardSparkAzureStorageCredentials", "true")\
    .option("dbTable", db_table)\
    .option("tempDir", tempDir)\
    .mode("append")\
    .save()
```

11. Run the following code which will overwrite the data in an existing dbo. Customer table.

```
customerDF.write \
    .format("com.databricks.spark.sqldw")\
    .option("url", sqlDwUrl)\
    .option("forwardSparkAzureStorageCredentials", "true")\
    .option("dbTable", db_table)\
    .option("tempDir", tempDir)\
    .mode("overwrite")\
    .save()
```

12. Run the following code to read data from Azure Synapse Dedicated SQL Pool using an Azure Synapse connector:

```
customerTabledf = spark.read \
    .format("com.databricks.spark.sqldw") \
    .option("url", sqlDwUrl) \
    .option("tempDir", tempDir) \
    .option("forwardSparkAzureStorageCredentials", "true") \
    .option("dbTable", db_table) \
    .load()
```

13. You can see the result in the DataFrame by using the following code:

```
customerTabledf.show()
```

14. Instead of table you can use query to read data from Dedicated SQL Pool. You can see from the following code that we have used option("query",query) to run a query on the database.

```
query= " select C_MKTSEGMENT, count(*) as Cnt from [dbo].
[customer] group by C_MKTSEGMENT"
df_query = spark.read \
    .format("com.databricks.spark.sqldw") \
    .option("url", sqlDwUrl) \
    .option("tempDir", tempDir) \
    .option("forwardSparkAzureStorageCredentials", "true")
```

```
      \
        .option("query", query) \
        .load()
```

15. You can execute the following code to display the results.

```
      display(df_query.limit(5))
```

By the end of this recipe, you have learnt how to read and write data from and to Synapse Dedicated SQL Pool using the Azure Synapse Connector from Azure Databricks.

How it works...

In Azure Synapse, data loading and unloading operations are performed by PolyBase and are triggered by the Azure Synapse connector through JDBC.

For Databricks Runtime 7.0 and above, the Azure Synapse connector through JDBC uses COPY to load data into Azure Synapse.

The Azure Synapse connector triggers Apache Spark jobs to read and write data to the Blob storage container.

We are using spark.conf.set (**acntInfo**, **blobAccessKey**) so that Spark connects to the Storage Blob container using the built-in connectors. We can use ADLS Gen-2 as well to the store the data read from Synapse or data written to Synapse Dedicated SQL Pool.

Spark connects to Synapse using the JDBC drivers with username and password. Azure Synapse connects to Azure Storage Blob account using account key and it can use Managed Service Identity as well to connect.

Following is the JDBC connection string used in the Notebook. In this case we have changed trustServerCertificate value to true from false (which is default value) and by doing so, Microsoft JDBC Driver for SQL Server won't validate the SQL Server TLS certificate. This change must be done only in test environments and not in production.

```
sqlDwUrl="jdbc:sqlserver://synapsetestdemoworkspace.sql.
azuresynapse.net:1433;database=sqldwpool1;user=sqladminuser@
synapsetestdemoworkspace;password=xxxxxxx;encrypt=true;
trustServerCertificate=true;hostNameInCertificate=*.sql.
azuresynapse.net;loginTimeout=30;"
```

If you are not creating the Master Key in the Synapse Dedicated SQL Pool you will be getting the following error while reading the data from the Dedicated SQL Pool from Azure Databricks Notebook.

```
Underlying SQLException(s):
    - com.microsoft.sqlserver.jdbc.SQLServerException: Please
create a master key in the database or open the master key
in the session before performing this operation. [ErrorCode =
15581] [SQLState = S0006]
```

When you are writing the data to Dedicated SQL Pools you will see the following messages while code is getting executed n the Notebook.

```
Waiting for Azure Synapse Analytics to load intermediate data
from wasbs://synapse@stgacccookbook.blob.core.windows.net/
tempDirs/2021-08-07/04-19-43-514/cb6dd9a2-da6b-4748-a34d-
0961d2df981f/ into "dbo"."customer" using COPY.
```

Spark is writing the csv files to the common Blob Storage as parquet files and then Synapse uses COPY statement to load the parquet files to the final tables. You can check in Blob Storage Account, and you will find the parquet files created. When you look at the DAG for the execution (you will learn more about DAG in upcoming recipes) you will find that Spark is reading the CSV files and writing to Blob Storage as parquet format.

When you are reading data from Synapse Dedicated SQL Pool tables you will see the following messages in the Notebook while the code is getting executed.

```
Waiting for Azure Synapse Analytics to unload intermediate
data under wasbs://synapse@stgacccookbook.blob.core.windows.
net/tempDirs/2021-08-07/04-24-56-781/esds43c1-bc9e-4dc4-bc07-
c4368d20c467/ using Polybase
```

Azure Synapse is writing the data from Dedicated SQL Pool to common Blob storage as parquet files first with snappy compression and then its is read by Spark and displayed to the end user when customerTabledf.show() is executed.

We are setting up the account key and secret for the common Blob Storage in the session configuration associated with the Notebook using spark.conf.set and setting the value **forwardSparkAzureStorageCredentials** as true. By setting the value as true, Azure Synapse connector will forward the Storage Account access key to the Azure Synapse Dedicated Pool by creating a temporary Azure Database Scoped Credentials.

Reading and writing data from and to Azure Cosmos DB

Azure Cosmos DB is Microsoft's globally distributed multi-model database service. Azure Cosmos DB enables you to manage your data scattered around different data centers across the world and also provides a mechanism to scale data distribution patterns and computational resources. It supports multiple data models, which means it can be used for storing documents and relational, key-value, and graph models. It is more or less a NoSQL database as it doesn't have any schema. Azure Cosmos DB provides APIs for the following data models, and their **software development kits (SDKs)** are available in multiple languages:

- **SQL API**

- **MongoDB API**

- **Cassandra API**

- **Graph (Gremlin) API**

- **Table API**

The Cosmos DB Spark connector is used for accessing Azure Cosmos DB. It is used for batch and streaming data processing and as a serving layer for the required data. It supports both the Scala and Python languages. The Cosmos DB Spark connector supports the core (SQL) API of Azure Cosmos DB.

This recipe explains how to read and write data to and from Azure Cosmos DB using Azure Databricks.

Getting ready

You will need to ensure you have the following items before starting to work on this recipe:

- An Azure Databricks workspace. Refer to *Chapter 1, Creating an Azure Databricks Service,* to create an Azure Databricks workspace.

- Download the Cosmos DB Spark connector.

- An Azure Cosmos DB account.

You can follow the steps mentioned in the following link to create Azure Cosmos DB account from Azure Portal.

```
https://docs.microsoft.com/en-us/azure/cosmos-db/create-
cosmosdb-resources-portal#:~:text=How%20to%20Create%20
a%20Cosmos%20DB%20Account%201,the%20Azure%20Cosmos%20DB%20
account%20page.%20See%20More.
```

Once the Azure Cosmos DB account is created create a database with name **Sales** and container with name **Customer** and use the **Partition key** as /C_MKTSEGMENT while creating the new container as shown in the following screenshot.

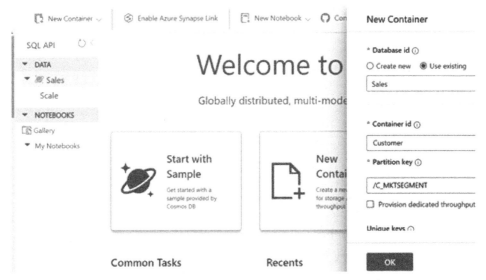

Figure 2.17 – Adding New Container in Cosmos DB Account in Sales Database

You can follow the steps by running the steps in the 2_6.Reading and Writing Data from and to Azure Cosmos DB.ipynb notebook in your local cloned repository in the Chapter02 folder.

Upload the csvFiles folder in the Chapter02/Customer folder to the ADLS Gen2 account in the rawdata file system.

Note

At the time of writing this recipe Cosmos DB connector for Spark 3.0 is not available.

You can download the latest Cosmos DB Spark `uber-jar` file from following link. Latest one at the time of writing this recipe was 3.6.14.

```
https://search.maven.org/artifact/com.microsoft.azure/azure-
cosmosdb-spark_2.4.0_2.11/3.6.14/jar
```

If you want to work with 3.6.14 version then you can download the `jar` file from following GitHub URL as well.

```
https://github.com/PacktPublishing/Azure-Databricks-Cookbook/
blob/main/Chapter02/azure-cosmosdb-spark_2.4.0_2.11-3.6.14-
uber.jar
```

You need to get the Endpoint and MasterKey for the Azure Cosmos DB which will be used to authenticate to Azure Cosmos DB account from Azure Databricks. To get the Endpoint and MasterKey, go to Azure Cosmos DB account and click on **Keys** under the **Settings** section and copy the values for **URI** and **PRIMARY KEY** under **Read-write Keys** tab.

How to do it...

Let's get started with this section.

1. Create a new Spark Cluster and ensure you are choosing the configuration that is supported by the Spark Cosmos connector. Choosing low or higher version will give errors while reading data from Azure Cosmos DB hence select the right configuration while creating the cluster as shown in following table:

Component	Version
Apache Spark	2.4.x, 2.3.x, 2.2.x, and 2.1.x
Scala	2.11
Azure Databricks runtime version	> 3.4

Table 2.2 – Configuration to create a new cluster

The following screenshot shows the configuration of the cluster:

Figure 2.18 – Azure Databricks cluster

2. After your cluster is created, navigate to the cluster page, and select the **Libraries** tab. Select **Install New** and upload the Spark connector `jar` file to install the library. This is the `uber jar` file which is mentioned in the *Getting ready* section:

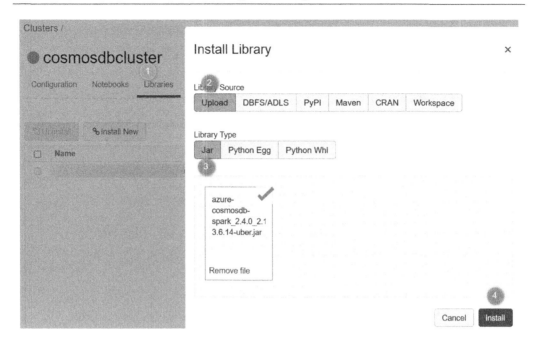

Figure 2.19 – Cluster library installation

3. You can verify that the library was installed on the **Libraries** tab:

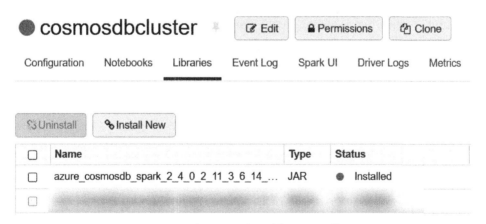

Figure 2.20 – Cluster verifying library installation

4. Once the library is installed, you are good to connect to Cosmos DB from the Azure Databricks notebook.

5. We will use the customer data from the ADLS Gen2 storage account to write the data in Cosmos DB. Run the following code to list the `csv` files in the storage account:

```
display(dbutils.fs.ls("/mnt/Gen2/ Customer/csvFiles/"))
```

6. Run the following code which will read the `csv` files from mount point into a DataFrame.

```
customerDF = spark.read.format("csv").
option("header",True).option("inferSchema", True).
load("dbfs:/mnt/Gen2Source/Customer/csvFiles")
```

7. Provide the cosmos DB configuration by executing the following code. `Collection` is the **Container** that you have created in the Sales Database in Cosmos DB.

```
writeConfig = (
   "Endpoint" : "https://testcosmosdb.documents.azure.
com:443/",
   "Masterkey" : "xxxxx-xxxx-xxx"
   "Database" : "Sales",
   "Collection" :"Customer",
   "preferredRegions" : "East US")
```

8. Run the following code to write the `csv` files loaded in customerDF DataFrame to Cosmos DB. We are using save mode as `append`.

```
#Writing DataFrame to Cosmos DB. If the Comos DB RU's
are less then it will take quite some time to write 150K
records. We are using save mode as append.
customerDF.write.format("com.microsoft.azure.cosmosdb.
spark") \
.options(**writeConfig)\
.mode("append")\
.save()
```

9. To overwrite the data, we must use save mode as overwrite as shown in the following code.

```
#Writing DataFrame to Cosmos DB. If the Comos DB RU's
are less then it will take quite some time to write 150K
records. We are using save mode as overwrite.
```

```
customerDF.write.format("com.microsoft.azure.cosmosdb.
spark") \
.options(**writeConfig)\
.mode("overwrite")\
.save()
```

10. Now let's read the data written to Cosmos DB. First, we need to set the `config` values by running the following code.

```
readConfig = {
  "Endpoint" : "https://testcosmosdb.documents.azure.
com:443/",
  "Masterkey" : "xxx-xxx-xxx",
   "Database" : "Sales",
   "Collection" : "Customer",
   "preferredRegions" : "Central US;East US2",
   "SamplingRatio" : "1.0",
   "schema_samplesize" : "1000",
   "query_pagesize" : "2147483647",
   "query_custom" : "SELECT * FROM c where c.C_MKTSEGMENT
='AUTOMOBILE'" #
}
```

11. After setting the `config` values, run the following code to read the data from Cosmos DB. In the `query_custom` we are filtering the data for AUTOMOBILE market segments.

```
df_Customer = spark.read.format("com.microsoft.azure.
cosmosdb.spark").options(**readConfig).load()
df_Customer.count()
```

12. You can run the following code to display the contents of the DataFrame.

```
display(df_Customer.limit(5))
```

By the end of this section, you have learnt how to load and read the data into and from Cosmos DB using Azure Cosmos DB Connector for Apache Spark.

How it works...

`azure-cosmosdb-spark` is the official connector for **Azure Cosmos DB** and **Apache Spark**. This connector allows you to easily read to and write from Azure Cosmos DB via Apache Spark DataFrames in **Python** and **Scala**. It also allows you to easily create a lambda architecture for batch processing, stream processing, and a serving layer while being globally replicated and minimizing the latency involved in working with big data.

Azure Cosmos DB Connector is a client library that allows Azure Cosmos DB to act as an input source or output sink for Spark jobs. Fast connectivity between Apache Spark and Azure Cosmos DB provides the ability to process data in a performant way. Data can be quickly persisted and retrieved using Azure Cosmos DB with the Spark to Cosmos DB connector. This also helps to solve scenarios, including blazing fast **Internet of Things (IoT)** scenarios, and while performing analytics, push-down predicate filtering, and advanced analytics.

We can use `query_pagesize` as a parameter to control number of documents that each query page should hold. Larger the value for `query_pagesize`, lesser is the network roundtrip which is required to fetch the data and thus leading to better throughput.

Reading and writing data from and to CSV and Parquet

Azure Databricks supports multiple file formats, including sequence files, Record Columnar files, and Optimized Row Columnar files. It also provides native support for CSV, JSON, and Parquet file formats.

Parquet is the most widely used file format in the Databricks Cloud for the following reasons:

1. **Columnar storage format**—Stores data column-wise, unlike row-based format files such as Avro and CSV.

2. **Open source**—Parquet is open source and free to use.

3. **Aggressive compression**—Parquet supports compression, which is not available in most file formats. Because of its compression technique, it requires slow storage compared to other file formats. It uses different encoding methods for compressions.

4. **Performance**—The Parquet file format is designed for optimized performance. You can get the relevant data quickly as it saves both data and metadata. The amount of data scanned is comparatively smaller, resulting in less **input/output (I/O)** usage.

5. **Schema evaluation**—It supports changes in the column schema as required. Multiple Parquet files with compatible schemas can be merged.

6. **Self-describing**—Each Parquet file contains metadata and data, which makes it self-describing.

Parquet files also support predicate push-down, column filtering, static, and dynamic partition pruning.

In this recipe, you will learn how to read from and write to CSV and Parquet files using Azure Databricks.

Getting ready

You can follow the steps by running the steps in the `2_7.Reading and Writing data from and to CSV, Parquet.ipynb` notebook in your local cloned repository in the `Chapter02` folder.

Upload the `csvFiles` folder in the `Chapter02/Customer` folder to the ADLS Gen2 storage account in the `rawdata` file system and in `Customer/csvFiles` folder.

How to do it...

Here are the steps and code samples for reading from and writing to CSV and Parquet files using Azure Databricks. You will find a separate section for processing CSV and Parquet file formats.

Working with the CSV file format

Go through the following steps for reading CSV files and saving data in CSV format.

1. Ensure that you have mounted the ADLS Gen2 Storage location. If not, you can refer to the *Mounting ADLS Gen2 and Azure Blob storage to Azure DBFS* recipe in this chapter to follow the steps for mounting a storage account.

2. Run the following code to list the CSV data files from the mounted ADLS Gen2 storage account:

```
#Listing CSV Files
dbutils.fs.ls("/mnt/Gen2Source/Customer/csvFiles")
```

3. Read the customer data stored in `csv` files in the ADLS Gen2 storage account by running the following code:

```
customerDF = spark.read.format("csv").
option("header",True).option("inferSchema", True).load("/
mnt/Gen2Source/Customer/csvFiles")
```

4. You can display the result of a Dataframe by running the following code:

```
customerDF.show()
```

5. By running the following code, we are writing customerDF DataFrame data to the location /mnt/Gen2Source/Customer/WriteCsvFiles in CSV format.

```
customerDF.write.mode("overwrite").option("header",
"true").csv("/mnt/Gen2Source/Customer/WriteCsvFiles")
```

6. To confirm that the data is written to the target folder in csv format, let's read the csv files from target folder by running the following code.

```
targetDF = spark.read.format("csv").
option("header",True).option("inferSchema", True).load("/
mnt/Gen2Source/Customer/WriteCsvFiles")
targetDF.show()
```

In the following section we will learn how to read data from and write data to parquet files.

Working with the Parquet file format

Let's get started.

1. You can use the same customer dataset for reading from the CSV files and writing into the Parquet file format.

2. We will use the targetDF DataFrame used in *Step 6* and save it as parquet format by running the following code. We are using save mode as overwrite in the following code. Using overwrite save option, existing data is overwritten in the target or destination folder mentioned.

```
#Writing the targetDF data which has the CSV data read as
parquet File using append mode
targetDF.write.mode("overwrite").option("header",
"true").parquet("/mnt/Gen2Source/Customer/
csvasParquetFiles/")
```

3. In the following code, we are reading data from csvasParquetFiles folder to confirm the data in parquet format:

```
df_parquetfiles=spark.read.format("parquet").
option("header",True).load("/mnt/Gen2Source/Customer/
csvasParquetFiles/")
display(df_parquetfiles.limit(5))
```

4. Let's change the save mode from `overwrite` to `append` by running the following code. Using save mode as `append`, new data will be inserted, and existing data is preserved in the target or destination folder:

```
#Using overwrite as option for save mode
targetDF.write.mode("append").option("header", "true").
parquet("/mnt/Gen2Source/Customer/csvasParquetFiles/")
```

5. Run the following code to check the count of records in the parquet folder and number should increase as we have appended the data to the same folder.

```
df_parquetfiles=spark.read.format("parquet").
option("header",True).load("/mnt/Gen2Source/Customer/
csvasParquetFiles/")
df_parquetfiles.count()
```

By the end of this recipe, you have learnt how to read from and write to CSV and Parquet files.

How it works...

The CSV file format is a widely used format by many tools, and it's also a default format for processing data. There are many disadvantages when you compare it in terms of cost, query processing time, and size of the data files. The CSV format is not that effective compared with what you will find in the Parquet file format. Also, it doesn't support partition pruning, which directly impacts the cost of storing and processing data in CSV format.

Conversely, Parquet is a columnar format that supports compression and partition pruning. It is widely used for processing data in big data projects for both reading and writing data. A Parquet file stores data and metadata, which makes it self-describing.

Parquet also supports schema evolution, which means you can change the schema of the data as required. This helps in developing systems that can accommodate changes in the schema as it matures. In such cases, you may end up with multiple Parquet files that have different schemas but are compatible.

Reading and writing data from and to JSON, including nested JSON

Spark SQL automatically detects the JSON dataset schema from the files and loads it as a DataFrame. It also provides an option to query JSON data for reading and writing data. Nested JSON can also be parsed, and fields can be directly accessed without any explicit transformations.

Getting ready

You can follow the steps by running the steps in the 2_8.Reading and Writing data from and to Json including nested json.iynpb notebook in your local cloned repository in the Chapter02 folder.

Upload the folder JsonData from Chapter02/sensordata folder to ADLS Gen-2 account having sensordata as file system . We are mounting ADLS Gen-2 Storage Account with sensordata file system to /mnt/SensorData.

The JsonData has two folders, SimpleJsonData which has files simple JSON structure and JsonData folder which has files with nested JSON structure.

> **Note**
> The code was tested on Databricks Runtime Version 7.3 LTS having Spark 3.0.1.

In the upcoming section we will learn how to process simple and complex JSON datafile. We will use sensordata files with simple and nested schema.

How to do it...

In this section, you will see how you can read and write the simple JSON data files:

1. You can read JSON datafiles using below code snippet. You need to specify multiline option as true when you are reading JSON file having multiple lines else if its single line JSON datafile this can be skipped.

```
df_json = spark.read.option("multiline","true").json("/
mnt/SensorData/JsonData/SimpleJsonData/")
display(df_json)
```

2. After executing the preceding code, you can see the schema of the json data.

```
1   df_json = spark.read.option("multiline","true")
2   .json("dbfs:/mnt/SensorData/JsonData/SimpleJsonData/")
3   display(df_json)
```

▶ (3) Spark Jobs

▼ ▦ df_json: pyspark.sql.dataframe.DataFrame
        Fuel: string
        Transmission: string
        _id: string
        about: string
        address: string
        color: string
        cost: string
        currentowner: string
        eventtime: string
        index: long
        latitude: double
        longitude: double
        phone: string
        seatingcapacity: string
        sellingcompany: string

Figure 2.21 – Simple Json Data

3. Writing json file is identical to a CSV file. You can use following code snippet to write json file using Azure Databricks. You can specify different mode options while writing JSON data like append, overwrite, ignore and error or errorifexists. error mode is the default one and this mode throws exceptions if data already exists.

```
multilinejsondf.write.format("json").mode("overwrite").
save("/mnt/SensorData/JsonData/SimpleJsonData/")
```

Very often, you will come across scenarios where you need to process complex datatypes such as arrays, maps, and structs while processing data.

To encode a struct type as a string and to read the struct type as a complex type, Spark provides functions such as to_json() and from_json(). If you are receiving data from the streaming source in nested JSON format, then you can use the from_json() function to process the input data before sending it downstream.

Similarly you can use to_json() method to encode or convert columns in DataFrame to JSON string and send the dataset to various destination like EventHub, Data Lake storage, Cosmos database, RDBMS systems like SQL server, Oracle etc. You can follow along the steps required to process simple and nested Json in the following steps.

1. Execute the following code to display the dataset from the mount location of storage account.

```
df_json = spark.read.option("multiline","true").
json("dbfs:/mnt/SensorData/JsonData/")
```

2. You can see that the vehicle sensor data has Owner's attribute in the multiline json format.

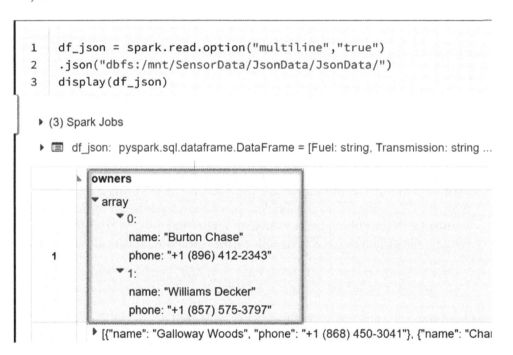

Figure 2.22 – Complex Json Data

3. To convert Owners attribute into row format for joining or transforming data you can use `explode()` function. Execute the following command for performing this operation. Here you can see using `explode()` function the elements of Array has been converted into two columns named name and phone.

```
1   from pyspark.sql.functions import explode
2   data_df = df_json.select("_id",
3       explode("owners").alias("vehicleOwnersExplode")
4   ).select("_id","vehicleOwnersExplode.*")
5   display(data_df)
```

▶ (2) Spark Jobs

▼ 🖾 data_df: pyspark.sql.dataframe.DataFrame
        _id: string
        name: string
        phone: string

	_id	name	phone
1	60f623d0f2861584c56e2660	Burton Chase	+1 (896) 412-2343
2	60f623d0f2861584c56e2660	Williams Decker	+1 (857) 575-3797

Figure 2.23 – Explode function

4. To encode or convert the columns in the DataFrame to JSON string, `to_json()` method can be used. In this example we will create new DataFrame with `json` column from the existing `DataFrame data_df` in preceding step. Execute the following code to create the new DataFrame with `json` column.

```
jsonDF = data_df.withColumn("jsonCol", to_
json(struct([data_df[x] for x in data_df.columns])))
.select("jsonCol")
display(jsonDF)
```

5. After executing the preceding command, you will get new DataFrame with column named jsonCol.

```
1   jsonDF = data_df.withColumn("jsonCol",
2                               to_json(struct([data_df[x] for x in data_df.columns])))
3                       .select("jsonCol")
4   display(jsonDF)
```

▶ (2) Spark Jobs

▶ 🖾 jsonDF: pyspark.sql.dataframe.DataFrame = [jsonCol: string]

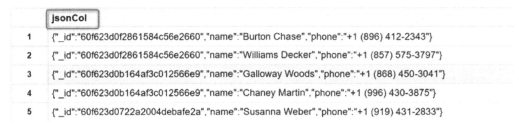

	jsonCol
1	{"_id":"60f623d0f2861584c56e2660","name":"Burton Chase","phone":"+1 (896) 412-2343"}
2	{"_id":"60f623d0f2861584c56e2660","name":"Williams Decker","phone":"+1 (857) 575-3797"}
3	{"_id":"60f623d0b164af3c012566e9","name":"Galloway Woods","phone":"+1 (868) 450-3041"}
4	{"_id":"60f623d0b164af3c012566e9","name":"Chaney Martin","phone":"+1 (996) 430-3875"}
5	{"_id":"60f623d0722a2004debafe2a","name":"Susanna Weber","phone":"+1 (919) 431-2833"}

Figure 2.24 – Encode To Json

6. Using to_json() method you have converted _id, name and phone column to a new json column.

How it works...

Spark provides you with options to process data from multiple sources and in multiple formats. You can process the data and enrich it before sending it to downstream applications. Data can be sent to a downstream application with low latency on streaming data or high throughput on historical data.

3
Understanding Spark Query Execution

To write efficient Spark applications, we need to have some understanding of how Spark executes queries. Having a good understanding of how Spark executes a given query helps big data developers/engineers work efficiently with large volumes of data.

Query execution is a very broad subject, and, in this chapter, we will start by understanding jobs, stages, and tasks. Then, we will learn how Spark lazy evaluation works. Following this, we will learn how to check and understand the execution plan when working with DataFrames or SparkSQL. Later, we will learn how joins work in Spark and the different types of join algorithms Spark uses while joining two tables. Finally, we will learn about the input, output, and shuffle partitions and the storage benefits of using different file formats.

Knowing about the internals will help you troubleshoot and debug your Spark applications more efficiently. By the end of this chapter, you will know how to execute Spark queries, as well as how to write and debug your Spark applications more efficiently.

We're going to cover the following recipes:

- Introduction to jobs, stages, and tasks

- Checking the execution details of all the executed Spark queries via the Spark UI

- Deep diving into schema inference

- Looking into the query execution plan

- How joins work in Spark

- Learning about input partitions

- Learning about output partitions

- Learning about shuffle partitions

- The storage benefits of different file types

Technical requirements

To follow along with the examples in this recipe, you will need to do the following:

- Create an Azure subscription and the required permissions for your subscription. These were mentioned in the *Technical requirements* section of *Chapter 1, Creating an Azure Databricks Service.*

- Create ADLS Gen-2 accounts. Go to the following link to create the required resources: `https://docs.microsoft.com/en-us/azure/storage/common/storage-account-create?tabs=azure-portal`.

- Acquire the relevant scripts. You can find the scripts for this chapter in the GitHub URL (`https://github.com/PacktPublishing/Azure-Databricks-Cookbook/tree/main/Chapter03`). The Chapter03 folder contains all the notebooks for this chapter.

- Acquire the relevant source files. You can find all the source files that were used in this chapter at `https://github.com/PacktPublishing/Azure-Databricks-Cookbook/tree/main/Common`.

Introduction to jobs, stages, and tasks

In this recipe, you will learn how Spark breaks down an application into job, stages, and tasks. You will also learn how to view **directed acyclic graphs** (**DAGs**) and how pipelining works in Spark query execution.

By the end of this recipe, you will have learned how to check the DAG you've created for the query you have executed and look at the jobs, stages, and tasks associated with a specific query.

Getting ready

You can follow along by running the steps in the `3-1.Introduction to Jobs, Stages, and Tasks` notebook. This can be found in your local cloned repository, in the `Chapter03` folder (`https://github.com/PacktPublishing/Azure-Databricks-Cookbook/tree/main/Chapter03`). Follow these steps before running the notebook:

1. Mount your ADLS Gen-2 account by following the steps mentioned in the *Mounting Azure Data Lake Storage (ADLS) Gen-2 and Azure Blob Storage to the Azure Databricks filesystem* recipe of *Chapter 2, Reading and Writing Data from and to Various Azure Services and File Formats.*

2. Clone the `Chapter03` folder and `Common` folder from `https://github.com/PacktPublishing/Azure-Databricks-Cookbook`.

3. Use the customer `csv` files at `https://github.com/PacktPublishing/Azure-Databricks-Cookbook/tree/main/Common/Customer/csvFiles` for this recipe.

How to do it...

Follow these steps to check the jobs, number of stages, and tasks Spark created while executing the query via the Spark UI:

1. Run the following command to create a DataFrame that will read the .csv files containing customer data from the mount point:

```
# Reading customer csv files in a DataFrame
df_cust= spark.read.format("csv").option("header",True).
load("dbfs:/mnt/Gen2/Customer/csvFiles")
```

2. Run the following command. We will learn how to check for the jobs associated with the query shortly:

```
display(df_cust.limit(10))
```

3. After executing the preceding query, you will find **Spark Jobs** associated with it, as shown in the following screenshot:

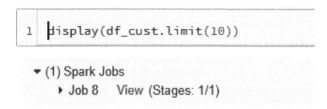

Figure 3.1 – Execution output of the query

4. Now, click on the **View** link under **Spark Jobs**, as shown in the preceding screenshot, and click on the **SQL** tab to view the jobs associated with the query. When you click on the **SQL** tab, you will see a list of queries that have been executed, along with the job IDs associated with them:

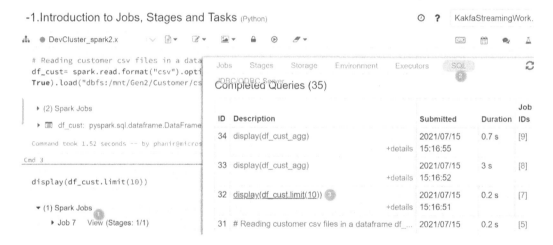

Figure 3.2 – Getting the DAG query

5. Now, click on **Description** (*Step 3*), as shown in the preceding screenshot. This can be found under **Completed Queries**. Here, you will see all the stages associated with that query. As shown in the preceding screenshot, it has read 10 files from the csvFiles folder, and that the total size of these files is 23.1 MB. Since we are displaying only 10 records from the DataFrame, **rowoutput** is **10** and **CollectLimit** is **DAG** since we are displaying the results using the display function:

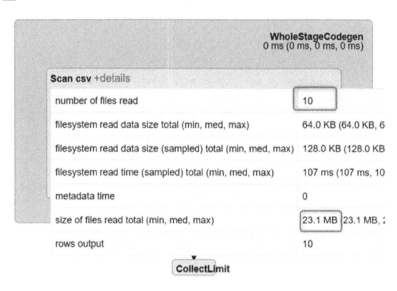

Jobs   Stages   Storage   Environment   Executors   SQL   JDBC/ODBC Server

Details for Query 3

Submitted Time: 2021/02/14 05:14:05
Duration: 0.3 s
Succeeded Jobs: 1

☑ Expand all the details in the query plan visualization

WholeStageCodegen
0 ms (0 ms, 0 ms, 0 ms)

Scan csv +details

number of files read	10
filesystem read data size total (min, med, max)	64.0 KB (64.0 KB, 6
filesystem read data size (sampled) total (min, med, max)	128.0 KB (128.0 KB
filesystem read time (sampled) total (min, med, max)	107 ms (107 ms, 10
metadata time	0
size of files read total (min, med, max)	23.1 MB 23.1 MB, 2
rows output	10

CollectLimit

Figure 3.3 – Reading the DAG

6. Now that we've looked at jobs and stages, let's look at the tasks associated with
    these stages. When you execute the query and expand the **Job** stage, as shown in
    following screenshot, you will see all the stages and the tasks associated with them.
    Here, we can see that **Job 1** has one stage and that there's one task in that stage:

```
1  display(df_cust.limit(10))
```

▼ (1) Spark Jobs
   ▼ Job 1   View (Stages: 1/1)
      Stage 1: 1/1 ❶

Figure 3.4 – Identifying the tasks associated with a job

7. Click on the **i** option to find all the tasks associated with that stage. You can see that the task's input size is 64 KB and that there are 10 records that we are displaying in the output:

Summary Metrics for 1 Completed Tasks

Metric	Min	25th percentile	Median	75th percentile	Max
Duration	0.2 s	0.2 s	0.2 s	0.2 s	0.2 s
GC Time	0 ms	0 ms	0 ms	0 ms	0 ms
Input Size / Records	64.0 KB / 10	64.0 KB / 10	64.0 KB / 10	64.0 KB / 10	64.0 KB / 10

▾Aggregated Metrics by Executor

Executor ID ⌃	Address	Task Time	Total Tasks	Failed Tasks	Killed Tasks	Succeeded Tasks	Input Size / Records	Blacklisted
0	stdout 10.139.64.5:42133 stderr	0.3 s	1	0	0	1	64.0 KB / 10	false

▾Tasks (1)

Index ⌃	ID	Attempt	Status	Locality Level	Executor ID	Host	Launch Time	Duration	GC Time	Input Size / Records	Errors
0	1	0	SUCCESS	PROCESS_LOCAL	0	10.139.64.5 stdout stderr	2021/02/14 05:14:05	0.2 s		64.0 KB / 10	

Figure 3.5 – Listing the completed task details

8. Let's run an aggregated query that provides a more complex DAG:

```
df_cust_agg = df_cust.groupBy("C_MKTSEGMENT")\
    .agg(sum("C_ACCTBAL").cast('decimal(20,3)').alias("sum_
acctbal"), \
        avg("C_ACCTBAL").alias("avg_acctbal"), \
        max("C_ACCTBAL").alias("max_bonus")).orderBy("avg_
acctbal",ascending=False)
```

9. Run the following command to display the DataFrame's output:

```
display(df_cust_agg)
```

10. You will receive the following output after executing the preceding code:

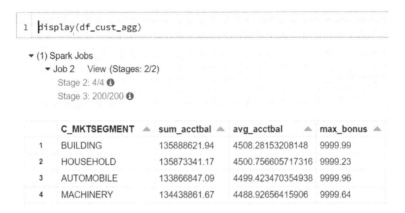

Figure 3.6 – Getting a DAG for an aggregated query

11. Under **Spark Jobs**, we can see that two stages have been created. Multiple stages are created when there is a shuffle involved. A shuffle operation is involved when the data is moved across the nodes, and this happens when we are using transformations such as average and sum. The sum transformation needs to collect data from various executors and send it to the driver node when actions such as **Show display** or **Limit** are called:

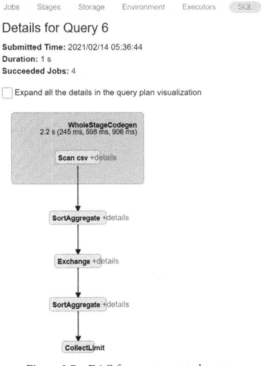

Figure 3.7 – DAG for an aggregated query

12. As you can see, there is an exchange operator involved as we are performing aggregations on the data that we read from the CSV file.

How it works...

It is very important to know how to identify the stages and tasks of a query you are executing, since this helps you identify how many stages have been created for the query and identify any issues. The Spark UI and DAG representations may change between Spark/Databricks runtime versions.

The following screenshot shows an additional tab called **Structured Streaming** that's available in Databricks runtime version 7.3. This tab is not available in Databricks runtime version 6.4:

Figure 3.8 – Jobs associated with a query

In the DAG, you can click on **Expand all the details in the query plan visualization** to view additional details regarding the number files that have been read, as well as the shuffled size of the data that is being sent over the network:

Succeeded Jobs:

☑ Expand all the details in the query plan visualization

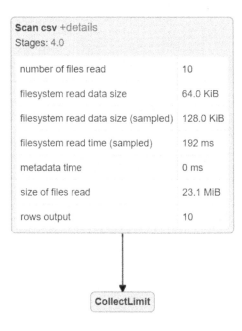

Figure 3.9 – Using the Expand all option in the DAG

Here, you can see that there are multiple sortAggregates in the DAG. One was created by the mapper, while another was created after the exchange operator. This happens before the results are given to the driver.

Checking the execution details of all the executed Spark queries via the Spark UI

In this recipe, you will learn how to view the statuses of all the running applications in your cluster. You will also look at various tasks you can use to identify if there are any issues with a specific application/query. Knowing this is useful as you will get holistic information about how your cluster is utilized in terms of tasks distribution and how your applications are running.

Getting ready

Execute the queries shown in the *Introduction to jobs, stages, and tasks* recipe of this chapter. You can either use a Spark 2.x (latest version) or Spark 3.x cluster.

How to do it...

Follow these steps to learn about the running applications/queries in your cluster:

1. When you are in your Databricks workspace, click on the **Clusters** option and then on the cluster that you are using. Then, click on the **Spark UI** tab, as shown in the following screenshot:

Figure 3.10 – Spark UI screen

2. When you click on the **Spark UI** tab, you will find a screen similar to the one shown in the *Introduction to jobs, stages, and tasks* recipe. Click on the **SQL** tab to see all the queries that have been completed or are still running:

Figure 3.11 – Listing all the executed queries in your cluster

3. You will see that will see every will have at least one job id associated with it. This screen shows all the queries twhich got completed and the duration of each query. Let's click on the query with highest duration, in this case it's the **ID196** which took 7 seconds and look at the **DAG** it has created and all the tasks for that Job.

4. Sort by **Duration** column to identify the queries which have taken the most time. This will help you to identify top duration queries and start optimizing those queries. Now click on **Description** column value for **ID 196** to view the DAG (**Step 3** in the preceding screenshot).

5. Now we will look at the stages for our Job **ID 0** that spark has created. From the same **SQL** tab, click on Job **Id 0** (for **ID 196**) which is a hyperlink as shown in the preceding screenshot and you will one stage for the job id:

Figure 3.12 – Job details

6. Now let's look into the stage which has multiple tasks. Click on **SQL** tab in **Spark UI** and click on **Job IDs 5** which has 10 tasks. Now click on the **Description** column value for the Stage which has 10 tasks, and you will find how many tasks have been executed on each executor. Since this cluster has 2 worker node there are two executors created for the aggregate query that we have executed:

Jobs   Stages   Storage   Environment   Executors   SQL   JDBC/ODBC Server   Structured Streaming

▸ Aggregated Metrics by Executor

Tasks (10)

Show 20 ∨ entries   Search:

Index ▲	Task ID	Attempt	Status	Locality level	Executor ID	Host	Logs	Launch Time	Duration	GC Time	Input Size / Records	Write Time	Shuffle Write Size / Records
0	23	0	SUCCESS	PROCESS_LOCAL	1	10.1.128.5	stdout stderr	2021-07-15 23:56:57	0.3 s		2.3 MiB / 15000	0.0 ms	75 B / 1
1	24	0	SUCCESS	PROCESS_LOCAL	0	10.1.128.4	stdout stderr	2021-07-15 23:56:57	0.2 s		2.3 MiB / 14999	0.0 ms	75 B / 1
2	25	0	SUCCESS	PROCESS_LOCAL	1	10.1.128.5	stdout stderr	2021-07-15 23:56:57	0.3 s		2.3 MiB / 15000	0.0 ms	75 B / 1

Figure 3.13 – Stage details

7. We can sort on the duration under the **Tasks (10)** and identify if there is any task which is taking more time than other tasks. If we see any task taking more time than others it's an indication of data skew.

How it works...

Every query that we execute on Spark has one or more job associated with it. If multiple actions are mentioned in the query, this means that multiple jobs will be created by the Spark execution engine while running the query.

Notice the aggregated metrics by executor. This information is very helpful for identifying how the tasks are split across the executors and for identifying if any executor is taking more time compared to others. The tasks are executed by the executors.

The following screenshot shows the time each executor took to execute the task:

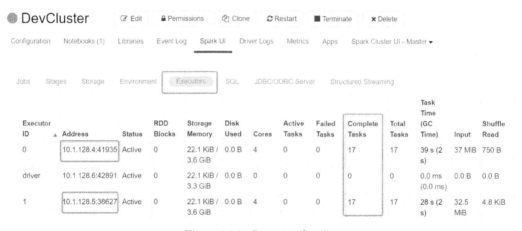

Figure 3.14 – Executor details

The **Address** column in the preceding screenshot shows the worker node's IP address and the **Input** shows the bytes and record read from the storage. **Shuffle Write Size / Records** describes the size of the data that the executor is processing and how much shuffle is involved in moving the data across the nodes.

Deep diving into schema inference

In this recipe, you will learn about the benefits of explicitly specifying a schema while reading any file format data from an **ADLS Gen-2** or **Azure Blob storage** account.

By the end of this recipe, you will have learned how Spark executes a query when a schema is inferred versus explicitly specified.

Getting ready

You need to ensure you have done the following before you start working on this recipe:

- An ADLS Gen-2 account mounted.
- Follow along by running the steps in the 3-3.Schema Inference notebook in your local cloned repository. This can be found in the Chapter03 folder (https://github.com/PacktPublishing/Azure-Databricks-Cookbook/tree/main/Chapter03).
- Upload the csvFiles folder in the Common/Customer folder (https://github.com/PacktPublishing/Azure-Databricks-Cookbook/tree/main/Common/Customer/csvFiles) to your ADLS Gen-2 account in the rawdata filesystem, inside the Customer folder.

How to do it...

You can learn about the benefits of specifying a schema while reading the files from your ADLS Gen-2 or Azure Blob storage account. First, we will read the set of files by inferring the schema from the file and explicitly specify the schema. Then, we will look at how Spark's execution differs in both scenarios:

1. Let's list the .csv files we are trying to read from the mount point:

   ```
   display(dbutils.fs.ls("/mnt/Gen2/Customer/csvFiles/"))
   ```

2. We will read the CSV files directly from the mount point without specifying any schema options:

   ```
   df_cust= spark.read.format("csv").option("header",True).
   option("inferSchema", True).load("dbfs:/mnt/Gen2/
   Customer/csvFiles")
   ```

3. Spark uses the concept of lazy evaluation, which means until an action is called, Spark will not execute the query. In the preceding query, we haven't invoked an action, and all transformation are lazy in nature. This means that you should not see a DAG when there are no actions in the query. However, in the following snippet and after executing the preceding query, you will see that the Spark optimizer has created a DAG:

```
# Reading customer csf files in a dataframe with specify
df_cust= spark.read.format("csv").option("header",True).
True).load("dbfs:/mnt/Gen2/Customer/csvFiles")
```

▼ (2) Spark Jobs

  ▶ Job 7   View (Stages: 1/1)

  ▶ Job 8   View (Stages: 1/1)

▶ 🖼 df_cust: pyspark.sql.dataframe.DataFrame = [C_CUSTKEY: intege

Figure 3.15 – Getting a DAG with an inferred schema

4. Now, we will create a schema and explicitly provide it while reading the .csv files in a DataFrame:

```
cust_schema = StructType([
    StructField("C_CUSTKEY", IntegerType()),
    StructField("C_NAME", StringType()),
    StructField("C_ADDRESS", StringType()),
    StructField("C_NATIONKEY", ShortType()),
    StructField("C_PHONE", StringType()),
    StructField("C_ACCTBAL", DoubleType()),
    StructField("C_MKTSEGMENT", StringType()),
    StructField("C_COMMENT", StringType())
])
```

5. Create the DataFrame by using the schema we created in the preceding step:

```
df_cust_sch= spark.read.format("csv").
option("header",True).schema(cust_schema).load("/mnt/
Gen2/Customer/csvFiles/")
```

6. After running the preceding query, you will see that Spark hasn't generated a DAG for the query and that the execution time has reduced from 1.6 seconds to 0.20 seconds:

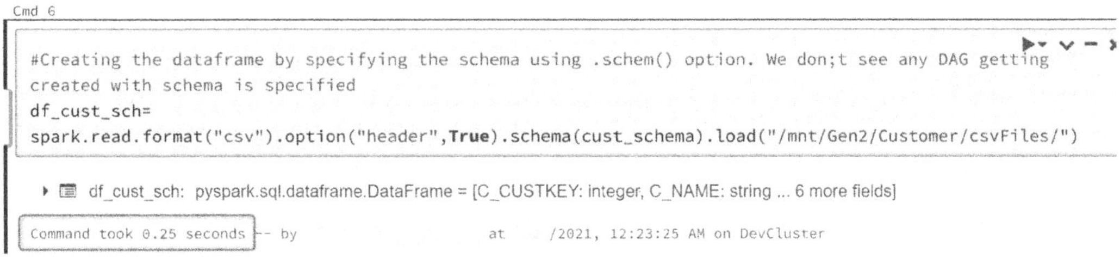

Cmd 6

```
#Creating the dataframe by specifying the schema using .schem() option. We don;t see any DAG getting
created with schema is specified
df_cust_sch=
spark.read.format("csv").option("header",True).schema(cust_schema).load("/mnt/Gen2/Customer/csvFiles/")
```

▸ ▦ df_cust_sch: pyspark.sql.dataframe.DataFrame = [C_CUSTKEY: integer, C_NAME: string ... 6 more fields]

Command took 0.25 seconds -- by   at   /2021, 12:23:25 AM on DevCluster

Figure 3.16 – Execution time with the explicit schema

7. Thus, it is always recommended to specify the schema wherever possible, as this will improve the performance of your queries. This is because you're not creating the DAG when no action is being triggered. But in scenarios where we don't have a schema at hand and we want to create one, we can read one file from the entire folder and get the schema for the underlying dataset:

```
df_cust_sch= spark.read.format("csv").
option("header",True).load("/mnt/Gen2/Customer/csvFiles/
part-00000-tid-3200334632332214470-9b4dec79-7e2e-495d-
8657-3b5457ed3753-108-1-c000.csv")
```

8. When the preceding query is executed, you will see that a DAG has been created but not multiple stages and that fewer tasks have been completed. You will also see that the execution duration is only 0.66 seconds.

9. After executing the preceding query, you can get the schema by running the df_cust_sch.printSchema() command, which you can use to define a schema and use it while reading the .csv files:

How it works...

By inferring the schema, you are asking Spark to identify all the columns and the data types of the column(s). Providing the schema while creating a DataFrame removes the overhead of reading the data types and columns we expect from the .csv files. Only at runtime does it validate whether the schema is matching the columns in the files. If the column(s) that are mentioned in the schema can't be found in the .csv files, then you will see NULL as the value in those columns. Ensure the column's name maps to the columns you have in the underlying .csv files.

As we mentioned in the preceding section, if you are not sure what the schema of the dataset it, you can get the schema by creating the DataFrame. Do this by reading only one file and printing the schema that Spark has inferred. You can use the schema that was identified by Spark, and then define the required schema that will be used to read all the .csv files and improve the performance of your query.

There's more...

To identify why it takes more time to read the .csv files when an action isn't performed, check the number of partitions that Spark created while reading the .csv files to infer the schema. You can do this by using the following command:

```
# Getting the number of partitions
print(f" Number of partitions with all files read = {df_cust.
rdd.getNumPartitions()
```

Based on the number of cores in your cluster, you will see a significantly high number, as shown in the following screenshot:

```
Cmd 4

1 # Getting the number of partitions
2 print(f" Number of partitions with all files read = {df_cust.rdd.getNumPartitions()}")

  Number of partitions with all files read = 10
```

Figure 3.17 – Getting the number of partitions while reading all files

If you specify just one file to infer the schema, you will see a different number for the partition count:

```
Cmd 8

1   #Getting the number of partitions by specifying only one csv file.
2   print(f" Number of partitions with 1 file read  = {df_cust_sch.rdd.getNumPartitions()}")


 Number of partitions with 1 file read   = 1
```

Figure 3.18 – Getting the number of partitions while reading one file

Here, you can see that only one partition was created and that the time it takes to read one file is much faster than reading all the files in the folder. We will discuss the different types of partitions later in this chapter.

Looking into the query execution plan

It's important to understand the execution plan and how to view its different stages when the Spark optimizer executes a query using a dataframe or the SparkSQL API.

In this recipe, we will learn how to create a logical and physical plan and the different stages involved. By the end of this recipe, you will have generated an execution plan using the dataframe API or the SparkSQL API and have a fair understanding of the different stages involved.

Getting ready

You can follow along by running the steps in the 3-4.Query Execution Plan notebook in your local cloned repository, which can be found in the Chapter03 folder (https://github.com/PacktPublishing/Azure-Databricks-Cookbook/tree/main/Chapter03).

Upload the csvFiles folder in the Common/Customer folder (https://github.com/PacktPublishing/Azure-Databricks-Cookbook/tree/main/Common/Customer/csvFiles) to your ADLS Gen-2 account. This can be found in the rawdata filesystem, inside the Customer folder.

You can execute this recipe on a Spark 2.x (latest version) or Spark 3.x cluster. You will find some differences in the output of the execution plan, but the process of getting there is the same.

How to do it...

Let's learn how to generate an execution plan using the dataframe API or SparkSQL API, understand the various stages involved, and identify how the execution plan can be viewed from the Spark UI.

Follow these steps to create an execution plan for Spark queries via the Spark UI and by using `Explain()` command:

1. Use the following code to create a DataFrame that reads all the `.csv` files from the `/mnt/Gen2/Customer/csvFiles` folder:

    ```
    df_cust_sch= spark.read.format("csv").
    option("header",True).schema(cust_schema).load("/mnt/
    Gen2/Customer/csvFiles/")
    ```

2. Now, let's create an aggregate query using market segment by running the following code:

    ```
    df_agg = df_cust_sch.groupBy("C_MKTSEGMENT").agg(avg("C_
    ACCTBAL").alias("AvgAcctBal"))
    ```

3. We will filter the DataFrame on the machinery market segment and get all the records where `AvgAcctBal>4500`. We can also check the execution plan, as shown here:

    ```
    df_agg.where(df_agg.C_MKTSEGMENT=="MACHINERY").where(df_
    agg.AvgAcctBal>4500).show()
    ```

4. After running the preceding query, we must get the DAG for the query we executed. You can find the steps for getting a DAG for a query in the *Introduction to jobs, stages, and tasks* recipe.

5. Click on **ID for your query**. When you scroll to the end, you will find details of the execution plan for the dataframe or SparkSQL API. It will contain the **Parsed Logical Plan, Analyzed Logical Plan, Optimized Logical Plan**, and **Physical Plan stages**:

Jobs	Stages	Storage	Environment	Executors	SQL	JDBC/ODBC Server	Structured Streaming

▼Details

```
== Parsed Logical Plan ==
GlobalLimit 21
+- LocalLimit 21
   +- Project [cast(C_MKTSEGMENT#2240 as string) AS C_MKTSEGMENT#2317, cast(AvgAcctBal#2284 as string) AS AvgAcctBa
      +- Filter (AvgAcctBal#2284 > cast(4500 as double))
         +- Filter (C_MKTSEGMENT#2240 = MACHINERY)
            +- Aggregate [C_MKTSEGMENT#2240], [C_MKTSEGMENT#2240, avg(C_ACCTBAL#2239) AS AvgAcctBal#2284]
               +- Relation[C_CUSTKEY#2234,C_NAME#2235,C_ADDRESS#2236,C_NATIONKEY#2237,C_PHONE#2238,C_ACCTBAL#2239,C

== Analyzed Logical Plan ==
C_MKTSEGMENT: string, AvgAcctBal: string
GlobalLimit 21
+- LocalLimit 21
   +- Project [cast(C_MKTSEGMENT#2240 as string) AS C_MKTSEGMENT#2317, cast(AvgAcctBal#2284 as string) AS AvgAcctBa
      +- Filter (AvgAcctBal#2284 > cast(4500 as double))
         +- Filter (C_MKTSEGMENT#2240 = MACHINERY)
```

Figure 3.19 – Getting the number of execution plans

6. Now, let's learn how to get the plan using the `Explain()` function. The plans that are generated using the dataframe API and SparkSQL API is the same. Create a `tempview`, as shown in the following command:

```
df_cust_sch.createOrReplaceTempView("df_Customer")
```

7. Now, execute the following command to generate an execution plan using both APIs:

```
# Note the plans are same using DF API or SQL API
sql = spark.sql("SELECT C_MKTSEGMENT, count(1) FROM df_Customer
GROUP BY C_MKTSEGMENT ")


dataframe = df_cust_sch\
  .groupBy("C_MKTSEGMENT")\
  .count()


sql.explain()
dataframe.explain()
```

8. The following is the output of executing the preceding code:

```
== Physical Plan ==
AdaptiveSparkPlan isFinalPlan=false
+- == Current Plan ==
   HashAggregate(keys=[C_MKTSEGMENT#2240], functions=[finalmerge_count(merge count#2357L) AS count(1)#2340L]
   +- Exchange hashpartitioning(C_MKTSEGMENT#2240, 200), true, [id=#2016]
      +- HashAggregate(keys=[C_MKTSEGMENT#2240], functions=[partial_count(1) AS count#2357L])
         +- FileScan csv [C_MKTSEGMENT#2240] Batched: false, DataFilters: [], Format: CSV, Location: InMemor
iles], PartitionFilters: [], PushedFilters: [], ReadSchema: struct<C_MKTSEGMENT:string>
+- == Initial Plan ==
   HashAggregate(keys=[C_MKTSEGMENT#2240], functions=[finalmerge_count(merge count#2357L) AS count(1)#2340L]
   +- Exchange hashpartitioning(C_MKTSEGMENT#2240, 200), true, [id=#2016]
      +- HashAggregate(keys=[C_MKTSEGMENT#2240], functions=[partial_count(1) AS count#2357L])
         +- FileScan csv [C_MKTSEGMENT#2240] Batched: false, DataFilters: [], Format: CSV, Location: InMemor
iles], PartitionFilters: [], PushedFilters: [], ReadSchema: struct<C_MKTSEGMENT:string>
```

```
== Physical Plan ==
AdaptiveSparkPlan isFinalPlan=false
+- == Current Plan ==
   HashAggregate(keys=[C_MKTSEGMENT#2240], functions=[finalmerge_count(merge count#2362L) AS count(1)#2352L]
   +- Exchange hashpartitioning(C_MKTSEGMENT#2240, 200), true, [id=#2062]
```

Figure 3.20 – Execution plan for both the dataframe API and the SparkSQL API

9. Here, you can see that the plan is similar to the query's, which was executed using two different APIs.

How it works...

You can use either the Spark UI or the `Explain()` command to get the execution plan for the query. Whether you use the dataframe API or the SparkSQL API, the execution plan that's generated by Spark is similar. This gives the developer the flexibility to use their API of choice.

If the data has been partitioned, you can also view the partition filters by using the appropriate partitions. This will help you avoid reading all the data. If there is a `where` clause, you can find the `PushedFilters` value that was populated for the predicate clause you are using in your query. The following example shows the where clause in the query:

```
df_agg.where(df_agg.C_MKTSEGMENT=="MACHINERY").where(df_agg.
AvgAcctBal>4500).show()
```

Now, you check the execution plan for the preceding query. Here, you will find `PushedFilters`, which helps in restricting the data that is fetched while reading the data:

```
DataFilters: [isnotnull(C_MKTSEGMENT#370), (C_MKTSEGMENT#370 = MACHINERY)], Format: CSV, Location:
InMemoryFileIndex[dbfs:/mnt/Gen2/Customer/csvFiles], PartitionFilters: [], PushedFilters:
[IsNotNull(C_MKTSEGMENT), EqualTo(C_MKTSEGMENT,MACHINERY)], ReadSchema:
struct<C_ACCTBAL:double,C_MKTSEGMENT:string>
```

Figure 3.21 – Pushed filters in the execution plan

At the core of SparkSQL is the Catalyst optimizer, which breaks down a query that's been submitted by the user into multiple phases. It does this by using optimization techniques, which efficiently execute the query:

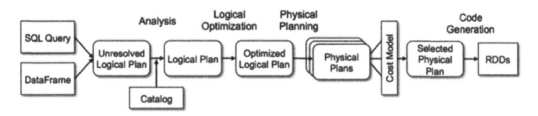

Figure 3.22 – Phases of the execution plan generated by the Catalyst optimizer

Here, we can see that there are multiple phases that the Spark Catalyst optimizer goes through. It shows how a query that's been submitted for execution is parsed into multiple logical and physical plans and then converted into RDD, which then gets executed.

How joins work in Spark

In this recipe, you will learn how query joins are executed by the Spark optimizer using different types of sorting algorithms such as SortMerge and BroadcastHash joins. You will learn how to identify which algorithm has been used by looking at the DAG that Spark generates. You will also learn how to use the hints that are provided in the queries to influence the optimizer to use a specific join algorithm.

Getting ready

To follow along with this recipe, run the cells in the 3-5.Joins notebook, which you can find in your local cloned repository, in the Chapter03 folder (https://github. com/PacktPublishing/Azure-Databricks-Cookbook/tree/main/ Chapter03).

Upload the `csvFiles` folders, which can be found in the `Common/Customer` and `Common/Orders` folders in your local cloned repository, to the ADLS Gen-2 account in the `rawdata` filesystem. You will need to create two folders called `Customer` and `Orders` in the `rawdata` filesystem:

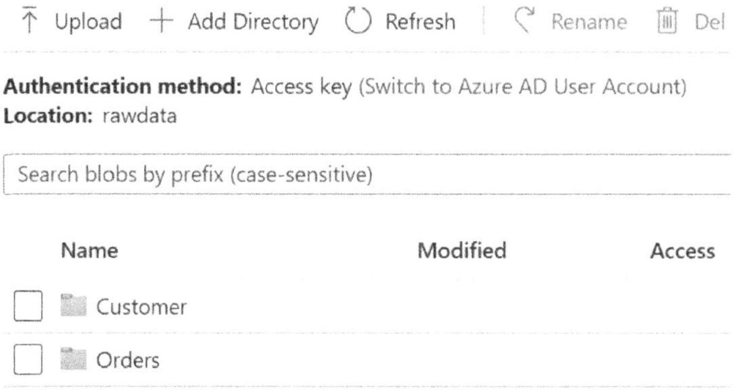

Figure 3.23 – ADLS Gen-2 folders

The preceding screenshot shows that two folders have been created and uploaded to the respective `csvFiles` folder from your locally cloned `Common/Customer` and `Common/Orders` folders. You can find the `Orders` and `Customer csvFiles` folders at `https://github.com/PacktPublishing/Azure-Databricks-Cookbook/tree/main/Common`.

You can use a Spark 2.x (latest version) or Spark 3.x cluster, but you will find little difference from using a Spark 3.0 cluster. We will discuss the optimizer changes for the join algorithm in the *There's more* section.

How to do it...

Let's learn how to identify the `join` algorithm the optimizer uses to join two DataFrames. Follow the steps mentioned in the `3-5.Joins` notebook to do so:

1. Create the schema mentioned in notebook cells 1, 2, and 3 and create the following two DataFrames:

    ```
    #Creating the Orders dataframe by specifying the schema
    df_ord_sch= spark.read.format("csv").
    option("header",True).schema(order_schema).load("/mnt/
    Gen2/Orders/csvFiles/")

    #Creating the dataframe by specifying the schema using
    .schema option. We don't see any DAG getting created with
    schema is specified.
    ```

```
df_cust_sch= spark.read.format("csv").
option("header",True).schema(cust_schema).load("/mnt/
Gen2/Customer/csvFiles/")
```

2. Get the default value for `autoBroadcastJoinThreshold` by running the following query:

```
spark.conf.get("spark.sql.autoBroadcastJoinThreshold")
```

3. The output of the preceding query should be **10485760**, which is 10 MB.

4. We will change the default value for `autoBroadcastJoinThreshold` to 2 MB from 10 MB to simulate that we are joining two large tables. The size of the customer DataFrame is around 5 MB:

```
spark.conf.set("spark.sql.
autoBroadcastJoinThreshold",2194304)
```

5. After executing the preceding command, we will execute a query that will perform an equijoin between the two DataFrames. Then, we will look at the DAG that Spark creates:

```
# Check the execution plan and you will find sort merge
join being used
df_ord_sch.join(df_cust_sch, df_ord_sch.O_CUSTKEY == df_
cust_sch.C_CUSTKEY, "inner").count()
```

6. Check the DAG for the preceding query by following the points mentioned in the following screenshot:

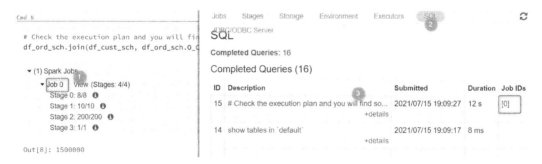

Figure 3.24 – Getting a DAG for a query

7. When you click on **ID 15** (this might be different while you are executing the task, so ensure you are selecting the right ID that maps to the query you have executed), you will find the following DAG. Here, we can see that the `SortMerge` join algorithm is being used. This algorithm is used by the Spark engine when both DataFrames/tables that are are used in joins are large (over 10 MB). This is the behavior of a Spark 2.x cluster:

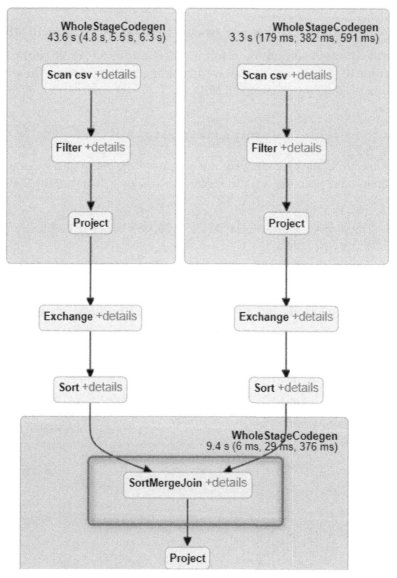

Figure 3.25 – DAG with the SortMerge join algorithm

8. Now, let's add a hint to our query. Here, we will find that the DAG that was generated for the query is different, and that the optimizer is not using a `SortMerge` join but a `BroadcastHash` join:

```
df_ord_sch.join(df_cust_sch.hint("broadcast"), df_ord_
sch.O_CUSTKEY == df_cust_sch.C_CUSTKEY, "inner").count()
```

9. If you set the `autoBroadcastJoinThreshold` value to 10 MB (which is its default value) and execute the join query without any hints, you will find that the DAG that is generated is the same as the one shown in the preceding snippet.

How it works...

The Spark query optimizer identifies which join algorithm should be used based on the size of the data in both tables/DataFrames that were used in the query. The `SortMerge` join is used when the size of both tables/DataFrames is large. If the table/DataFrame that's used in the join size is less than 10 MB, then the `BroadcastHash` join algorithm will be used. So, when we are joining a big table to another big table, the `SortMerge` join will be used, while if we are joining a big table to a small table, then the `BroadcastHash` join will be used.

In the `BroadcastHash` join, there is `BroadcastExchange`. Here, a smaller dataset is transferred to every executor on the worker nodes, and it avoids data shuffle between the nodes. This approach improves the query's performance as no shuffle operation happens. This is because all the executors have the smaller table cached locally, in memory. The optimizer checks if the size of the smaller table is less than 10 MB and then broadcasts the smaller table to all the executors. If the size of the table(s) is greater than 10 MB, then the `SortMerge` algorithm will be used to join the two DataFrames/tables in a Spark 2.4.5 cluster. Spark 3.0.x or later, the behavior is a little different. We will see the DAG for it in the following section to understand what algorithm is used.

There's more...

When we use a Spark 3.0.x cluster, the optimizer generates a different DAG when we set the value for `autoBroadcastJoinThreshold` to less than 10 MB.

When we change the `autoBroadcastJoinThreshold` value to 2 MB by attaching the notebook to a Spark 3.x cluster, the Spark engine will use a `BroadcastHash` join algorithm to execute the query. Let's take a look:

1. Execute the following code and check the execution plan. You will see the join that is being used by the Spark engine. Change `autoBroadcastJoinThreshold` to 2 MB:

```
spark.conf.set("spark.sql.
autoBroadcastJoinThreshold",2194304)
```

2. Now, execute the join query. You will see that the `BroadcastHash` join is being used, not the `SortMerge` join we saw in the Spark 2.4.5 cluster:

```
df_ord_sch.join(df_cust_sch, df_ord_sch.O_CUSTKEY == df_
cust_sch.C_CUSTKEY, "inner").count()
```

3. In the preceding query's DAG, we can see that the `BroadcastHash` join was used instead of `SortMerge`. To force a `sortmerge` join, Spark 3.0.x and later has introduced a new hint called **merge**. We can use this to force the optimizer to use a `SortMerge` join. Execute the following query and check the DAG for `SortMerge`:

```
df_ord_sch.join(df_cust_sch.hint("merge"), df_ord_sch.O_
CUSTKEY == df_cust_sch.C_CUSTKEY, "inner").count()
```

4. By using the DAG, you will see that the Spark query optimizer is using a `SortMerge` join to join the two dataframes.

Learning about input partitions

Partitions are subsets of files in memory or storage. In Spark, partitions are more utilized compared to the Hive system or SQL databases. Spark uses partitions for parallel processing and to gain maximum performance.

Spark and Hive partitions are different; Spark processes data in memory, whereas Hive partitions are in storage. In this recipe, we will cover three different partitions; that is, the input, shuffle, and output partitions.

Let's start by looking at input partitions.

Getting ready

Apache Spark has a layered architecture, and the driver nodes communicate with the worker nodes to get the job done. All the data processing happens in the worker nodes. When the job is submitted for processing, each data partition is sent to the specific executors. Each executor processes one partition at a time. Hence, the time it takes each executor to process data is directly proportional to the size and number of partitions. The more partitions there are, the more work will be distributed across the executors. There will also be fewer partitions. This means that processing will be done faster and in larger chunks.

You can manipulate partitions to speed up data processing.

While sending the partition to each executor, you can control the size of the partitions to get optimized performance.

To complete this recipe, run the steps in the 3-6.InputPartition notebook, which can be found in your local cloned repository, in the Chapter03 folder.

How to do it...

Let's learn how to change the spark.files.maxPartitionBytes configuration value by tweaking the number of input partition files:

1. Display the customer csv files that have been mounted in the chapter02 folder from the Azure Data Lake Storage account using the following code. /mnt/Gen2/ has the customer csv files.:

    ```
    display(dbutils.fs.ls("/mnt/Gen2/"))
    ```

2. By specifying the spark.sql.files.maxPartitionBytes parameter, you can control the number of bytes that can be packed into single partition. You can do this while reading data from JSON, ORC, and Parquet files. Execute the following code snippet to see the default block size, which is 134,217,728 bytes:

    ```
    print(spark.conf.get("spark.sql.files.
    maxPartitionBytes"))
    ```

3. Load the dataframe using the following code:

    ```
    df = spark.read.format("csv").option("header","true").
    load("/mnt/Gen2/")
    ```

4. Execute the following code to see the number of partitions that were created for the dataframe. Considering the default block size, 10 partitions will be created:

```
df.rdd.getNumPartitions()
```

5. Now, you can change the default partition size to 1 MB by executing the following code:

```
spark.conf.set("spark.sql.files.maxPartitionBytes",
"1048576")
```

6. Now, when you load the dataframe and check the number of partitions, you will see that 30 partitions have been created:

```
df = spark.read.format("csv").option("header","true").
load("/mnt/Gen2/")
```

```
df.rdd.getNumPartitions()
```

7. You can tweak the partitions of the files to achieve better parallelism. You can test this by creating partitions based on the number of cores in your cluster.

How it works...

Spark reads a HDFS file as a single partition for each file split. Spark's default block size is 128 MB.

Let's understand this by taking an example of 60 GB uncompressed text data files that have been stored in a HDFS filesystem. As you already know, the default block size is 128 MB, so 480 blocks will be created. There will also be 480 partitions. If the data can't be divided, then Spark will use the default number of partitions.

Learning about output partitions

Saving partitioned data using the proper condition can significantly boost performance while you're reading and retrieving data for further processing.

Reading the required partition limits the number of files and partitions that Spark reads while querying data. It also helps with dynamic partition pruning.

But sometimes, too many optimizations can make things worse. For example, if you have several partitions, data is scattered within multiple files, so searching the data for particular conditions in the initial query can take time. Also, memory utilization will be more while processing the metadata table as it contains several partitions.

While saving the in-memory data to disk, you must consider the partition sizes as Spark produces files for each task. Let's consider a scenario: if the cluster configuration has more memory for processing the dataframe and saving it as larger partition sizes, then processing the same data even further with a smaller cluster configuration may cause issues while you're reading the saved data.

Getting ready

In this recipe, you will learn how to manage partitions while writing the DataFrame.

You can follow along by running the steps in the 3-7.OutputPartition notebook. This can be found in your local cloned repository, in the Chapter03 folder.

How to do it...

There are two ways to manage partitions: by using the **repartitioning** and **coalesce** operations.

Let's learn how to implement both:

1. First, load the customer csv files data into the dataframe from the ADLS mounted location ./mnt/Gen2/ has customer csv files.

    ```
    df = spark.read.format("csv").option("header","true").
    load("/mnt/Gen2/")
    ```

2. Execute the following code snippet to see the number of stages that have been created to process the task by Spark:

    ```
    spark.conf.set("spark.sql.files.maxPartitionBytes",
    "134217728") # 128 MB
    ```
    ```
    df = spark.read.format("csv").option("header","true").
    load("/mnt/Gen2/")
    ```
    ```
    print(f"Number of partitions = {df.rdd.
    getNumPartitions()}")
    ```
    ```
    df.write.mode("overwrite").option("path",
    "dbfs:/tmp/datasources/customerSingleFile/").
    saveAsTable("customerSingleFile")
    ```

After executing the preceding code snippet, you will see that 10 tasks have been created for 10 partitions. Spark created 10 tasks to achieve parallelism:

Figure 3.26 – Multiple tasks for a query

3. If you have a very large file, you can increase the number of output partitions that Spark will write the output to using many cores.

4. You can repartition the existing dataframe using the `repartition` function. Use the following code snippet and verify that the partition count has been reduced to 8:

```
repartitionedDF = df.repartition(8)
print('Number of partitions: {}'.format(repartitionedDF.
rdd.getNumPartitions()))
```

5. You can also pass the name of the column where you want the data to be partitioned:

```
repartitionedDF = df.repartition('C_MKTSEGMENT')
print('Number of partitions: {}'.format(repartitionedDF.
rdd.getNumPartitions()))
```

6. The `coalesce` method is used to reduce parallelism while processing data. It avoids fully shuffling data by reducing the number of partitions. You should be careful when applying `coalesce` as it may also reduce the number of partitions you are expecting, which will impact parallel processing and performance.

7. You can remediate the problem we mentioned in the preceding step by passing `shuffle = true`. This adds a shuffle step, but reshuffled partitions will use full cluster resources wherever they're required:

```
coalescedDF = df.coalesce(2)
print('Number of partitions: {}'.format(coalescedDF.rdd.
getNumPartitions()))
```

8. You can use the `maxRecordsPerFile` parameter to control the size of the files. With this parameter we are asking Spark to create files with certain number of records:

```
df.write.option("maxRecordsPerFile", 1000).
mode("overwrite").partitionBy("C_MKTSEGMENT").
option("path", "dbfs:/tmp/datasources/customer/parquet/
maxfiles/").saveAsTable("customer_maxfiles")
```

```
%fs ls dbfs:/tmp/datasources/customer/parquet/maxfiles/C_
MKTSEGMENT=BUILDING/
```

```
df_read = spark.read.format("parquet").
option("inferSchema","True").load("dbfs:/tmp/datasources/
customer/parquet/maxfiles/C_MKTSEGMENT=BUILDING/part-
00000-tid-2745561518541164111-d6e0dd05-db1c-4716-b1ae-
604c8817099a-177-302.c000.snappy.parquet")
df_read.count()
```

How it works...

The **repartitioning** operation reduces or increases the number of partitions that the data in the cluster will be split by. This is an expensive operation and involves fully shuffling the data over the network and redistributing the data evenly. When this operation is performed, data is serialized, moved, and then deserialized.

You should only use repartitioning when you understand when it can speed up data processing by Spark jobs. The **coalesce** operation uses existing partitions and reduces the number of partitions to minimize the amount of data that's shuffled. Coalesce results in partitions that contain different amounts of data. In this case, the coalesce operation executor leaves data in a minimum number of partitions and only moves data from redundant nodes. Therefore, the coalesce operation usually runs faster than the repartition operation. But sometimes, when there is a significant difference in the partition sizes, it is slower.

Learning about shuffle partitions

In this recipe, you will learn how to set the `spark.sql.shuffle.partitions` parameter and see the impact it has on performance when there are fewer partitions.

Most of the time, in the case of wide transformations, where data is required from other partitions, Spark performs a data shuffle. Unfortunately, you can't avoid such transformations, but we can configure parameters to reduce the impact this has on performance.

Wide transformations uses shuffle partitions to shuffle data. However, irrespective of the data's size or the number of executors, the number of partitions is set to 200.

The data shuffle procedure is triggered by data transformations such as `join()`, `union()`, `groupByKey()`, `reduceBykey()`, and so on. The `spark.sql.shuffle.partitions` configuration sets the number of partitions to use during data shuffling. The partition numbers are set to 200 by default when Spark performs data shuffling.

Getting ready

You can follow along by running the steps in the `3-8.ShufflePartition` notebook. This can be found in your local cloned repository, in the `Chapter03` folder.

How to do it...

Let's learn how the execution time gets reduced when the number of shuffle partitions are reduced for small datasets:

1. First, load your dataframe from the customer `csv` files using the following code:

```
df = spark.read.format("csv").option("header","true").
load("/mnt/Gen2/")
```

2. Execute the following code snippet and see how long it takes to execute. Note that the time varies according to the volume of data in the dataframe:

```
spark.conf.set("spark.sql.shuffle.partitions", 200)
mktSegmentDF = df.groupBy("C_MKTSEGMENT").count().
collect()
```

3. The preceding code took 1.43 seconds to execute on the cluster we used with
   `spark.sql.shuffle.partitions` set to 200 (default value).

```
1  # Check the duration of execution with default 200 partitions
2  spark.conf.set("spark.sql.shuffle.partitions", 200)
3  mktSegmentDF = df.groupBy("C_MKTSEGMENT").count().collect()
```

▶ (2) Spark Jobs

Command took 1.43 seconds -- by ▓▓▓▓▓▓▓▓▓▓▓▓▓▓▓▓▓▓▓▓▓▓ on CookBookCluster

Figure 3.27 – Execution time with more partitions

4. Now, change the value of the `spark.sql.shuffle.partitions` parameter to
   30 and look at the execution time for the same query:

```
spark.conf.set("spark.sql.shuffle.partitions", 30)
mktSegmentDF = df.groupBy("C_MKTSEGMENT").count().
collect()
```

5. Following is the output for the preceding code and note that the execution time
   when `spark.sql.shuffle.partitions` is
   set to 30 is 0.61 seconds:

```
1  # Check the duration of execution with default 30 partitions
2  spark.conf.set("spark.sql.shuffle.partitions", 30)
3  mktSegmentDF = df.groupBy("C_MKTSEGMENT").count().collect()
```

▶ (2) Spark Jobs

Command took 0.61 seconds -- ▓▓▓▓▓▓▓▓▓▓▓▓▓▓▓▓▓▓▓▓▓▓ on CookBookCluster

Figure 3.28 – Execution time with fewer partitions

6. You will see that the time taken after changing the number of partitions to 30
   is comparatively less than when the `spark.sql.shuffle.partitions`
   parameter value was 200.

How it works...

Spark shuffling can increase or decrease the performance of your job, so based on your memory, data size, and processor, the `spark.sql.shuffle.partitions` configuration value must be set. When the data is small, then the number of partitions should be reduced; otherwise, too many partitions containing less data will be created, resulting in too many tasks with less data to process. However, when the data size is huge, having a higher number for the shuffle partition from default 200 might improve the query execution time. There is no direct formula to get the right number for shuffle partitions. It depends on the cluster size and the size of data you are processing.

Storage benefits of different file types

Storage formats are a way to define how data is stored in a file. Hadoop doesn't have a default file format, but it supports multiple file formats for storing data. Some of the common storage formats for Hadoop are as follows:

- Text files
- Sequence files
- Parquet files
- **Record-columnar (RC)** files
- **Optimized row columnar (ORC)** files
- Avro files

Choosing a write file format will provide significant advantages, such as the following:

- Optimized performance while reading and writing data
- Schema evaluation support (allows us to change the attributes in a dataset)
- Higher compression, resulting in less storage space being required
- Splittable files (files can be read in parts)

Let's focus on columnar storage formats as they are widely used in big data applications because of how they store data and can be queried by the SQL engine. The columnar format is very useful when a subset of data needs to be referred to. However, when most of the columns in a dataset need to be fetched, then row-oriented storage formats are beneficial.

The following are some columnar file formats:

- **RC files**: This stands for **record columnar files**. They provide many advantages over non-columnar files, such as fast data loading, quick query processing, and highly efficient storage space utilization. RC files are a good option for querying data, but writing them requires more memory and computation. Also, they don't support schema evolution.

- **ORC files**: This stands for **optimized row columnar files**. They have almost the same advantages and disadvantages as RC files. However, ORC files have better compression. They were designed for Hive and cannot be used with non-Hive MapReduce interfaces such as Pig, Java, or Impala.

- **Parquet files**: Parquet is a columnar data format that is suitable for large-scale queries. Parquet is just as good as RC and ORC in terms of performance while reading data, but it is slower when writing compared to other columnar file formats. Parquet supports schema evolution, which is not supported in RC and ORC file formats. Parquet also supports column pruning and predicate pushdown, which are not supported in CSV or JSON.

Now, let's look at partition pruning and predicate pushdown:

- **Partition pruning**: When you are dealing with terabytes of data, it is very difficult to retrieve the required data in a performant way. In this case, if files support partition pruning, then data can be retrieved faster. Partition pruning is a performance optimization technique that restricts the number of files and partitions that Spark can read while querying data. When partitioning is done, data is stored according to the partitioning scheme that's been segregated in the hierarchical folder structure and when data is queried, only a particular partition where data is available will be searched.

- **Predicate pushdown**: This is a condition in Spark queries that's used to filter the data that's restricting the number of records being returned from databases, thus improving the query's performance. While writing Spark queries, you need to ensure that the partition key columns are included in the filter condition of the query. Using predicate pushdown lets you skip over huge portions of the data while you're scanning and processing.

In this recipe, you will learn about and compare the different storage spaces that are required while saving the data in different file formats.

Getting ready

You can follow along by running the steps in the `3-9.FileFormats` notebook. This can be found in your local cloned repository, in the `Chapter03` folder.

How to do it...

Let's learn how to load data from a data file into a dataframe and then write that dataframe in different file formats:

1. Load the customer data into your dataframe from the ADLS mounted location using the following code snippet:

```
df = spark.read.format("csv").option("header","true").
load("/mnt/Gen2/")
```

2. Sort the customer data on the C_CUSTKEY column:

```
sortDF = df.sort('C_CUSTKEY')
display(sortDF)
```

You can verify the sorted result after executing the preceding code:

```
sortDF = df.sort('C_CUSTKEY')
display(sortDF)
```

▶ (1) Spark Jobs

▶ 🖬 sortDF: pyspark.sql.dataframe DataFrame = [C_CUSTKEY: string, C_NAME: string ... 6 more fields]

	C_CUSTKEY ▲	C_NAME ▲	C_ADDRESS ▲	C_NATIONKEY ▲	C_PHONE
1	1	Customer#000000001	IVhzIApeRb ot,c,E	0	10-989-741-2988
2	10	Customer#000000010	Lbrg3ElDiel0B10bB0Aymm	0	10-741-346-9870
3	100	Customer#000000100	mFowluhnHjp2GjCiYYavkW kUwOjlaTCQ	0	10-749-445-4907
4	1000	Customer#000001000	Ne,bJD40ae8ZXo XFrOkEmACe	0	10-730-275-2976
5	10000	Customer#000010000	OI7fOBe9O7SEIX7xSxqR	0	10-923-910-819
6	100000	Customer#000100000	GIw,RrxSCw6UDA5	0	10-488-516-6598

Figure 3.29 – Sorted dataframe

3. Write the sorted and unsorted dataframes in different file formats, such as Parquet and JSON:

```
sortDF.write.mode("overwrite").format("parquet").
option("path", "/tmp/customer/sortedData/").
saveAsTable("sortedData")
```

```
df.write.mode("overwrite").format("parquet").
option("path", "/tmp/customer/unsortedData").
saveAsTable("unsortedData")
```

```
df.write.mode("overwrite").format("json").option("path",
"/tmp/customer/jsonData").saveAsTable("jsonData")
```

4. Compare the storage space that was taken up by each file. You will observe that the sorted data is the smallest, followed by unsorted and then JSON:

```
%fs ls /tmp/customer/sortedData/
```

```
%fs ls /tmp/customer/unsortedData/
```

```
%fs ls /tmp/customer/jsonData/
```

The preceding code will list the files from each folder, along with their occupied storage space.

How it works...

Parquet supports all the features that are provided by the RC and ORC file formats. It stores data in binary files with metadata. Using this metadata information, Spark can easily determine data types, column names, and compression by parsing the data files. Because of these features, it is widely used in big data applications.

4
Working with Streaming Data

As data ingestion pipelines evolve and change, we see a lot of streaming sources, such as Azure Event Hubs and Apache Kafka, being used as sources or sinks as part of data pipeline applications. Streaming data such as temperature sensor data and vehicle sensor data has become common these days. We need to build our data pipeline application in such a way that we can process streaming data in real time and at scale. Azure Databricks provides a great set of APIs, including Spark Structured Streaming, to process these events in real time. We can store the streaming data in various sinks, including **Databricks File System (DBFS)**, in various file formats, in various streaming systems, such as Event Hubs and Kafka, and in databases such as Azure SQL databases, Azure Synapse Dedicated SQL pools, or in NoSQL databases such as Azure Cosmos. In this chapter, we will learn how to read data from various streaming sources using Azure Databricks Structured Streaming APIs and write the events to Delta tables, DBFS in Parquet format, and learn some internals on how checkpoints and triggers are used and how this guarantees fault tolerance of streaming queries.

By the end of this chapter, you will know how to use Spark Structured Streaming APIs to consume the data from various streaming sources such as Kafka, Event Hubs, and Kafka-enabled Event Hubs. This will establish the foundation required to work on end-to-end data pipelines using streaming and batch data.

We're going to cover the following main topics:

- Reading streaming data from Apache Kafka
- Reading streaming data from Azure Event Hubs
- Reading data from Event Hubs for Kafka
- Streaming data from log files
- Understanding trigger options
- Understanding window aggregation on streaming data
- Understanding offsets and checkpoints

Technical requirements

To follow along with the examples shown in the recipes, the following is required:

- An Azure subscription and the requisite permissions in relation to the subscription mentioned in the *Technical requirements* section of *Chapter 1*, *Creating an Azure Databricks Service.*
- A Python editor such as Visual Studio Code, PyCharm, or any other editor of your choice.
- An Azure Databricks cluster with runtime version 8.1
- You can find the scripts for this chapter in the GitHub URL at `https://github.com/PacktPublishing/Azure-Databricks-Cookbook/tree/main/Chapter04/Code`.

Reading streaming data from Apache Kafka

In this recipe, you will learn how to use Apache Kafka connectors for structured streaming in Azure Databricks to read data from Apache Kafka and write the streaming data to Delta tables and to Parquet files in the default DBFS location.

Getting ready

Before you start working on this recipe, please ensure you have gone through all the following points.

- Creating an Azure HD Insight Apache Kafka cluster (version 3.6 or later) that has Kafka version Kafka 0.10+. Perform the steps mentioned in the following document:

  `https://docs.microsoft.com/en-us/azure/hdinsight/kafka/apache-kafka-get-started#:~:text=Table%201%20%20%20%20Property%20%20,a%20region%20...%20%205%20more%20rows`

- You can use the following Python script, `https://github.com/PacktPublishing/Azure-Databricks-Cookbook/blob/main/Chapter04/PythonCode/Kafka_producer.py`, which will push the data to the Apache Kafka cluster as a streaming data producer.

- To run the Python script, you need Kafka broker hostnames or IPs, which we will use in the Python script. You can perform the steps mentioned in the following screenshot to get the broker's hostname and IP from **Ambari** homepage:

Figure 4.1 – Kafka broker host

- The following screenshot has the steps to get the broker host IP. The worker node IP's name starts with wn:

Figure 4.2 – Kafka broker host IP

- Before you run the Kafka producer script, you should change the config value for **auto.create.topics.enabled** from **False** to **True** from the Ambari portal. This is used where you are not pre-creating the topics in Kafka and wish to create them as part of the Kafka producer Python script. The following screenshot includes the steps to change the config value:

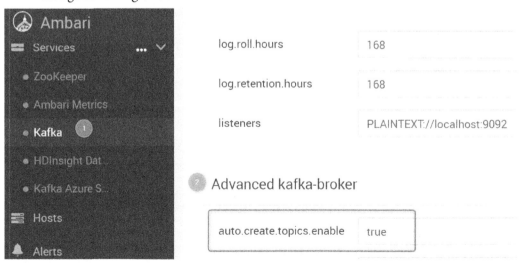

Figure 4.3 – Kafka topic enabling

- Once you have the broker hostname or IP, you can use the details in the Python script to produce events in Kafka:

```
producer = KafkaProducer(bootstrap_servers=['10.0.0.16:9092','10.1.0.14:9092',
                                            '10.1.0.15:9092'],
                    value_serializer=lambda x:
                    dumps(x).encode('utf-8'))
```

Figure 4.4 – Kafka Broker details

> **Note**
>
> You can either use Visual Studio Code or any IDE of your choice to run the Python code. There will be cases when running `kafka import KafkaProducer` in the IDE is failing to import the library. You can alternatively use the Python terminal to run the commands mentioned in the script to produce/push events to Kafka.

How to do it...

In this section, you will learn how to read data from Kafka topics using structured streaming in Azure Databricks, parse the JSON data received, write the data into a Delta table, and then write the data to the DBFS as Parquet files:

1. Our vehicle sensor information has id, `timestamp`, `rpm`, `speed`, and `kms`. Every event that we read from Kafka has these fields in the `value` column of the Kafka message.

2. We will first create a schema for `json`, which we will parse in the Kafka message:

```
jsonschema = StructType() \
.add("id", StringType()) \
.add("timestamp", TimestampType()) \
.add("rpm", IntegerType()) \
.add("speed", IntegerType()) \
.add("kms", IntegerType())
```

3. We will read the streaming data from the Kafka brokers by running the following code:

```
kafkaDF = spark.readStream.format("kafka") \
.option("kafka.bootstrap.servers", "10.1.0.13:9092,10.1.0
.11:9092") \
.option("subscribe", "VehicleDetails") \
.option("group.id", "Cookbook-demo") \
.option("startingOffsets","latest" ) \
.load()
```

4. Run the following code to check whether streaming has started and get the schema for the dataframe:

```
print( kafkaDF.isStreaming)
print( kafkaDF.printSchema())
```

5. You will find the data type for the key and the value columns for the Kafka dataframe will be binary. We need to convert them to a string so that we can parse the JSON value from the value column of the dataframe:

```
newkafkaDF=kafkaDF.selectExpr("CAST(key AS STRING)",
"CAST(value AS STRING)")
```

6. Run the following code to add a new column to the dataframe and use the from_ json function to parse the JSON object:

```
newkafkaDF=newkafkaDF.withColumn('vehiclejson', from_
json(col('value'),schema=jsonschema))
```

7. The new column (vehiclejson) in the preceding step is of the struct type and we will include all the columns of vehiclejson, along with the key and value columns, in a new dataframe:

```
kafkajsonDF=newkafkaDF.select("key","value",
"vehiclejson.*")
```

8. Now we will write the `kafkajsonDF` data to a Delta table by running the following code. Delta tables will be discussed in more detail in the upcoming chapters:

```
kafkajsonDF.selectExpr(
                "id"        \
                ,"timestamp"       \
                ,"rpm"    \
                ,"speed" \
                ,"kms" )  \
.writeStream.format("delta") \
.outputMode("append") \
.option("checkpointLocation", "dbfs:/Vehiclechkpoint_
Demo/") \
.option("mergeSchema", "true") \
.start("dbfs:/Vehiclechkpoint_Delta")
```

9. Run the following code, which will create a Delta table in the `dbfs:/Vehiclechkpoint_Delta` location where the streaming data is written:

```
%sql
-- Creating the table on delta location
CREATE TABLE IF NOT EXISTS VehicleDetails_Delta
USING DELTA
LOCATION "dbfs:/Vehiclechkpoint_Delta/"
```

10. You can now query the Delta table created in the preceding step:

```
%sql
select * from VehicleDetails_Delta limit 10
```

11. We have seen how to write the streaming data to the Delta table. Now we will learn how to write the input stream data to a Parquet file the in DBFS. First, let's create folders in the default DBFS mounted path by running the following code:

```
dbutils.fs.mkdirs("dbfs:/VehiclechData/parquetFiles/")
```

12. Once the folder is created, we will run the following command to write the stream data to the `DBFS` folder created and store the output as Parquet format:

```
kafkajsonDF.selectExpr(
                "id"         \
                ,"timestamp"       \
                ,"rpm"    \
                ,"speed" \
                ,"kms"  ) \
.writeStream.format("parquet").queryName("veh_details").
option("checkpointLocation", "dbfs:/Vehiclechkpoint_Demo_
Parquet/").start("dbfs:/VehiclechData/parquetFiles")
```

13. You can check the files created in the folder using the following command:

```
%fs ls dbfs:/VehiclechData/parquetFiles
```

14. You can use these Parquet files for any further analytics.

How it works...

We are using the Python script to produce events in Kafka and the Python script is generating 10 random vehicle IDs. For each vehicle ID, it is generating 20 events.

We are using the following code to read events from Kafka:

```
kafkaDF = spark.readStream.format("kafka") \
.option("kafka.bootstrap.servers", "10.1.0.13:9092,10.1.0
.11:9092") \
.option("subscribe", "VehicleDetails") \
.option("group.id", "Cookbook-demo") \
.option("startingOffsets","latest" ) \
.load()
```

In the preceding code, we need to make sure to understand what each option is:

- `kafka.bootstrap.servers`: This is the Kafka hostname or IP and the port needs to be 9092.

- `subscribe`: This is the name of the topic to which the producer is sending events. The producer in our demo is the Python script, which is sending events to a topic named `VehicleDetails`.

- `group.id`: This can be any unique name that you can provide.
- `startingOffsets`: It can have three values – the latest, the earliest, or a JSON string, specifying the offset for topic partition. It describes from which offset point you want the query to start.

Reading streaming data from Azure Event Hubs

In this recipe, you will learn how to connect an Azure Event Hubs streaming data source from Azure Databricks to process data in real time. You will set up the data process using Azure Event Hubs and read messages coming from the Event Hub using Azure Databricks. To access the streaming data, you will set up a streaming data producer application in Python to ingest vehicle information.

Getting ready

Before you start working on this recipe, please ensure you have gone through the following points:

- You can create an Event Hub namespace and an Event Hub within the namespace in accordance with the Microsoft documentation available at `https://docs.microsoft.com/en-us/azure/event-hubs/event-hubs-create`.

- You can use the Python script, `Event_producer.py`, which will push the data to Azure Event Hubs as a streaming data producer You can get the Python script from `https://github.com/PacktPublishing/Azure-Databricks-Cookbook/blob/main/Chapter04/PythonCode/Kafkaeventhub_producer.py`.

- You will need an Azure Databricks workspace. Refer to the recipes in *Chapter 1, Creating an Azure Databricks Service*, for information on how to create the Azure Databricks workspace.

- The connection string to access the Event Hubs namespace. The connection string should have a format similar to `Endpoint=sb://<namespace>.servicebus.windows.net/;SharedAccessKeyName=<key name>;SharedAccessKey=<key value>`.

- A shared access policy name and a connection string-primary key for the Event Hub namespace. You can refer to the following link to get the connection string-primary key value and **Primary key** value or the policy from the Azure portal. We are adding a policy with name `readwrite` which has read, write, and manage permissions. This is the policy name that we will be using in the Python script and in the Databricks notebook.

```
https://docs.microsoft.com/en-us/azure/event-hubs/event-
hubs-get-connection-string#get-connection-string-from-the-
portal.
```

- Following is the screenshot after adding the readwrite policy.

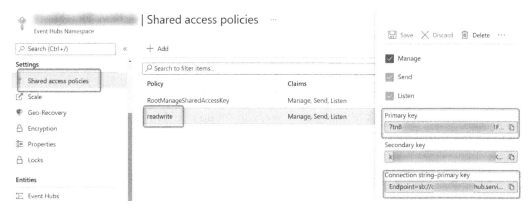

Figure 4.5 – Output after adding the readwrite policy

- Install the following library from the Maven coordinates, `com.microsoft.` `azure:azure-eventhubs-spark_2.12:2.3.20`, or higher. Search for azure-eventhubs-spark in the `Maven Central` and select the latest `Artifact Id` for com.microsoft.azure and the latest `Release`. You can refer to the following link on how to install libraries in the Databricks cluster Use the latest **Artifact Id** that is available. This code was tested on `com.microsoft.azure:azure-eventhubs-spark_2.12:2.3.20`.

```
https://docs.microsoft.com/en-us/azure/databricks/
libraries/workspace-libraries#--maven-or-spark-package:
```

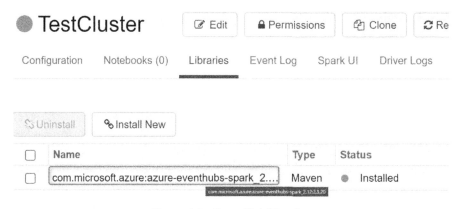

Figure 4.6 – Event Hub libraries

You should see the status for the Azure Event Hubs spark connector as installed in the cluster libraries section.

How to do it...

In this section, you will learn how to read data from Azure Event Hubs using structured streaming in Azure Databricks, parse the JSON data received, and write the data into a Delta table:

1. Our vehicle sensor information has id, timestamp, rpm, speed, and kms. Every message that is read from Azure Event Hubs has these fields in the body column of the message.

2. You can read the streaming data from Azure Event Hubs by running the following code. Here, the Azure Event Hub details, such as **Namespace**, **Shared access policy name**, and **Shared access key**, are required. Replace the variable values as per your environment before executing the code. We have created a new **Shared access** policy name readwrite which we have used in the following code and in the Python code to push data to Event Hubs.

```
from pyspark.sql.functions import *
from pyspark.sql.types import *


#Eventhub namespace and required keys
EH_NAMESPACE_NAME = "CookbookEventHub"
EH_KEY_NAME = "readwrite"
EH_KEY_VALUE = "xxxxxxxxxxxxx-xxxxxxx-xxxxx"
# connection string of Event Hubs Namespace
connectionString = "Endpoint=sb://{0}.servicebus.windows.
net/;SharedAccessKeyName={1};SharedAccessKey={2};
EntityPath=ingestion".format(EH_NAMESPACE_NAME, EH_KEY_
NAME, EH_KEY_VALUE)


ehConfig = {}
ehConfig['eventhubs.connectionString'] = connectionString


ehConfig['eventhubs.connectionString'] = sc._
jvm.org.apache.spark.eventhubs.EventHubsUtils.
encrypt(connectionString)


EventHubdf = spark.readStream.format("eventhubs").
options(**ehConfig).load()
```

3. Execute the following code to verify whether data streaming has started and to verify the schema:

```
print( EventHubdf.isStreaming)
print( EventHubdf.printSchema())
```

You will observe that the output of the previous commands is true and that the schema of the message is also displayed:

```
print( EventHubdf.isStreaming)
print( EventHubdf.printSchema())
```

```
True
root
 |-- body: binary (nullable = true)
 |-- partition: string (nullable = true)
 |-- offset: string (nullable = true)
 |-- sequenceNumber: long (nullable = true)
 |-- enqueuedTime: timestamp (nullable = true)
 |-- publisher: string (nullable = true)
 |-- partitionKey: string (nullable = true)
 |-- properties: map (nullable = true)
 |    |-- key: string
 |    |-- value: string (valueContainsNull = true)
 |-- systemProperties: map (nullable = true)
 |    |-- key: string
 |    |-- value: string (valueContainsNull = true)
```

Figure 4.7 – Dataframe schema

4. The JSON schema will be required to parse the body attribute in the message as the body in the message will always be in binary format:

```
jsonschema = StructType() \
.add("id", StringType()) \
.add("timestamp", TimestampType()) \
.add("rpm", IntegerType()) \
.add("speed", IntegerType()) \
.add("kms", IntegerType())
```

5. As the `body` column for the Azure Event Hub message is binary, we need to cast it as a string so that it can be parsed:

```
newEventHubDf=EventHubdf.selectExpr("CAST(body AS
STRING)")
```

6. Run the following code to add a new column to the dataframe, using the `from_json` function to parse the `json` object:

```
newEventHubDf=newEventHubDf.withColumn('vehiclejson',
from_json(col('body'),schema=jsonschema))
```

7. The new column (`vehiclejson`) in the preceding step is of the struct type and we will extract all the columns of `vehiclejson`, along with the `body` column, into a new dataframe:

```
newEventHubjsonDF=newEventHubDf.select("body",
"vehiclejson.*")
```

8. Now we can write data to a Delta table by running the following code. Delta tables will be discussed in more detail in the upcoming chapters:

```
newEventHubjsonDF.selectExpr(
                "id"      \
                ,"timestamp"     \
                ,"rpm"    \
                ,"speed" \
                ,"kms"  )  \
.writeStream.format("delta") \
.outputMode("append") \
.option("checkpointLocation", "dbfs:/Vehiclechkpoint_
AzureEventHub_Demo/") \
.option("mergeSchema", "true") \
.start("dbfs:/Vehiclechkpoint_AzureEventHub_Delta")
```

9. We can query the Delta table and list the files in the Delta table location in accordance with the steps mentioned in the *How to do it...* section of the *Reading streaming data from Apache Kafka* recipe earlier in this chapter.

How it works...

In this example, vehicle sensor data is being generated using a Python application. Details regarding this can be found in the *Reading streaming data from Apache Kafka* recipe earlier in this chapter.

Now we will understand how the following code is working to read the Azure Event Hub data:

```
from pyspark.sql.functions import *
from pyspark.sql.types import *


#Eventhub namespace and required keys
EH_NAMESPACE_NAME = "CookbookEventHub"
EH_KEY_NAME = "readwrite"
EH_KEY_VALUE = "xxxxxxxxxxxxx-xxxxxxx-xxxxx"
# connection string of Event Hubs Namespace
connectionString = "Endpoint=sb://{0}.servicebus.windows.
net/;SharedAccessKeyName={1};SharedAccessKey={2};
EntityPath=ingestion".format(EH_NAMESPACE_NAME, EH_KEY_NAME,
EH_KEY_VALUE)


ehConfig = {}
ehConfig['eventhubs.connectionString'] = connectionString


ehConfig['eventhubs.connectionString'] = sc._jvm.org.apache.
spark.eventhubs.EventHubsUtils.encrypt(connectionString)


EventHubdf = spark.readStream.format("eventhubs").
options(**ehConfig).load()
```

Let's go through the preceding code.

- Import the required classes of Spark SQL and dataframes. These are required to use the methods of the imported classes in your notebook for data processing.

- Variable values for EH_NAMESPACE_NAME, EH_KEY_NAME, and EH_KEY_VALUE are provided as per the environment.

- The connection string of the Azure Event Hub is formed based on the variable's values in the preceding step.

- Event Hub configurations are saved in the Event Hub configuration dictionary. The `connectionString` variable value is also assigned to the Event Hub connection string property. Additionally, there are lots of optional configurations that will be useful in different use cases. Refer to the following resource link to read more about them:

  ```
  https://docs.microsoft.com/en-us/python/api/azure-
  eventhub/azure.eventhub.aio.eventhubconsumerclient?view=az
  ure-python
  ```

- The connection string needs to be stored securely, so it is encrypted using the `eventhubs.EventHubsUtils.encrypt()` method.

- Finally, the data from the Event Hub is read using the `readStream` method as we are processing streaming data. The format in this use case is `eventhubs` and, in the option, the Event Hub configuration dictionary is passed.

Reading data from Event Hubs for Kafka

In this recipe, you will learn how Event for Kafka provides an endpoint that is compatible with Kafka and can be used as a streaming source. We will learn how Azure Databricks can consume the data from Event Hubs for Apache Kafka.

Getting ready

Before starting, you need to ensure that you have contributor access to the subscription or owner of the resource group and have gone through the *Technical requirements* section:

- You can create an Event Hub namespace and Event Hub within the namespace in accordance with the Microsoft documentation available at `https://docs.microsoft.com/en-us/azure/event-hubs/event-hubs-create`.

- You can use the Python script, `https://github.com/PacktPublishing/Azure-Databricks-Cookbook/blob/main/Chapter04/PythonCode/Kafkaeventhub_producer.py`, which will push the data to Event Hub for Kafka as a streaming data producer.

- To run the Python script, you need the Event Hub connection string, which we will use in the Python script. You can perform the steps mentioned in the following screenshot to get the connection string details. We are adding a policy with name `sendreceivekafka` which has read, write, and manage permissions. This is the policy name that we will be using in the Databricks notebook.

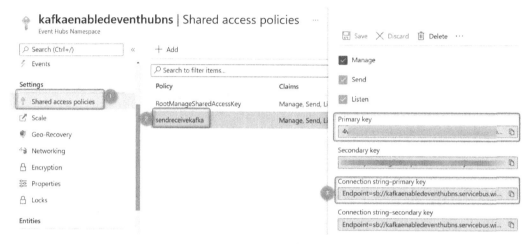

Figure 4.8 – Event Hub policies

- You can find more details about getting the connection string from the following link: `https://docs.microsoft.com/en-us/azure/event-hubs/event-hubs-get-connection-string`.

- You can copy the **Connection string-primary key** value and use that in the Python code for the config value, `sasl.password`.

- For the `bootstrap.servers` config value in the Python script, provide the name of the `Eventhub` namespace; it should be `{Your Event Hub namespace}.servicebus.windows.net:9093`.

- We are using Confluent Kafka for pushing the events to Event Hub for Kafka. You can install Confluent Kafka by running `pip install confluent_kafka`.

- You can follow along by running the steps in the notebook at `https://github.com/PacktPublishing/Azure-Databricks-Cookbook/blob/main/Chapter04/Code/4.3-Reading%20Data%20from%20Kafka%20Enabled%20EventHub.ipynb`.

How to do it...

In this section, you will learn how to read data from Event Hubs for Kafka using structured streaming in Azure Databricks, parse the `json` data received, write the data into a Delta table, and store it in the DBFS as Parquet files as well:

1. Our vehicle sensor information has `id`, `timestamp`, `rpm`, `speed`, and `kms`. Every event that we read from Kafka has these fields in the `value` column of the Kafka message.

2. We will first create a schema for the `json` data, which we will parse in the Kafka message:

```
jsonschema = StructType() \
.add("id", StringType()) \
.add("timestamp", TimestampType()) \
.add("rpm", IntegerType()) \
.add("speed", IntegerType()) \
.add("kms", IntegerType())
```

3. We need to get the bootstrap server and topic details before we can read the streaming data. You need to set the `BOOTSTRAP_SERVERS` and `EH_SASL` values for the topic:

```
TOPIC = "kafkaenabledhub" -This is the name of eventhub
--Use the Event Hub namespace for bootstrap server
BOOTSTRAP_SERVERS = "kafkaenabledeventhubns.servicebus.
windows.net:9093"
--Password is the connection string that we have seen in
Getting ready section
EH_SASL = "kafkashaded.org.apache.kafka.common.security.
plain.PlainLoginModule required username=
\"$ConnectionString\" password=\"Endpoint=sb:
//kafkaenabledeventhubns.servicebus.windows.
net/;SharedAccessKeyName=sendreceivekafka;
SharedAccessKey=2dsaddsdasdasd0+xxxxxxvoVE=\";"
```

4. We will read the streaming data from Azure Event Hubs for Kafka by running the following code:

```
kafkaDF = spark.readStream \
    .format("kafka") \
    .option("subscribe", TOPIC) \
    .option("kafka.bootstrap.servers", BOOTSTRAP_SERVERS) \
    .option("kafka.sasl.mechanism", "PLAIN") \
    .option("kafka.security.protocol", "SASL_SSL") \
    .option("kafka.sasl.jaas.config", EH_SASL) \
    .option("kafka.request.timeout.ms", "60000") \
    .option("kafka.session.timeout.ms", "60000") \
    .option("kafka.group.id", "POC") \
    .option("failOnDataLoss", "false") \
    .option("startingOffsets", "latest") \
    .load()
```

5. You will ascertain that the data type for the `key` and `value` columns for the `kafkaDF` dataframe is binary and that we need to convert it to a string so that we can parse the `json` value from the `value` column of the dataframe:

```
newkafkaDF=kafkaDF.selectExpr("CAST(key AS STRING)",
"CAST(value AS STRING)")
```

6. Run the following code to add a new column to the dataframe and use the `from_json` function to parse the `json` object:

```
newkafkaDF=newkafkaDF.withColumn('vehiclejson', from_
json(col('value'),schema=jsonschema))
```

7. The new column (`vehiclejson`) in the preceding step is of the struct type and we will include all the columns of `vehiclejson`, along with the `key` and `value` columns, in a new dataframe:

```
kafkajsonDF=newkafkaDF.select("key","value",
"vehiclejson.*")
```

8. Now we will write the `kafkajsonDF` data to a Delta table by running the following code. Delta tables will be discussed in more detail in the upcoming chapters:

```
kafkajsonDF.selectExpr(
                    "id"          \
                   ,"timestamp"        \
                   ,"rpm"      \
                   ,"speed" \
                   ,"kms" ) \
.writeStream.format("delta") \
.outputMode("append") \
.option("checkpointLocation", "dbfs:/
Vehiclechkpointkafkaeventhub_Demo /") \
.option("mergeSchema", "true") \
.start("dbfs:/VehiclechkpointKafkaEventHub_Delta")
```

9. Run the following code, which will create a Delta table in the `VehiclechkpointKafkaEventHub_Delta` location where the streaming data is written:

```
%sql
-- Creating the table on delta location
CREATE TABLE IF NOT EXISTS VehicleDetails_
KafkaEnabledEventHub_Delta
USING DELTA
LOCATION "dbfs:/VehiclechkpointKafkaEventHub_Delta /"
```

10. You can now query the Delta table created in the preceding step:

```
%sql
select * from VehicleDetails_KafkaEnabledEventHub_Delta
limit 10
```

11. We have seen how to write the stream data to the Delta table. Now we will learn how to write the stream data to a Parquet file. First, let's create folders in the default DBFS filesystem by running the following code:

```
dbutils.fs.mkdirs("dbfs:/VehiclechData_
KafkaEnabledEventHub/parquetFiles/")
```

12. After the folder is created, we will run the following command to write the stream data to the DBFS and store the data in Parquet format:

```
kafkajsonDF.selectExpr(
                    "id"          \
                    ,"timestamp"      \
                    ,"rpm"    \
                    ,"speed" \
                    ,"kms" ) \
.writeStream.format("parquet").queryName("veh_details1").
option("checkpointLocation", "dbfs:/VehiclechData_
KafkaEnabledEventHub/chkpoint/").start("dbfs:/
VehiclechData_KafkaEnabledEventHub/parquetFiles")
```

13. You can check the files created in the folder using the following command:

```
%fs ls dbfs:/VehiclechData_KafkaEnabledEventHub/
parquetFiles
```

14. You can use these Parquet files for any further analytics.

How it works...

We are using the Python script to produce events in Kafka and the Python script is generating 10 random vehicle IDs. For each vehicle ID, it is generating 20 events.

We are using the following code to read events from Kafka:

```
kafkaDF = spark.readStream \
    .format("kafka") \
    .option("subscribe", TOPIC) \
    .option("kafka.bootstrap.servers", BOOTSTRAP_SERVERS) \
    .option("kafka.sasl.mechanism", "PLAIN") \
    .option("kafka.security.protocol", "SASL_SSL") \
    .option("kafka.sasl.jaas.config", EH_SASL) \
    .option("kafka.request.timeout.ms", "60000") \
    .option("kafka.session.timeout.ms", "60000") \
    .option("kafka.group.id", "POC") \
    .option("failOnDataLoss", "false") \
    .option("startingOffsets", "latest") \
    .load()
```

In the preceding code, we need to make sure to understand what each option is:

- `kafka.bootstrap.servers`: This will be `{EventHub namespace}.servicebus.windows.net:9093`.

- `subscribe`: This is the name of the Event Hub to which the producer is sending events. The producer in our demo is the Python script that is sending events to `kafkaenabledhub`.

- `group.id`: This can be any unique name that you provide.

- `kafka.sasl.jaas.config`: This is the connection string value and the following is the value for it:

  `"kafkashaded.org.apache.kafka.common.security.plain.PlainLoginModule required username=\"$ConnectionString\" password=\"Endpoint=sb://kafkaenabledeventhubns.servicebus.windows.net/;SharedAccessKeyName=sendreceivekafka;SharedAccessKey=4cscasdasdd+asdasdVxxxxxx=\";"`

  `kafkaenabledeventhubns` is the name of the Event Hubs namespace.

  `SharedAccessKeyName` is the primary key for the Event Hubs namespace.

You can learn more about Event Hubs for Kafka by going through the following document:

`https://docs.microsoft.com/en-us/azure/event-hubs/event-hubs-for-kafka-ecosystem-overview`.

Streaming data from log files

Nowadays, most enterprises are maintaining a lot of applications and each application has its log files. Extracting the required information from log files or monitoring the log file data is becoming a cumbersome task for administrators. To salvage some of the workloads from the shoulders of administrators, Azure Databricks is a great help. Using Databricks, you can process the log files and interactively query the log data to extract the required information.

Getting ready

You can follow along by running the steps in the "4-4.StreamingLogFiles" notebook in your local cloned repository in the Chapter04 folder (https://github. com/PacktPublishing/Azure-Databricks-Cookbook/tree/main/ Chapter04).

Upload the LogFiles folder in the Common/LogData folder to the ADLS Gen-2 account in the rawdata filesystem under the Log Files folder.

In this recipe, the use case that we are going to examine is the application logs being generated in the ADLS Gen-2 location and using Azure Databricks, you will process the information in the log files and extract the required information for further analysis.

How to do it...

Let's see how to use Databricks to create a streaming application to process the log files using the dataframe API:

1. You can verify the content of the directory using the following code snippet:

    ```
    display(dbutils.fs.ls("/mnt/Gen2/LogFiles"))
    ```

    These are json log files that have been uploaded as part of the *Getting ready* section of this recipe:

    ```
    display(dbutils.fs.ls("/mnt/Gen2/LogFiles"))
    ```

    ▸ (2) Spark Jobs

	path	name	size
1	dbfs:/mnt/Gen2/LogFiles/Log1.json	Log1.json	211
2	dbfs:/mnt/Gen2/LogFiles/Log2.json	Log2.json	209
3	dbfs:/mnt/Gen2/LogFiles/Log3.json	Log3.json	209
4	dbfs:/mnt/Gen2/LogFiles/Log4 - Copy.json	Log4 - Copy.json	209
5	dbfs:/mnt/Gen2/LogFiles/Log4.json	Log4.json	209

    Figure 4.9 – Listing log files

2. You can verify the content of the JSON file by executing the following code snippet:

    ```
    %fs head /mnt/Gen2/Log1.json
    ```

The file contains data from different applications with the same schema. Each file contains a log_type, which specifies whether the log file includes an error, warning, or information:

```
%fs head dbfs:/mnt/Gen2/LogFiles/Log3.json
```

```json
{
    "source": "Application 1",
    "data": "Log data example 1",
    "IP": "10.22.135.7",
    "log_level": "DEBUG",
    "log_type": "Error",
    "log_app": "app",
    "log_timestamp": "2020-08-25T17:45:13+07:00"
}
```

Figure 4.10 – Log file data

3. You can define the schema of the dataframe, which will be built on top of the data in the file, and provide the table name. Here, we are using the read() method to extract the data from static files:

```python
from pyspark.sql.types import *

logFilePath = "/mnt/Gen2/LogFiles/"
logSchema = StructType([ StructField("source",
StringType(), True), StructField("data",
StringType(), True), StructField("IP", StringType(),
True), StructField("log_level", StringType(),
True),StructField("log_type", StringType(),
True),StructField("log_app", StringType(), True),
StructField("log_timestamp", TimestampType(), True) ])


LogDF = (
  spark
    .read
    .schema(logSchema)
    .option("multiline","true")
```

```
        .json(logFilePath)
)
```

```
display(LogDF)
```

4. Let's take the example of a scenario where you want to get a count of the number of logs based on `log_type` from all the log files:

```
from pyspark.sql.functions import *
logCountDF = (
  LogDF
    .groupBy(col("log_type"))
    .count()
)
display(logCountDF)
```

5. You can apply window functions such as `rank()`, `denserank()`, `percentRank()`, and `rowNumber()` on the `LogDF` dataframe as per your use case. Refer to the following resource to get more details on the window function in Spark: `https://spark.apache.org/docs/latest/sql-ref-syntax-qry-select-window.html`.

6. You can also read the log files as a streaming source by running the following code snippet. This code is reading file by file and you should see the count for the `log_type` getting changed.

```
from pyspark.sql.types import *
from pyspark.sql.functions import *
logFilePath = "/mnt/Gen2/LogFiles/"

logSchema = StructType([ StructField("source",
StringType(), True), StructField("data",
StringType(), True), StructField("IP", StringType(),
True), StructField("log_level", StringType(),
True),StructField("log_type", StringType(),
True),StructField("log_app", StringType(), True),
StructField("log_timestamp", TimestampType(), True) ])
streamingLogDF = (
  spark
    .readStream
    .schema(logSchema)
```

```
        .option("multiline","true")
        .option("maxFilesPerTrigger", 1)
        .json(logFilePath)
)
streamingDataCountDF = (
    streamingLogDF
        .groupBy(col("log_type"))
        .count()
)
display(streamingDataCountDF)
```

7. Run the following code, which is using memory as the sink to write the input streaming data. The following query will always overwrite the complete data from the input streaming source. If you add new files to the Log folder you will see the counts getting updated in near real time by running the following code as well as from the previous code. To simulate the scenario, you can upload the same JSON files by changing their names.

```
report = (
    streamingDataCountDF
        .writeStream
        .format("memory")
        .queryName("counts")
        .outputMode("complete")
        .start()
)
```

8. Here, counts is the name of the table that can be queried for near real-time data.

9. You can run the following code to query the data from the counts table:

```
%sql
select * from counts
```

How it works...

Files can be read as a static data source and streaming data source as well. In both cases, the methods are different: read() is used for reading the static data, whereas readstream() is used for reading the data as a streaming source. maxFilesPerTrigger is the parameter to specify the numbers of files that will be processed in each execution.

Understanding trigger options

In this recipe, we will understand various trigger options that are available in Spark Structured Streaming and learn under which scenarios a specific type of trigger option can be used. The trigger option for a streaming query identifies how quickly streaming data needs to be processed. It defines whether the streaming query needs to be processed in micro-batch mode or continuously. The following are the different types of triggers that are available:

- **Default** (when unspecified): New data is processed as soon as the current micro-batch completes. No interval is set in this option.

- **Fixed Interval** – micro-batch: We define a processing time that controls how often the micro-batches are executed. This is preferred in many use cases.

- **One Time** – micro-batch: This will execute as a micro-batch only once, process all the data that is available, and then stop. It can be used in scenarios where data arrives once every hour or so.

- **Continuous Mode**: With this option, a query runs in milliseconds and with low latency. This option is still at the experimental stage.

Getting ready

We will use the same Python script as we used in the *Reading data from Kafka-enabled Event Hubs* recipe to push the data to Event Hubs.

You can follow along by running the steps in the notebook at `https://github.com/PacktPublishing/Azure-Databricks-Cookbook/blob/main/Chapter04/Code/4.5-Understanding%20Trigger%20Options.ipynb`.

Code was tested on Databricks Runtime version 7.3 LTS with Spark 3.0.1.

How to do it...

Let's learn how to use different trigger options and check from the UI how often the write stream will look for new data and write to the sink:

1. Run the Python code used in the recipe *Reading Data from Event Hubs for Kafka* which generates streaming data. We are reading from Event Hubs for Kafka.

2. We will read the streaming data from Azure Event Hubs for Kafka by running the following code:

```
kafkaDF = spark.readStream \
    .format("kafka") \
```

```
.option("subscribe", TOPIC) \
.option("kafka.bootstrap.servers", BOOTSTRAP_SERVERS) \
.option("kafka.sasl.mechanism", "PLAIN") \
.option("kafka.security.protocol", "SASL_SSL") \
.option("kafka.sasl.jaas.config", EH_SASL) \
.option("kafka.request.timeout.ms", "60000") \
.option("kafka.session.timeout.ms", "60000") \
.option("kafka.group.id", "POC") \
.option("failOnDataLoss", "false") \
.option("startingOffsets", "latest") \
.load()
```

3. You will ascertain that the data type for the key and the value columns for the
    kafkaDF dataframe are binary and that we need to convert them to a string so that
    we can parse the JSON value from the value column of the dataframe:

```
kafkaDF=kafkaDF.selectExpr("CAST(key AS STRING)",
"CAST(value AS STRING)")
```

4. Run the following code to add a new column to the dataframe and use the from_
    json function to parse the json object:

```
newkafkaDF=newkafkaDF.withColumn('vehiclejson', from_
json(col('value'),schema=jsonschema))
```

5. The new column (vehiclejson) in the preceding step is of the struct type and
    we will extract all the columns of vehiclejson, along with the key and value
    columns, into a new dataframe:

```
kafkajsonDF=newkafkaDF.select("key","value",
"vehiclejson.*")
```

6. In the following code, we are not specifying any trigger option, and the default
    behavior is to run the data in micro-batches and process data as soon as one micro-
    batch completes:

```
kafkajsonDF.selectExpr(
                "id"          \
                ,"timestamp"        \
                ,"rpm"     \
                ,"speed"  \
                ,"kms"  )  \
```

```
.writeStream.format("delta") \
.outputMode("append") \
.option("checkpointLocation", "dbfs:/
Vehiclechkpointkafkaeventhub_Demo_triffer /") \
.option("mergeSchema", "true") \
.start("dbfs:/VehiclechkpointKafkaEventHub_Delta_
trigger")
```

7. Run the following code to create a Delta table:

```
%sql
-- Creating the table on delta location
CREATE TABLE IF NOT EXISTS VehicleDetails_
KafkaEnabledEventHub_Delta_trifer
USING DELTA
LOCATION "dbfs:/VehiclechkpointKafkaEventHub_Delta /"
```

8. Run the following code to check the count of records from the Delta table:

```
%sql
-- You can keep running this cell continuously and you
will find the numbers growing as data is processed as it
arrives.
select count(*) from VehicleDetails_KafkaEnabledEventHub_
Delta_Trigger
```

9. After running Step 6, you will find that the **Last updated** value, as shown in the following screenshot, varies between 5, 10, and 15 seconds:

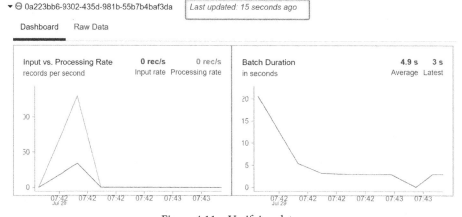

Figure 4.11 – Verifying data

10. Now we will run the write stream at fixed intervals by specifying the option trigger (`processingTime='30 seconds'`). Stop the existing write stream and run the following code:

```
kafkajsonDF.selectExpr(
                "id"      \
               ,"timestamp"      \
               ,"rpm"    \
               ,"speed" \
               ,"kms" ) \
.writeStream.format("delta") \
.outputMode("append") \
.option("checkpointLocation", "dbfs:/
Vehiclechkpointkafkaeventhub_Demo_trigger/") \
.option("mergeSchema", "true") \
.trigger(processingTime='30 seconds') \
.start("dbfs:/VehiclechkpointKafkaEventHub_Delta_
trigger")
```

11. Now, run the Python code to push data to Event Hubs and you will find that the write stream will read new data every 30 seconds from the source. You can see from the following snippet that the write stream performs a check every 30 seconds:

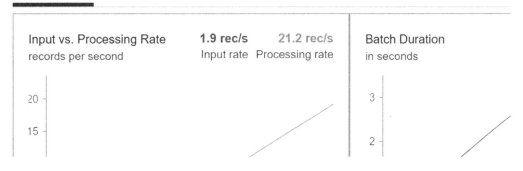

Figure 4.12 – Write stream data

12. You can run the following `select` statement and you will discover that the rows are updated every 30 seconds and not immediately:

```sql
%sql
-- You can keep running this cell continuously and you
will find the numbers don't change continuously, it gets
updates after every 30 seconds.
select count(*) from VehicleDetails_KafkaEnabledEventHub_
Delta_Trigger
```

13. Now we will run the write stream with the continuous trigger option by specifying the option trigger (`continuous='1 second'`). This option is not completely production-ready:

```
kafkajsonDF.selectExpr(
                    "id"           \
                    ,"timestamp"        \
                    ,"rpm"     \
                    ,"speed" \
                    ,"kms" ) \
.writeStream.format("Console") \
.format("console") \
.trigger(continuous='1 second') \
.start()
```

14. You will establish that the data is continuously read as soon as the data is found from the input stream and that the latency is a few milliseconds.

15. Now we will run the write stream with trigger once option by specifying the option trigger (**once=True**). This option will read streaming data in micro batch once from the last offset till end of the stream that it finds at the time of execution and stops on its own. If you want to invoke the Notebook from an ADF pipeline and want to trigger the execution once every 2-3 hours, then you can use this option rather than streaming the data continuously.

```
kafkajsonDF.selectExpr(
                    "id"      \
                    ,"timestamp"            \
                    ,"rpm"         \
                    ,"speed" \
                    ,"kms" ) \
```

```
.writeStream.format("delta") \
.outputMode("append") \
.option("checkpointLocation", "dbfs:/
Vehiclechkpointkafkaeventhub_Demo_trigger/") \
.option("mergeSchema", "true") \
.trigger(once=True) \
.start("dbfs:/VehiclechkpointKafkaEventHub_Delta_
trigger")
```

By now you have learned the different trigger option that can be used based on the streaming requirements.

How it works...

We need to ensure that we understand that the next micro-batch will run when the currently running micro-batches complete within 30 seconds or take more than 30 seconds to complete.

- *If it takes less than 30 seconds*: If the current micro-batch is executed in, say, 10 seconds, then the next micro-batch will be executed after 20 seconds as we have mentioned that the `processingTime` is 30 seconds.

- *Takes more than 30 seconds*: If the current micro-batch takes, say, 45 seconds, then the next micro-batch gets executed immediately as the current batch took more than 30 seconds.

For the continuous trigger option, the following are the supported sources and sinks:

- **Kafka source**: All options are supported.

- **Rate source**: Good for testing. The only options that are supported in continuous mode are `numPartitions` and `rowsPerSecond`.

- **Kafka sink**: All options are supported.

- **Memory sink**: Good for debugging.

- **Console sink**: Good for debugging. All options are supported. Note that the console will print every checkpoint interval that you have specified in the continuous trigger.

Understanding window aggregation on streaming data

We often encounter situations where we don't want the streaming data to be processed as is and want to aggregate the data and then perform some more transformation before data is written to the destination. Spark provides us with an option for performing aggregation on data using a Windows function for both non-overlapping and overlapping windows. In this recipe, we will learn how to use aggregations using the window function on streaming data.

Getting ready

We will be using Event Hubs for Kafka as the source for streaming data.

You can use the Python script, `https://github.com/PacktPublishing/Azure-Databricks-Cookbook/blob/main/Chapter04/PythonCode/KafkaEventHub_Windows.py`, which will push the data to Event Hubs for Kafka as the streaming data producer. Change the topic name in the Python script to `kafkaenabledhub1`.

You can refer to the *Reading data from Kafka-enabled Event Hubs* recipe to understand how to get the bootstrap server details and other configuration values that are required to run the Python script.

For Spark code, you can follow along by running the steps in the notebook at `https://github.com/PacktPublishing/Azure-Databricks-Cookbook/blob/main/Chapter04/Code/4.6-Event%20time%20for%20Window%20aggregation%20on%20Streaming%20Data.ipynb`.

How to do it...

We will learn how to use tumbling and overlapping windows with sliding intervals to aggregate the input streaming data and write to Delta tables.

The following steps demonstrate how to use the tumbling window method for aggregating the input stream data on the vehicle `id` and `Timestamp` columns:

1. The following code will aggregate the data every minute and create windows of 1 minute on the timestamp column to group and count by `id` value every minute:

    ```
    kafkajsonDF.groupBy(window('timestamp',"1
    minutes"),'id').count().orderBy('window') \
    .writeStream.format("delta") \
    .outputMode("complete") \
    ```

```
.option("truncate", "false") \
.option("checkpointLocation", "dbfs:/
Vehiclechkpointkafkaeventhub_Agg_Chkpoint_Tumbling/") \
.option("mergeSchema", "true") \
.start("dbfs:/VehiclechkpointKafkaEventHub_Delta_Agg_
Tumbling")
```

2. Create a Delta table in Spark based on the file location used in the preceding code:

```
%sql
CREATE TABLE IF NOT EXISTS VehiclechkpointKafkaEventHub_
Delta_Agg_Tumbling
USING DELTA
LOCATION "dbfs:/VehiclechkpointKafkaEventHub_Delta_Agg_
Tumbling/"
```

3. Now, run the Python code mentioned in the *Getting ready* section to push the data to the Event Hub.

4. After pushing the data, we will query the Delta table and check for the IDs and the window column in the output by running the following code:

```
%sql
SELECT * FROM VehiclechkpointKafkaEventHub_Delta_Agg_
Tumbling ORDER BY Window desc
```

5. By running the preceding code block, you will see the following screenshot by way of output:

```
%sql
SELECT * FROM VehiclechkpointKafkaEventHub_Delta_Agg_Tumbling ORDER BY Window desc
```

▶ (1) Spark Jobs

	window	id	count
1	▶ {"start": "2021-07-30T01:53:00.000+0000", "end": "2021-07-30T01:54:00.000+0000"}	19eeda6f-0489-4c68-937a-f91ba866643b	6
2	▶ {"start": "2021-07-30T01:53:00.000+0000", "end": "2021-07-30T01:54:00.000+0000"}	afa56211-c75c-4d76-9f17-2e550cd51fa8	5
3	▶ {"start": "2021-07-30T01:53:00.000+0000", "end": "2021-07-30T01:54:00.000+0000"}	66ce2ce6-3b23-4f92-a3b7-a7dfd3fe7caf	5
4	▶ {"start": "2021-07-30T01:53:00.000+0000", "end": "2021-07-30T01:54:00.000+0000"}	a529fb2a-5f7c-4aa1-976c-e4b683b919f2	5
5	▶ {"start": "2021-07-30T01:53:00.000+0000", "end": "2021-07-30T01:54:00.000+0000"}	c7bb7aa9-cc1c-453f-a86e-ca171c710e85	5
6	▶ {"start": "2021-07-30T01:53:00.000+0000", "end": "2021-07-30T01:54:00.000+0000"}	c91ff0d5-bffc-458f-9a15-25fac0fc6cc8	6

Showing all 10 rows.

Figure 4.13 – Window aggregation

6. Wait for a few minutes and then run the Python code again and you will see additional window times for the aggregated data captured. After running the Python code, re-run the `select` statement and you should see output similar to the following screenshot. You can see that the data is aggregated for 1-minute intervals, as defined in the write stream dataframe code:

```sql
%sql
SELECT * FROM VehiclechkpointKafkaEventHub_Delta_Agg_Tumbling ORDER BY Window desc
```

▶ (1) Spark Jobs

	window	id	count
1	▶ {"start": "2021-07-30T01:55:00.000+0000", "end": "2021-07-30T01:56:00.000+0000"}	a1a4b4ba-7f9c-4058-aa15-b79f3fd5dd7d	2
2	▶ {"start": "2021-07-30T01:55:00.000+0000", "end": "2021-07-30T01:56:00.000+0000"}	c7bb7aa9-cc1c-453f-a86e-ca171c710e85	1
3	▶ {"start": "2021-07-30T01:55:00.000+0000", "end": "2021-07-30T01:56:00.000+0000"}	67f5187f-d1c0-431b-844a-2f99f49d59e3	1
4	▶ {"start": "2021-07-30T01:55:00.000+0000", "end": "2021-07-30T01:56:00.000+0000"}	45e71b4f-f46e-4e58-959d-e2afa7830875	2
5	▶ {"start": "2021-07-30T01:55:00.000+0000", "end": "2021-07-30T01:56:00.000+0000"}	66ce2ce6-3b23-4f92-a3b7-a7dfd3fe7caf	1
6	▶ {"start": "2021-07-30T01:55:00.000+0000", "end": "2021-07-30T01:56:00.000+0000"}	a529fb2a-5f7c-4aa1-976c-e4b683b919f2	1

Showing all 30 rows.

Figure 4.14 – Window incremental data

7. Now we will simulate late-arriving data by running the following piece of Python code and confirming that the later arriving data gets updated in the correct window. This code is inserting data that was generated at 2021-03-14 10:46:31.043358 and arriving after 11 A.M. for a specific device ID:

```python
reading = {'id': 'c7bb7aa9-cc1c-453f-a86e-ca171c710e85',
'timestamp':str(datetime.datetime.utcnow()-datetime.
timedelta(minutes=55)), 'rpm': random.randrange(100),
'speed': random.randint(70, 100), 'kms': random.
randint(100, 1000)}
```

```python
msgformatted = json.dumps(reading)
```

```python
p.produce(topic, msgformatted, callback=delivery_
callback)
```

```python
p.flush()
```

8. Now, run the following code in the notebook and you will see that the count of devices will change from 1 to 2 and that the Spark engine is updating the right window in the `timestamp` column:

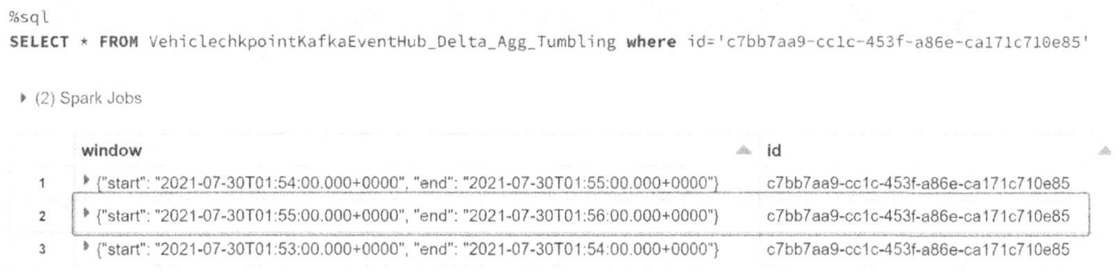

```
%sql
SELECT * FROM VehiclechkpointKafkaEventHub_Delta_Agg_Tumbling where id='c7bb7aa9-cc1c-453f-a86e-ca171c710e85'
```

▶ (2) Spark Jobs

	window	id
1	▶ {"start": "2021-07-30T01:54:00.000+0000", "end": "2021-07-30T01:55:00.000+0000"}	c7bb7aa9-cc1c-453f-a86e-ca171c710e85
2	▶ {"start": "2021-07-30T01:55:00.000+0000", "end": "2021-07-30T01:56:00.000+0000"}	c7bb7aa9-cc1c-453f-a86e-ca171c710e85
3	▶ {"start": "2021-07-30T01:53:00.000+0000", "end": "2021-07-30T01:54:00.000+0000"}	c7bb7aa9-cc1c-453f-a86e-ca171c710e85

Figure 4.15 – Window count of devices

9. The preceding snippet shows the value of the count changing from 1 to 2 for the device ID 'c7bb7aa9-cc1c-453f-a86e-ca171c710e85', where the counts are updated for the correct window of event time.

The following steps demonstrate how to use overlapping windows by specifying both the window length and the sliding interval for aggregating the input stream data:

1. The following code will aggregate the data with windows of 2 minutes and with a 1-minute sliding interval to group and count the number of vehicle IDs:

```
kafkajsonDF.groupBy(window('timestamp',"2 minutes","1
minutes"),'id').count().orderBy('window') \
.writeStream.format("delta") \
.outputMode("complete") \
.option("truncate", "false") \
.option("checkpointLocation", "dbfs:/
VehiclechkpointkafkaeventHub_Agg_Chkpoint_Overlapping4/")
\
.option("mergeSchema", "true") \
.start("dbfs:/VehiclechkpointKafkaEventHub_Delta_Agg_
Overlapping4")
```

2. Create a Delta table in Spark based on the file location used in the preceding code:

```
%sql
CREATE TABLE IF NOT EXISTS VehiclechkpointKafkaEventHub_
Delta_Agg_Overlapping
USING DELTA
LOCATION "dbfs:/VehiclechkpointKafkaEventHub_Delta_Agg_
Overlapping4/"
```

3. Now, run the Python code to push the data to the Event Hub.

4. After pushing the data, query the Delta table and check for the IDs and the `Window` column in the output by running the following code:

```sql
%sql
SELECT * FROM VehiclechkpointKafkaEventHub_Delta_Agg_
Tumbling
where id ='c2c7cb35-2f97-4fab-ab23-62fe24eca7af'
ORDER BY Window desc
```

5. The following snippet is the output of the `select` statement. Your output may vary slightly based on the number of times you run the Python code to push the data. You will find overlapping window intervals such as rows 3 and 4, which have timestamps for {`"start"`: `"2021-07-30T03:07:00.000+0000"`, `"end"`: `"2021-07-30T03:09:00.000+0000"`} and {`"start"`: `"2021-07-30T03:06:00.000+0000"`, `"end"`: `"2021-07-30T03:08:00.000+0000"`}. Here, data with the timestamp `2021-07-30T03:08:00.000+0000` will fall into both windows:

```sql
%sql
select * from VehiclechkpointKafkaEventHub_Delta_Agg_Overlapping
where id ='c2c7cb35-2f97-4fab-ab23-62fe24eca7af'
order by window desc
```

▸ (1) Spark Jobs

	window	id	count
1	▸ {"start": "2021-07-30T03:08:00.000+0000", "end": "2021-07-30T03:10:00.000+0000"}	c2c7cb35-2f97-4fab-ab23-62fe24eca7af	1
2	▸ {"start": "2021-07-30T03:07:00.000+0000", "end": "2021-07-30T03:09:00.000+0000"}	c2c7cb35-2f97-4fab-ab23-62fe24eca7af	13
3	▸ {"start": "2021-07-30T03:06:00.000+0000", "end": "2021-07-30T03:08:00.000+0000"}	c2c7cb35-2f97-4fab-ab23-62fe24eca7af	34
4	▸ {"start": "2021-07-30T03:05:00.000+0000", "end": "2021-07-30T03:07:00.000+0000"}	c2c7cb35-2f97-4fab-ab23-62fe24eca7af	28
5	▸ {"start": "2021-07-30T03:04:00.000+0000", "end": "2021-07-30T03:06:00.000+0000"}	c2c7cb35-2f97-4fab-ab23-62fe24eca7af	6

Figure 4.16 – Data verification

6. Now we will simulate late-arriving data by running the following piece of Python code and confirm that the later arriving data gets updated in the required overlapping windows. This code is inserting data that was generated at `3:08:30.661780 A.M.` and arriving after 3:10 A.M. for a specific device ID:

```python
reading = {'id': 'c2c7cb35-2f97-4fab-ab23-62fe24eca7af',
'timestamp':str(datetime.datetime.utcnow()-datetime.
timedelta(minutes=32)), 'rpm': random.randrange(100),
'speed': random.randint(70, 100), 'kms': random.
randint(100, 1000)}
```

```
msgformatted = json.dumps(reading) # Convert the reading
into a JSON object.

p.produce(topic, msgformatted, callback=delivery_
callback)

p.flush()
```

7. Now, run the following code in a notebook and you will see that the count of devices changed for rows 1 and 2, as highlighted, and you can compare the values with the output of *Step 5*:

```sql
%sql
select * from VehiclechkpointKafkaEventHub_Delta_Agg_Overlapping
where id ='c2c7cb35-2f97-4fab-ab23-62fe24eca7af'
order by window desc
```

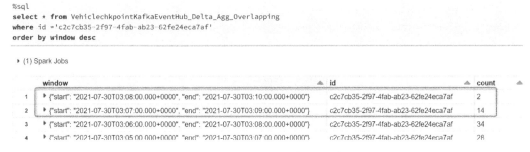

Figure 4.17 – Incremental data verification

8. You can see from the preceding snippet that since the event time (03:08:30.661780) is between two overlapping windows, the count is updated in both the windows, as highlighted in red in the preceding screenshot.

How it works...

The window function on streaming data provides us with the option to aggregate the data based on event time and additional columns from the source data. As we have seen in the *How to do it...* section of the recipe, there are two options in terms of using the window function, one that is non-overlapping, called a tumbling window, and the second an overlapping window with sliding intervals.

The tumbling window is a fixed window option where the data is grouped based on the fixed interval we specified in the dataframe write stream window (event time, column, duration).

The overlapping window with a sliding interval option creates multiple overlapping windows using the sliding interval option. Explaining how entire tumbling and overlapping windows work is a vast topic and beyond the scope of this book.

Handling data that arrives late is a big challenge in most streaming systems. Databricks automatically handles the late-arriving data and ensures that it puts the new data in the correct window. The main challenge is how old the late data can be, and which old, aggregated data should not be updated. To handle this, Databricks has introduced a concept known as watermarking, and we will learn about watermarking in the *Understanding offsets and checkpoints* recipe next.

Understanding offsets and checkpoints

In this recipe, you will learn how a Spark Streaming query recovers from failure or any unexpected server crash using checkpointing, where it stores the process and the state of the query as and when it is executing. The information that the checkpointing stores is the range of offsets that are processed in each trigger (you can refer to the *Understanding trigger options* recipe to learn more about triggers).

Getting ready

We will be using Event Hubs for Kafka as the source for streaming data.

You can use the Python script available at `https://github.com/PacktPublishing/Azure-Databricks-Cookbook/blob/main/Chapter04/PythonCode/KafkaEventHub_Windows.py`, which will push the data to Event Hubs for Kafka as the streaming data producer. Change the topic name in the Python script to `kafkaenabledhub2`.

You can refer to the *Reading data from Kafka-enabled Event Hubs* recipe to understand how to get the bootstrap server details and other configuration values that are required to run the Python script.

For Spark code, you can follow along by running the steps in the notebook at `https://github.com/PacktPublishing/Azure-Databricks-Cookbook/blob/main/Chapter04/Code/4.7-Watermarking%20Offset%20and%20Checkpointing.ipynb`.

How to do it...

We will learn how to check the offset value and the state that the Spark engine creates while processing aggregating streaming data.

The following steps demonstrate how to use the tumbling window method for aggregating the input stream data on the vehicle's id and Timestamp columns. We are using Azure Blob storage to mount to the DBFS, and the mount point is /mnt/Blob:

1. The following code will aggregate the data every minute and create windows of 1 minute on the timestamp column to group and count according to the number of IDs every minute and create one file for every trigger and for every ID:

```
kafkajsonDF.withWatermark("timestamp","4 minutes").
groupBy(window('timestamp',"1 minutes"),'id').count().
coalesce(1) \
.writeStream.format("delta") \
.outputMode("complete") \
.option("truncate", "false") \
.option("checkpointLocation", "/mnt/Blob/
Vehiclechkpointkafkaeventhub_Agg_Chkpoint_Delta11/") \
.start("/mnt/Blob/VehiclechkpointKafkaEventHub_Delta_Agg_
Delta11/")
```

2. Create a Delta table in Spark based on the file location used in the preceding code:

```
%sql
CREATE TABLE IF NOT EXISTS Vehicle_Agg
USING delta
LOCATION "/mnt/Blob/Vehicle_Agg/"
```

3. Now, run the Python code mentioned in the *Getting ready* section to push the data to the Event Hub.

4. After pushing the data, we will query the Delta table and check for the IDs and the Window column in the output by running the following code:

```
%sql
SELECT * FROM VehiclechkpointKafkaEventHub_Delta_Agg_
Tumbling ORDER BY Window desc
```

5. Now we will check the state details that the Spark engine will create in the checkpoint location. For that, go to the **Blob storage** account that you have mounted to the DBFS and you will find the folder as per the following screenshot. The two folders we have created are one for the checkpoint and the other for storing the Delta table files:

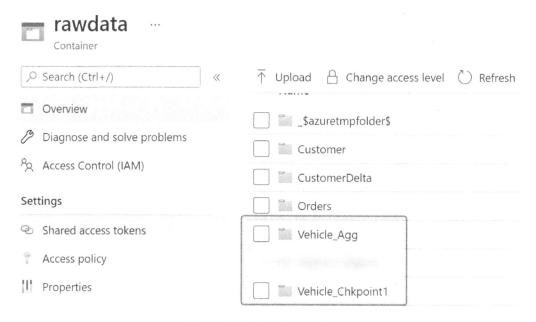

Figure 4.18 – Blob Storage data

6.   If you go to `Vehicle_Chkpoint`, you will find multiple folders and, when you look in the `state` folder, you will find multiple files for every state that Spark generates. As data is aggregated, Spark creates states prior to the start of every trigger:

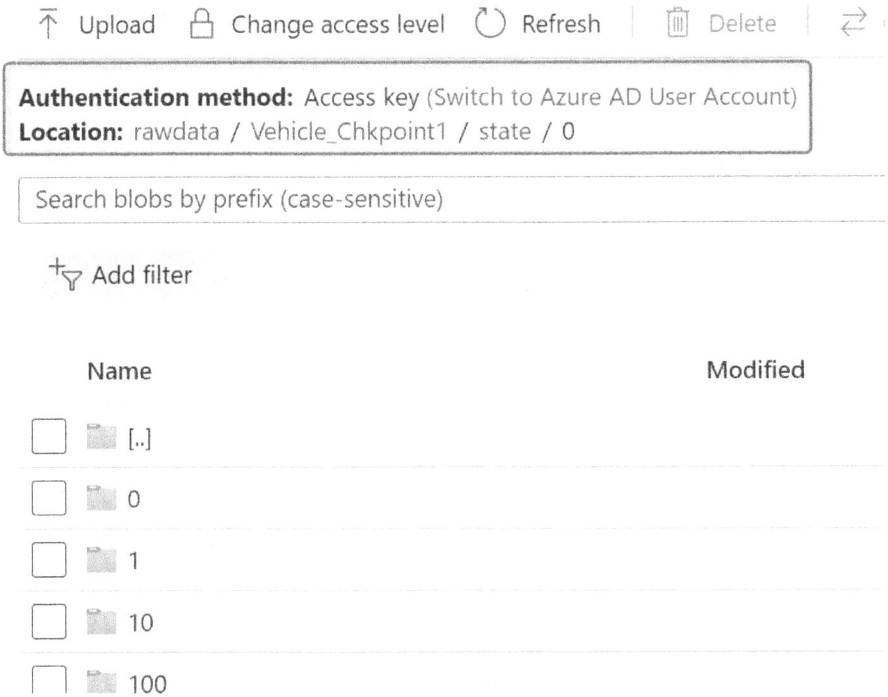

↑ Upload   🔒 Change access level   ↺ Refresh   🗑 Delete   ⇄

Authentication method: Access key (Switch to Azure AD User Account)
Location: rawdata / Vehicle_Chkpoint1 / state / 0

Search blobs by prefix (case-sensitive)

⁺▽ Add filter

Name	Modified
[..]	
0	
1	
10	
100	

Figure 4.19 – Blob Storage folders

7. To check the offset information, you can go to the `Vehicle_Chkpoint` folder, and, in that location, you will find a folder with the name **offsets**. This folder contains information about the latest offset that has been read by the Spark Streaming query. If you want to go back to the checkpoint every few days to get the data from the source, then you need to find the offset point. Every file in the offset folder contains the offset information that Spark last read. The offset value fetched from these files can be used in the read stream query:

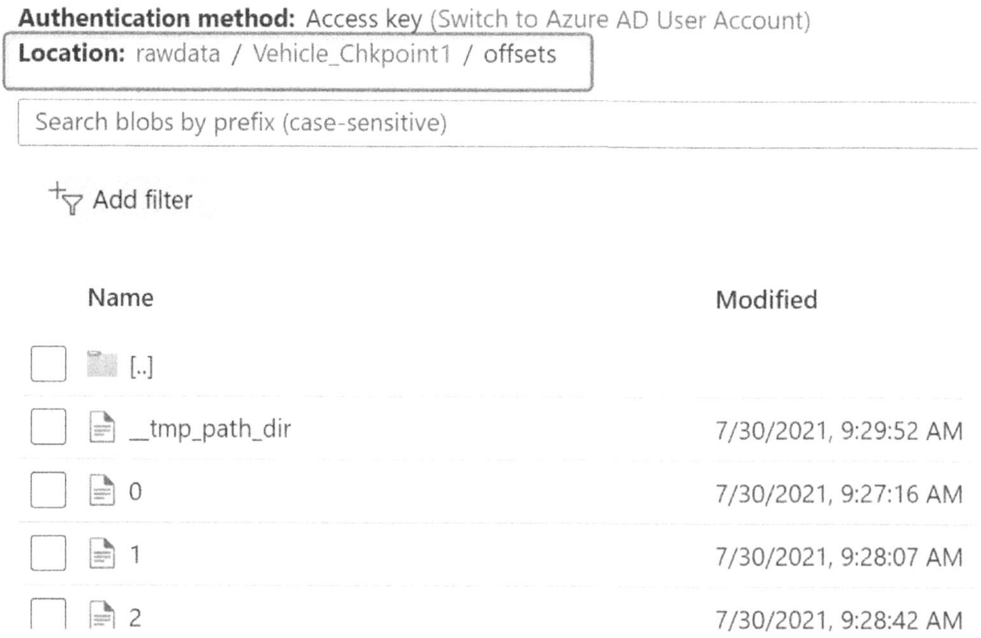

Authentication method: Access key (Switch to Azure AD User Account)

Location: rawdata / Vehicle_Chkpoint1 / offsets

Search blobs by prefix (case-sensitive)

+ Add filter

Name	Modified
[..]	
__tmp_path_dir	7/30/2021, 9:29:52 AM
0	7/30/2021, 9:27:16 AM
1	7/30/2021, 9:28:07 AM
2	7/30/2021, 9:28:42 AM

Figure 4.20 – Checkpoint offsets

8. When you look at the file content, you will see the `eventhub` name from which the data was read (source for streaming) and the offset information for the trigger run:

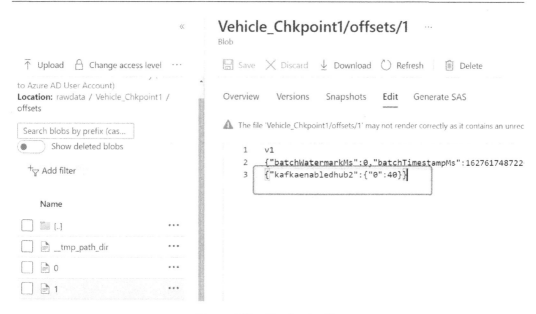

Figure 4.21 – Checkpoint file

Each file has offset information that you can use as the starting point in a Spark read stream query instead of specifying the earliest or latest.

How it works...

There are two types of stream processing; one is stateless, where the data from the source is received and loaded as is in any sink, such as Blob or Delta tables. In this case, the Spark SQL engine doesn't have to remember any previous incoming data as there is no old data that needs to be updated. This method is straightforward.

The second type of stream processing is stateful stream processing, where we are performing aggregations such as `count`, `min`, `max`, and `avg` on the incoming streaming data, and data is processed in micro-batches. A state is an intermediate version that the Spark SQL engine generates between two micro-batches.

For every trigger, a new micro-batch is started and the Spark engine reads the previous state value, such as the `count` and `avg` values, and then updates the value of the current micro-batch.

When the streaming aggregation query is being executed, the Spark SQL engine internally maintains the intermediate aggregations as a fault-tolerant state. The structure of the state is stored as a key-value pair. The value is the intermediate aggregation that Spark generates and stores in the executor's memory. For every trigger, the state value is read and updated and is committed to write-ahead logs, which are in the checkpoint location that we have specified in the write stream query. In case of any server crash or abrupt termination, the Spark engine gets the required version of the state from the checkpoint location and executes the streaming query. This functionality ensures fault tolerance and guarantees precisely one-time processing of the message.

5
Integrating with Azure Key Vault, App Configuration, and Log Analytics

These days, most data processing or data ingestion pipelines read or write data from or to various external sources such as Azure Blob/ADLS Gen-2, SQL, Cosmos, and Synapse. To access these sources, you will need credentials. Storing these credentials, such as a storage account key or SQL password, in a notebook is not an option from a security standpoint and not a recommended approach when deploying these data ingestion or processing pipelines to production. To overcome these problems, Microsoft provides **Azure Key Vault**, where you can store credentials such as username and password, and access them securely from your notebooks. Apart from Key Vault, we can also use **App Configuration** to store these passwords and access them from **Databricks** notebooks.

By the end of this chapter, you will have learned how to create an Azure Key Vault from the **Azure portal** and the **Azure CLI**, as well as how to access Key Vault from Databricks notebooks. You will have also learned how to use App Configuration to store passwords and how to integrate Log Analytics with an Azure Databricks workspace.

We're going to cover the following recipes in this chapter:

- Creating an Azure Key Vault to store secrets using the UI
- Creating an Azure Key Vault to store secrets using ARM templates
- Using Azure Key Vault secrets in Azure Databricks
- Creating an App Configuration resource
- Using App Configuration in an Azure Databricks notebook
- Creating a Log Analytics workspace
- Integrating a Log Analytics workspace with Azure Databricks

Technical requirements

To follow along with the examples in this chapter, you will need the following:

- An Azure subscription and the required permissions for that subscription, as we mentioned in the *Technical requirements* section of *Chapter 1, Creating an Azure Databricks Service*.
- An Azure Databricks workspace premium tier.
- Secret paths in a Spark configuration property or environment variable available in Databricks Runtime Version 6.4 and above.
- The necessary scripts. You can find the scripts for this chapter at `https://github.com/PacktPublishing/Azure-Databricks-Cookbook/tree/main/Chapter05/Code`. The `Chapter05` folder contains all the notebooks for this chapter.

- The Azure CLI installed in your machine. You can download and install it from the following URL:

```
https://docs.microsoft.com/en-us/cli/azure/install-azure-
cli-windows?tabs=azure-cli.
```

Creating an Azure Key Vault to store secrets using the UI

In this recipe, you will learn how to create an *Azure Key Vault* instance via the *Azure portal* and how to create secrets in the Azure Key Vault. Once the Key Vault instance and secrets have been created, we can refer to these secrets in the notebook so that we are not exposing passwords to our users. By the end of this recipe, you will have learned how to create an Azure Key Vault via the Azure portal and how to create secrets in the Azure Key Vault.

Getting ready

Before starting, you need to ensure you have contributor access to the subscription or are the owner of the resource group.

How to do it...

In this section, you will learn how to create an Azure Key Vault via the Azure portal. Let's get started:

1. From the Azure portal home page, search for `Key Vault` and select the **Create** button.

2. Provide the **Resource group** name, **Key vault name**, and select the **Standard** pricing tier:

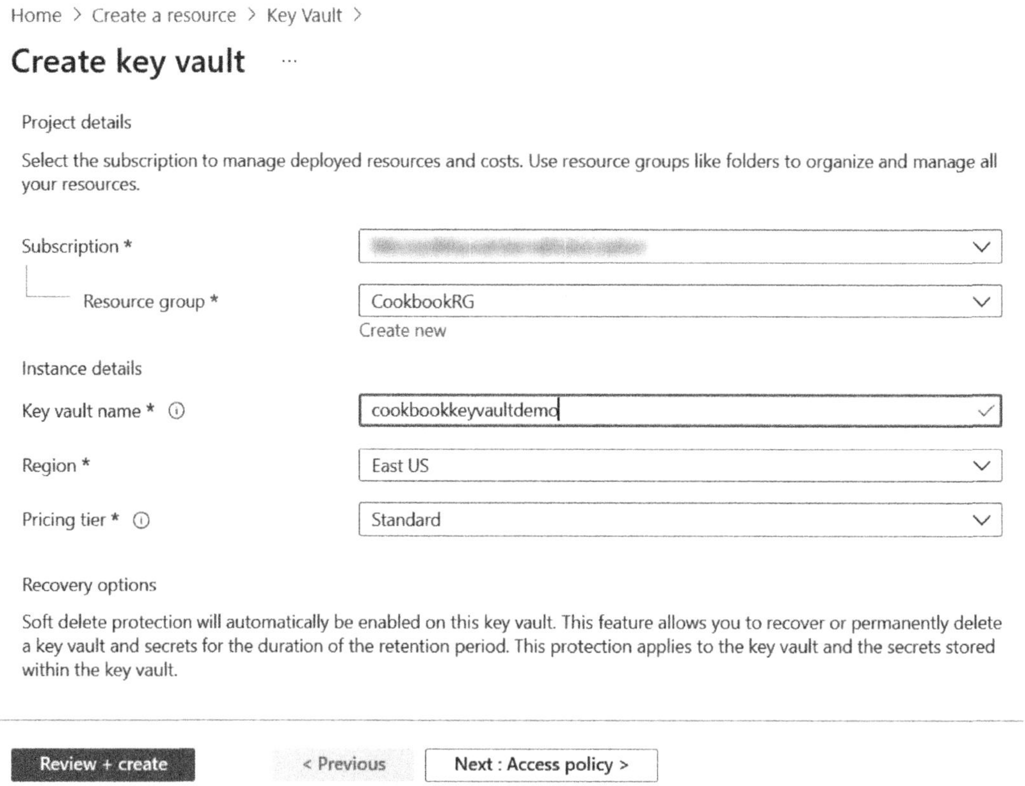
Home > Create a resource > Key Vault >
Create key vault
Project details
Select the subscription to manage deployed resources and costs. Use resource groups like folders to organize and manage all your resources.
Subscription *
Resource group *
CookbookRG
Create new
Instance details
Key vault name *
cookbookkeyvaultdemo
Region *
East US
Pricing tier *
Standard
Recovery options
Soft delete protection will automatically be enabled on this key vault. This feature allows you to recover or permanently delete a key vault and secrets for the duration of the retention period. This protection applies to the key vault and the secrets stored within the key vault.
Review + create
< Previous
Next : Access policy >

Figure 5.1 – Create key vault page

3. You can keep the default values under **Access policy**. Then, select **Next: Networking**:

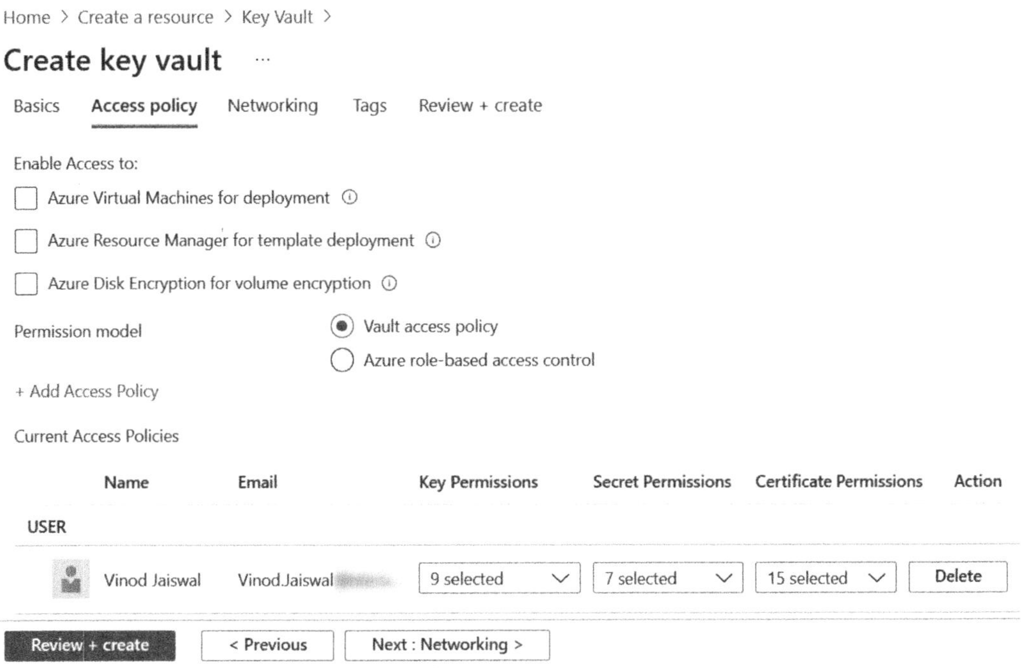

Home > Create a resource > Key Vault >

Create key vault   ...

Basics   **Access policy**   Networking   Tags   Review + create

Enable Access to:

☐ Azure Virtual Machines for deployment ⓘ

☐ Azure Resource Manager for template deployment ⓘ

☐ Azure Disk Encryption for volume encryption ⓘ

Permission model   ⦿ Vault access policy
                                       ◯ Azure role-based access control

\+ Add Access Policy

Current Access Policies

	Name	Email	Key Permissions	Secret Permissions	Certificate Permissions	Action
USER						
👤	Vinod Jaiswal	Vinod.Jaiswal	9 selected ⌄	7 selected ⌄	15 selected ⌄	Delete

[Review + create]   [< Previous]   [Next : Networking >]

Figure 5.2 – Create key vault – Access policy

4. For networking, select **Public endpoint (all networks)** and click the **Review + create** button:

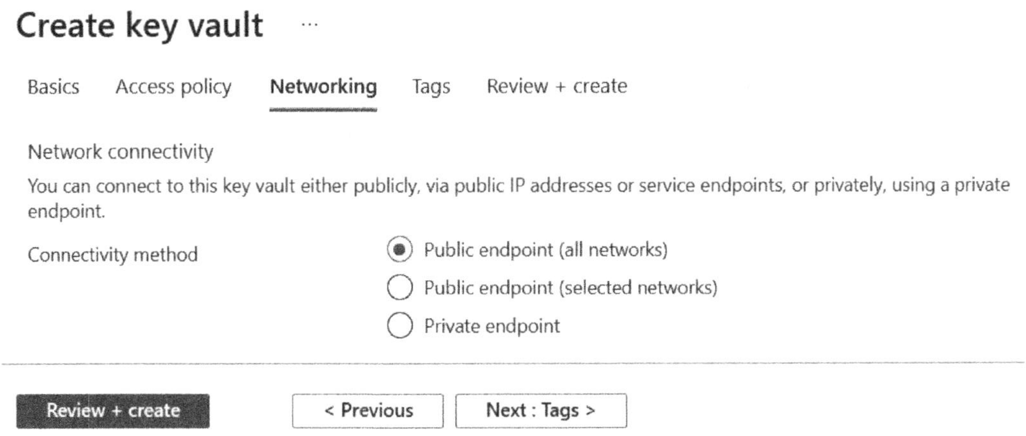

Create key vault   ...

Basics   Access policy   **Networking**   Tags   Review + create

Network connectivity

You can connect to this key vault either publicly, via public IP addresses or service endpoints, or privately, using a private endpoint.

Connectivity method   ⦿ Public endpoint (all networks)
                                       ◯ Public endpoint (selected networks)
                                       ◯ Private endpoint

[Review + create]   [< Previous]   [Next : Tags >]

Figure 5.3 – Create key vault – Networking

5. Once the resource has been created, you will find a Key Vault resource called **democookbookkeyvault** in the resource group you selected while creating the Azure Key Vault instance.

To create a secret, select the **Secrets** option under **Settings**, as shown in the following screenshot. Then, select the **+ Generate/import** option:

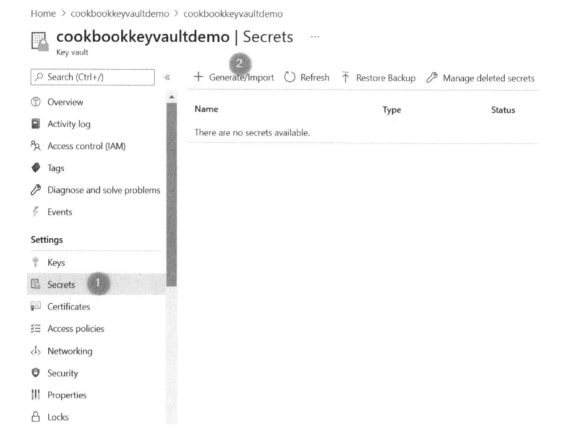

Figure 5.4 – Creating secrets in Azure Key Vault

6. Provide the name of the secret, along with the secret's value. Here, we are providing the storage key for the Azure Blob storage account and deselecting the activation and expiry dates. Now, click the **Create** button:

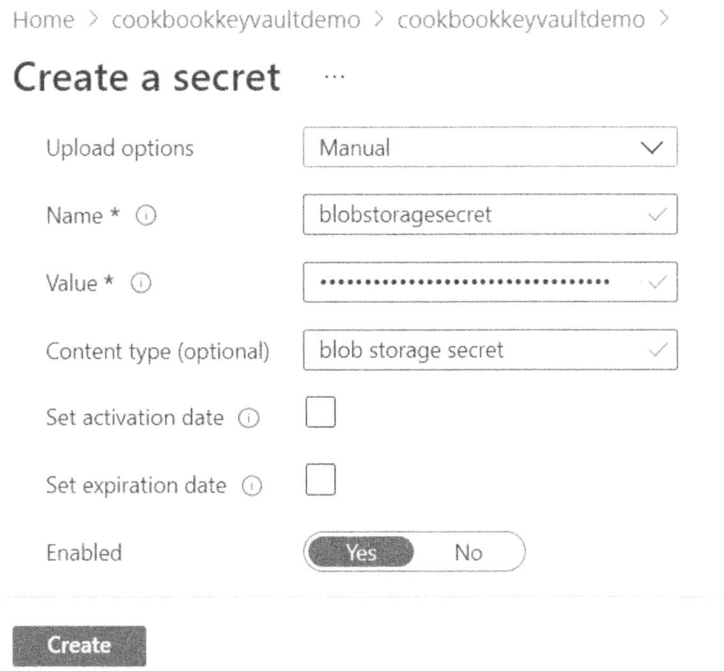

Home > cookbookkeyvaultdemo > cookbookkeyvaultdemo >

Create a secret   ...

Upload options	Manual ⌄
Name * ⓘ	blobstoragesecret ✓
Value * ⓘ	•••••••••••••••••••••••••••••••• ✓
Content type (optional)	blob storage secret ✓
Set activation date ⓘ	☐
Set expiration date ⓘ	☐
Enabled	**Yes** No

Create

Figure 5.5 – Create a secret page

7. You should see that a secret called **blobstoragesecret** has been created.

How it works...

There are various versions of a secret that can be generated for organization policy requirements, and we must change the secret's value every 3 months. We can list all the versions of the secret and identify the latest version from the Key Vault page.

Click on the secret you created (**blobstoragesecret**) to view all the different versions. You can also identify which versions are currently enabled:

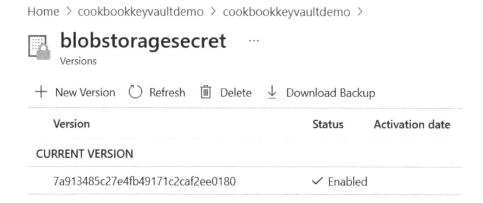

Figure 5.6 – Secret versions

You can generate a new version by selecting +**New Version**. You will find a new version and see whether it is enabled.

Creating an Azure Key Vault to store secrets using ARM templates

In this recipe, you will learn how to create an Azure Key Vault instance and secrets using the *Azure CLI* and *ARM templates*. It is very useful to know how to deploy templates using the CLI, which helps you automate the task of deploying from your *DevOps pipeline*.

Getting ready

In this recipe, we will use a **service principal** to authenticate to Azure so that we can create an Azure Key Vault resource from the Azure CLI. Follow the steps mentioned in the following link to create a service principal:

```
https://docs.microsoft.com/en-us/azure/active-directory/
develop/howto-create-service-principal-portal#:~:text=Option%20
1:%20Upload%20a%20certificate.%201%20Select%20Run,key,%20
and%20export%20to%20a%20.CER%20file
```

You can find the ARM template JSON files and the required PowerShell script at `https://github.com/PacktPublishing/Azure-Databricks-Cookbook/tree/main/Chapter05/Code`.

You can find the Parquet files that were used in the recipe at `https://github.com/PacktPublishing/Azure-Databricks-Cookbook/tree/main/Common/Customer/parquetFiles`.

You must run the PowerShell `DeployKeyVault.PS1` script to create an Azure Key Vault resource.

How to do it...

Before running the PowerShell script, ensure you make the following changes:

1. Change the variable values that are used in the script and assign the values for the service principal and resource group name you just created:

```
$appId=""
$appSecret="xxxxxxxEpQv6H_3Vxxxxx~.xxxxx8jg~~5"
$tenantId="xxxxx-0bfm-xx-xxxx-276cdxxxxxx"
$subscriptionName="Pay As You Go"
$resourceGroup = "CookbookRG"
```

2. `AzureDeploy.json` is the main template file and specifies how to deploy to Azure Key Vault and create a secret. Update the parameter values for `keyVaultName`, `objectId`, `secretName`, and `secretValue` in the parameter file (`azuredeploy.parameters.json`).

3. The following is what the `azuredeploy.parameters.json` file looks like after changing the parameter values:

```
{
    "$schema": "https://schema.management.azure.com/
schemas/2019-04-01/deploymentParameters.json#",
    "contentVersion": "1.0.0.0",
    "parameters": {
      "keyVaultName": {
        "value": "AzureKeyVault-Prod"
      },
      "objectId": {
        "value": "GEN-AZUREAD-OBJECTID"
      },
      "secretName": {
        "value": "blobstorage"
```

```
    },
    "secretValue": {
      "value": "xxxxxxxxxxxxx"
    }
  }
}
```

4. `objectId` is the user you are providing access to secrets. You can find the object by running the `Az` command from PowerShell:

```
Get-AzADUser -UserPrincipalName foo@domain.com
```

5. `secretValue`, in the parameter file, will be the account storage key or SQL Database login password, or any password you want to store.

6. From the PowerShell terminal, go to the folder that contains the PowerShell file, along with the JSON file, and run the PowerShell script:

```
PS C:\CreateWorkspace> .\CreateDatabricksWorkspace.ps1
```

7. After executing the preceding command, you will see that a new Azure Key Vault resource has been created in the **CookbookRG** resource group, along with a secret called `AzureKeyVault-Prod`.

How it works...

Azure Resource Manager helps you implement Infrastructure as Code for your **Azure solutions**. The template helps you define the infrastructure and all the configurations for the project and resource you are deploying. A SKU represents a purchasable **Stock Keeping Unit (SKU)** for a product. Refer to the following link to find out more about SKU properties:

https://docs.microsoft.com/en-us/partner-center/develop/product-resources#sku

We are using an ARM template and a command line to deploy the resource. In the `az login` script, the service principal is used to authenticate to Azure. This is used instead of a username and password as using a service principal is the preferred method. We are granting a `List` permission for the `ObjectId` property we specify in the `Parameter` file. We can provide additional permissions based on the user's role, such as reading and writing to the secret value.

Using Azure Key Vault secrets in Azure Databricks

In this recipe, you will learn how to use the secrets stored in Azure Key Vault in an Azure Databricks notebook. You can store information such as storage account keys or SQL Database passwords in Azure Key Vault as secrets, ensuring sensitive information is not exposed.

Getting ready

To use Azure Key Vault secrets in Databricks notebooks, we must create a **secret scope** in Databricks. The following steps will show you how to create a secret scope in Azure Databricks:

1. Open Databricks and create a scope URL called `<Databricks URL>/#secrets/createScope`. You can find the Databricks URL on the Azure Key Vault **Overview** page. The following screenshot shows the Databricks URL. The secret scope URL will be similar to `https://xxxxxx.azuredatabricks.net/#secrets/createScope`:

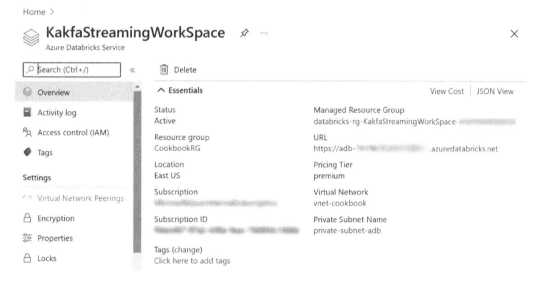

Figure 5.7 – Databricks service URL

2. Once you have opened the Secret scope URL, provide any name for your scope. **Manage Principal** can be either **Creator** or **All Users**. Provide a **DNS Name** for Key Vault, which you can find on the Azure Key Vault **Overview** page, and a **Resource ID**:

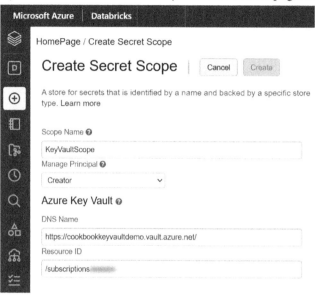

Figure 5.8 – Databricks scope

3. You can find the **Resource ID** value on the Azure Key Vault **Properties** page. Once you've provided the required details, click the **Create** button to create the Secret scope:

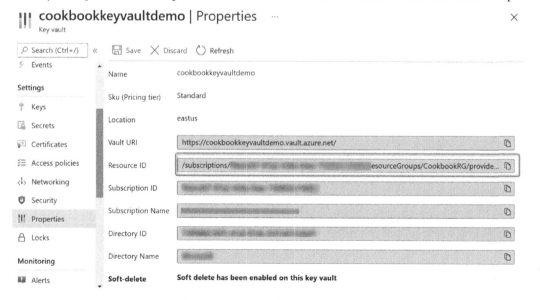

Figure 5.9 – Key vault – Resource ID

4. The Secret scope we created in the preceding steps can be used in notebooks to retrieve secret values from Azure Key Vault.

You can follow along by running the steps in the 5_1, Using Azure Key-Vault Secrets in Notebooks notebook https://github.com/PacktPublishing/Azure-Databricks-Cookbook/tree/main/Chapter05/.

How to do it...

In this section, you will learn how to read data, read the secrets from the Secret scope that we created in Azure Databricks (which stores information about Azure Key Vault), and use it in notebooks. You will retrieve the storage account key from Azure Key Vault and use it to mount the *Azure Blob* storage to DatabaseFS and read Parquet files from the mounted folder:

1. Run the following code, which will mount the Azure Blob storage to DatabaseFS by reading the storage key that is stored in Azure Key Vault. The following PySpark code reads the secrets and mounts the Azure Blob storage account to DatabaseFS. We are mounting the Blob account to /mnt/KeyVaultBlob:

```
#Storage account key is stored in Azure Key-Vault as
a sceret. The secret name is blobstoragesecret and
KeyVaultScope is the name of the scope we have created.
We can also store the storage account name as a new
secret if we don't want users to know the name of the
storage account.

storageAccount="cookbookblobstorage1"
storageKey = dbutils.secrets.
get(scope="KeyVaultScope",key="blobstoragesecret")
mountpoint = "/mnt/KeyVaultBlob"
storageEndpoint =   "wasbs://rawdata@{}.blob.core.
windows.net".format(storageAccount)
storageConnSting = "fs.azure.account.key.{}.blob.core.
windows.net".format(storageAccount)

try:
   dbutils.fs.mount(
   source = storageEndpoint,
```

```
    mount_point = mountpoint,
      extra_configs = {storageConnSting:storageKey})
  except:
      print("Already mounted...."+mountpoint)
```

2. Run the following code, which will read the files that are available in the Azure Blob storage account:

```
display(dbutils.fs.ls("/mnt/KeyVaultBlob/Customer/
parquetFiles"))
```

3. We will load Parquet files into a dataframe by running the following code:

```
df_cust= spark.read.format("parquet").
option("header",True).load("databasefs:/mnt/KeyVaultBlob/
Customer/parquetFiles/*.parquet")
```

4. Run the following code, which will display 10 rows of the dataframe:

```
display(df_cust.limit(10))
```

5. By doing this, you can read the storage key from a Key Vault instance, mount the Blob account to DatabaseFS, and load the parquet files into a dataframe, which can be used for further data processing.

How it works...

Using Azure Key Vault provides a centralized location for storing all your secrets. It also provides a seamless experience for developers to integrate Key Vault into their applications.

To read secrets from Key Vault, we can use `dbutils.secrets.` `get(scope="KeyVaultScope",key="blobstoragesecret")`. **KeyVaultScope** is the name of the secret scope that we created in Azure Databricks, while the **key** value is the secret name that we created in the Azure Key Vault. It stores the storage account key value. We can also store the storage account name in the Key Vault and read the secret name in the Notebooks. This is helpful when dev, test, and UAT have different names for a storage account. We won't need to change anything to store the storage Blob account name in the Key Vault, as we will be using variables to store the storage account name that was read.

Creating an App Configuration resource

Azure App Configuration is a service that's used to manage application configuration settings such as flags or any other static keys that are required across applications. It provides a centralized location to store configurations that can be referred to later. When you are working in a cloud environment, many components are distributed across multiple machines, and having the application configurations for each component can cause issues such as inconsistencies in the configuration values, which makes it hard to troubleshoot errors. In such scenarios, you can use Azure App Configuration to store your application settings in a centralized location that can be changed dynamically without requiring any deployment.

In this recipe, you will learn how to create an App Configuration resource in the Azure portal using a UI.

Getting ready

Before starting, you need to ensure you have contributor access to the subscription or are the owner of the resource group.

How to do it...

Let's learn how to create an App Configuration resource using the Azure portal UI. In the upcoming recipes, we will integrate with a Databricks notebook to refer to the configuration values that we will create in App Configuration.

The following steps demonstrate how to create an App Configuration resource:

1. From the Azure portal home page, search for `App Configuration` and click the **Create** button:

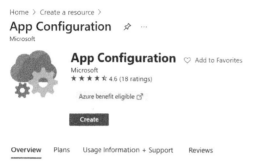

Home > Create a resource >

App Configuration   📌   ...
Microsoft

App Configuration   ♡ Add to Favorites
Microsoft
★ ★ ★ ★ ★ 4.6 (18 ratings)

Azure benefit eligible ☑️

Create

Overview   Plans   Usage Information + Support   Reviews

Azure App Configuration allows developers to store, retrieve and manage access to application settings all in one place. It is easy to set up and simple to use from any application. It gives developers the ability to modify an application's behavior on demand without having to redeploy the application. App Configuration offers the following benefits:

Figure 5.10 – Creating an App Configuration resource

2. Once you've clicked on the **Create** button, you will be redirected to **App Configuration** to create the necessary page.

3. Select your **Subscription** from the dropdown and provide a **Resource group**, **Resource name**, **Location**, and **Pricing tier**, as shown in the following screenshot:

Home > Create a resource > Marketplace > App Configuration >

Create App Configuration   ...

Azure App Configuration provides a service to centrally manage application settings and feature flags. Modern programs, especially programs running in a cloud, generally have many components that are distributed in nature. Spreading configuration settings across these components can lead to hard-to-troubleshoot errors during an application deployment. Use App Configuration to store all the settings for your application and secure their accesses in one place. Learn more

Project Details

Subscription *	▼
Resource group *	CookbookRG ▼
	Create new

Instance Details

Resource name *	Enter resource name
Location *	East US ▼
Pricing tier *	Standard ▼
	View full pricing details

Review + create   < Previous   Next: Tags >

Figure 5.11 – Create App Configuration page

4. Once the service has been created, you must create a key-value for the storage account access key to be stored in the App Configuration service. On the App Configuration **Service** page, click on **Configuration explorer** on the left-hand pane, under **Operations**, as shown in the following screenshot. Click on **+ Create** and select **Key-Value**. Provide any name for our **Key** (we have created a key called **StorageKey**). **Value** will be the access key for the storage account that contains the files we want to read:

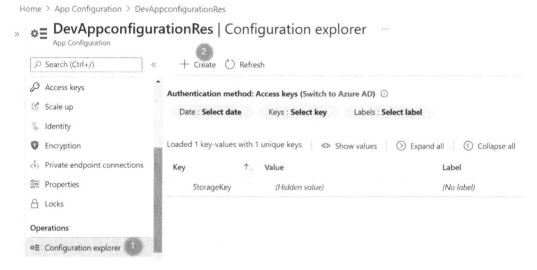

Figure 5.12 – Creating a key-value configuration value

5. Here, you can see that we have created a key called **StorageKey**.

How it works...

In the App Configuration service, we can create configuration values in two ways:

- **Key-Value**: Create a key and its value, which is stored in the App Configuration.

- **Key Vault reference**: We can refer to the secret in Azure Key Vault and just create a key via the Configuration explorer. The secret value is picked up from the Key Vault details that we provided while creating the configuration value.

In our example, we used the key-value method to create the configuration values, which is the secret for the Azure Blob storage account. You can find out more about the App Configuration service at `https://docs.microsoft.com/en-us/azure/azure-app-configuration/concept-key-value`.

In the next recipe, you will learn how to use the configuration values from the App Configuration service in a Databricks notebook.

Using App Configuration in an Azure Databricks notebook

In this recipe, you will learn how to use the secrets stored as configuration values in the App Configuration service in an Azure Databricks notebook.

Getting ready

You can follow along by running the steps in the `5_2.Using App Config in Notebooks` notebook at `https://github.com/PacktPublishing/Azure-Databricks-Cookbook/tree/main/Chapter05/`.

You can find the Parquet files that will be used in this recipe at `https://github.com/PacktPublishing/Azure-Databricks-Cookbook/tree/main/Common/Customer/parquetFiles`.

To execute the code mentioned in the notebook, we need to get the connection string of the App Configuration service we have created. The following screenshot shows how to get the connection string for your App Configuration service. The name of the App Configuration service in this example is **DevAppconfigurationRes**:

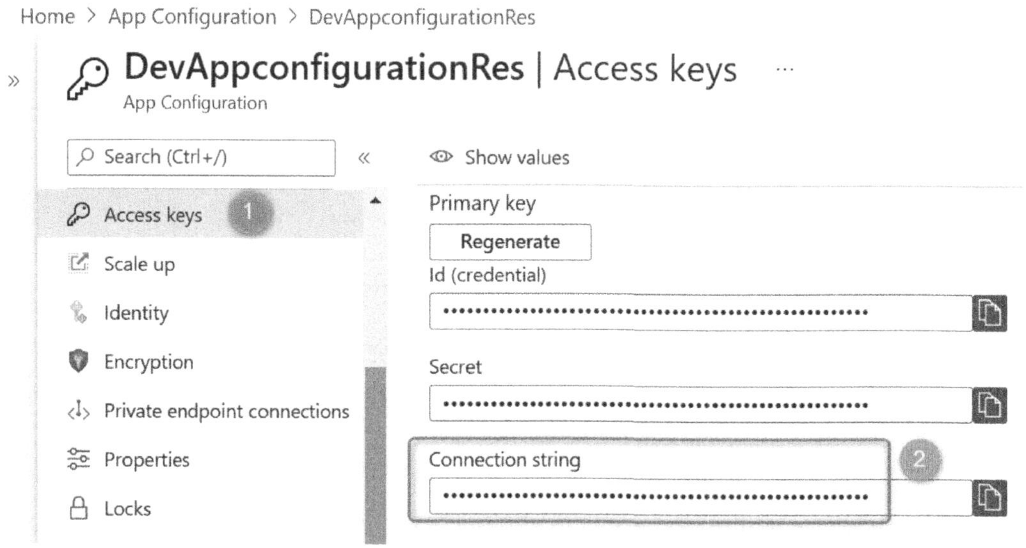

Figure 5.13 – Creating a key-value configuration value

In the next section, you will learn how to read the configuration key-value using Python APIs.

How to do it...

In this section, you will learn how to read the value of the configuration key (which is the secret value) and use it in notebooks. You will retrieve the storage account key from the App Configuration service and use it to mount the Azure Blob storage to DatabaseFS, as well as to read Parquet files from the mounted folder:

1. We are going to use the Python API to read the key and value from the App Configuration service. First, we need to install the required Python libraries to read the App Configuration connection string. Execute the following code, which is mentioned in the Databricks notebook:

    ```
    %pip install azure-appconfiguration
    ```

2. Now, let's import the libraries into the Notebook by executing the following code:

    ```
    from azure.appconfiguration import
    AzureAppConfigurationClient, ConfigurationSetting
    ```

3. The name of key that we have created in App Configuration is **StorageKey**. This key holds the value of the access key for the cookbookblobstorage1 storage account. Using Python code, we will read the secret value for the key called **StorageKey** that's been created in App Configuration.

4. Run the following code to get the secret value for StorageKey. Once we have read the secret, we can store the value in the storageKey variable:

    ```
    try:
        connection_string = "Endpoint=https://
    devappconfigurationres.azconfig.io;Id=V/Ri-10-s0:vKdwORQd
    asdasdGuClo2oi0K;Secret=zz-zzzx--xx--xxxx"
        app_config_client = AzureAppConfigurationClient.from_
    connection_string(connection_string)
        retrieved_config_setting = app_config_client.get_
    configuration_setting(key='StorageKey')
        storageKey= retrieved_config_setting.value
    except Exception as ex:
        print('Exception:')
        print(ex)
    ```

5. Run the following code to mount the Azure Blob storage to DatabaseFS by reading the storage key stored in the Azure App Configuration service. The following PySpark code reads the secrets and mounts the Azure Blob storage account to DatabaseFS. We are mounting the Blob account to /mnt/AppConfigBlob here:

```
storageAccount="cookbookblobstorage1"
mountpoint = "/mnt/AppConfigBlob "
storageEndpoint =   "wasbs://rawdata@{}.blob.core.
windows.net".format(storageAccount)
storageConnSting = "fs.azure.account.key.{}.blob.core.
windows.net".format(storageAccount)

try:
  dbutils.fs.mount(
  source = storageEndpoint,
  mount_point = mountpoint,
  extra_configs = {storageConnSting:storageKey})
except:
    print("Already mounted...."+mountpoint)
```

6. Run the following code, which will read the files that are available in the Azure Blob storage account:

```
display(dbutils.fs.ls("/mnt/AppConfigBlob /Customer/
parquetFiles"))
```

7. Load some Parquet files into a dataframe by running the following code:

```
df_cust= spark.read.format("parquet").
option("header",True).load("databasefs:/mnt/AppConfigBlob
/Customer/parquetFiles/*.parquet")
```

8. Run the following code, which will display 10 rows from the dataframe:

```
display(df_cust.limit(10))
```

9. With that, you have read the storage key from the App Configuration service, mounted the Blob account to DatabaseFS, and loaded the Parquet files into a dataframe that can be used for further data processing.

How it works...

We are using the `azure-appconfiguration` Python library to work with the App Configuration service. You can also use *.NET Core*, Java, and Spring to work with the App Configuration service. In this recipe, we hardcoded the value for the App Configuration connection string. But in production, you can use Azure Key Vault to store the connection string for App Configuration. App Configuration would be a better option when your project's configurations are only stored in an App Config service. Some of its advantages and uses are mentioned in the following link:

```
https://docs.microsoft.com/en-us/azure/azure-app-
configuration/overview
```

Creating a Log Analytics workspace

As more and more Azure services are being used to build enterprise solutions, there needs to be a centralized location where we can collect performance and application metrics for various Azure services. This will help us understand how the service is functioning. Every Azure resource has a set of resource logs that provides information about the operations that are performed on the Azure service, as well as the health of that service. With the help of Azure Monitor Logs, we can collect data from resource logs, as well as performance metrics from applications and virtual machines, into a common *Log Analytics workspace*. We can also use these metrics to identify any specific trends, understand the performance of the service, or even find any anomalies. We can analyze the data that has been captured in a Log Analytics Workspace using *Log Query*, which was written in **Kusto Query Language** (**KQL**), and perform various types of Data Analytics operations. In this recipe, you will learn how to create a Log Analytics Workspace. Then, in the following recipe, you will learn how to integrate a Databricks service with a Log Analytics workspace, as well as how to analyze data stored in a Log Analytics workspace.

Getting ready

Before starting, we need to ensure we have access to a subscription and have contributor access to that subscription.

How to do it...

Let's learn how to create a new Log Analytics workspace that can be used to receive Databricks metrics and Spark application metrics.

The following steps demonstrate how to create a Log Analytics workspace:

1. From the Azure portal home page, search for Log Analytics workspaces and click the **Create log analytics workspace** button.

2. Provide the resource group, workspace, and region name, as shown in the following screenshot:

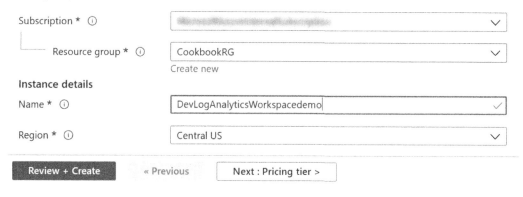

Figure 5.14 – Create Log Analytics workspace page

3. Set **Pricing tier** to **Pay-as-you-go** and click on the **Review + create** button to create the resource:

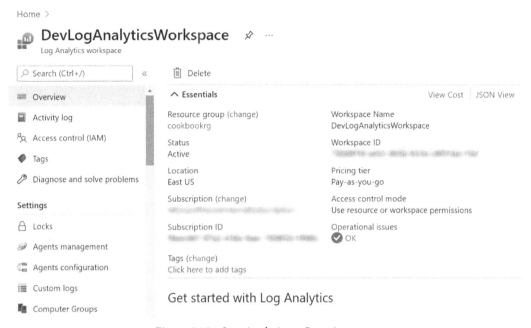

Figure 5.15 – Log Analytics – Overview page

Now, you will see that a new Log Analytics workspace resource has been created in your resource group.

How it works...

Now that you have created the workspace, you can send logs from different Azure services to the same workspace. Select the **Logs** option of the Log Analytics workspace resource to query the data that is available in that workspace:

Figure 5.16 – Log Analytics – Logs

When you click on **Queries**, you will find a list of precreated queries that we can use for various services, all of which are integrated with your Log Analytics workspace:

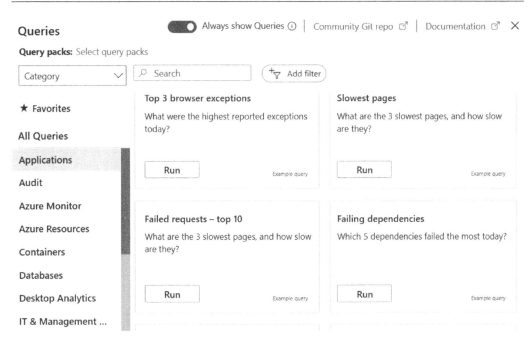

Figure 5.17 – Log Analytics – existing queries

You can write your own query using KQL to perform any kind of analysis on the data that's collected in the workspace.

Integrating a Log Analytics workspace with Azure Databricks

In this recipe, you will learn how to integrate a Log Analytics workspace with Azure Databricks. You will also learn how to send Databricks service metrics and Databricks application metrics to the Log Analytics workspace.

Getting ready

Before starting, we need to ensure we have access to a subscription and have contributor access to that subscription. To send Databricks service metrics to a Log Analytics workspace, we will need the Azure Databricks Premium tier.

You can follow along by running the steps in the 5_1.Using Azure Key Vault Secrets in Notebooks notebook. This will allow you to send Databricks log data to a Log Analytics workspace (https://github.com/PacktPublishing/Azure-Databricks-Cookbook/tree/main/Chapter05/).

How to do it...

To send metrics to the Log Analytics workspace, we need to turn on diagnostics in the Azure Databricks service. Following this, we must send the service or application metrics to the workspace.

Follow these steps to enable the diagnostic settings of the Databricks service:

1. Go to the Databricks service in your resource group and under the **Monitoring** section, select **Turn on Diagnostics**. Now, select **Add diagnostic settings**, which will send Databricks service metrics to your Log Analytics workspace, as shown in the following screenshot:

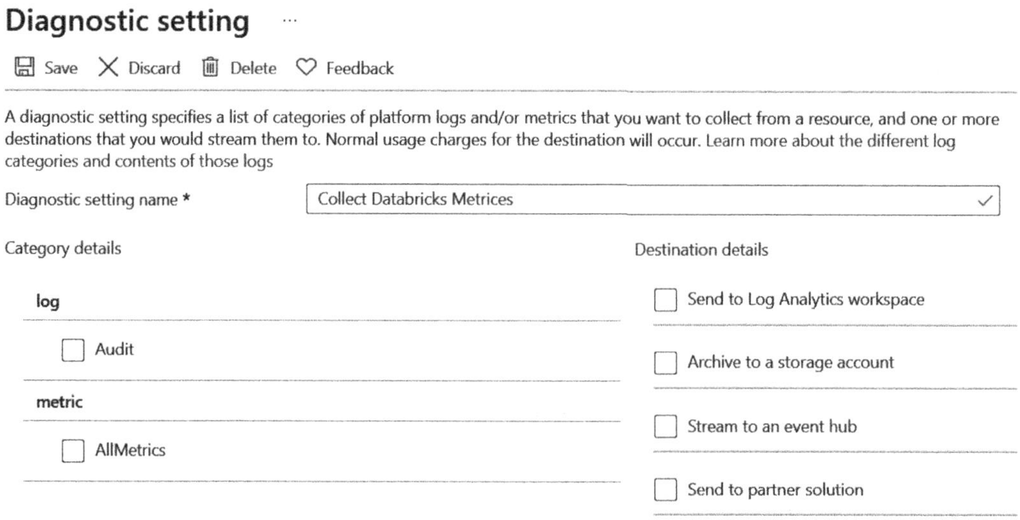

Diagnostic setting   ···

🖫 Save   ✕ Discard   🗑 Delete   ♡ Feedback

A diagnostic setting specifies a list of categories of platform logs and/or metrics that you want to collect from a resource, and one or more destinations that you would stream them to. Normal usage charges for the destination will occur. Learn more about the different log categories and contents of those logs

Diagnostic setting name * | Collect Databricks Metrices   ✓ |

Category details

Destination details

log

☐ Send to Log Analytics workspace

☐ Audit

☐ Archive to a storage account

metric

☐ Stream to an event hub

☐ AllMetrics

☐ Send to partner solution

Figure 5.18 – Diagnostics settings page

2. You can use any name for the diagnostic setting. Then, select the **Send to Log Analytics workspace** checkbox.

3. Select the log data you want to send to the workspace, such as **DBFS** or **clusters**. You can see these under in the **Category details** section of the preceding screenshot. Select all the available log categories. Then, click **Save**:

Diagnostic setting ⋯

🖫 Save   ✕ Discard   🗑 Delete   ♡ Feedback

A diagnostic setting specifies a list of categories of platform logs and/or metrics that you want to collect from a resource, and one or more destinations that you would stream them to. Normal usage charges for the destination will occur. Learn more about the different log categories and contents of those logs

Diagnostic setting name *

| Collect Databricks Metrices | ✓ |

Category details

log

   ☑ Audit

metric

   ☑ AllMetrics

Destination details

☑ Send to Log Analytics workspace

Subscription

| ▓▓▓▓▓▓▓▓▓▓▓▓▓▓▓▓▓▓ | ∨ |

Log Analytics workspace

| DevLogAnalyticsWorkspace (eastus) | ∨ |

☐ Archive to a storage account

☐ Stream to an event hub

☐ Send to partner solution

Figure 5.19 – Selecting all logs

4. Once you have added some diagnostic settings, you can find a new entry under the **Diagnostics settings** section.

Now, let's learn how to use KQL to analyze the data that is sent to the Log Analytics workspace:

1. For data to get into a Log Analytics workspace, we need to perform operations such as starting a Databricks cluster, running notebooks, and reading data from DatabaseFS. It will take up to 5 minutes for information to be loaded into the Log Analytics workspace. Once you've performed activities such as starting a cluster or running a notebook, wait 3-5 minutes before querying the data from the Log Analytics workspace.

2. Next, start or restart the Databricks cluster and run the 5_1, Using Azure Key-Vault Secrets in Notebooks notebook at https://github. com/PacktPublishing/Azure-Databricks-Cookbook/tree/main/ Chapter05/.

3.   To view the data that was sent to the workspace, go to the Log Analytic workspace we created in the *Creating a Log Analytics workspace* recipe:

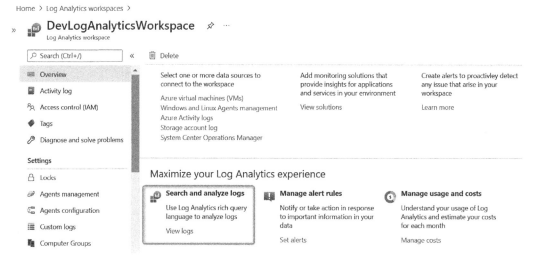

Figure 5.20 – The Search and analyze logs option

4.   Click on **View logs**, as highlighted in the preceding screenshot, to open the query editor. Here, you can query the tables that we created, as shown in the following screenshot:

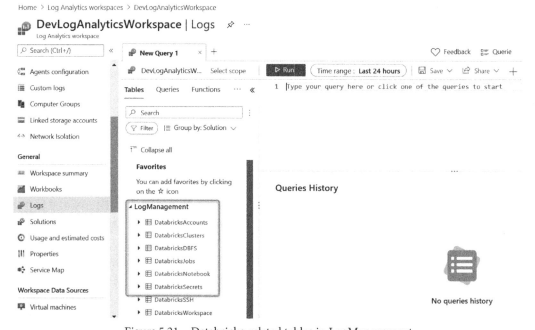

Figure 5.21 – Databricks-related tables in LogManagement

5. As you can see, there are multiple Databricks tables under **LogManagement**. These provide details about the notebooks that have been executed, as well as cluster operations, and DatabaseFS.

6. You can execute the following query to list the Notebooks that have been executed. This will list all the notebooks that have been executed in the last 12 hours:

```
DatabricksNotebook
 | where TimeGenerated > ago(12h)
```

7. The following is the output of the preceding query. As you can see, we have received information about `clusterid`, `notebookid`, and their action details, as well as other information that is very helpful for analysis:

	ActionName		RequestId		Response		RequestParams		Type
	attachNotebook		68156378-2965-451d-b944-259d12e8...		{"statusCode":2...		{"notebookId":"452834995439556","clusterId":"0302-165541-d...		DatabricksNo
	attachNotebook		987de542-72e4-4105-999c-ae718f6f4...		{"statusCode":2...		{"notebookId":"452834995439556","clusterId":"0302-165541-d...		DatabricksNo
	attachNotebook		b2577f28-3d95-45d9-acd5-5c5bb5e...		{"statusCode":2...		{"notebookId":"452834995439556","clusterId":"0302-165541-d...		DatabricksNo

Figure 5.22 – Databricks notebook query output

8. Similarly, you can query other Databricks-related tables you see in the Log Analytics workspace to find out more about, for example, the mount points that were queried and when the cluster was started, as well as the name of the Key Vault secret that was used in the notebooks.

How it works...

You can use the same Log Analytics workspace to send all Azure service data or application data so that you can perform data analytics and troubleshoot any errors. We can even create a dashboard in the Log Analytics workspace to get an overview of the health of our Azure services. The KQL is used to query and aggregate data that is stored in a Log Analytics workspace. The following link provides more details on how to use KQL to query data:

```
https://docs.microsoft.com/en-us/azure/data-explorer/kusto/
query/
```

6
Exploring Delta Lake in Azure Databricks

Delta Lake is an open source storage layer that sits on a cloud object store such as **Azure Data Lake Storage**. Recently, many organizations have opted for data lake for their big data solution as they can keep all the data (batch and streaming data) in one location and later use it for various analytics and machine learning work. The main challenges with a data lake is that there is no schema enforcement, it does not guarantee consistency of the data, and does not provide **Atomicity, Consistency, Isolation, and Durability** (ACID) transactions. To overcome these challenges, Databricks has introduced Delta Lake. Delta Lake provides a lot of key benefits including ACID transactions, schema enforcements, schema evolution, update/delete operations on the data in the Delta Lake, and metadata handling.

By the end of this chapter, you will get to know how you can use Delta Lake and adopt Lakehouse patterns in your big data projects.

In this chapter, we will cover the following recipes:

- Delta table operations – create, read, and write
- Streaming read and writes to Delta tables
- Delta table data format
- Handling concurrency

- Delta table performance optimization
- Constraints in Delta tables
- Versioning in Delta tables

Technical requirements

To follow along with the examples shown in the recipes, you need the following:

- An Azure subscription and the required permissions on that subscription mentioned in the *Technical requirements* section of *Chapter 1, Creating an Azure Databricks Service.*

- An Azure Databricks workspace standard or premium tier with a **Spark 3.0.x cluster**. All the notebooks used in this chapter are executed on a Spark 3.0.x cluster.

- You can find the scripts for this chapter in the GitHub repo at (`https://github.com/PacktPublishing/Azure-Databricks-Cookbook/tree/main/Chapter06`). The `Chapter06` folder contains all the notebooks for this chapter.

Delta table operations – create, read, and write

In this recipe, you will learn how to create, read, and write to Delta tables. You will learn how to write batch data to the Delta table. You will also learn how to perform DML operations such as insert, update, and delete on the Delta table.

Getting ready

Before starting, you need to ensure you have contributor access to the subscription or are an owner of the resource group.

For this recipe, you can follow along by running the steps in the `6.1-Reading Writing to Delta Tables` notebook at `https://github.com/PacktPublishing/Azure-Databricks-Cookbook/tree/main/Chapter06/`.

Copy the `Customer` and `Orders` Parquet files from the following GitHub link. You will find folders named `csvFiles` and `ParquetFiles` – make sure to copy the files from the `ParquetFiles` folder at the following URL:

`https://github.com/PacktPublishing/Azure-Databricks-Cookbook/tree/main/Common`

We are mounting the *ADLS Gen2* account and mounting to **Databricks File System** (**DBFS**). You can follow along with the steps mentioned in the same notebook. We have a container named **rawdata** and have copied the **Customer** and **Orders** Parquet folders. The following is the screenshot from the portal:

Location: rawdata

Search blobs by prefix (case-sensitive)

Name	Modified
☐ Customer	
☐	
☐	
☐ Orders	

Figure 6.1 – Folders in the rawdata container

In the **Orders** folder, we have two folders created as shown in the following screenshot. **parquetFiles** contains the first 26 files copied from `https://github.com/PacktPublishing/Azure-Databricks-Cookbook/tree/main/Common/Orders/parquetFiles` and the last 4 files are copied to **newParquetFiles**. In total there are 30 files in `https://github.com/PacktPublishing/Azure-Databricks-Cookbook/tree/main/Common/Orders/parquetFiles`:

Authentication method: Access key (Switch to Azure
Location: rawdata / Orders

Search blobs by prefix (case-sensitive)

Name
☐ [..]
☐ newParquetFiles
☐ parquetFiles

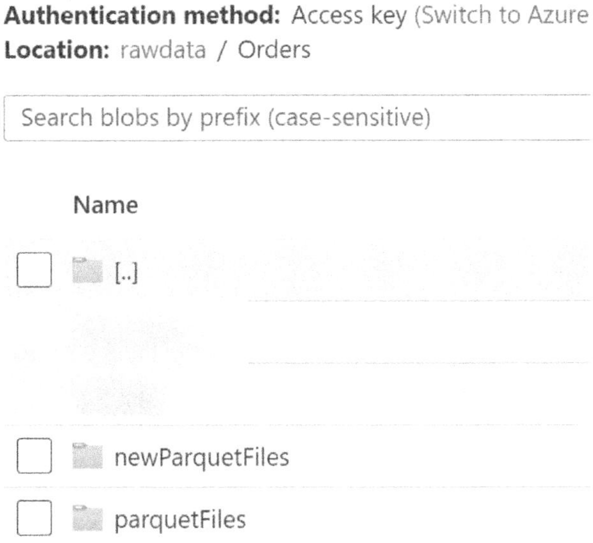

Figure 6.2 – Multiple folders for the Orders Parquet files

This is done to show how to perform inserts and updates with new data.

How to do it...

In this section, you will read `Customer` and `Orders` Parquet files and load them in a Delta table. You will learn how to join Delta tables and perform DML operations.

1. We are mounting an ADLS Gen2 storage account to `/mnt/Gen2Source`. You can find the details in the notebook mentioned in the preceding *Getting ready* section to find out how to mount the ADLS Gen2 account. To find more details about how to create a service principal, you can refer to the *Mounting ADLS Gen2 and Blob to Azure Databricks File System* recipe in *Chapter 2, Reading and Writing Data from and to Various Azure Services and File Formats*.

2. We read the `Customer` Parquet files from the mount point and save them in `delta` format by running the following code:

```
cust_path = "/mnt/Gen2Source/Customer/parquetFiles"
```

```
df_cust = (spark.read.format("parquet").load(cust_path)
        .withColumn("timestamp", current_timestamp()))
```

```
df_cust.write.format("delta").mode("overwrite").save("/
mnt/Gen2Source/Customer/delta")
```

3. We must use `format("delta")` to save the data in `delta` format. By running the following code, we are creating a Delta table at the location mentioned in *Step 2*:

```
%sql
-- Creating Delta table
DROP TABLE IF EXISTS Customer;
CREATE TABLE Customer
USING delta
location "/mnt/Gen2Source/Customer/delta"
```

4. Run the following code to view the format for the table we created in the preceding step and the location for the Delta table. You will see the provider's name as `delta` and along with the location and the name of the Delta table:

```
%sql
describe formatted Customer
```

5. Run the following code to read the `Orders` Parquet files, save them in `delta` format, and create a Delta table:

```
ord_path = "/mnt/Gen2Source/Orders/parquetFiles"
```

```
df_ord = (spark.read.format("parquet").load(ord_path)
       .withColumn("timestamp", current_timestamp())
       .withColumn("O_OrderDateYear", year(col("O_
OrderDate")))
      )
df_ord.write.format("delta").partitionBy("O_
OrderDateYear").mode("overwrite").save("/mnt/Gen2Source/
Orders/delta")
%sql
DROP TABLE IF EXISTS Orders;
CREATE TABLE Orders
USING delta
location "/mnt/Gen2Source/Orders/delta"
```

6. Run the following code to join the `Orders` and `Customer` Delta tables and perform a few aggregations:

```
%sql
-- Getting total customer based on priority and total
account balance by joining the delta tables
SELECT o.O_ORDERPRIORITY,count(o.O_CustKey) As
TotalCustomer,Sum(c.C_AcctBal) As CustAcctBal
FROM Orders o
INNER JOIN Customer c on o.O_CustKey=c.C_CustKey
WHERE o.O_OrderDateYear>1997
GROUP BY o.O_OrderPriority
ORDER BY TotalCustomer DESC;
```

7. You can use the Python API to work with Delta tables. You can run the following code to read the Delta files, convert them to a DataFrame, and display a few records:

```
deltaTable = spark.read.format("delta").load("/mnt/
Gen2Source/Orders/delta/")
```

```
deltaTable.show()
```

8. Delta tables support DML operations such as `insert`, `update`, and `delete`. You can run the following code to create a daily `Orders` Delta table and then run the `MERGE` command that will update if the record exists in the final table, else it performs an insert from the daily table:

```
new_ord_path = "/mnt/Gen2Source/Orders/newParquetFiles"

df_new_order = (spark.read.format("parquet").load(new_
ord_path)
        .withColumn("timestamp", current_timestamp())
        .withColumn("O_OrderDateYear", year(col("O_
OrderDate")))
    )

df_new_order.write.format("delta").partitionBy("O_
OrderDateYear").mode("overwrite").save("/mnt/Gen2Source/
Orders/dailydata_delta")
%sql
DROP TABLE IF EXISTS Orders_Daily;
CREATE TABLE Orders_Daily
USING delta
location "/mnt/Gen2Source/Orders/dailydata_delta"
%sql
-- Merging into Orders from Orders_Daily table. If
records matche on OrderKey then perform update eles
insert
MERGE INTO Orders AS o
USING Orders_daily AS d
ON o.O_ORDERKEY = D.O_ORDERKEY
WHEN MATCHED THEN
  UPDATE SET *
WHEN NOT MATCHED
  THEN INSERT *;
```

9. You can run the following command to delete the records from the Delta table:

```
%sql
-- Deleting from Delta table
DELETE FROM Orders WHERE O_ORDERKEY=1359427
```

10. Delta Lake supports statements for deleting, inserting, and updating data in Delta tables.

How it works...

You can use SQL, Python, or Scala APIs to work with Delta tables. You can read from multiple formats and load the data into a Delta table. We have used `overwrite` mode while saving the data in `delta` format, but you can also use `append` mode, with which you are only adding new data to the Delta table. This can be helpful when the data source provides only new data every day with no updates to old data.

There's more...

If you have a folder that has a lot of Parquet files, then you can run the following code to implicitly convert the Parquet files to `delta` format and you can create a Delta table pointing to that location. We have created a new folder named `ParquetOutputFormatted` and copied all the 30 `Orders` Parquet files to that folder in the mounted folder:

```
%sql CONVERT TO DELTA parquet.`dbfs:/mnt/Gen2Source/Orders/
ParquetOutputFormatted`
```

Run the following code to create a Delta table pointing to the location in the preceding code snippet:

```
%sql
CREATE TABLE Orders_Test
USING DELTA
LOCATION "/mnt/Gen2Source/Orders/ParquetOutputFormatted"
```

Using this approach, we can directly convert files in place to create an unmanaged table.

Streaming reads and writes to Delta tables

In this recipe, you will learn how to write streaming data coming from event hubs to Delta tables and later reading data from Delta tables as a streaming source that can be used by other downstream consumers. You will learn how data from multiple event hubs are written to the same Delta table.

Getting ready

Before starting you need to ensure you have contributor access to the subscription or are the owner of the resource group.

- You can follow along by running the cells in the `6.2-Streaming Read & Writes to Delta Table` notebook in the `https://github.com/PacktPublishing/Azure-Databricks-Cookbook/tree/main/Chapter06/` folder.

- You should set up Azure Event Hub for Kafka with two event hubs named **eventhubsource1** and **eventhubsource2**. The following link has steps on how to create an event hub in Azure:

- `https://docs.microsoft.com/en-us/azure/event-hubs/event-hubs-create`

- You can use the Python script at `https://github.com/PacktPublishing/Azure-Databricks-Cookbook/tree/main/Chapter06/PythonCode/KafkaEventHub_Session1.py` that will push the data to the `eventhubsource1` event hub and `https://github.com/PacktPublishing/Azure-Databricks-Cookbook/tree/main/Chapter06/PythonCode/KafkaEventHub_Session2.py`, which will push the data to `eventhubsource2`.

- You can find out more about how to get the broker's information used in the Python script and in the notebook from the *Reading data from Kafka-enabled event hubs* recipe in *Chapter 4, Working with Streaming Data*.

How to do it...

In this section, you will learn how we can use Delta tables to store data coming from multiple event hubs and later use a Delta table as a source for streaming dat:

1. Run both the `KafkaEventHub_Session1.py` and `KafkaEventHub_Session2.py` Python scripts, which will push data to two different event hubs (`eventhubsource1` and `eventhubsource2`).

2. Assign the bootstrap server to a variable by running the following code:

```
BOOTSTRAP_SERVERS = "kafkaenabledeventhubns.servicebus.
windows.net:9093"
```

```
EH_SASL = "kafkashaded.org.apache.kafka.common.
security.plain.PlainLoginModule required
username=\"$ConnectionString\" password=\"Endpoint=sb://
kafkaenabledemodeventhubns.servicebus.windows.net/;Shared
AccessKeyName=sendreceivekafka;SharedAccessKey=xxxxx-xxx-
xxx\";"
```

```
GROUP_ID = "$Default"
```

3. Run the following code to create a function that will accept the event hub name –
    we can use this by calling the function twice, passing different event hub names.
    This function reads the data from the event hub and extracts the JSON from the
    `Value` column of the DataFrame. Once the JSON is extracted, we extract the
    columns from the JSON and write them to the Delta table:

```
# Function to read data from EventHub and writing as
delta format
def append_kafkadata_stream(topic="eventhubsource1"):
  kafkaDF = (spark.readStream \
    .format("kafka") \
    .option("subscribe", topic) \
    .option("kafka.bootstrap.servers", BOOTSTRAP_SERVERS) \
    .option("kafka.sasl.mechanism", "PLAIN") \
    .option("kafka.security.protocol", "SASL_SSL") \
    .option("kafka.sasl.jaas.config", EH_SASL) \
    .option("kafka.request.timeout.ms", "60000") \
    .option("kafka.session.timeout.ms", "60000") \
    .option("kafka.group.id", GROUP_ID) \
    .option("failOnDataLoss", "false") \
    .option("startingOffsets", "latest") \
    .load().withColumn("source", lit(topic)))

  newkafkaDF=kafkaDF.selectExpr("CAST(key AS
STRING)", "CAST(value AS STRING)","source").
withColumn('vehiclejson', from_
json(col('value'),schema=jsonschema))
```

```
    kafkajsonDF=newkafkaDF.select("key","value","source",
"vehiclejson.*")


    query=kafkajsonDF.selectExpr(
                    "id"             \
                    ,"timestamp"         \
                    ,"rpm"       \
                    ,"speed" \
                    ,"kms"
                    ,"source") \
            .writeStream.format("delta") \
            .outputMode("append") \
            .option("checkpointLocation",checkpoint_
dir()) \
            .start("/mnt/Gen2Source/Vehicle_Delta/")


    return query
```

4. Running the following code will start streaming the data from the
    eventhubsource1 event hub:

    ```
    query_source1 = append_kafkadata_
    stream(topic='eventhubsource1')
    ```

5. Running the following code will start streaming the data from the
    eventhubsource2 event hub:

    ```
    query_source2 = append_kafkadata_
    stream(topic='eventhubsource2')
    ```

6. Running the following code will create a Delta table on the location mentioned in
    the append_kafkadata_stream function:

    ```
    %sql
    -- Creating the table on delta location
    CREATE DATABASE IF NOT EXISTS Vehicle;
    CREATE TABLE IF NOT EXISTS Vehicle.VehicleDetails_Delta
    USING DELTA
    LOCATION "/mnt/Gen2Source/Vehicle_Delta/"
    ```

7. We will use `readStream` on the Delta table to view changes in real time. This data can be written to another event hub, SQL database, or Blob/ADLS storage. Run the following code to read data as streaming data from the Delta table. Run the Python code to generate more data and push it to the event hub:

```
display(spark.readStream.format("delta").table("Vehicle.
  VehicleDetails_Delta").groupBy("source").count().
  orderBy("source"))
```

8. As and when data is flowing into the event hub, we see the count of records changing.

How it works...

We are running both the `KafkaEventHub_Session1.py` and `KafkaEventHub_Session2.py` Python scripts to push data into the event hub. As you can see from the following screenshot that we are running two write stream sessions writing to the same Delta table:

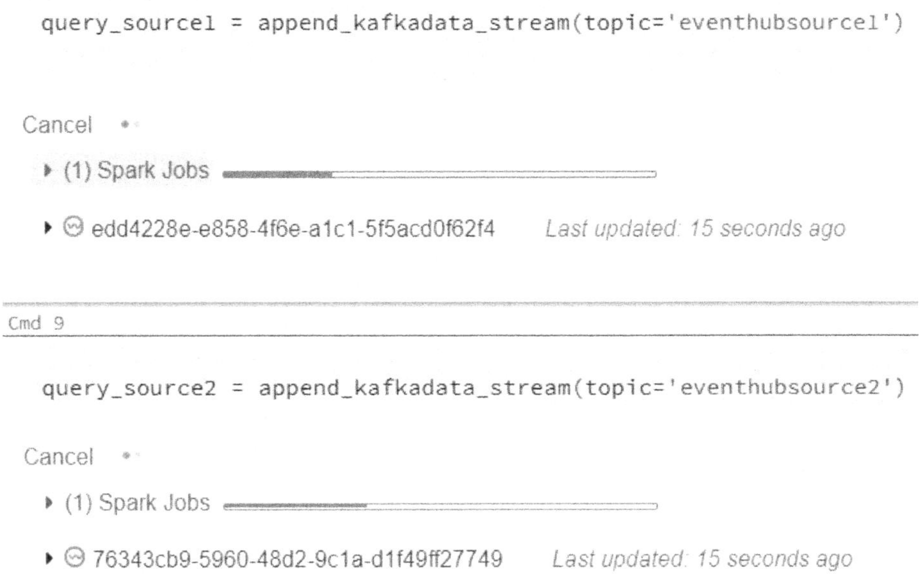

```
query_source1 = append_kafkadata_stream(topic='eventhubsource1')
```

Cancel   •

▸ (1) Spark Jobs ▬▬▬▬▬▬▬▬▬▬▬▬▬▬▬▬▬▬▬▬▬▬▬▬▬▬▬▬▬

▸ ☺ edd4228e-e858-4f6e-a1c1-5f5acd0f62f4   *Last updated: 15 seconds ago*

Cmd 9

```
query_source2 = append_kafkadata_stream(topic='eventhubsource2')
```

Cancel   •

▸ (1) Spark Jobs ▬▬▬▬▬▬▬▬▬▬▬▬▬▬▬▬▬▬▬▬▬▬▬▬▬▬▬▬▬

▸ ☺ 76343cb9-5960-48d2-9c1a-d1f49ff27749   *Last updated: 15 seconds ago*

Figure 6.3 – Streaming from multiple event hubs

By running the following code, you can create real-time reports on the data coming from multiple event hubs:

```
display(spark.readStream.format("delta").table("Vehicle.
VehicleDetails_Delta").groupBy("source").count().
orderBy("source"))
```

The following screenshot is the bar chart representation of the group by query:

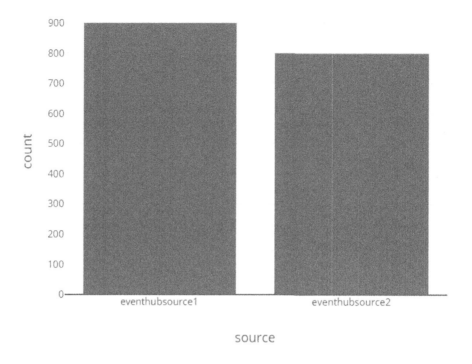

Figure 6.4 – Real-time counts from Delta Table

We can see the values changing in real time as and when data is written to the Delta tables from multiple event hubs.

Delta table data format

In this recipe, you will learn how data is stored in Delta tables and how Delta tables keep track of the history of all DML operations.

Delta Lake's transaction log (the DeltaLog) records every transaction that has been performed on a Delta table since it was created. When a user performs a DML operation, Delta Lake breaks down the operation into multiple steps that each have one or more actions associated with them, as follows:

- **Add file** – Adds a data file to Delta Lake
- **Remove file** – Removes a data file

- **Update metadata** – Updates the table metadata including changing the table name adding partitioning

- **Set transaction** – Records the commit using a Structured Streaming micro-batch job with a given ID

- **Change protocol** – Enables features by switching the Delta Lake transaction log to the newest software protocol

- **Commit info** – Contains information around the commit and the details about the operation like who did it, from where, and at what time

In the next section, we will cover the prerequisites to get started on this recipe.

Getting ready

Before starting you need to ensure you have contributor access to the subscription or are the owner of the resource group.

- You can follow along by running the steps in the `6.3-Delta Table Data Format` notebook in the `https://github.com/PacktPublishing/Azure-Databricks-Cookbook/tree/main/Chapter06/` folder.

- Copy the `Customer` Parquet files from the following GitHub link. You will find folders with the names `csvFiles` and `parquetFiles` and you can copy files from the `parquetFiles` folder from the GitHub link to the `ADLS Gen2` folder:

  `https://github.com/PacktPublishing/Azure-Databricks-Cookbook/tree/main/Common`

- We are using the ADLS Gen2 account and mounting it to DBFS. You can follow along the steps mentioned in the Notebook to learn how to mount. We have created a container named **rawdata** in ADLS Gen2 and copied the `Customer` Parquet files in the `rawdata` container.

- In the `Customer` folder, we have two folders created as shown in the following screenshot. **parquetFiles** has the first seven files copied from `https://github.com/PacktPublishing/Azure-Databricks-Cookbook/tree/main/Common/Customer/parquetFiles` and the last three are files copied to **parquetFiles_Daily** folder. In total, there are 10 files in `https://github.com/PacktPublishing/Azure-Databricks-Cookbook/tree/main/Common/Customer/parquetFiles`:

Authentication method: <u>Access</u> key (Switch

Location: rawdata / Customer

Search blobs by prefix (case-sensitive)

	Name	Modified
☐	[..]	
☐		
☐		
☐		
☐	parquetFiles	
☐	parquetFiles_Daily	

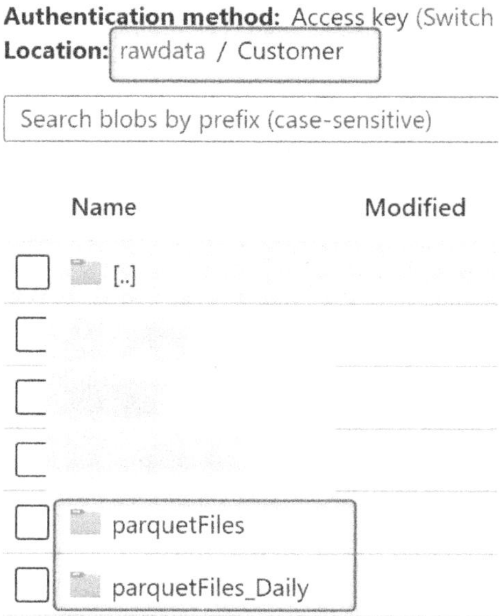

Figure 6.5 – Customer historical and daily files

- This is done to show what information is stored in the DeltaLog after performing a few DML operations.

How to do it...

In this recipe, you will learn what file format Delta Lake uses to store the data, as well as some more details about the DeltaLog:

1. We will load the data from the `parquetFiles` folder that contains data in Parquet format, load it into Delta Lake, and create a table:

```
#Reading parquet files and adding a new column to the
dataframe and writing to delta table
cust_path = "/mnt/Gen2Source/Customer/parquetFiles"
```

```
df_cust = (spark.read.format("parquet").load(cust_path)
       .withColumn("timestamp", current_timestamp()))


df_cust.write.format("delta").mode("overwrite").save("/
mnt/Gen2Source/Customer/delta")


%sql
-- Creating Delta table
DROP TABLE IF EXISTS Customer;
CREATE TABLE Customer
USING delta
location "/mnt/Gen2Source/Customer/delta"
```

2. After you write the Parquet files to Delta Table, you will find your data saved in Parquet files as shown in the following screenshot. You can see from the following screenshot that it has created one compressed Parquet file with Snappy compression used:

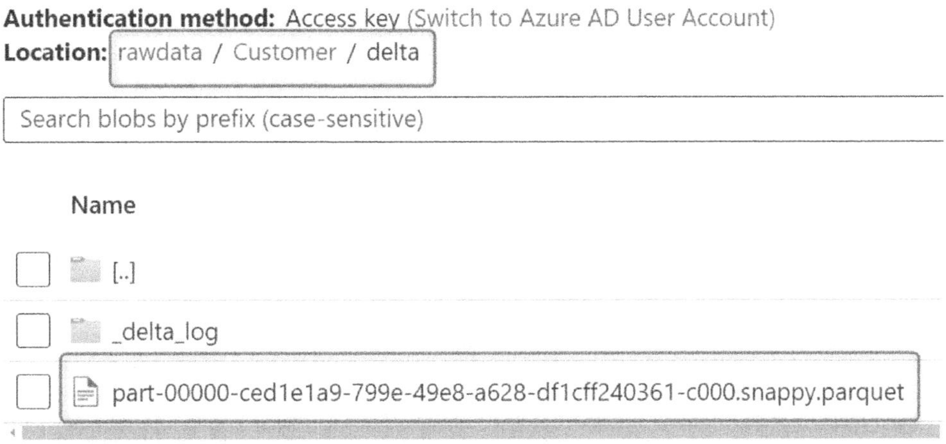

Authentication method: Access key (Switch to Azure AD User Account)
Location: rawdata / Customer / delta

Search blobs by prefix (case-sensitive)

Name

[..]

_delta_log

part-00000-ced1e1a9-799e-49e8-a628-df1cff240361-c000.snappy.parquet

Figure 6.6 – Compressed Parquet file created for the Delta table

3. You will find a folder created with the name _delta_log when you write to Delta Tables. And inside the _delta_log folder, there are CRC and JSON files for every transaction:

Figure 6.7 – DeltaLog JSON and CRC files

4. These JSON files have information about commitInfo (when they were committed), the protocol, any metadata, and details about the Parquet file created as part of our insert into the Delta table, as shown in the following screenshot. commitinfo has details about how many records have been written as part of the transaction and the number of files created, along with clusterId and notebookid:

Figure 6.8 – DeltaLog JSON file information

5. The CRC file has details about the table size and number of files in the Delta table:

Figure 6.9 – Details in the CRC file

6. Now let's go ahead and append more data to the Delta table by running the following code:

```
daily_cust_path = "/mnt/Gen2Source/Customer/parquetFiles_
Daily"

df_cust_daily = (spark.read.format("parquet").load(daily_
cust_path)
        .withColumn("timestamp", current_timestamp()))

df_cust_daily.write.format("delta").mode("append").
save("/mnt/Gen2Source/Customer/delta")
```

7. If you check the _delta_log folder you will find additional JSON and CRC files created. The operation in the JSON file is WRITE, as shown in the following screenshot. Also, you can see the save mode **Append** being used while writing data to the Delta Tables.

Figure 6.10 – DeltaLog operation information after data is inserted into the Delta table

8. Now we will delete a record from the Delta table and check what is stored in the DeltaLog by running the following code:

```sql
%sql
-- Deleting from Delta table
DELETE FROM Customer WHERE C_CUSTKEY=82533
```

9. You will find new files added to the `delta_log` folder. As we have deleted a record, it marks the old Parquet file as stale and does not physically delete the file from the folder. The new Parquet file is added, and all the data is copied from the old Parquet file. You will find the new Parquet file has 149,999 records, as we have deleted one record from the table. This isn't shown in the following screenshot, but when you open the JSON file and scroll to the right, you will find details about the number of records in the Parquet file:

Figure 6.11 – Addition of Parquet file details in the DeltaLog

10. Run the following code to identify what is stored in the Delta file when we update a record in the Delta table:

```sql
%sql
UPDATE Customer SET C_MKTSEGMENT="BUILDING" WHERE C_
CUSTKEY=101275
```

11. After the preceding code is executed, you will find a new JSON file added to the `_delta_log` folder. The following is the metadata information about the operation performed:

Customer/delta/_delta_log/00000000000000000003.json

Blob

Save   Discard   Download   Refresh   Delete

Overview   Versions   **Edit**   Generate SAS

```
1  com""operation":"UPDATE","operationParameters":{"predicate":"(C_CUSTKEY#4112 = 101275)"},"notebook":{"notebookId":
2  imestamp":1628417846199,"dataChange":true,"extendedFileMetadata":true,"partitionValues":{},"size":8620958}}
3  ues":{},"size":8620802,"modificationTime":1628417847000,"dataChange":true,"stats":"{\"numRecords\":104999,\"minValu
4
```

Figure 6.12 – DeltaLog update operation details

12. You can see from the preceding screenshot that the operation performed was UPDATE, and it even tracks the predicate clause on which the update was performed.

13. Information in the JSON files helps the Delta table to travel to a specific point in time and get the information from the Delta Table requested by the end user.

How it works...

The Delta Lake transaction log, also called the DeltaLog, tracks every transaction in a linear ordered fashion that has ever happened on that Delta table. If we delete records from the Delta table, the file from the storage is not deleted immediately as that information is used for time travel queries (you can learn more about it in the *Versioning in Delta tables* recipe). Using techniques such as VACUUM, stale and unused files can be deleted.

There's more...

Let's look at how Spark records transaction information when streaming data. We will be using the same Python code used in the *Streaming reads and writes to Delta tables* recipe to push the record to an event hub. We will learn what information is stored in the JSON files when Spark Structured Streaming writes data to a Delta table. You can follow along with the code in the 6.3-Delta Table Data Format notebook for writing streaming data to the Delta table.

1. Run the Python code in KafkaEventHub_Session1.py, found in the https://github.com/PacktPublishing/Azure-Databricks-Cookbook/tree/main/Chapter06/PythonCode/ folder, to push the data to the event hub.

2. Running the following code will start writing the streaming data to the Delta table:

```
query_source1 = append_kafkadata_
stream(topic='eventhubsource1')
```

3. Let's check what information is logged in the JSON file (/mnt/Gen2Source/Vehicle_Delta) in the DeltaLog. We can see from the following screenshot that the operation logged is STREAMING UPDATE, as we have used outputMode("Append") in the stream write method:

Vehicle_Delta/_delta_log/00000000000000000000.json   ...
Blob

🖫 Save   ✕ Discard   ↓ Download   ◯ Refresh   🗑 Delete

Overview   Versions   Edit   Generate SAS

```
1    ","operation":"STREAMING UPDATE","operationParameters":{"outputMode":"Append","queryId":"76             277  ",
2
```

Figure 6.13 – DeltaLog operation details for streaming data

4. In the JSON file, we can see all details about how many Parquet files have been added and the number of rows in the Parquet file:

Overview   Versions   **Edit**   Generate SAS

```
1    tionMetrics":{"numRemovedFiles":"0","numOutputRows":"75","numOutputBytes":"3440","numAddedFiles":"1"}}}
2
3    d-4e91-ba08-1f5cd3dd◆\",\"timestamp\":\"2021-04-16T16:59:57.818Z\",\"rpm\":99,\"speed\":100,\"kms\":995
4
```

Figure 6.14 – DeltaLog details on records inserted by streaming writes

5. The JSON file provides information on how many records are inserted in the files and finds the max and min values stored in the Parquet files.

Handling concurrency

One of the most common problems in big data systems is that they are not compliant with ACID properties, or to put it more simply, let's say they only support some properties of ACID transactions between reads and writes, and even then, they still have a lot of limitations. But with Delta Lake, ACID compliance is possible, and you can now leverage the features of ACID transactions that you used to get in **Relational Database Management Systems** (**RDBMSes**). Delta Lake uses optimistic concurrency control for handling transactions.

Optimistic concurrency control provides a mechanism to handle concurrent transactions that are changing data in the table. It ensures that all the transactions are completed successfully. A Delta Lake write operation is performed in three stages:

1. **Read** – The latest version of the table in which the file needs to be modified is read.

2. **Write** – New data files are written.

3. **Validate and commit** – Validate for the conflicting changes that might have been caused by any other transactions before committing the changes. In case of conflicts, instead of corrupting the table, the write operation fails with a concurrent modification exception.

Conflicts occur when two or more operations are performed on the same files. For example, the following commands process the same set of files if the table is not partitioned on the Date column:

```
UPDATE Table WHERE Date > '2021-04-10'
DELETE Table WHERE Date < '2021-04-10'
```

In the preceding example, to avoid conflicts the table must be partitioned on the date column. Similarly, in other cases the table must be partitioned on the conditions that are commonly used for processing data.

These will significantly reduce conflicts. Also, you must take care that you don't overpartition columns, leading to higher cardinality, as it may lead to other performance issues due to many small files.

But this does not mean Delta Lake will be able to handle all conflicts. There are a few exceptions that will occur that cannot be resolved by an optimistic approach.

The following list outlines the exceptions caused due to conflicts between transactions:

- **ConcurrentAppendException**: This exception is thrown when one operation is reading data from a partition where concurrent operations are processing files in the same partition or in an unpartitioned table, due to INSERT, UPDATE, DELETE, or MERGE operations causing conflicts. This can be avoided by separating the conditions in the script.

- **ConcurrentDeleteReadException**: This exception is thrown when one process reads a file, and the same file is deleted by another concurrent process. It is caused by UPDATE, DELETE, or MERGE operations that rewrite files.

- **ConcurrentDeleteDeleteException**: This exception is thrown when a concurrent operation deletes a file and another operation is also trying to delete the same file.

- **MetadataChangedException**: This exception is thrown when a concurrent operation updates the metadata of a Delta table. It is caused by the ALTER table operation or any operation causing a change in the metadata of the Delta table.

- **ConcurrentTransactionException**: This exception is thrown when a concurrent streaming query uses the same checkpoint location and tries to write the streaming data to a Delta table at the same time.

- **ProtocolChangedException**: This exception is thrown when the Delta table is upgraded. Delta Lake must be upgraded so that further operations on the Delta table succeed.

We will see all of these exception causes in the queries in the upcoming section.

Getting ready

Before starting we need to ensure that we have a valid Azure subscription with contributor access, a Databricks workspace, and an ADLS Gen2 storage account.

- Copy the Customer Parquet files from following github link. You will find folders with the names csvFiles and parquetFiles and you can copy files from the folder parquetFiles from the GitHub link to ADLS Gen-2 folder.

  https://github.com/PacktPublishing/Azure-Databricks-Cookbook/tree/main/Common

- You can follow along by running the steps in the 6_4.
  ConcurrencyExceptions and 6_4_1.ConcurrencyTest notebooks
  at https://github.com/PacktPublishing/Azure-Databricks-
  Cookbook/tree/main/Chapter06/.

In this section, we will cover two scenarios and demonstrate the exceptions due to read/
write operations in concurrent transactions.

Let's go through the prerequisite steps for this recipe:

1. Load the customer data into the DataFrame from the mounted location using the
   following code snippet:

   ```
   df_parquet = spark.read.format("parquet").
   option("header",True).load("/mnt/Gen2Source/Customer/
   parquetFiles")
   ```

2. 2.Write the loaded Dataframe in Delta format with append mode using the
   following code snippet. We are executing this command in for loop to generate
   close to 3 million records in the delta table. We are generating more data to simulate
   the concurrency issue.

   ```
   for i in range (1,20):
   df_parquet.write.format("delta").mode("append").save("/
   mnt/Gen2Source/CustomerDelta")
   ```

3. Create a Delta table named CustomerDelta using the preceding delta location.
   Note that this Delta table is not partitioned:

   ```
   spark.sql("CREATE TABLE CustomerDelta USING DELTA
   LOCATION '/mnt/Gen2Source/CustomerDelta/'")
   ```

4. Using the same DataFrame, let's create another Delta table that will be partitioned
   on the C_MKTSEGMENT column. We are running in a loop to generate more data in
   the Delta table which is partitioned by C_MKTSEGMENT

   ```
   for i in range (1,20):
      df_parquet.write.format("delta").partitionBy("C_
   MKTSEGMENT").mode("append").save("/mnt/Gen2Source/
   CustomerDeltaPartition")
   ```

5. Let's create a new Delta Table on the location /mnt/Gen2Source/
    CustomerDeltaPartition by running the following code:

```
#Creating CustomerDeltaPartition table
spark.sql("CREATE TABLE CustomerDeltaPartition
USING DELTA LOCATION '/mnt/Gen2Source/
CustomerDeltaPartition/'")
```

In the next section, you will learn how handle concurrent transactions.

How to do it...

Let's go through both the scenarios and learn how conflicts occur in both the cases
of concurrent transactions when the Delta table is not partitioned, and with the
Serializable and WriteSerializable isolation level (the default isolation level
for Delta tables).

Scenario 1: In this scenario, you will learn how to handle concurrency exceptions
when concurrent transactions are updating and deleting data from partitioned and
non-partitioned Delta tables.

1. Update the non-partitioned Delta table using the following code. This is a simple
    UPDATE statement where we are updating MACHINERY market segment records
    in the table and setting their C_NATIONKEY columns to 4. As soon as you
    execute the following code you should immediately go to the Notebook **6_4.
    ConcurrencyExceptions.ipynb** and execute code mentioned in *Step 2* so that
    we can encounter the exceptions. With small data it is difficult to simulate the
    concurrency scenario.

```
%sql
-- Updating non partitioned table
UPDATE CustomerDelta SET C_NATIONKEY = 4 WHERE C_
MKTSEGMENT='MACHINERY'
```

2. Now execute the following DELETE statement in the 6_4.1.ConcurrencyTest
    notebook. Here we will try to delete some records based on the following condition
    at the same time as the preceding update statement is executed:

```
%sql
DELETE FROM CustomerDelta WHERE C_MKTSEGMENT='FURNITURE'
```

3. When the `DELETE` command is executed, you will get a
    ConcurrentAppendException error. The error message clearly says that files were
    added to the table by a concurrent update. You will find the **update** query gets
    execute successfully.

```
%sql
DELETE FROM CustomerDelta WHERE C_MKTSEGMENT='FURNITURE'
```

▶ (3) Spark Jobs

⊟Error in SQL statement: [ConcurrentAppendException: Files were added to the root of the table by a concurrent update.] Please try the operation again.

Figure 6.15 – Non-partitioned table concurrency exception

4. Since the state of the table has changed due to the `UPDATE` statement, the `DELETE`
    command execution will not succeed and throws an exception because the changes
    by the `DELETE` command cannot be committed.

5. Now we will try to execute the same `UPDATE` and `DELETE` commands on the
    partitioned Delta table and see whether the exception still occurs or not. Execute
    the following code snippet to update the data in the partitioned Delta table:

```
%sql
UPDATE CustomerDeltaPartition SET C_NATIONKEY = 4 WHERE
C_MKTSEGMENT='MACHINERY'
```

6. Execute the following code to delete the data from the partitioned table:

```
%sql
DELETE FROM CustomerDeltaPartition WHERE C_
MKTSEGMENT='FURNITURE'
```

7. This time we will not get an exception as the data files are residing in their
    respective partitions. Using the partitioning approach like this, we can resolve
    concurrency conflicts:

```
%sql
DELETE FROM CustomerDeltaPartition WHERE C_MKTSEGMENT='FURNITURE'
```

▶ (4) Spark Jobs

OK

Figure 6.16 – Concurrency in the partitioned table

Scenario 2: In this scenario, we will learn how the isolation level of the Delta table impacts concurrent transactions on the partitioned Delta table:

1. Now let's see the second scenario, where we will see the impact of concurrent transactions with different isolation levels. Execute the following code snippet to change the isolation level of the table to `Serializable`:

```sql
%sql

ALTER TABLE CustomerDeltaPartition SET TBLPROPERTIES
('delta.isolationLevel' = 'Serializable')
```

2. To create more data, we call the following code block to append data in Delta table in the `for` loop for i in range (1,20):

```
df_parquet.where(col("C_MKTSEGMENT")=="MACHINERY").
write.format("delta").mode("append").
partitionBy("C_MKTSEGMENT").save("/mnt/Gen2Source/
CustomerDeltaPartition")
```

3. Now execute the following `DELETE` command from the `6_4_1.`
`ConcurrencyTest` notebook:

```sql
%sql
DELETE FROM CustomerDeltaPartition WHERE C_
MKTSEGMENT='MACHINERY' AND C_CUSTKEY=1377
```

4. You will observe that you are again getting a **ConcurrentAppendException** error with the partitioned table:

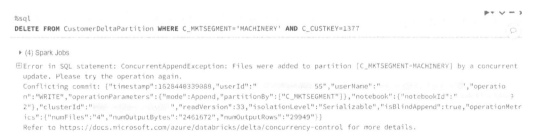

Figure 6.17 – Concurrency issue with the Serializable isolation level

5. Now you can try with the default isolation level of the Delta table, which is `WriteSerializable`. Execute the following command to change the isolation level of the Delta table:

```sql
%sql


ALTER TABLE CustomerDeltaPartition SET TBLPROPERTIES
('delta.isolationLevel' = 'WriteSerializable')
```

6. Repeat *Steps 2* and *3* again and you will not get an exception this time because `WriteSerializable` is a weaker isolation level than `Serializable`. It ensures data is consistent and available for common operations:

```sql
%sql
DELETE FROM CustomerDeltaPartition WHERE C_MKTSEGMENT='MACHINERY' AND C_CUSTKEY=1377
```

▶ (8) Spark Jobs

OK

Figure 6.18 – WriteSerializable isolation level

7. `WriteSerializable` allows transactions to read tables that do not exist in the DeltaLog.

How it works...

In RDBMS, conflicts are handled using the locks, but in the filesystem, there is no locking mechanism. Hence when there are conflicts, the write operation fails with exceptions instead of corrupting the data in the table. In the preceding section, we saw concurrent transactions trying to update the same files. As you know, the Delta tables maintain versions. So, whenever there are concurrent transactions, Delta Lake handles both mutually exclusively, meaning one transaction will be accepted and the other will be rejected. It handles them optimistically and updates the table for one transaction creating a new version of the table. The second transaction will have the older version of the table and does not match the version recently committed by another transaction. You can learn more about concurrency conflicts at `https://docs.microsoft.com/en-us/azure/databricks/delta/concurrency-control#write-conflicts`.

Delta table performance optimization

Delta engine is a high-performance query engine and most of the optimization is taken care of by the engine itself. However, there are some more optimization techniques that we are going to cover in this recipe.

Using Delta Lake on Azure Databricks, you can optimize the data stored in cloud storage. The two algorithms supported by Delta Lake on Databricks are bin-packing and Z-ordering:

- **Compaction (bin-packing)** – The speed of read queries can be optimized by compacting small files into large ones. So, whenever data is required, instead of searching for data in a large number of small files, the Spark engine efficiently reads the Delta files up to 1 GB.

- **Z Order** – Delta Lake on Databricks provides a technique to arrange related information in the same set of files. This helps in reducing the amount of data that needs to be read. You specify the column name ZORDER by clause to collocate the data.

- **VACUUM** – You can use the VACUUM command to delete the compacted files. The default value for deleting the files is 7 days. That means the files that were compacted before 7 days will get deleted when the VACUUM command is executed.

Getting ready

Before starting we need to ensure that we have valid a subscription with contributor access, a Databricks workspace, and an ADLS Gen2 storage account.

You can follow along by running the steps in the 6_5. DeltaTablePerformanceOptimization notebook in the https://github. com/PacktPublishing/Azure-Databricks-Cookbook/tree/main/ Chapter06/ folder.

You can find the Parquet files used in the recipe at https://github.com/ PacktPublishing/Azure-Databricks-Cookbook/tree/main/Common/ Orders/parquetFiles.

How to do it...

In this section, you will learn how to use the OPTIMIZE, ZORDER, and VACUUM commands for performance improvement. We will use the Orders data files for creating the Delta table and see the difference when the data is read from the Delta table after applying the OPTIMIZE and ZORDER commands.

1. Execute the following command to load Order data in the DataFrame. Note that we are also deriving a new column called O_OrderYear from the O_ORDERDATE column. This new derived column will be used later while creating the Delta table:

```
from pyspark.sql.functions import count, year

ordersDF = spark.read.format("parquet").load("/mnt/
Gen2/Orders/parquetFiles/").withColumn('O_OrderYear',f.
year("O_ORDERDATE"))
```

2. Now you can execute the following command to get the number of open orders for each year based on order priority. After executing the query, observe the time taken to return the result:

```
import pyspark.sql.functions as f
display(ordersDF.filter("O_ORDERSTATUS = 'O'").
groupBy("O_OrderYear","O_ORDERPRIORITY").agg(count("*").
alias("TotalOrders")).orderBy("TotalOrders",
ascending=False).limit(20))
```

In our case, the query took **1.7 seconds** to execute:

```
display(ordersDF.filter("O_ORDERSTATUS =
'O'").groupBy("O_OrderYear","O_ORDERPRIORITY").agg(count("*").alias("TotalOrde
ascending=False).limit(20))
```

▶ (2) Spark Jobs

	O_OrderYear	O_ORDERPRIORITY	TotalOrders
1	1996	1-URGENT	46014
2	1996	4-NOT SPECIFIED	45776
3	1997	4-NOT SPECIFIED	45754
4	1997	2-HIGH	45689
5	1997	1-URGENT	45662
6	1996	3-MEDIUM	45657
7	1996	5-LOW	45639

Showing all 20 rows.

Command took 1.70 seconds --

Figure 6.19 – Normal query execution

In the next step, we will see the execution time of the same query with OPTIMIZE.

3. Let's overwrite the same table using the following command:

```
ordersDF.write.format("delta").mode("overwrite").
partitionBy("O_OrderYear").save("/mnt/Gen2/Orders/
OrdersDelta/")
```

4. Before running the query to read the data, let's run OPTIMIZE and ZORDER and compare the difference in the execution time. Execute the following code to optimize the data stored in the table:

```
display(spark.sql("DROP TABLE  IF EXISTS Orders"))

display(spark.sql("CREATE TABLE Orders USING DELTA
LOCATION '/mnt/Gen2/Orders/OrdersDelta'"))

display(spark.sql("OPTIMIZE Orders ZORDER BY (O_
ORDERPRIORITY)"))
```

5. Once the commands are executed, you will see the operation performed in the table where you are applying OPTIMIZE and ZORDER:

```
display(spark.sql("DROP TABLE  IF EXISTS Orders"))

display(spark.sql("CREATE TABLE Orders USING DELTA LOCATION '/mnt/Gen2Source/Orders/OrdersDelta'"))

display(spark.sql("OPTIMIZE Orders ZORDER BY (O_ORDERPRIORITY)"))
```

▶ (17) Spark Jobs

OK

OK

path	metrics
null	▶ {"numFilesAdded": 7, "numFilesRemoved": 28, "filesAdded": {"min": 2178106, "max": 3726077, "avg": 3452511, "totalFiles": 7, "totalSize": 24167579}, "filesRemoved": {"min": 443929, "max": 1024790, "avg": 887174, "totalFiles": 28, "totalSize": 24840888}, "partitionsOptimized": 7, "zOrderStats": {"strategyName": "minCubeSize(107374182400)", "inputCubeFiles": {"num": 0, "size": 0}, "inputOtherFiles": {"num": 28, "size": 24840888}, "inputNumCubes": 0, "mergedFiles": {"num": 28, "size": 24840888}, "numOutputCubes": 7, "mergedNumCubes": null}, "numBatches": 1}

Figure 6.20 – Optimize and Zorder

6. Now execute the following command to fetch the Orders data using the same query as used in *step 2*:

```
from pyspark.sql.functions import count
ordersDeltaDF = spark.read.format("Delta").load("/mnt/
Gen2/Orders/OrdersDelta/")
display(ordersDeltaDF.filter("O_ORDERSTATUS = 'O'").
groupBy("O_OrderYear","O_ORDERPRIORITY").agg(count("*").
alias("TotalOrders")).orderBy("TotalOrders",
ascending=False).limit(20))
```

7. You will observe a significant difference in the execution time after changing the table to a Delta table and running the OPTIMZE and ZORDER commands:

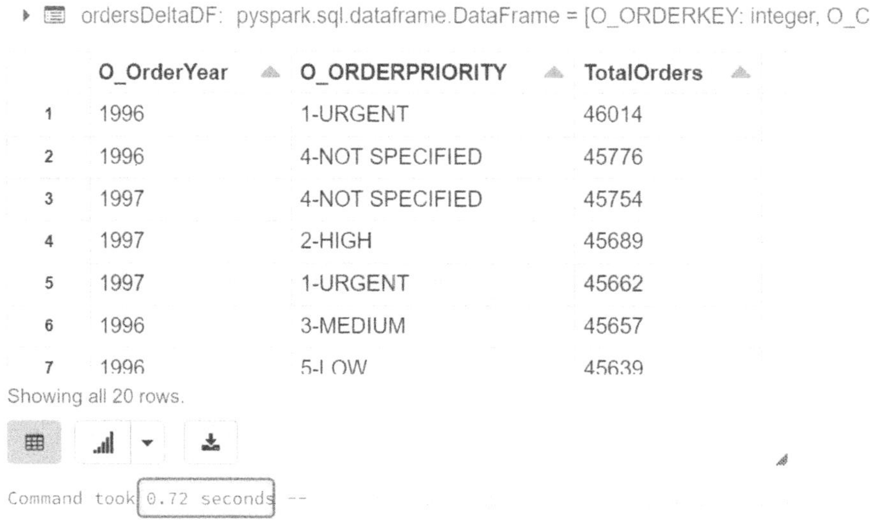

> ▸ ▦ ordersDeltaDF: pyspark.sql.dataframe.DataFrame = [O_ORDERKEY: integer, O_C

	O_OrderYear	O_ORDERPRIORITY	TotalOrders
1	1996	1-URGENT	46014
2	1996	4-NOT SPECIFIED	45776
3	1997	4-NOT SPECIFIED	45754
4	1997	2-HIGH	45689
5	1997	1-URGENT	45662
6	1996	3-MEDIUM	45657
7	1996	5-LOW	45639

Showing all 20 rows.

Command took 0.72 seconds --

Figure 6.21 – Execution time with Optimize and Zorder

8. The decrease in the execution time depends on the cluster configuration, but you should get faster results compared to the non-Delta tables.

9. You can compare the number of files created after running the OPTIMIZE command using the following command:

```
display(dbutils.fs.ls("dbfs:/mnt/Gen2Source/Orders/
OrdersDelta/O_OrderYear=1993/"))
```

10. As the files are now compacted, you will observe the number of files has been reduced when compared to the numbers of data files prior to changing to a Delta table.

11. You can delete the data files that are no longer queried and are older than the retention threshold period (7 days by default) using the VACUUM command. Log files are deleted automatically once the checkpoint operations are done. The default value for the retention period of log files is 30 days but it is configurable and can be changed using the delta.logRetentionDuration property with the ALTER TABLE SET TBLPROPERTIES SQL method. Also, note after running the VACUUM command, you will lose the ability to use time travel to go to a version older than the retention interval. You can use the following command to run VACUUM on a data file location or Delta table:

```
%sql
VACUUM ordersDeltaDF  -- Based on the Delta table name
VACUUM '/mnt/Gen2/Orders/OrdersDelta/' -- Based on the
Delta table files location
```

By running VACUUM periodically, we can proactively control the size of the storage in ADLS Gen2 by deleting files that we don't need for queries.

How it works...

The Small File Problem is very common in big data systems. It occurs when the data is written to very small files that may be spread across multiple machines sitting in multiple data centers. When the data is read, the execution will be very slow because of network latency and the volume of small files. OPTIMIZE is the solution for this Small File Problem – it compacts many small files into large files up to 1 GB. The OPTIMZE command uses the bin-packing algorithm for coalescence operations.

You can see in the following snippet the number of files added is 7, with 56 removed after applying the OPTIMIZE command:

```
display(spark.sql("DROP TABLE  IF EXISTS Orders"))

display(spark.sql("CREATE TABLE Orders USING DELTA LOCATION '/mnt/Gen2Source/Orders/OrdersDelta'"))

display(spark.sql("OPTIMIZE Orders ZORDER BY (O_ORDERPRIORITY)"))
```

▶ (20) Spark Jobs

OK

OK

	path	▲	metrics	▲
1	null		▶ {"numFilesAdded": 7, "numFilesRemoved": 28, "filesAdded": {"min": 2178106, "max": 3726077, "avg": 3452511, "totalFiles": 7, "totalSize": 24167579}, "filesRemoved": {"min": 443929, "max": 1024790, "avg": 887174, "totalFiles": 28, "totalSize": 24840888}, "partitionsOptimized": 7, "zOrderStats": {"strategyName": "minCubeSize(107374182400)", "inputCubeFiles": {"num": 0, "size": 0}, "inputOtherFiles": {"num": 28, "size": 24840888}, "inputNumCubes": 0, "mergedFiles": {"num": 28, "size": 24840888}, "numOutputCubes": 7, "mergedNumCubes": null}, "numBatches": 1}	

Figure 6.22 – OPTIMIZE and ZORDER results

ZORDER takes the files within a partition, maps its rows based on the ordered column, and writes the data in the sorted order into new Parquet files. Note, you cannot use the column on which the table has been partitioned in ZORDER column.

Constraints in Delta tables

Delta tables support constraints to ensure data integrity and quality. When the constraint conditions are not met by the data then InvariantViolationException is thrown, and data is not added to the table.

The following types of constraints are supported by the Delta table:

- **CHECK**: Evaluate a given Boolean expression for each input row.

- **NOT NULL**: Check that the column under constraint does not have a null value.

Getting ready

Before starting we need to ensure that we have a valid subscription with contributor access, a Databricks workspace, and an ADLS Gen2 storage account.

You can follow along by running the steps in the 6_6.Constraints notebook in the https://github.com/PacktPublishing/Azure-Databricks-Cookbook/blob/main/Chapter06/6_6.Constraints.ipynb. Upload the file to Customer folder in the rawdata container in your ADLS Gen-2 account which is mounted.

CustomerwithNullCName.csv file has 4 rows and one row has C_NAME as NULL value.

How to do it...

In this recipe, you will learn the syntax for adding and dropping the constraints supported by Delta tables. Constraints are a good way to implement data validation during ingestion. Hence, it is always a good practice to create constraints on the tables to maintain data integrity. Not all the constraints of other common databases (such as SQL Server or Oracle) are supported by the Delta table. We will learn the commands for the NOT NULL and CHECK constraints:

1. The NOT NULL constraint can be added at column level while defining the schema of the Delta table and can be dropped using the ALTER TABLE CHANGE COLUMN command. Execute the following code create customer Delta table which has C_CUSTKEY and C_NAME marked as NOT NULL columns:

```sql
%sql
DROP TABLE IF EXISTS customer;
CREATE TABLE customer(
    C_CUSTKEY INT NOT NULL,
    C_NAME STRING NOT NULL,
    C_ADDRESS STRING,
    C_NATIONKEY INT,
```

```
    C_PHONE STRING,
    C_ACCTBAL Double,
    C_MKTSEGMENT STRING,
    C_COMMENT STRING
) USING DELTA;

ALTER TABLE customer CHANGE COLUMN C_NAME DROP NOT NULL;
```

2. Run the following code to load the csv file CustomerwithNullCName.csv into a DataFrame.

```
df_cust = spark.read.format("csv").option("header",True).
option("inferSchema",True).load("/mnt/Gen2Source/
Customer/CustomerwithNullCName.csv")
```

3. Now let's write the DataFrame to Customer Delta table by running the following code.

```
df_cust.write.format("delta").mode("append").
saveAsTable("customer")
```

4. Since C_NAME column is marked as NOT NULL, inserting NULL values will throw the following error.

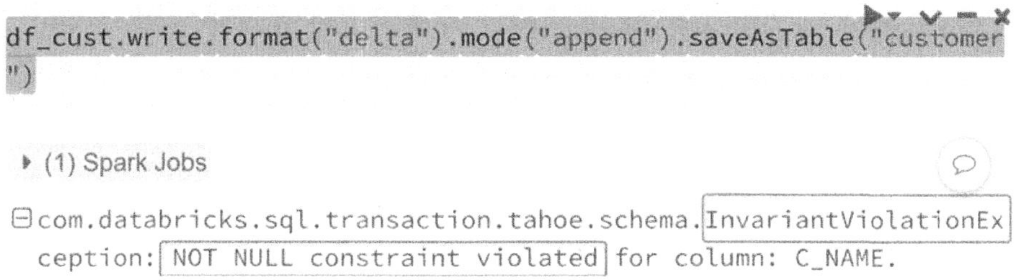

```
df_cust.write.format("delta").mode("append").saveAsTable("customer
")
```

▶ (1) Spark Jobs

com.databricks.sql.transaction.tahoe.schema.InvariantViolationEx
ception: NOT NULL constraint violated for column: C_NAME.

Figure 6.23 –NOT NULL constraint violation

5. Let's drop the NOT NULL constraint in the Customer table by running the following code. After running the following code, when you re-run the code mentioned in *Step 3* it will succeed.

```
ALTER TABLE customer CHANGE COLUMN C_NAME DROP NOT NULL;
```

6. NOT NULL constraint can be added to the existing Delta table using following command. Before we enable, make sure there are no rows in the Delta table which has NULL values for C_NAME else the following command will fail.

```
%sql
ALTER TABLE customer CHANGE COLUMN C_CUSTKEY SET NOT
NULL;
```

7. A nested column in an array or map type does support the NOT NULL constraint. However, if there is a NOT NULL constraint on a nested column in a struct, then the parent struct is also NOT NULL.

8. You can add or drop the CHECK constraint using the ALTER TABLE ADD CONSTRAINT and ALTER TABLE DROP CONSTRAINT commands. Execute the following script for creating customer Delta table adding the CHECK constraint on Delta table. Here we are adding CHECK constraint C_MKTSEGMENT column and expecting all the rows which are getting inserted into the Delta table has the value BUILDING.

```
%sql
CREATE TABLE customer(
  C_CUSTKEY INT,
  C_NAME STRING ,
  C_ADDRESS STRING,
  C_NATIONKEY INT,
  C_PHONE STRING,
  C_ACCTBAL DOUBLE,
  C_MKTSEGMENT STRING,
  C_COMMENT STRING
) USING DELTA;
ALTER TABLE customer ADD CONSTRAINT MKTSEGMENT CHECK (C_
MKTSEGMENT = 'BUILDING');
ALTER TABLE customer DROP CONSTRAINT MKTSEGMENT;
```

9. Now let's load the df_cust DataFrame into Customers Delta table by running the following code and it will fail with error **InvariantViolationException: CHECK constraint mktsegment**. DataFrame df_cust has only one row with BUILDING as value for C_MKTSEGMENT column and rest of the rows have different values.

```
df_cust.write.format("delta").mode("append").
saveAsTable("customer")
```

10. To drop the CHECK constraint run the following code.

```sql
%sql
ALTER TABLE customer DROP CONSTRAINT MKTSEGMENT;
```

11. Execute the following command to create the CHECK constraint C_NATIOKEY in a Delta table:

```sql
%sql
ALTER TABLE customer ADD CONSTRAINT MKTSEGMENT CHECK (C_
NATIONKEY = 0));
```

12. Execute the following code to view the table properties on the Delta table which includes the constraints on the table:

```sql
%sql
DESCRIBE DETAIL customer;
```

13. Refer to the following screenshot to see the output of this command:

Figure 6.24 – Output of the DESCRIBE command

The preceding output will show the properties of the table, including createdAt, lastModified, partitionColumns, numFiles, and constraints as well.

How it works...

Constraints are applied before inserting the data row in the table. If the constraint condition does not match, then the data row is not inserted or updated. In case of failure due to constraints on the table, an InvariantViolationException exception is thrown.

Versioning in Delta tables

In today's world, data is growing day by day and sometimes we need to access the historical data. To access the data for a particular period, data needs to be saved at a point in time, meaning a snapshot of the data at an interval of time. Having such a snapshot will make it easy to audit data changes and perform rollbacks for bad writes or accidentally deleted data.

When the data is written into Delta Lake, every transaction is versioned, and it can be accessed at any point in time. This is called *Time Travel*. It provides the flexibility to travel back to a previous time and access the data of the current Delta table as it was then. The transaction log contains the versioning information of the Delta table.

Delta Lake always provides backward compatibility, but sometimes suffers from forward-compatibility breaks, meaning a lower version of the Databricks runtime may not be able to read and write data that was written using a higher version of the Databricks runtime.

Delta Lake selects the required protocol version depending on a table peculiarity such as the schema or its properties. The default protocol version can be set using the SQL configuration. The following configuration shows the default value for the protocol version of Delta Lake:

```
spark.databricks.delta.properties.defaults.minWriterVersion = 2
spark.databricks.delta.properties.defaults.minReaderVersion = 1
```

Let's see how to use the Delta Lake Time Travel capabilities in the upcoming section.

Getting ready

Before starting we need to ensure we have an Azure subscription with contributor access and an ALDS Gen2 storage account.

You can follow along by running the steps in the `6_7.DeltaTableVersioning` notebook in the `https://github.com/PacktPublishing/Azure-Databricks-Cookbook/tree/main/Chapter06/` folder to get Databricks to send log data to a Log Analytics workspace.

How to do it...

You can access the different versions of the Delta table data in two ways. The first one is by using TIMESTAMP and the second is by using the version number. We will explore both ways and see how the retrieve the point-in-time data:

1. Use the DESCRIBE HISTORY command to get the history of changes in the table. You can also get the same details from the UI:

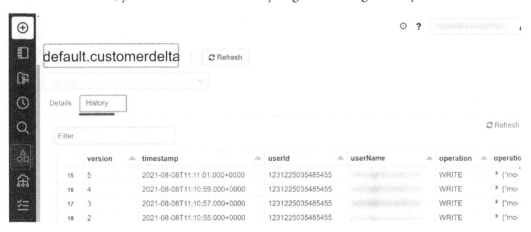

Figure 6.25 – Checking the history with a command

2. From the UI, you check the table history to get the change history:

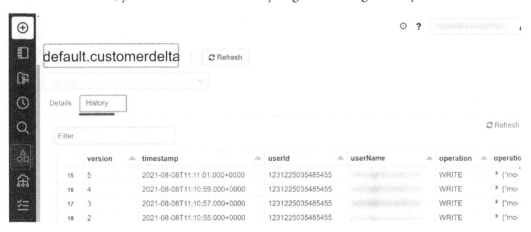

Figure 6.26 – Checking the history from the UI

3. You can provide a datetime stamp as an option to the DataFrame to receive data based on the datetime. Execute the following code to fetch the Customer data:

```
df = spark.read \
  .format("delta") \
  .option("timestampAsOf", "2021-04-
10T19:08:54.000+0000") \
  .load("/mnt/Gen2Source/CustomerDelta/")
```

4. You can use the following SQL query to fetch the point-in-time data using a datetime stamp:

```sql
%sql
SELECT * FROM CustomerDelta TIMESTAMP AS OF "2021-04-
10T19:08:54.000+0000"
```

5. You can use the version number that you see in the *Step 2* output to use time travel and fetch the records for that specific version:

```
df = spark.read \
  .format("delta") \
  .option("versionAsOf", "1") \
  .load("/mnt/Gen2/CustomerDelta/")
```

6. You can use the SQL query to fetch the point-in-time data using the version number:

```sql
%sql
SELECT * FROM CustomerDelta VERSION AS OF 1
```

7. Using time travel, you can easily fix data that has been deleted accidentally or in the case of a rollback. By running the following command, you are inserting the records into `CustomerDelta` for the `BUILDING` market segment that was deleted at a specific timestamp. Using versioning we fetch the records from the table from before they were deleted, and load the records back to the table:

```sql
%sql
INSERT INTO CustomerDelta
SELECT * FROM CustomerDelta TIMESTAMP AS OF "2021-04-
10T19:08:54.000+0000"
WHERE C_MKTSEGMENT = = 'BUILDING'
```

Versioning provides a convenient way to undo any human errors made on the Delta table, such as deleting records or updating records that are invalid.

How it works...

The Delta table transaction log contains the version information. For time travel, the log and data files of the previous versions must be retained. The version number starts from 0 and goes on as logs are committed to the `_delta_log` directory. This folder contains the transaction log of the Delta table that keeps the version information. Each commit in the Delta table is written in a JSON file inside the log folder. The JSON filenames start with `000000.json` and are subsequently increased in ascending numerical order. So, when the next commit is done, a file named `000001.json` will be created. The following is a snippet of the `_delta_log` folder:

Location: rawdata / CustomerDelta

Search blobs by prefix (case-sensitive)

Name	Modified	Access tier
[..]		
_delta_log		
part-00000-0625ed...	8/8/2021, 4:41:10 PM	Hot (Inferred)
part-00000-0885cb...	8/8/2021, 4:40:55 PM	Hot (Inferred)

Figure 6.27 – Delta log folder structure

Parquet is the files having the data. Delta Lake also automatically creates checkpoint files for every 10 commits.

7
Implementing Near-Real-Time Analytics and Building a Modern Data Warehouse

Azure has changed the way data applications are designed and implemented and how data is processed and stored. As we see more data coming from various disparate sources, we need to have better tools and techniques to handle streamed, batched, semi-structured, unstructured, and relational data together. Modern data solutions are being built in such a way that they define a framework that describes how data can be read from various sources, processed together, and stored or sent to other streaming consumers to generate meaningful insights from the raw data.

In this chapter, we will learn how to ingest data coming from disparate sources such as **Azure Event Hubs**, **Azure Data Lake Storage Gen2** (ADLS Gen2) storage, and **Azure SQL Database**, and how this data can be processed together and stored as a data warehouse model with Facts and Dimension **Azure Synapse Analytics**, and store processed and raw data in Delta lake and in Cosmos DB for near real time analytics. We will learn how to create a basic data visualization in Power BI and in Azure Databricks on the data that is in Delta Lake and create a near-real-time dashboard for the streaming data that is ingested in **Azure Databricks**.

By the end of this chapter, you will have learned how you can use Delta Lake and adopt Lakehouse patterns in your big data projects.

We're going to cover the following recipes in this chapter:

- Understanding the scenario for an **end-to-end** (**E2E**) solution
- Creating required Azure resources for the E2E demonstration
- Simulating a workload for streaming data
- Processing streaming and batch data using Structured Streaming
- Understanding the various stages of transforming data
- Loading the transformed data into Azure Cosmos DB and a Synapse dedicated pool
- Creating a visualization and dashboard in a notebook for near-real-time analytics
- Creating a visualization in Power BI for near-real-time analytics
- Using **Azure Data Factory** (**ADF**) to orchestrate the E2E pipeline

Technical requirements

To follow along with the examples shown in the recipes, you will need to have the following:

- An Azure subscription and required permissions on the subscription, as mentioned in the *Technical requirements* section of *Chapter 1*, *Creating an Azure Databricks Service*.
- An Azure Databricks workspace with a Spark 3.x cluster. All the notebooks used in this chapter are executed on a Spark 3. 0.1 cluster.
- You can find the scripts for this chapter in the GitHub repository at `https://github.com/PacktPublishing/Azure-Databricks-Cookbook/tree/main/Chapter07`. The `Chapter07` folder contains all the notebooks, Python code, and a few Parquet files required for the demonstration.

Understanding the scenario for an end-to-end (E2E) solution

In this recipe, you will learn about an E2E solution that you will be building in this chapter. We will look at various components used in the solution and the data warehouse model that we will be creating in a Synapse dedicated pool.

Getting ready

You need to ensure you read the following chapters before starting on this recipe if you are new to Azure Databricks:

- *Chapter 2, Reading and Writing Data from and to Various Azure Services and File Formats*

- *Chapter 4, Working with Streaming Data*

- *Chapter 6, Exploring Delta Lake in Azure Databricks*

Also, you will need to have a basic understanding of facts and dimension tables in a data warehouse.

How to do it...

In this section, you will understand an E2E data pipeline scenario along with the modern data warehouse model that will be created as part of the solution. The following points list down all the stages of the data pipeline, right from creating **JavaScript Object Notation** (**JSON**) source files up to creating curated Delta tables and a data warehouse in Azure Synapse Analytics.

1. We are simulating vehicle sensor data that tracks information about cars in the New York City (NYC) area. Information transmitted by the sensor is in JSON format. Vehicle sensor information is sent to Event Hubs for Kafka, using a Python script. The Python script generates the required data as a producer and will send it to Event Hubs for Kafka.

2. We have the streaming data coming from Event Hubs for Kafka, and there is historical vehicle sensor data on ADLS Gen2 storage. We will be loading data from both batch and streaming sources to Synapse dedicated pools, Cosmos DB, and Delta tables after performing various transformations.

3. Delta tables would have the aggregated data that will be the source for Power BI reports along with other Delta tables. The sensor data will be loaded into a Synapse dedicated pool and to Cosmos DB.

The architecture is illustrated in the following diagram:

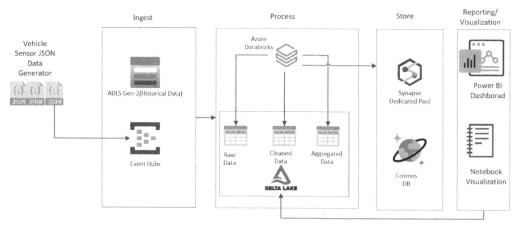

Figure 7.1 – E2E architecture

4. *Figure 7.*1 is an E2E diagram for the solution we will be building in this chapter.

5. Data coming from Event Hubs is loaded as is in the raw Delta table, and we do some cleansing on the raw data and then load the cleansed data into another Delta table. This cleansed data will be loaded to Synapse dedicated pool staging tables. We will run some aggregation and load the aggregated data to another Delta table (Gold zone Delta tables).

6. We will create stored procedures in a dedicated pool that will load the data from the staging tables to fact and dimension tables:

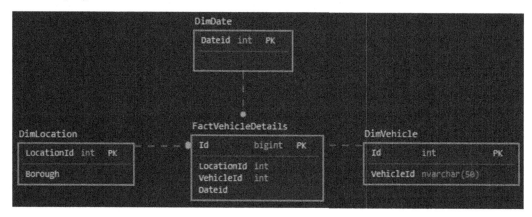

Figure 7.2 – Data warehouse model

7. *Figure 7.2* is a data model for the vehicle sensor data that is stored in the Synapse dedicated pool. We have one fact table and three dimension tables created in the dedicated pool, and details about the tables are provided here:

   a) `FactVehicleDetails`: Has core vehicle information such as vehicle **identifier (ID)**, **kilometers (kms)**, **low fuel indicator (LFI)**, **revolutions per minute (RPM)**, speed, and **engine repair indicator (ERI)**

   b) `DimVehicle`: Has the make and model details, along with the vehicle name for the vehicle ID, which is part of the JSON data received from Event Hubs

   c) `DimLocation`: Has details about the latitude, longitude, and the location name

   d) `DimDate`: This table is typical Date dimension which is generated using t-sql scripts in any Data warehouse

8. All the tasks mentioned in the preceding steps will be orchestrated using an Azure Data Factory pipeline or through a Databricks job.

By the end of this recipe, you will have understood the E2E solution that will be built as part of this chapter.

How it works...

We are using Python code to simulate the vehicle sensor data, which also sends the data in JSON format to Event Hubs for Kafka. Using Azure Databricks Spark Structured Streaming, we are processing the data in near real time and storing the aggregated data in the Delta table. We will create a Power BI dashboard and a notebook dashboard for showing near-real-time data from the Delta table.

The non-aggregated data will be stored in a Synapse dedicated pool and Cosmos DB for further reporting and any application usage. By the end of this chapter, you will be building an E2E data ingestion pipeline in Azure Databricks, along with some near-real-time dashboards.

Creating required Azure resources for the E2E demonstration

In this recipe, you will create Azure resources required for an E2E solution for implementing batch processing, real-time analytics, and building a modern warehouse solution using Azure Stack.

Getting ready

Before starting, we need to ensure we have access to the subscription and have contributor access to the subscription, or are the owner of the resource group.

Before we begin, ensure that you have completed the recipes in *Chapter 2, Reading and Writing Data from and to Various Azure Services and File Formats*, and *Chapter 4, Working with Streaming Data*.

How to do it...

In this section, you will learn how to get the required information for various components to establish a connection.

1. Refer to the *Reading and writing data from and to Azure Cosmos* recipe from *Chapter 2, Reading and Writing Data from and to Various Azure Services and File Formats* to learn how to read and write data to and from a Cosmos DB account. You can also refer to the following link to find out more about Azure Cosmos DB account creation: `https://docs.microsoft.com/en-us/azure/cosmos-db/create-cosmosdb-resources-portal`.

2. Open a provisioned Cosmos DB account and traverse to the **Keys** section, as shown in the following screenshot, to get the required connection string and keys from the Azure Cosmos DB account:

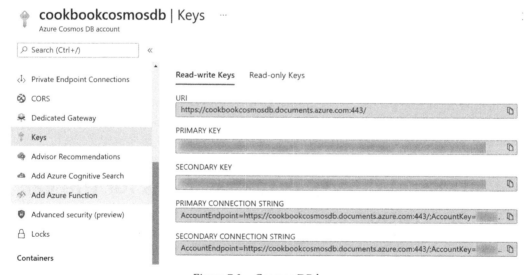

Figure 7.3 – Cosmos DB keys

3. Refer to the *Reading data from Kafka-enabled event hubs* recipe from *Chapter 4, Working with Streaming Data,* to learn how to read from a Kafka-enabled event hub.

4. Refer to the *Reading and writing data from and to ADLS Gen2* recipe from *Chapter 2, Reading and Writing Data from and to Various Azure Services and File Formats,* to learn how to read and write data to and from ADLS Gen2. You can also refer to the following link to find out how to configure an ADLS Gen2 account in Azure: `https://docs.microsoft.com/en-us/azure/storage/blobs/ create-data-lake-storage-account`.

5. Open a provisioned ADLS Gen2 account and traverse to the **Access keys** section under **Security Networking** to grab the required connection strings and keys. Refer to the following screenshot from the Azure portal:

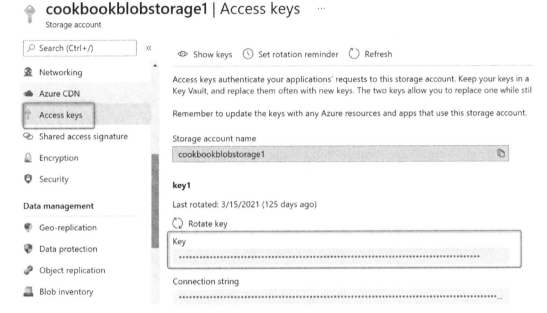

Figure 7.4 – ADLS Gen2 keys

6. Refer to the *Reading and writing data from and to an Azure SQL database using native connectors* recipe from *Chapter 2, Reading and Writing Data from and to Various Azure Services and File Formats,* to learn how to read and write data to and from an Azure **Structured Query Language** (**SQL**) database. You can also refer to the following link to learn how to create an Azure SQL database using the Azure portal: `https://docs.microsoft.com/en-us/azure/azure-sql/ database/single-database-create-quickstart?tabs=azure- portal`.

7. Open a provisioned Azure SQL database resource and click on **Connection strings** under **Settings** section section. Refer to the following screenshot from the Azure portal:

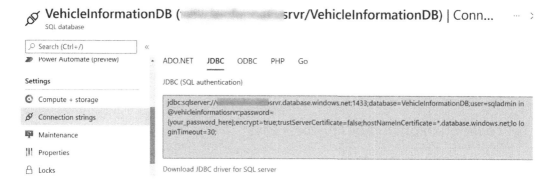

Figure 7.5 – SQL database connection string

8. Refer to the *Reading and writing data from and to Azure Synapse Dedicated SQL Pool using native connectors* recipe from *Chapter 2, Reading and Writing Data from and to Various Azure Services and File Formats,* to learn how to read and write data to and from Azure Synapse. You can also refer to the following link to learn how to configure an Azure Synapse workspace: `https://docs.microsoft.com/ en-us/azure/synapse-analytics/quickstart-create-workspace`.

9. Go to the provisioned Azure Synapse workspace SQL pool and traverse to the **Connection strings** section to grab the JDBC connection string. Refer to the following screenshot from the Azure portal:

Figure 7.6 – Synapse dedicated pool

You can pick the connection string based on your application connection type. We are using a **JavaScript Database Connectivity** (**JDBC**) connection string for connection to the Azure Synapse Dedicated SQL Pool and Azure SQL DB. In the next recipe, you will be learning how to generate the vehicle sensor data, which will be the source for this solution.

How it works...

We will require the connection strings and keys grabbed in the preceding section to connect the resources such as Azure Cosmos DB, ADLS Gen2 Storage Account, Event Hub for Kafka, and the Azure Synapse Dedicated SQL Pool. These connection strings and keys will be stored in Azure Key Vault and then they will be read into the Azure Databricks notebooks to access the required Azure resources.

Simulating a workload for streaming data

In this recipe, you will learn how to simulate the vehicle sensor data that can be sent to Event Hubs. In this recipe, we will be running a Python script that will be generating the sensor data for 10 vehicle IDs and learn how the events can be pushed to Event Hubs for Kafka.

Getting ready

Before you start on this recipe, make sure you have the latest version of Python installed on the machine from which you will be running the Python script. The Python script was tested on Python 3.8.

- You need to install `confluent_kafka` libraries by running `pip install confluent_kafka` from `bash`, PowerShell, or Command Prompt.

- You need to have Azure Event Hubs for Kafka, which is mentioned in the previous recipe, *Creating required Azure resources for the E2E demonstration.* In the mentioned recipe, you can find out how to get the Event Hubs connection string that will be used for the `bootstrap.servers` notebook variable.

- The Python script will need a `ccacert.pem` file, which you can find at `https://github.com/PacktPublishing/Azure-Databricks-Cookbook/tree/main/Chapter07/pythoncode`.

- You can find the Python script that needs to be executed at the following GitHub **Uniform Resource Locator (URL)**:

  `https://github.com/PacktPublishing/Azure-Databricks-Cookbook/blob/main/Chapter07/pythoncode/KafkaEventHub_EndtoEnd.py`

How to do it...

You will learn how to generate vehicle sensor data using a Python script with Event Hubs for Kafka. We have seen this approach in other chapters, but in this recipe, we are adding additional fields to the JSON code so that we can do different analytics on the vehicle sensor data.

1. You will be generating vehicle sensor data with 10 unique vehicles for which we have the make and model details in Azure SQL Database:

```
#Reading parquet files and adding a new column to the #
Sensor data is generated for on below 10 Vehicles
devices = ['4b1e829f-5f32-4ae9-b415-9e7f0eb15401',
'115e6d02-4a43-4131-b6af-9d2a8d642073', '90ccea91-416e-
453f-b582-e6f04f02ee40', 'aa7e09d0-92cb-4cc0-99e2-
04602ab0f85a', 'b51480fc-af07-491d-b914-fec46d7d7d47',
'5cb4ae8e-19de-40e1-96b5-874ffc43210b', 'c79935cc-0b88-
44ae-9765-a68d3c0fd37d', '04ac43cf-ed3c-4fb7-a15e-
2dabd3c8342e', '2832b3ec-222c-4049-9af5-45a8d66d6b58',
'288e3ee8-ea29-489b-9c3d-07e7c6d6ee99']
```

Here, we are capturing the latitude and longitude information about the vehicle at the time the sensor data is emitted. For this demonstration, we are using the latitude and longitude of Manhattan, Brooklyn, Staten Island, the Bronx, and Queens:

```
latlong =[[40.730610,-73.984016],[40.650002, -73.949997],
[40.579021, -74.151535],[40.837048,
-73.865433],[40.742054, -73.769417]]
```

2. We will get the location and vehicle master details from Azure SQL Database, which has the make, model, location, and borough details.

3. Here is the code we are using to send the data to Event Hubs. Change the topic name if you are using a different name for the event hub before running the code:

```
topic= 'VehicleSensorEventHub' #Event Hub name
for dev in devices:
    for y in range(0,random.randrange(20)): # For each
device, produce up to 20 events max.
        lfi=0
        if(y%2==0):
            lfi=random.randint(0,1)
        try:
        # Create a dummy vehicle reading.
            print(y)
            latlonglocal = random.choice(latlong)
            reading = {'id': dev, 'eventtime':
str(datetime.datetime.utcnow()+timedelta(hours=y)),
'rpm': random.randrange(100), 'speed': random.randint(70,
120), 'kms': random.randint(100, 10000),'lfi':
lfi,'lat':latlonglocal[0],'long':latlonglocal[1]}


            msgformatted = json.dumps(reading) # Convert
the reading into a JSON object.
            p.produce(topic, msgformatted,
callback=delivery_callback)
            p.flush()
            # time.sleep(1)


        except BufferError as e:
            sys.stderr.write('some error')


sys.stderr.write('%% Waiting for %d deliveries\n' %
len(p))
p.flush()
```

4. For every vehicle ID, we are generating up to 20 events and simulating the scenario of sending data every hour. Each vehicle is sending information to Event Hubs for Kafka (`VehicleSensorEventHub`) on an hourly basis:

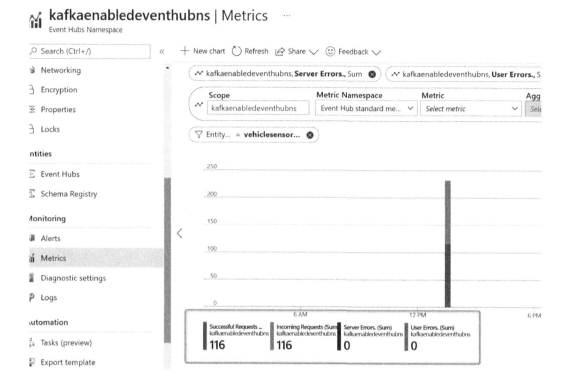

Figure 7.7 – Event Hubs incoming requests

5. *Figure 7.7* is a screenshot from `VehicleSensorEventHub`, showing all the messages were consumed and there is no error.

6. The following screenshot shows that in total, there were 200 messages received by the event hub:

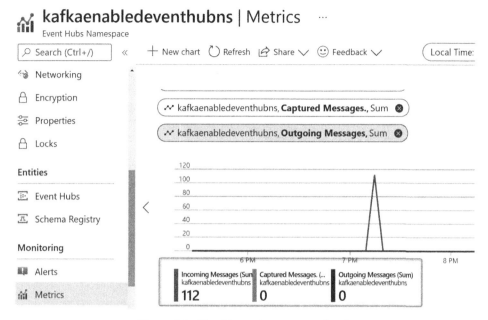

Figure 7.8 – Total incoming message details

With the help of our Python script, we were able to simulate vehicle sensor data and send the streaming data to Event Hubs.

How it works...

The Python script generates upto 20 events per vehicle and in total for single execution of Python script you are sending max 200 messages to the Event Hubs for Kafka. You can change the number of messages per vehicle as well if you want to send more or fewer messages to Event Hubs.

These are the fields of the JSON message:

- `id`—Vehicle ID
- `eventtime`—Date and time when the message was captured from the vehicle
- `rpm`—Rotations per minute of the vehicle
- `speed`—Speed of the vehicle captured
- `kms`—How many kilometers the vehicle has run so far
- `lfi`—Low fuel indicator
- `lat`—Latitude of the vehicle at the time of the event capture
- `long`—Longitude of the vehicle at the time of the event capture

We will use this information to create a data warehouse model and create Power BI reports for some interesting insights in upcoming recipes of this chapter. In the next recipe, we will learn how to consume the data from Event Hubs and store the sensor data in different sinks.

Processing streaming and batch data using Structured Streaming

We tend to see scenarios where we need to process batch data in **comma-separated values** (**CSV**) or Parquet format stored in ADLS Gen2 and from real-time streaming sources such as Event Hubs together. In this recipe, we will learn how we use Structured Streaming for both batch and real-time streaming sources and process the data together. We will also fetch the data from Azure SQL Database for all metadata information required for our processing.

Getting ready

Before starting, you need to have a valid subscription with contributor access, a Databricks workspace (Premium), and an ADLS Gen2 storage account. Also, ensure that you have been through the previous recipes of this chapter.

We have executed the notebook on Databricks Runtime Version 7.5 having Spark 3.0.1.

You can follow along by running the steps in the following notebook:

https://github.com/PacktPublishing/Azure-Databricks-Cookbook/blob/main/Chapter07/7.1-End-to-End%20Data%20Pipeline.ipynb

We have created a /mnt/SensorData mount point for the ADLS Gen2 storage account that has a container named sensordata, as shown in the following screenshot:

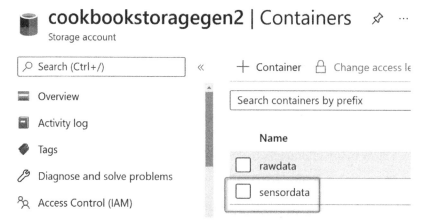

Figure 7.9 – ADLS Gen2 folder details

You can find the Parquet files at `https://github.com/PacktPublishing/Azure-Databricks-Cookbook/tree/main/Chapter07/HistoricalData` and copy them to `/mnt/SensorData/historicalvehicledata/Hist/data`:

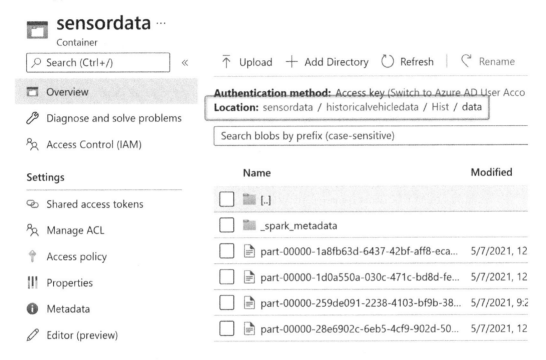

Figure 7.10 – Vehicle sensor historical data

Data in the `Hist` folder will be used as the source for historical data used in the notebook.

We are storing the master data for the vehicle and location in Azure SQL Database. Create a SQL database with the name `VehicleInformationDB` and run the SQL scripts, which will create a required master table and populate them. You can get the SQL scripts from `https://github.com/PacktPublishing/Azure-Databricks-Cookbook/tree/main/Chapter07/sqlscripts`.

How to do it...

Let's understand how to use Structured Streaming for reading data from both ADLS Gen2 and Event Hubs for Kafka and combine the data from two different types of sources for further processing.

1. Run the following command, which will create a connection string required to read data from Azure SQL Database:

```
sqldbusername = dbutils.secrets.get
(scope="KeyVaultScope",key="VehicleInformationDBUserId")

sqldbpwd=dbutils.secrets.
get(scope="KeyVaultScope",key="VehicleInformationDBPwd")


jdbcHostname = "vehicledemosensorsqlsrv.database.windows.
net"

jdbcDatabase = "VehicleInformationDB"

jdbcPort = 1433

jdbcUrl = "jdbc:sqlserver://
{0}:{1};database={2};user={3};password={4}".
format(jdbcHostname, jdbcPort, jdbcDatabase,
sqldbusername, sqldbpwd)

connectionProperties = {
    "user" : sqldbusername,
    "password" : sqldbpwd,
    "driver" : "com.microsoft.sqlserver.jdbc.
SQLServerDriver"
}
```

2. As you can see from the preceding code, we are using Azure Key Vault to get the password for `sqluser`.

3. Run the following command, which will read `dbo.VehicleInformation` and `dbo.LocationInfo` tables from Azure SQL Database and put it in a DataFrame:

```
vehicleInfo = "(select
VehicleId,Make,Model,Category,ModelYear from dbo.
VehicleInformation) vehicle"

df_vehicleInfo = spark.read.jdbc(url=jdbcUrl,
table=vehicleInfo, properties=connectionProperties)

display(df_vehicleInfo)

locationInfo = "(select
Borough,Location,Latitude,Longitude from dbo.
LocationInfo) vehicle"

df_locationInfo = spark.read.jdbc(url=jdbcUrl,
table=locationInfo, properties=connectionProperties)

display(df_locationInfo)
```

4. In this recipe, we are reading data from Gen2 storage using the `readStream` **Application Programming Interface (API)**. You can run the following code to start `readstream` on the `/mnt/SensorData/historicalvehicledata/Hist/data` folder:

```
kafkaDF = (spark.readStream \
   .schema(jsonschema)
  .format("parquet") \
   .load(hist_dir("Hist")).withColumn("source",
lit(topic)))
```

5. We have created a function that will keep checking for new data in `/mnt/SensorData/historicalvehicledata/Hist/data` and load data into a Delta table that is on `/mnt/SensorData/vehiclestreamingdata/Hist/delta/`. Run the following code to create a function to read data from a historical location and write it to a Delta location:

```
# Function to read data from ADLS gen-2 and writing as
delta format
def append_batch_source():
  topic ="historical"
  kafkaDF = (spark.readStream \
     .schema(jsonschema)
    .format("parquet") \
     .load(hist_dir("Hist")).withColumn("source",
lit(topic)))

  query=kafkaDF.selectExpr(
            "id"            \
            ,"eventtime"        \
            ,"rpm"    \
            ,"speed" \
            ,"kms" \
            ,"lfi" \
            ,"lat" \
            ,"long" \
            ,"source"
            ) \
        .writeStream.format("delta") \
```

```
                  .option("checkpointLocation",checkpoint_
dir("Hist")) \
                .outputMode("append") \
                .start(delta_dir("Hist"))


    return query
```

6. Running the following commands will read data from Event Hubs for Kafka and ADLS Gen2 and will continuously write data to a Delta table as and when data is available in the source:

```
# Reading data from EventHubs for Kafka
query_source1 = append_kafkadata_
stream(topic='vehiclesensoreventhub')


# Reading data from Historical location ( in this example
its from ADLS Gen-2 having historical data for Vehicle
Sensor.)
# There may be cases where historical data can be added
to this location from any other source where the schema
is same for all the files. In such scenarios using
readStream API on Gen-2 location will keep polling for
new data and when available, it will be ingested
query_source2 = append_batch_source()
```

7. Run the following code to create a Delta table for historical data:

```
#Create historical table
spark.sql("CREATE TABLE IF NOT EXISTS VehicleSensor.
VehicleDelta_Historical USING DELTA LOCATION '{}'".
format(delta_dir("Hist")))
```

At this point, we have two streaming queries running that are reading data from Event Hubs for Kafka and writing to Delta tables and other reading data from the ADLS Gen2 storage and writing to a different Delta table continuously.

How it works...

The reason we are using a streaming API for batch data as well is to handle scenarios where we expect historical data to come at a later point in time. To avoid making any changes to the existing code or running any ad hoc code to handle new batch data, we are using the readstream API that checks for any new file; if found, it will be ingested and loaded into a historical Delta table. Without using streaming APIs for historical batch source, we might have to put in additional logic to identify when to handle historical data.

Understanding the various stages of transforming data

Building a near-real-time warehouse is being used these days as a common architectural pattern for many organizations who want to avoid the delays that we see in on-premises data warehouse systems. Customers want to view the data in near real time in their new modern warehouse architecture and they can achieve that by using Azure Databricks Delta Lake with Spark Structured Streaming APIs. In this recipe, you will learn the various stages involved in building a near-real-time data warehouse in Delta Lake. We are storing the data in a denormalized way in Delta Lake, but in a Synapse dedicated SQL pool, we are storing the data in facts and dimension tables to enhance reporting capabilities.

As part of data processing in Delta Lake, you will be creating three Delta tables, as follows:

1. **Bronze table**: This will hold the data as received from Event Hubs for Kafka.

2. **Silver table**: We will implement the required business rules and data cleansing process and join with **lookup tables (LUTs)** to fetch additional details and load these into the Silver table. This table will store cleansed data.

3. **Gold table**: This table will store the aggregated data from the Silver Delta table, which can be used by downstream consumers or for reporting purposes.

In the previous recipe, we saw how to read streaming data from Event Hubs for Kafka and ADLS Gen2. In this recipe, you will learn how to join the streaming data, join with LUTs, and do some data processing to load it into Bronze, Silver, and Gold Delta tables.

Getting ready

You can follow along by running the steps in the following notebook:

```
https://github.com/PacktPublishing/Azure-Databricks-Cookbook/
blob/main/Chapter07/7.1-End-to-End%20Data%20Pipeline.ipynb
```

How to do it...

In this section, you will be learning how to join data from streaming sources and LUTs, and how to perform certain transformations on the data received from streaming and batch sources.

1. Execute the following code to create the Bronze Delta table:

```sql
%sql
-- Creating the delta table on delta location for Bronze
data
CREATE DATABASE IF NOT EXISTS VehicleSensor;
CREATE TABLE IF NOT EXISTS VehicleSensor.VehicleDelta_
Bronze
USING DELTA
LOCATION "dbfs:/mnt/SensorData/vehiclestreamingdata/
Bronze/delta"
```

2. Run the following command to start streaming data from the Bronze Delta table, and we can apply some business logic to load incremental data to the Silver Delta tables:

```
#Streaming Data from Bronze Delta Table. This will help
in only extracting new data coming from Event Hubs to be
loaded into Silver Delta tables.
df_bronze=spark.readStream.format("delta").
option("latestFirst", "true").table("VehicleSensor.
VehicleDelta_Bronze")
#Creating Temp View on Bronze DF
df_bronze.createOrReplaceTempView("vw_TempBronze")
```

3. Run the following command to join the streaming data from the historical Delta table and the Bronze Delta table:

```
#Joining both historical and Bronze Streaming Data
df_bronze_hist = df_bronze.union(df_historical)
```

4. Running the following code will create a Silver Delta table:

```
# We are always combining data from streaming and batch
data by using Structured streaming


df_silver= spark.sql("select s.*,m.Make,m.Model,m.
Category, Year(eventtime) as Year, month(eventtime) as
Month,day(eventtime) as Day, \
```

```
                    hour(eventtime) as Hour,l.Borough,l.
Location   \
                    from vw_TempBronzeHistorical s \
                    left join vw_VehicleMaster m on s.id
= m.VehicleId \
                    left join vw_LocationMaster l on
s.lat = l.Latitude and s.long = l.Longitude") \
            .writeStream.format("delta").
option("MergeSchem","True") \
            .outputMode("append") \
            .option("checkpointLocation",checkpoint_
dir("Silver"))   \
            .start(delta_dir("Silver"))
```

5. The following command creates a Silver Delta table at the location mentioned in *Step 4*:

```
%sql
CREATE TABLE IF NOT EXISTS VehicleSensor.VehicleDelta_
Silver
USING DELTA
LOCATION "dbfs:/mnt/SensorData/vehiclestreamingdata/
Silver/delta/"
```

6. The last step for building a near-real-time warehouse in Delta Lake is to create final Delta tables that store all the aggregated data (Gold Delta tables):

```
df_gold=(spark.readStream.format("delta").
option("latestFirst", "true").table("VehicleSensor.
VehicleDelta_Silver") \

.groupBy(window('eventtime',"1
hour"),"Make","Borough","Location","Month","Day","Hour").
count()) \

                              .writeStream.
format("delta") \

.outputMode("complete") \

.option("checkpointLocation",checkpoint_dir("Gold"))   \

.start(delta_dir("Gold"))
```

At this stage, we have all the required Delta tables created that are required for building near-real-time dashboards and visualizations. As and when data is getting ingested from Event Hubs, we will see the counts changing dynamically as we are streaming data from these Delta tables.

How it works...

We have used `outputmode("complete")` as we are not handling a late-coming data scenario. You can use `outputmode("append")` and use watermarking logic so that you can drop data that is older than the specified time. Using `outputmode("complete")`, we are overwriting the aggregated data at every trigger, provided new data is found. This aggregated table can grow huge if we are receiving millions of records every day and, in such scenarios, it's best to go with aggregating data with watermarking logic so that only incremental data is processed and not the entire history from Silver delta tables.

In our next recipe, you will see how we will take the Silver Delta table data and load it into an Azure Synapse dedicated SQL pool and create a data warehouse with the required facts and dimensions tables.

Loading the transformed data into Azure Cosmos DB and a Synapse dedicated pool

In this recipe, we will learn how to write the transformed data into various sinks such as Azure Cosmos DB and a Synapse dedicated SQL pool. The processed data needs to be saved in a different destination for further consumption or to build a data warehouse. Azure Cosmos DB is one of the most widely used NoSQL databases and acts as a source for web portals. Similarly, an Azure Synapse dedicated SQL pool is used for creating a data warehouse.

Customers want to view data in near real time in their warehouse or web application so that they can get insights from the data in real time. In the following section, you will learn how to read data from the Silver zone (Delta table), do some data processing, and then finally load the data into Cosmos DB and to a Synapse dedicated SQL pool.

Getting ready

In the previous recipe, we saw how data was loaded into Bronze, Silver, and Gold Delta tables. In this recipe, we will learn how to load the processed data from the Silver zone to final destinations such as Azure Cosmos DB and an Azure Synapse dedicated SQL pool. You can follow along by running the steps in the following notebook to ingest data in Cosmos DB: `https://github.com/PacktPublishing/Azure-Databricks-Cookbook/tree/main/Chapter07` 7-4.Writing to Cosmos DB.

> **Note**
>
> The Cosmos DB connector is not supported in Spark version 3.0 at the time of writing this recipe, hence you need to run this notebook on a cluster having a Spark version earlier than 3.0. You can refer to the *Reading and writing data from and to Azure Cosmos DB* recipe from *Chapter 2, Reading and Writing Data from and to Various Azure Services and File Formats,* for more information on the Cosmos DB connector. We have executed this notebook on Databricks Runtime Version 6.4 having Spark 2.4.5

You can follow along by running the steps in the following notebook for ingesting data into an Azure Synapse dedicated SQL pool:

```
https://github.com/PacktPublishing/Azure-Databricks-Cookbook/
tree/main/Chapter07/7-5.Writing to Synapse Dedicate Pool
```

There are two separate sets of notebooks for ingesting data into Cosmos DB and to an Azure Synapse dedicated pool, as the Cosmos DB connector is not supported in a higher Spark version (3.0 and above), whereas there is no dependency as such on the cluster configuration for ingesting data into an Azure Synapse dedicated SQL pool.

Before proceeding, we need endpoint, master key, database, and collection details from the provisioned Azure Cosmos DB account. Also, you need a JDBC connection string for the Azure Synapse dedicated pool.

1. Go to the Azure portal and search for the Azure Cosmos DB account. Refer to the *Creating required Azure resources for the E2E demonstration* recipe from the current chapter if you have not created an Azure Cosmos DB account:

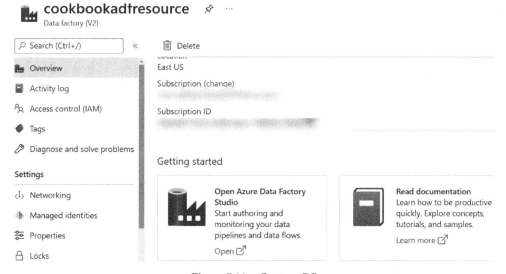

Figure 7.11 – Cosmos DB

2. After browsing to the Cosmos DB account, go to the **Keys** section to copy the **Uniform Resource Identifier** (**URI**) and PRIMARY key. These will be required in the notebook for establishing a connection with the Cosmos DB.

3. Go to the **Data Explorer** section and create a database and collection named vehicle and vehicleinformation with the default settings:

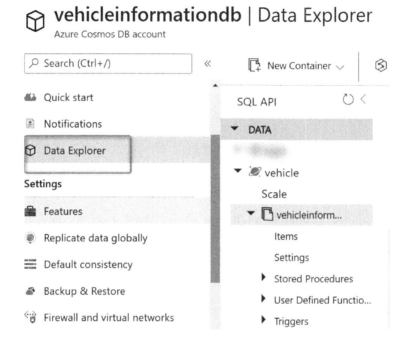

Figure 7.12 – Cosmos DB container

4. You can get the JDBC connection string of the Azure Synapse dedicated SQL pool from the **Connection strings** section:

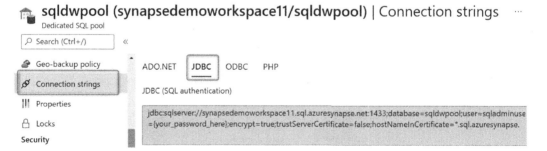

Figure 7.13 – Azure Synapse JDBC connection string

> **Note**
>
> The data warehouse model we are creating in this recipe is a simple model. It is just to illustrate how we can get started on loading near-real-time data into a Synapse dedicated SQL pool and build a warehouse model. We are not following any best practices for building a data warehouse model for this demonstration as this is out of the scope of this book.

How to do it...

In this section, you will learn how to save the enriched data from the Silver zone Delta tables to destinations such as Cosmos DB and an Azure Synapse dedicated SQL pool.

1. Once you install the Cosmos connector libraries in your Databricks cluster, replace the URI, master key, database name, and collection name copied from the preceding *Getting ready* section in the following code to connect the Azure Cosmos DB account:

```
writeConfig = {
    "Endpoint": "https://vehicleinformationdb.
documents.azure.com:443/",
    "Masterkey": "xxxxxxxxxxxxxxxxxxxxxxxxxxx",
    "Database": "vehicle",
    "Collection": "vehicleinformation",
    "Upsert": "true",
    "WritingBatchSize": "500"
}
```

2. Run the following command to read the data loaded into the Silver Delta tables using streaming API. Using this option data is continuously read from the Delta table:

```
vehicledf = spark.readStream.format("delta").
option("latestFirst", "true").table("VehicleSensor.
VehicleDelta_Silver")
```

3. Run the following command to insert the data read from the Silver table to Cosmos DB:

```
changeFeed = (vehicledf
              .writeStream
              .format("com.microsoft.azure.cosmosdb.
spark.streaming.CosmosDBSinkProvider")
              .outputMode("append")
              .options(**writeConfig)
```

```
            .option("checkpointLocation", "/mnt/
SensorData/vehiclestreamingdata/cosmos/chkpnt/")
            .start())
```

4. After executing the preceding command, you can verify the data in the Cosmos DB collection:

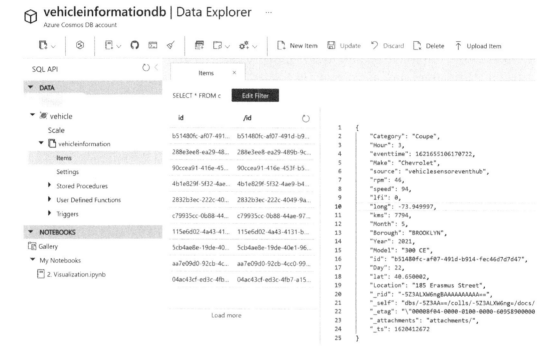

Figure 7.14 – Cosmos DB table details

5. You can see the data has been inserted into the Cosmos DB and can be consumed by other downstream applications. As and when new data is loaded in the Silver Delta table, the same data is ingested into Cosmos DB continuously.

Now, let's go through the steps to save the data in an Azure Synapse SQL pool.

1. Open **SQL Server Management Studio** (**SSMS**) and execute the following query to create a table called `vehicleinformation` in the database. This is a staging table for the streaming data and in the following steps, we will see how to transform data from this table to a fact table:

```
CREATE TABLE [dbo].[vehicleinformation]
(
    id [varchar](100),
    eventtime Datetime,
    rpm [int],
    speed [int],
    kms [int],
    lfi [int],
    lat decimal(10,6),
    long decimal(10,6),
    source [varchar](50),
    Make [varchar](50),
    Model [varchar](50),
    Category [varchar](50),
    Year [int],
    Month [int],
    Day [int],
    Hour [int],
    Borough [varchar](50),
    Location [varchar](50)
)
WITH
(
    CLUSTERED COLUMNSTORE INDEX
)
GO
```

2. The following code is specifying ADLS Gen2 details such as storage account name, blob container name, and the primary key:

```
blobStorage = "demosynapsestorageacct.blob.core.windows.
net"
blobContainer = "demo"
blobAccessKey = "xxxxxxxxxxxxxxxxxxxxxxxxxx"
tempDir = "wasbs://" + blobContainer + "@" + blobStorage
+"/tempDirs"
```

3. Execute the following code to set the Hadoop configuration associated with the Spark context. This is shared by all the notebooks:

```
acntInfo = "fs.azure.account.key."+ blobStorage
sc._jsc.hadoopConfiguration().set(acntInfo,
blobAccessKey)
```

4. We are using the `readStream` streaming API to read the data from `VehicleSensor.VehicleDelta_Silver` Delta Table:

```
vehicledf = spark.readStream.format("delta").
option("latestFirst", "true").table("VehicleSensor.
VehicleDelta_Silver")
```

5. Execute the following code by replacing the `url` connection string with the value you have captured in *Step 4* of the *Getting ready* section. The following code is writing the data to the `vehicleinformation` staging table in the Azure Synapse dedicated SQL pool:

```
vehicledf.writeStream
.format("com.databricks.spark.sqldw")
.option("url", "jdbc:sqlserver://synapsedemoworkspace11.
sql.azuresynapse.net:1433;database=sqldwpool;user=xxxx;
password=xxxxxx;encrypt=true;trustServerCertificate=false;
hostNameInCertificate=*.sql.azuresynapse.net;
loginTimeout=30;authentication=ActiveDirectoryPassword")
.option("tempDir", tempDir)
.option("forwardSparkAzureStorageCredentials", "true")
.option("dbTable", "vehicleinformation")
.option("checkpointLocation", "/mnt/SensorData/
vehiclestreamingdata/Synapse/chkpnt/")
.start()
```

Now, we will learn how to build a data warehouse in Azure Synapse using the streaming vehicle sensor data available in the [dbo].[vehicleinformation] staging table.

1. Execute the following SQL script to create dimension tables named Dim_VehicleMaster and Dim_Location with the master data populated:

   https://github.com/PacktPublishing/Azure-Databricks-Cookbook/blob/main/Chapter07/sqlscripts/masterData.sql

2. Execute the following code to provide the details of the blob container. Replace the blob storage account name, container, and access key as per your storage account. You can use Azure Key Vault to store the access keys:

   ```
   blobStorage = "xxx.blob.core.windows.net"
   blobContainer = "synapse"
   blobAccessKey = "xxxxxxxxx"
   ```

3. Running the following code will set up a temporary directory for the Azure Synapse dedicated SQL pool:

   ```
   tempDir = "wasbs://" + blobContainer + "@" + blobStorage +"/tempDirs"
   print(tempDir)
   ```

4. The following code sets up blob storage configuration for the Spark context:

   ```
   spark.conf.set("fs.azure.account.key.xxxx.blob.core.windows.net","xxxxxxx")
   ```

5. Execute the following code to read the Silver zone data from the Delta table:

   ```
   vehicledf = spark.readStream.format("delta").option("latestFirst", "true").table("VehicleSensor.VehicleDelta_Silver")
   ```

6. To save the vehicle sensor data to an Azure Synapse Dedicated SQL Pool table, run the following code. We are using the writeStream API to continuously write data to Synapse dedicated SQL pool staging tables. Using this approach, you can build a near-real-time data warehouse in a Synapse Dedicated SQL Pool:

   ```
   vehicledf.writeStream \
     .format("com.databricks.spark.sqldw") \
     .trigger(once=True) \
     .option("url", "jdbc:sqlserver://synapsedemoworkspace11.sql.azuresynapse.net:1433;database=sqldwpool;
   ```

```
user=xxxx@synapsedemoworkspace11;password=xxxx;
encrypt=false;trustServerCertificate=false;
hostNameInCertificate=*.sql.azuresynapse.net;
loginTimeout=30;") \
    .option("tempDir", tempDir) \
    .option("forwardSparkAzureStorageCredentials", "true") \
    .option("dbTable", ]"stgvehicleinformation") \
    .option("checkpointLocation", "/mnt/SensorData/
vehiclestreamingdata/Synapse/chkpnt3/") \
    .option("truncate", "true") \
    .start()
```

7. Open SSMS and connect to your Azure Synapse dedicated SQL pool. You can see the dimension tables and staging table containing the vehicle information data:

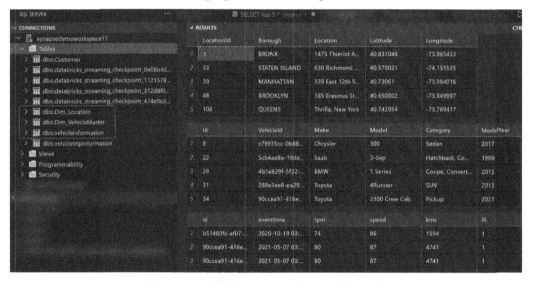

Figure 7.15 – Tables in Azure Synapse SQL pool

Once all the steps are executed successfully, you will see the data is available in Azure Synapse SQL dedicated pool tables. Once the data is loaded into staging tables, run through the following steps to populate fact and dimension tables.

8. Execute the following query to create a fact table:

```
SET ANSI_NULLS ON

GO


SET QUOTED_IDENTIFIER ON
```

```
GO

CREATE TABLE [dbo].[dbo.vehicletripinformation]
(
        [RecordId] bigint PRIMARY KEY NONCLUSTERED NOT
ENFORCED identity(1,1),
        [LocationId] int NOT NULL,
        [VehilceId] int NOT NULL,
        [eventtime] [datetime2](7) NULL,
        [rpm] [int] NULL,
        [speed] [int] NULL,
        [kms] [int] NULL,
        [lfi] [int] NULL,
        [source] [varchar](50) NULL,
        [Year] [int] NULL,
        [Month] [int] NULL,
        [Day] [int] NULL,
        [Hour] [int] NULL


)
WITH
(
        DISTRIBUTION = ROUND_ROBIN,
        CLUSTERED COLUMNSTORE INDEX
)
GO
```

> **Note**
>
> An explanation of data warehouse concepts is out of the scope of this cookbook and readers are expected to know the basics of these.

9.　In the preceding step, we have created a fact table and we will now create a stored procedure that will populate the fact table based on the data coming into the staging table. Execute the following script to create a stored procedure in the SQL database that will read the data from the staging table and insert the data into the fact table after resolving the dimension keys. In this demonstration, we are expecting only new data and no updates to existing data, hence we are only inserting data into the fact table:

```
CREATE PROC dbo.usp_PopulateVehicleTripFact
AS
BEGIN

    INSERT INTO [dbo].[vehicletripinformation](
[LocationId],[VehilceId],[eventtime],[rpm],[speed],[kms],
[lfi],[source],[Year],[Month],[Day],[Hour])
    SELECT
    DL.[LocationId],
    VM.id,
    [eventtime],
    [rpm],
    [speed],
    [kms],
    [lfi],
    [source],
    [Year],
    [Month],
    [Day],
    [Hour]
    FROM [dbo].[vehicleinformation] VI
    INNER JOIN [dbo].[Dim_Location] DL
    ON VI.[Lat]= DL.[Latitude] AND  VI.[Long]=DL.
[Longitude]
    INNER JOIN [dbo].[Dim_VehicleMaster] VM
    ON VI.[id]=VM.[VehicleId]
END
```

This stored procedure can be executed manually to populate the fact table. We will learn how to automate this entire data flow in the upcoming recipe, *Using ADF for orchestrating the E2E pipeline*.

How it works...

We have read the streaming data from Event Hubs, processed it, and saved data in different zones such as Silver, Bronze, and Gold. Data from the Silver zone is then ingested into Cosmos DB using the Spark connector. Similarly, the same data is also ingested into an Azure Synapse SQL pool database using the JDBC connector. Dimension table data is loaded into the Synapse SQL pool using the SQL scripts, and the fact table is populated using a stored procedure. Our data warehouse is ready for data analysis. We can build reports for data analysis on the fact and dimension tables. We are not building the `dbo.DimDate` but you can create and populate the table using any method you are aware of

Creating a visualization and dashboard in a notebook for near-real-time analytics

Azure Databricks provides the capability to create various visualizations using Spark SQL and to create dashboards from various visualizations. This helps data engineers and data scientists to create quick dashboards for near-real-time analytics. In this recipe, you will learn how to create visualizations in a notebook and how to create a dashboard for static and near-real-time reporting. The dashboard capabilities of Azure Databricks are very limited when compared to reporting tools such as Power BI. If you need more drill-downs and various levels of slicing and dicing, then you can use Power BI for reporting purposes.

Getting ready

Before starting, we need to ensure we have executed the following notebook. The following notebook creates the required Delta tables on which we can build our visualizations and dashboard in the notebook:

```
https://github.com/PacktPublishing/Azure-Databricks-Cookbook/
blob/main/Chapter07/7.1-End-to-End%20Data%20Pipeline.ipynb
```

How to do it...

We will explore how to create various visualizations in a notebook and how to create a dashboard that will display near-real-time data as new data is ingested.

1. Run the following code to create a view on the `VehicleSensor.VehicleDelta_Silver` table:

   ```
   df_silver_agg=(spark.readStream.format("delta").table
   ("VehicleSensor.VehicleDelta_Silver"))

   df_silver_agg.createOrReplaceTempView("vw_AggDetails")
   ```

2. Run the following code to create aggregations for a bar chart:

```sql
%sql
SELECT Make,Model,coalesce(Borough,"UnKnown")AS Borough,lfi
AS LowFuelIndicator,Location,Year,Month,Day,COUNT(*) as
TotalVehicles
FROM vw_AggDetails
WHERE lfi=1
GROUP BY Year,Make,Model,coalesce(Borough,"UnKnown"),
Location,Month,Day,lfi
ORDER BY Year DESC,Month DESC,TotalVehicles DESC
```

3. After executing the preceding code, click on the **Display Bar Chart** option, as
    shown in the following screenshot.

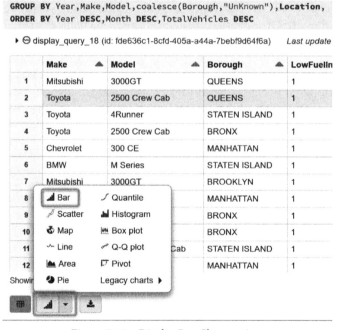

Figure 7.16 – Display Bar Chart option

4. After you get the bar chart visualization, click on **Plot Options…** and select the required columns in **Keys**, **Series groupings**, and **Values**, as shown in the following screenshot:

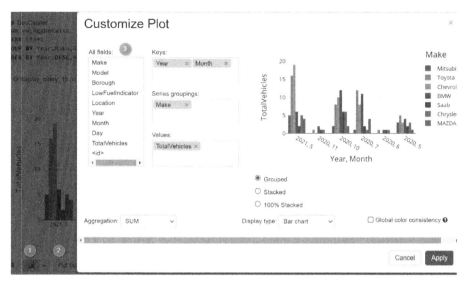

Figure 7.17 – Creating a visualization with aggregation

5. Run the following command to create another visualization and follow the same steps mentioned previously to do this, but this time we are creating a pie chart instead of a bar chart:

```
%sql
SELECT Make,Borough,Year,Month,COUNT(*) as TotalVehicles
FROM vw_AggDetails
GROUP BY Make,Borough,Year,Month
```

6. The following screenshot will be the output after running the preceding command
    and picking a pie chart for visualization:

```
SELECT Make,Borough,Year,Month,COUNT(*) as TotalVehicles
FROM vw_AggDetails
GROUP BY Make,Borough,Year,Month
```

▸ (1) Spark Jobs

▸ ⊖ display_query_19 (id: 228f3487-e444-4c83-8e17-cd953db6137c)   *Last upd*

Lost connection to cluster. The notebook may have been detac
yError.

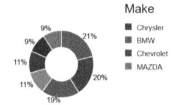

Figure 7.18 – Pie chart visualization

7. To create a dashboard in the notebook, we should select a visualization and create
    a dashboard for the first time, and for other visualizations, we need to select the
    dashboard we have already created. The following screenshot shows the steps to
    create a dashboard and pin visualizations to the dashboard:

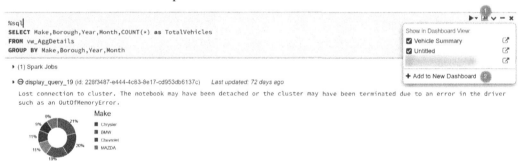

Figure 7.19 – Creating a dashboard

8. When you click on **Add to New Dashboard**, as shown in the preceding screenshot, a new tab will be opened where you can give a name for your dashboard. After creating a dashboard, you can pin a visualization from a different cell to the same dashboard:

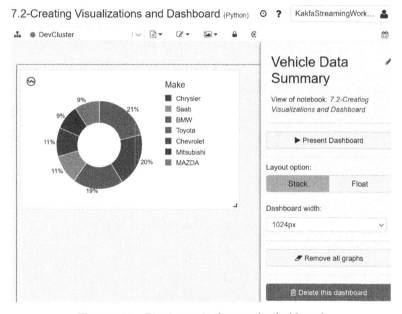

Figure 7.20 – Pinning a pie chart to the dashboard

9. As you can see from the following screenshot, we are adding another visualization to the same dashboard:

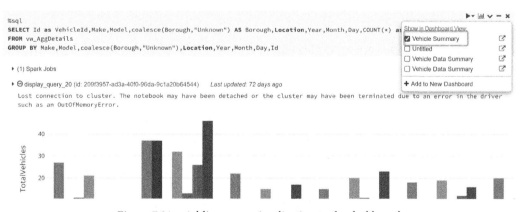

Figure 7.21 – Adding more visualization to the dashboard

10. The following screenshot depicts visualizations being pinned to the dashboard:

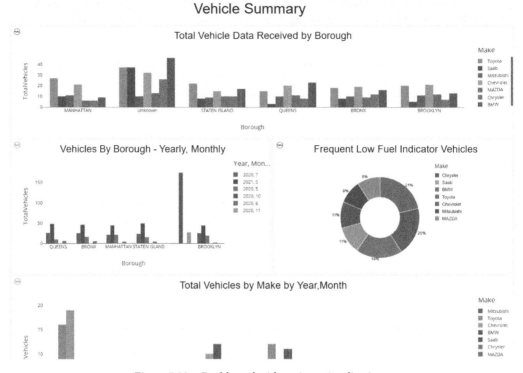

Figure 7.22 – Dashboard with various visualizations

All the visualizations in the dashboard will show near-real-time data as and when new data is ingested, and you don't have to refresh the page.

How it works...

Creating a dashboard in Azure Databricks is a quick way to view and analyze data in near real time and can be shared with other users. You can pin both streaming queries and static data to the same dashboard.

Creating a visualization in Power BI for near-real-time analytics

Before starting, we need to ensure we have executed the following notebook. This notebook creates the required tables on which we can build out visualizations and dashboards in the notebook: `https://github.com/PacktPublishing/Azure-Databricks-Cookbook/blob/main/Chapter07/7.1-End-to-End%20 Data%20Pipeline.ipynb`.

Getting ready

Before starting to work on this recipe, you need to get the **server hostname** and the **HyperText Transfer Protocol (HTTP) path details** for the Azure Databricks clusters.

Go to the **Clusters** tab in the Azure Databricks workspace and select the cluster you are using. Under **Configuration**, you will find advanced options—select the **JDBC/ODBC** option to get the details about the server hostname and HTTP path, as shown in the following screenshot:

Figure 7.23 – Cluster configuration details

Copy the entire string for the server hostname and HTTP path that you will use in this recipe. Details about Power BI visualization settings are outside the scope of this book. We are showing ways in which you can connect to a Delta table from Power BI for near-real-time reports. You can create any kind of visualization that you need.

How to do it...

In this recipe, you will learn the steps involved to create visualizations on the `VehicleSensor.VehicleDeltaAggregated` Delta table that was created by running the `/7.1-End-to-End Data Pipeline.ipynb` notebook.

1. Open Power BI Desktop, select **Get data**, and search for `azure databricks`, as shown in the following screenshot, then select the **Azure Databricks** connector and click on **Connect**:

Figure 7.24 – Connecting to Delta table from Power BI

2. You will be prompted to enter values for the **Server Hostname** and **HTTP path** fields. You can paste the values that you captured in the *Getting ready* section of this recipe. Select the **DirectQuery** option as we want the data to change as and when new data is ingested:

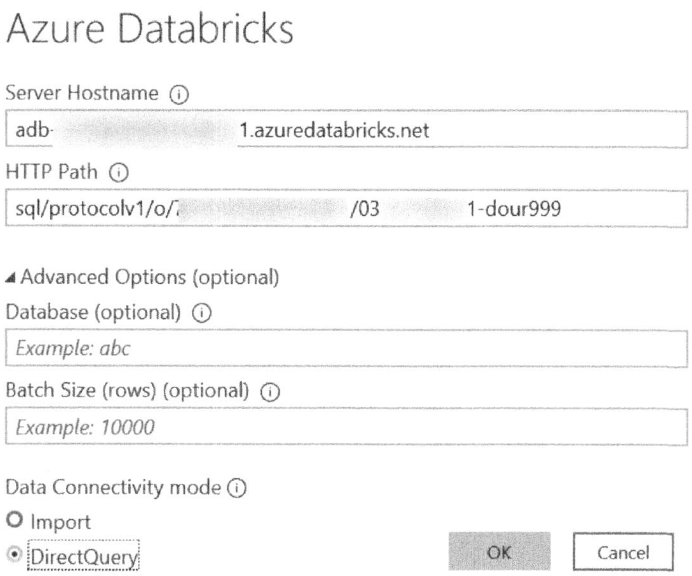

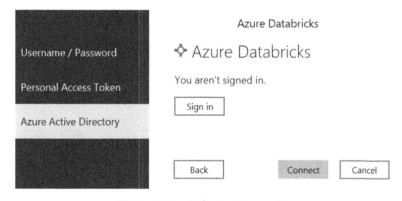

Figure 7.25 – Connecting to Delta table from Power BI (continued)

3. Next, Power BI will prompt you for authentication. You can choose any option —we are using **Azure Active Directory** for this demonstration:

Figure 7.26 – Authentication option

4. After connecting, select a database and table on which you want to create the various visualizations, as shown in the following screenshot:

Figure 7.27 – Loading data

5. You can click on **Load** and create a visualization of your choice on this data. Here is a screenshot of a dashboard you can create:

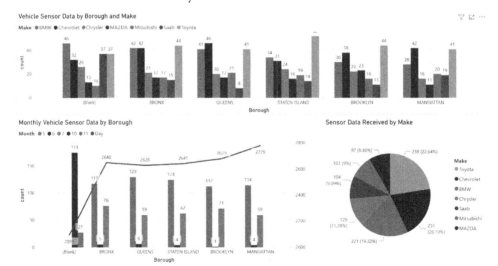

Figure 7.28 – Power BI visualization

You can add various visualizations as per your needs and reporting requirements to prepare a dashboard.

How it works...

Power BI is a preferred reporting tool in Azure and can combine data from various sources. We have used the native Azure Databricks connector that allows us to directly query the Delta Lake without worrying about the size of the data. Azure Databricks **Open Database Connectivity** (**ODBC**) drivers provide reduced query latency for providing near-real-time data.

Using Azure Data Factory (ADF) to orchestrate the E2E pipeline

ADF is a serverless data integration and data transformation Azure service. It's a cloud **Extract Transform Load** (**ETL**)/**Extract Load Transform** (**ELT**) service in the Microsoft Azure platform. In this recipe, we will learn how to orchestrate and automate a data pipeline using ADF.

Getting ready

Before starting with this recipe, you need to ensure that you have a valid Azure subscription, valid permission to create an ADF resource, and Azure Databricks workspace details with an access token.

> **Note**
> Explaining ADF is beyond the scope of this book and readers are expected to have basic knowledge of creating an ADF pipeline and how to schedule it.

How to do it...

In this section, we learn how to invoke a Databricks notebook in an ADF pipeline and how to schedule an E2E data pipeline using an ADF trigger.

1. Open an ADF workspace from the Azure portal and click on the **Author & Monitor** link to create a new pipeline:

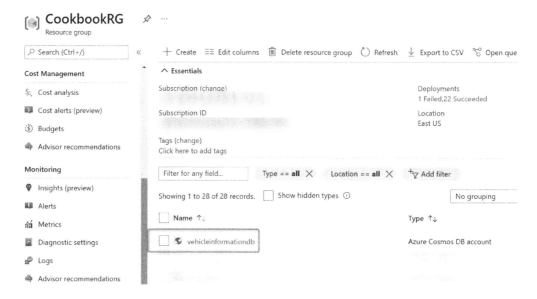

Figure 7.29 – Authoring a pipeline

2. Click on **Create pipeline** and you will get an option to create a new pipeline. Expand **Databricks activities** from the toolbar pane and drag and drop the **Notebook** activity:

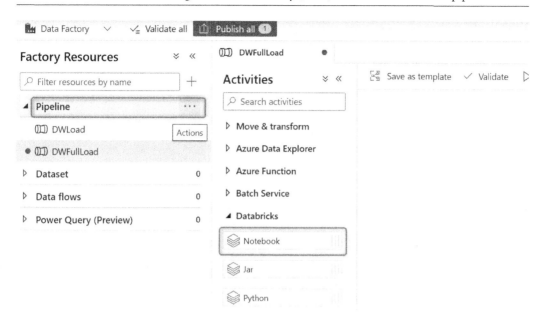

Figure 7.30 – Adding the Notebook activity to the pipeline

3. Create a linked service connecting to your Azure Databricks workspace. Get the access token from your Databricks workspace and provide the Databricks workspace URL:

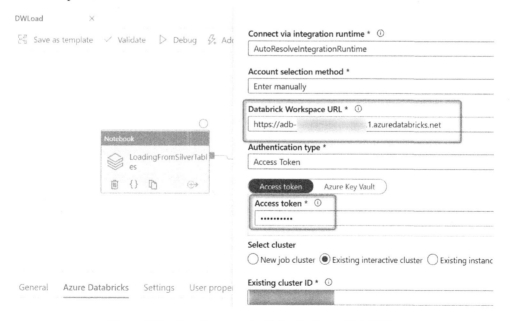

Figure 7.31 – Creating a service linked to Azure Databricks

4. We will call a stored procedure to load data in fact and dimension tables. Here is a screenshot showing what happens after calling `notebook` and `stored proc`:

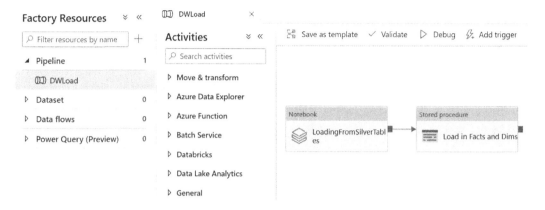

Figure 7.32 – Creating a service linked to Azure Databricks (continued)

5. You can schedule it to run every 15 minutes, which will load the data from Silver Delta tables and load it into an Azure Synapse dedicated pool.

How it works...

This is one way to load data every 15 minutes into a Synapse dedicated SQL pool. You can avoid ADF and load data into a dedicated SQL pool by invoking the `writeStream` API in the continuously running notebook, and this method can be more real time than running it every 15 minutes from ADF.

8
Databricks SQL

Databricks SQL provides a great experience for SQL developers, BI developers, analysts, and data scientists to run ad hoc queries on large volumes of data in a data lake, creating various visualizations and rich dashboards.

Databricks SQL provides the following features:

- A fully managed SQL endpoint for running all SQL queries
- A query editor for writing SQL queries
- Visualizations and dashboards for providing various insights into the data
- Integration with Azure Active Directory, providing enterprise-level security for data by controlling the access to tables using role-based access controls
- Integration with Power BI for creating rich visualizations and sharing meaningful insights from the data in a data lake
- The ability to create alerts on a field returned by a query on meeting a threshold value and notifying users

By the end of this chapter, you will have learned how you can use Databricks SQL to write ad hoc queries and create various visualizations and dashboards.

We're going to cover the following recipes:

- How to create a user in Databricks SQL
- Creating SQL endpoints
- Granting access to objects to the user
- Running SQL queries in Databricks SQL
- Using query filters and parameters
- Introduction to visualizations in Databricks SQL
- Creating dashboards in Databricks SQL
- Connecting Power BI to Databricks SQL

Let's look at the prerequisites of this chapter in the next section.

Technical requirements

To follow along with the examples shown in the recipes, you will need to have the following:

- An Azure subscription and the required permissions on the subscription that was mentioned in the *Technical requirements* section in *Chapter 1, Creating an Azure Databricks Service*.
- An Azure Databricks premium workspace with a Spark 3.x cluster.
- Databricks SQL is in public preview.

> **Important Note**
> The UI and some features of Databricks SQL may change in the future when it goes to **General Availability** (**GA**) as it is still in public preview.

In the next section, you will learn how to create a user in Databricks SQL.

How to create a user in Databricks SQL

In this recipe, you will learn how to create a user for running queries, creating dashboards, or performing data analysis on top of the data available in Delta Lake.

Getting ready

Before starting with this recipe, you need to ensure that you have the resources mentioned in the *Technical requirements* section of this chapter.

How to do it...

Let's go through the steps for creating a Databricks SQL user:

1. Open your Databricks workspace with Databricks SQL access:

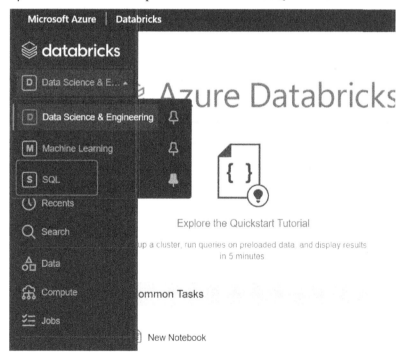

Figure 8.1 – Databricks SQL workspace

2. Click on **Admin Console** and go to the **Users** tab to add a user:

Figure 8.2 – Databricks workspace Admin Console

3. Click on the **Add User** button and enter the email ID of the user whom you want to add. You can only add users who belong to the Azure Active Directory tenant of your Azure Databricks workspace. Click on **OK** to add the user to the Databricks workspace:

Figure 8.3 – Add a Databricks SQL user

4. Once the user is added, click the **Databricks SQL access** checkbox to provide access to Databricks SQL to the newly added user. You will get a prompt to turn on Databricks SQL for that user as shown in the following screenshot. Click on **Confirm** to provide Databricks SQL access to the user:

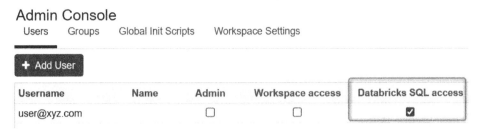

Figure 8.4 – Databricks SQL access

You can see the user has been added in the preceding screenshot and in the next recipe you will learn how to create SQL endpoints.

How it works...

Once the user is provided with access to the Databricks SQL workspace, they are set to write SQL commands to perform ad hoc queries and create visualizations, dashboards, and alerts on the data available in Delta Lake.

Creating SQL endpoints

SQL endpoints are computation resources using which you can run SQL queries on data objects in Azure Databricks environments. SQL endpoints are fully managed SQL-optimized compute clusters that autoscale based on user load to support a better experience for user concurrency and performance. They are computing clusters, very similar to clusters that we have already used in the Azure Databricks environment.

Getting ready

Let's go through the permissions required for creating and managing SQL endpoints in the Azure Databricks workspace.

The user must have the **Allow** cluster creation permission in the Azure Databricks workspace. You can check this permission from **Admin Console** | the **Users** tab or the **Groups** tab depending on whether access needs to be granted to an individual user or group. Refer to the following screenshot from the workspace:

Admin Console

Users   Groups   Global Init Scripts   Workspace Settings   ⊘   ?   ADE

+ Add User

Username	Name	Admin	Workspace access	Databricks SQL access	Allow cluster creation
user@xyz.com		☐	☐	☑	☑

Figure 8.5 – Databricks SQL cluster creation

After permission is granted, the user or group can create clusters.

How to do it...

In this section, you will learn how to create and manage a SQL endpoint from the Azure portal. It can also be done using SQL Endpoint APIs. Refer to the following article to learn how to work with APIs:

```
https://docs.microsoft.com/en-us/azure/databricks/sql/api/
sql-endpoints
```

Let's run through the following steps to create and manage a SQL Endpoint from the Azure portal UI:

1. Go to the **Databricks SQL** page by selecting **SQL** option as shown in *Figure 8.1*.
2. From the Databricks SQL home page, click on the **SQL Endpoints** icon in the sidebar and click on the **Create SQL Endpoint** button:

Figure 8.6 – Create a new SQL endpoint

3. Enter the following properties in the window to create a new SQL endpoint:

   a) **Name**: Enter the name of the SQL endpoint as per your choice.

   b) **Cluster Size**: Choose the cluster size as per your requirements. The default value is **X-Large**. It is a number of cluster workers and the size of the coordinator. A larger cluster size reduces the latency of queries. The coordinator size and the number of cluster workers depend on the size of the cluster.

   c) **Auto Stop**: Using this option, you can stop the SQL endpoint if it's idle for a specified time in minutes. The default value is 120 minutes.

   d) **Multi-cluster Load Balancing**: This is the minimum and maximum number of clusters on which the queries are distributed. The default value is **Off**. Enable load balancing and increase the cluster count to handle more concurrent users.

e) **Photon**: This is a polymorphic vectorized execution engine that speeds up the execution engine. The default is **Off**. To enable it, select **On**. You can read more about this at the following URL:

```
https://azure.microsoft.com/en-us/updates/accelerate-
analytics-and-ai-workloads-with-photon-powered-delta-
engine-on-azure-databricks/
```

f) **Tags**: These are annotations that can identify who uses the endpoint:

New SQL Endpoint ^{Preview} ... ✕

Name:	DemoSQLendpoint
Cluster Size ⓘ :	2X-Small	4 DBU ∨
Auto Stop:	⬤ After 60	minutes of inactivity.
Multi-cluster Load Balancing ⓘ : Preview	◯ Cluster Count: Min 1	Max 1
Photon ⓘ :	◯
Tags ⓘ :	Key	Value

Cancel   Create

Figure 8.7 – SQL endpoint settings

4. After entering the required details, click on the **Create** button to create the SQL endpoint.

5. After completing the preceding steps, you should be able to see the SQL endpoint created and running:

Figure 8.8 – SQL endpoint state

We will see how SQL queries are executed using a SQL endpoint in the upcoming recipe.

How it works...

Azure Databricks provides a scalable platform, and it gives options to work with multiple languages such as SQL, Scala, Python, and R to create data engineering pipelines.

Data engineers or data analysts with SQL skills can use the SQL editor interface and can write queries as they are used to doing with databases such as Azure SQL, Microsoft SQL, or Azure Synapse, and so on. Databricks SQL also provides capabilities to create visual dashboards.

Databricks SQL endpoints are special Azure Databricks clusters, dedicated to serving BI/ad hoc analytics queries and access the same data that's visible to conventional clusters, but they isolate their workloads, providing greater concurrency. These clusters are provisioned based on "T-shirt" sizes and avoid the need to specify the number and type of master and worker nodes that are required while creating conventional clusters in a Databricks environment. Refer to the following URL to get more details on the cluster driver size and workers count:

```
https://docs.microsoft.com/en-us/azure/databricks/sql/admin/
sql-endpoints#cluster-size
```

Also, users have the option to choose autoscaling, allowing additional clusters to be provisioned, and de-provisioned, based on workload demands. Autoscaling is enabled by selecting **Multi-cluster Load Balancing**. BI tools and other query clients can connect to a single endpoint and are not aware of the existence of the multiple clusters in the backend. Whenever queries are fired to an endpoint, requests will be sent to a particular cluster.

Granting access to objects to the user

In this recipe, you will learn how to grant access to objects to users so that they can write queries for analyzing data. We have already seen how users are created in the *How to create a user in Databricks SQL* recipe of this chapter.

Getting ready

Before you start on this recipe, make sure you have gone through the *How to create a user in Databricks SQL* recipe in this chapter and that all the resources mentioned in the *Technical requirements* section are ready for usage.

Also, run the following notebook to create **Customer** and **Orders** external Delta tables:

```
https://github.com/PacktPublishing/Azure-Databricks-Cookbook/
blob/main/Chapter06/6_1.Reading%20Writing%20to%20Delta%20
Tables.ipynb.
```

How to do it...

Let's run through the following commands to grant access to a user:

1. Execute the following command to grant access to a user or principal to the default database:

    ```
    GRANT USAGE ON DATABASE default TO `user@xyz.com`;
    ```

2. After granting access to the database, execute the following command to grant the SELECT permission to the user or principal on the table:

    ```
    GRANT SELECT ON TABLE default.customer TO `user@xyz.com`;
    ```

    The metadata of the table can be accessed using the following command. This command grants the privilege to read the metadata of the table to the user or group:

    ```
    GRANT READ_METADATA on TABLE default.customer TO `user@
    xyz.com`;
    ```

3. To validate the access granted to a particular user or group, execute the following:

    ```
    SHOW GRANT `user@xyz.com` ON TABLE default.customer;
    ```

4. After executing the preceding command, you will see the permissions granted to the user:

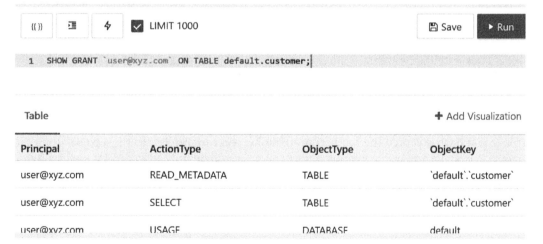

Figure 8.9 – SHOW GRANT command result

The user user@xyz.com has the USAGE permission on the default database and READ_METADATA and SELECT permissions on the **Customer** table.

How it works...

The GRANT command provides access to a user or principal. Granting privileges on the database level provides privileges to all the objects in the database.

The SHOW GRANT command displays all access (revoked, granted, and inherited) to the specified object. You must be a Databricks SQL administrator, the owner of the object, or the specified user to run this command.

Running SQL queries in Databricks SQL

SQL queries in Databricks SQL allows BI users or data analysts to create and run ad hoc SQL queries on data in a data lake and schedule the queries to run at regular intervals. BI users or analysts can create reports based on business requirements and it's easy for traditional BI users to be onboarded to Databricks SQL to write SQL queries and get a similar experience they are used to in on-prem databases.

Getting ready

Before starting, execute the following notebooks:

- `https://github.com/PacktPublishing/Azure-Databricks-Cookbook/blob/main/Chapter06/6_1.Reading%20Writing%20to%20Delta%20Tables.ipynb`.

  Running the preceding notebook will create **Customer** and **Orders** external Delta tables.

- `https://github.com/PacktPublishing/Azure-Databricks-Cookbook/blob/main/Chapter07/7.1-End-to-End%20Data%20Pipeline.ipynb`

  Running the preceding notebook will create the VehicleSensor-related Delta tables.

You need to create the SQL endpoints and the required users as mentioned in the *Creating SQL endpoints* and *Granting access to objects to the user* recipes.

Once you have executed the required notebooks, you can proceed to the next section. You can also execute any one notebook, but the queries will be limited to objects created by the notebook you execute.

How to do it...

In this section, you will learn how to write SQL queries in Databricks SQL and learn how to look at the history of all queries executed in Databricks SQL:

1. On the Databricks SQL home page, you will find an option called **Queries** where you can write queries. Once you select **Queries**, click on the **Create Query** option as shown in the following screenshot:

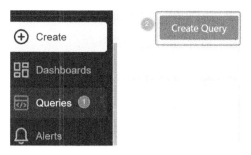

Figure 8.10 – Databricks SQL Create Query

2. In the query editor, write the following query and name the query Customer Query:

```
select COUNT(*),C_MKTSEGMENT FROM default.customer
group by C_MKTSEGMENT
order BY COUNT(*) desc
```

3. Once you execute the preceding query, you have options to export the result to CSV, TSV, or Excel, or even add the output to a dashboard as shown in the following screenshot. We will learn about dashboards in upcoming recipes:

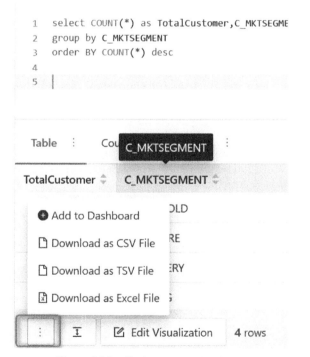

Figure 8.11 – Customer count output

4. You will find all the databases and the objects such as tables and views in the SQL editor as shown in the following screenshot:

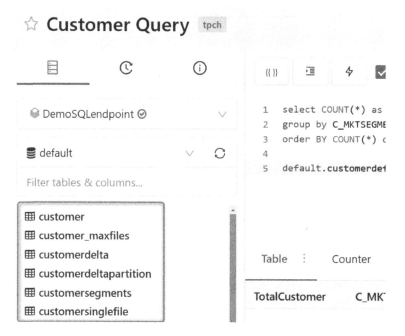

Figure 8.12 – Customer Query

5. You can view the history of all queries executed in the past few days and can select queries executed by a specific user. On the Databricks SQL home page, you will find the **History** option and by selecting it, you will find all the queries executed in the last 14 days as the default filter, as shown in the following screenshot:

Figure 8.13 – Query History

6. If you have multiple endpoints, you can also filter by a single endpoint. Select any one of the queries and you will get the details about the query start time; the end time; the status – whether failed (along with an error message), running, or finished; and which endpoint was used to execute the query, as shown in the following screenshot:

Figure 8.14 – Query History details

7. Once you have written the queries, you can schedule them so that the data is refreshed automatically. To do this, you need to schedule a refresh for the query you have written. Select **Customer Query**, select the **Query Info** option, and change **Refresh Schedule** from **Never** to every 30 mins. You can set it to a minimum of **1 minute** as shown in the following screenshot:

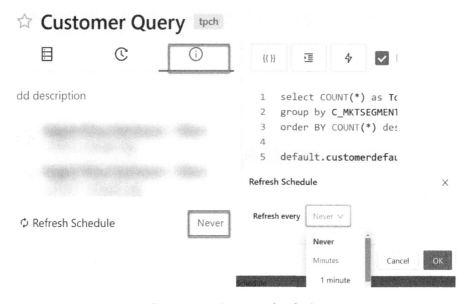

Figure 8.15 – Query result refresh

8. By running *Step 7*, the data for the **Customer Query** page will get refreshed/updated every 30 minutes.

Databricks SQL provides a great experience for data analysts, BI developers, and data scientists to write complex SQL queries and get good IDE experience, such as IntelliSense and the live autocomplete feature, while writing queries.

How it works...

You can use the **History** feature to do various kinds of auditing. You can identify how much time is taken for compilation, execution, and result fetching. Hover over the **Duration** value or select **Execution Details** in **Query details** in **Query History** and you will find the details about the execution and compilation along with the fetch time as shown in the following screenshot:

Query History

	Query	SQL Endpoi..
⊘	select * from customer limit 100000	DemoSQLe...
⊘	select * from customer LIMIT 1000	DemoSQLe...
⊘	Listing columns 'catalog : null, sch...	DemoSQLe...
⊘	Listing tables 'catalog : null, sche...	DemoSQLe...
⊘	select * from customer LIMIT 1000	DemoSQLe...
⊘	Listing columns 'catalog : null, sch...	DemoSQLe...
⊘	Listing tables 'catalog : null, sche...	DemoSQLe...

Me (▢) ⌄   Last

Overview   Execution Details

Duration ▦	5.07 s	100%
○ Loading metadata & optimizing ⓘ	383 ms	8%
• Execution ⓘ	2.13 s	42%
● Result fetching ⓘ	2.56 s	51%
Rows returned	100,000	

IO
Rows read	135,000
Bytes read	10.58 MB
Bytes read from cache	0 %
Bytes written	0 bytes

Files & Partitions
Files read	3
Partitions read	0

Figure 8.16 – Query Execution Details

You can also get the DAG for the query execution. Select a query in the **History** tab and in the **Overview** tab, you will find **Details** with a link to the Spark UI as shown in the following screenshot:

	Query	SQL Endpoint
⊘	select * from customer LIMIT 1000	DemoSQLe...
⊘	Listing columns 'catalog : null, sch...	DemoSQLe...
⊘	Listing tables 'catalog : null, sche...	DemoSQLe...
⊘	select * from customer LIMIT 1000	DemoSQLe...
⊘	Listing columns 'catalog : null, sch...	DemoSQLe...
⊘	Listing tables 'catalog : null, sche...	DemoSQLe...
⊘	Listing columns 'catalog : null, sch...	DemoSQLe...
⊘	Listing tables 'catalog : null, sche...	DemoSQLe...
⊘	Listing columns 'catalog : null, sch...	DemoSQLe...
⊘	Listing tables 'catalog : null, sche...	DemoSQLe...

```
5   limit
6      100000
```

ID	3ccf8e6b-364c-421c-a9ee-cea
Status	⊘ Finished
Start time	2021-07-21 15:23:15.478
End time	2021-07-21 15:23:21.663
Duration	5.07 s
User	▢
SQL Endpoint	DemoSQLendpoint
Details	Open ↗

Figure 8.17 – Query execution DAG link

When you click on the **Open link**, you will see the Spark UI screen with DAG and execution plan details as shown in the following screenshot:

Details for Query 52   📷 Download screen as png

Submitted Time: 2021/07/21 09:53:17
Duration: 2 s
Succeeded Jobs: 12 13

☑ Expand all the details in the query plan visualization

Scan parquet default.customer +details Stages: 20.0 21.0	
cache writes size (uncompressed) total (min, med, max)	20.5 MiB (6.8 MiB, 6.8 MiB, 6.8 MiB)
time spent waiting fetching data from cloud storage total (min, med, max)	592 ms (163 ms, 213 ms, 215 ms)
time spent in the cache locality manager in milliseconds total (min, med, max)	5 ms (0 ms, 0 ms, 5 ms)
number of files read	3
filesystem read data size total (min, med, max)	10.6 MiB (3.5 MiB, 3.5 MiB, 3.5 MiB)
cache async file status fetch waiting time total (min, med, max)	0 ms (0 ms, 0 ms, 0 ms)
scan time total (min, med, max)	763 ms (212 ms, 263 ms, 288 ms)
filesystem read data size (sampled) total (min, med, max)	21.2 MiB (7.0 MiB, 7.0 MiB, 7.1 MiB)
filesystem read time (sampled) total (min, med, max)	824 ms (268 ms, 276 ms, 280 ms)
metadata time	0 ms
size of files read	10.6 MiB
cache hits size total (min, med, max)	0.0 B (0.0 B, 0.0 B, 0.0 B)

Figure 8.18 – DAG

The **Query History** tab provides great information to admins and users to troubleshoot any specific query or get more details about which query is taking a longer duration to complete. In the next recipe, you will learn how to provide values to the SQL queries at runtime.

Using query parameters and filters

Query parameters and filters are ways to filter the data that is returned to the end user. A query parameter will substitute the values in a query at runtime before getting executed, whereas a query filter will limit the data after it has been loaded into the browser. Query filters should be used only for small datasets and not for large volumes of data since it does not filter the data at runtime. In this recipe, you will learn how to use query filters and parameters in SQL queries.

Getting ready

Before starting, you need to ensure you execute the following notebooks:

- `https://github.com/PacktPublishing/Azure-Databricks-Cookbook/blob/main/Chapter06/6_1.Reading%20Writing%20to%20Delta%20Tables.ipynb`

  Running the preceding notebook will create Customer and Orders external Delta tables.

- `https://github.com/PacktPublishing/Azure-Databricks-Cookbook/blob/main/Chapter07/7.1-End-to-End%20Data%20Pipeline.ipynb`

  Running the preceding notebooks will create **Customer**, **Orders**, and VehicleSensor-related Delta tables. The example used in the next section is based on the tables created by running the preceding notebooks.

How to do it...

In this section, you will learn how to use query parameters and query filters in Databricks SQL queries.

Let's run through the following steps to use query parameters in SQL queries:

1. You need to use {{ }} to substitute the value in the query at runtime. Writing the following query will add two variables with the names `BoroughName` and `MakeValue` even before executing:

```
SELECT
    COUNT(*),
    SUM(count) AS TotalCountofVehicles
FROM
    vehiclesensor.vehicledeltaaggregated
  WHERE Borough={{ BoroughName }} and Make ={{ MakeValue
}}
```

2.   The following is the screenshot you will see after writing the preceding query in the query editor even before executing the query:

```
1   SELECT
2     COUNT(*),
3     SUM(count) AS TotalCountofVehicles
4   FROM
5     vehiclesensor.vehicledeltaaggregated
6   WHERE Borough={{ BoroughName }} and Make ={{ MakeValue }}
7
8
```

BoroughName	⚙	MakeValue	⚙

Figure 8.19 – Query parameters

3.   Provide the values as STATEN ISLAND and Toyota and execute the preceding query. You can also provide the datatype for the parameter as well. To do that, click on **Add New Parameter** (*Ctrl + P*) and provide the name of the keyword and the title. Both values can be the same or different and you can choose the type of the variable. Select the drop-down list and you will find various types such as number, date time, and date range and you can create a drop-down list based on the set of values or from another query:

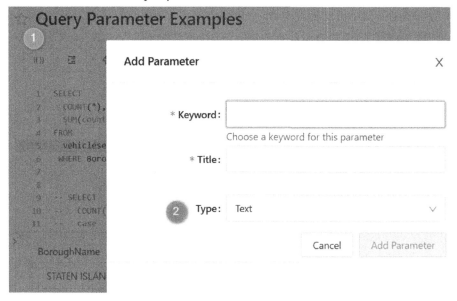

Figure 8.20 – Add query parameters

4. Run the following query, which will get the total count of vehicles based on the low fuel indicator. The parameter type used is DATERANGE:

```
SELECT
    COUNT(*) AS    TotalVehicles,
    case
      when lfi = 0 then "Low"
      else "High"
    end as LowFuelIndicator
FROM
    vehiclesensor.vehicledelta_silver
WHERE
    eventtime BETWEEN '{{ DATERANGE.start }}' AND ' {{
DATERANGE.end }} '
    group BY LowFuelIndicator
```

5. The following is the screenshot of the output for the preceding query execution. We are looking for the **Daterange** between May 23 and 24:

Figure 8.21 – Query Daterange output

6. You can also use a date range such as *last 30 days* or *last month.* Click on the flash-type icon that is near to **Daterange** shown in the following screenshot and you can select values such as **Last week** and **Last 14 days**:

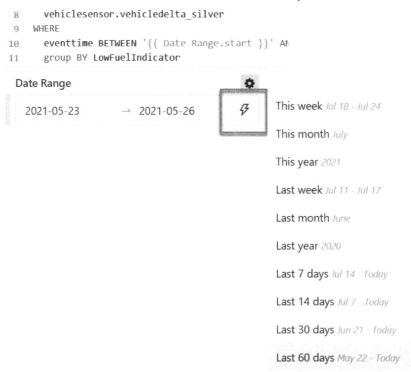

```
 8     vehiclesensor.vehicledelta_silver
 9    WHERE
10      eventtime BETWEEN '{{ Date Range.start }}' AN
11      group BY LowFuelIndicator
```

Date Range

| 2021-05-23 | → | 2021-05-26 | ⚡ |

This week *Jul 18 - Jul 24*

This month *July*

This year *2021*

Last week *Jul 11 - Jul 17*

Last month *June*

Last year *2020*

Last 7 days *Jul 14 - Today*

Last 14 days *Jul 7 - Today*

Last 30 days *Jun 21 - Today*

Last 60 days *May 22 - Today*

Figure 8.22 – Change Daterange

7. Run the following query to get the data for the last 7 days with the DATERANGE parameter value set as **Last 7 days**:

```
SELECT
   COUNT(*) AS   TotalVehicles,
   case
     when lfi = 0 then "Low"
      else "High"
   end as LowFuelIndicator
FROM
   vehiclesensor.vehicledelta_silver
WHERE
   eventtime > '{{ DATERANGE.start }}'
   group BY LowFuelIndicator
```

8. The following is the screenshot of the **DATERANGE** parameter with **Last 7 days** selected:

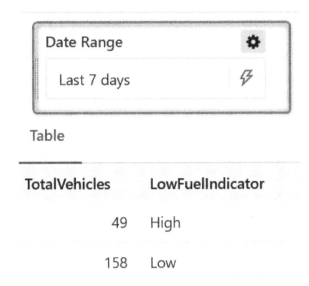

Figure 8.23 – Last 7 days DATERANGE

9. Create a new query with the name `Borough` and execute the following query:

```
SELECT DISTINCT Borough FROM vehiclesensor.
vehicledeltaaggregated
WHERE Borough IS NOT null
```

10. We will create a query-based drop-down list parameter and use the `Boroughs` query created in the preceding step as the query parameter.

11. Run the following query, which uses the `Boroughs` query for the query parameter, which will be in the drop-down list:

```
SELECT
   COUNT(*) AS   TotalVehicles,
   case
     when lfi = 0 then "Low"
     else "High"
   end as LowFuelIndicator,
   Borough
FROM
```

```
    vehiclesensor.vehicledelta_silver
WHERE
    Borough  in  ({{ Boroughs }})
    group BY LowFuelIndicator,Borough
    order by Borough
```

12. The following is the screenshot for the `Boroughs` parameter used in the query. We are enabling **Allow multiple values** so that we can enable multi-select from the list:

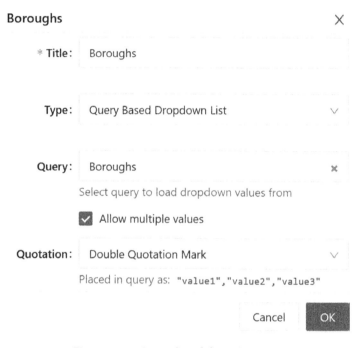

Figure 8.24 – Query-based drop-down list

13. Once you create the query parameter, you can select for which borough you want the query to execute against. In the following screenshot, we are selecting two boroughs and running the query:

```
12    Borough  in ({{ Boroughs }})
13    group BY LowFuelIndicator,Borough
```

Figure 8.25 – Multi-select parameter

Let's run through the following steps to use query filters in the SQL queries:

14. Run the following, which will create a parameter with list values fetched from the Borough column in the vehicledelta_silver table. To create a query filter, you need to use an alias for the column on which you want to create a filter. Here, we are creating the alias for the Borough column as Borough::filter, which creates a single SELECT drop-down list with all boroughs:

```
SELECT
   COUNT(*) AS    TotalVehicles,
   case
     when lfi = 0 then "Low"
      else "High"
   end as LowFuelIndicator,
   Borough as `Borough::filter`
FROM
   vehiclesensor.vehicledelta_silver
WHERE Borough IS NOT NULL
group BY LowFuelIndicator,Borough
order by Borough
```

15. The following is the output after executing the preceding query. You can see a new drop-down list with the name `Borough` is added, and its single `SELECT` drop-down list:

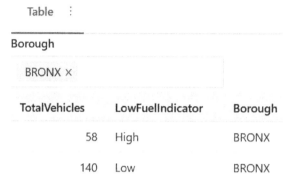

Figure 8.26 – Single SELECT filter

16. `Borough::filter` creates a single `SELECT` filter. To create a multi-select filter, you should use `Borough::multi-filter` as the alias for the `Borough` column. The following is the screenshot with a multi-select filter on the `Borough` column:

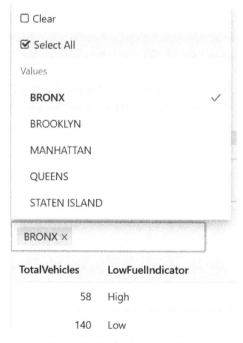

Figure 8.27 – Multi-select filter

Using filters and parameters, we can filter the data based on the business requirements and it provides us with the flexibility to change the values at runtime.

How it works...

Query parameters and filters provide BI developers and analysts with the ability to change the values of SQL queries at runtime. Using a query drop-down list, we can obfuscate the logic of using the values in the *in-clause* and restrict the data that needs to be fetched from the underlying tables.

In the following recipes, we will learn how to create different visualizations and build dashboards from various queries.

Introduction to visualizations in Databricks SQL

In this recipe, we will learn how to create different visualizations in Databricks SQL queries and how to change certain properties of visualizations.

Getting ready

Before starting, you need to ensure you execute the following notebook so that the tables used in the queries are created:

- `https://github.com/PacktPublishing/Azure-Databricks-Cookbook/blob/main/Chapter06/6_1.Reading%20Writing%20to%20Delta%20Tables.ipynb`

- `https://github.com/PacktPublishing/Azure-Databricks-Cookbook/blob/main/Chapter07/7.1-End-to-End%20Data%20Pipeline.ipynb`

Running the preceding notebooks will create **Customer**, **Orders**, and **VehicleSensor** related Delta tables. Ensure you complete the *Running SQL queries in Databricks SQL* and *Using query parameters and filters* recipes as you will be using the queries created in those recipes.

How to do it...

In this section, you will learn how to create visualizations by running through the following steps:

1. Run the following query, which we created in the previous recipe, *Using query parameters and filters*:

```
SELECT
    COUNT(*) AS    TotalVehicles,
    case
        when lfi = 0 then "Low"
        else "High"
    end as LowFuelIndicator,
    Borough
FROM
    vehiclesensor.vehicledelta_silver
WHERE
    Borough   in ({{ Boroughs }})
    group BY LowFuelIndicator,Borough
    order by Borough
```

2. After the query is executed, click on the + **Add Visualization** option as shown in the following screenshot:

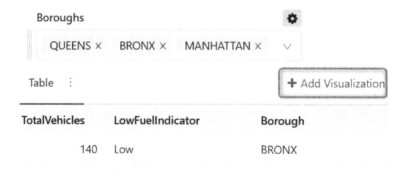

Figure 8.28 – Add Visualization

3. Once you click on the + **Add visualization** option, provide the value for **X Column** and other details to create a bar chart as shown in the following screenshot:

General   X Axis   Y Axis   Series   Colors   Data Labels

Chart Type

|ıl.ı| Bar

Horizontal Chart

X Column

Borough

Y Columns

TotalVehicles ×

Group By

LowFuelIndicator

Figure 8.29 – Visualization Editor

4. You can change the colors and add data labels to the chart by going to the **Colors** and **Data Labels** tabs in **Visualization Editor** as shown in the following screenshot. Go to the **Data Labels** tab and select **Show Data Labels** to add data labels to the chart:

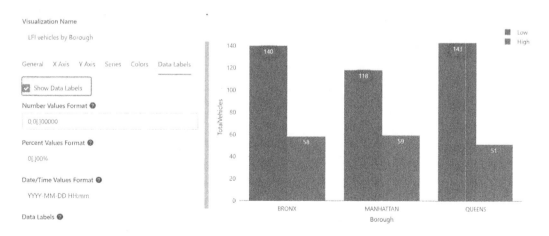

Figure 8.30 – Visualization Data Labels

5.   We will add another visualization called `Funnel` for the same query. Click on
+ Add Visualization, select the visualization type as **Funnel**, and use the values
for the **Value** column and other details as shown in the following screenshot:

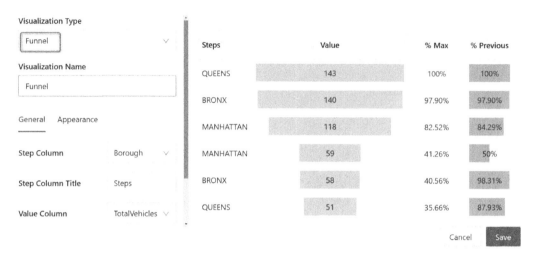

Figure 8.31 – Visualization Type – Funnel

6.   You can also duplicate the existing visual by clicking on the ellipsis on the
Funnel Visual tab and selecting the **Duplicate** option:

Figure 8.32 – Visualization –Duplicate

In Databricks SQL, you can create different types of visualizations such as bar charts,
funnels, maps, pivot tables, and lots of other visualizations that you can find under
the **Visualization** type in the editor. In the next recipe, you will learn how to create
a dashboard using the visualizations we have created in this recipe.

Creating dashboards in Databricks SQL

Azure Databricks Databricks SQL allows users to create various dashboards based on the queries and visualizations that are already built. This helps businesses to get a visual representation of data for various KPIs.

In this recipe, you will learn how to create visualizations in Databricks SQL and how to pin a visualization from various queries to the dashboard.

Getting ready

Before starting, we need to ensure we have executed the following notebook. The following notebook creates the required tables on which we can build our visualizations and dashboard:

`https://github.com/PacktPublishing/Azure-Databricks-Cookbook/blob/main/Chapter07/7.1-End-to-End%20Data%20Pipeline.ipynb`

Also create the visualization as mentioned in the *Introduction to visualizations in Databricks SQL recipe*.

How to do it...

Let's learn how to create a dashboard by running through the following steps:

1. From the Databricks SQL homepage go to the **Dashboards** tab, click on **+ New Dashboard**, and give the name as `Vehicle and Customer Stats`.

2. On the dashboard screen, click on **Add Visualizations** and select the query that has the visual we want to add to the dashboard. We are using the **Customer Query**, which has the following query text:

```
select COUNT(*) as TotalCustomer,C_MKTSEGMENT FROM
default.customer
group by C_MKTSEGMENT
order BY COUNT(*) desc
```

3. Once you have created a query with the name `Customer Query`, select **Query name** and from the drop-down list, select the visualization you want to add as shown in the following screenshot. Select **Table** as the visualization to add the table to the dashboard:

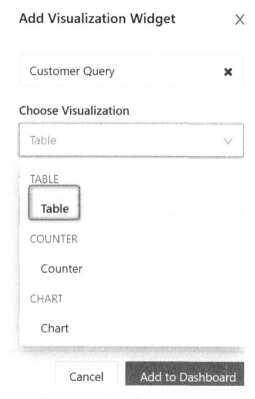

Figure 8.33 – Visualization options

4. Let's add another visualization, and this time, we will select the **LFI vehicles by Borough** query we created in the previous recipe, as shown in the following screenshot. Since the query has a parameter, the same parameter list will be added to the dashboard:

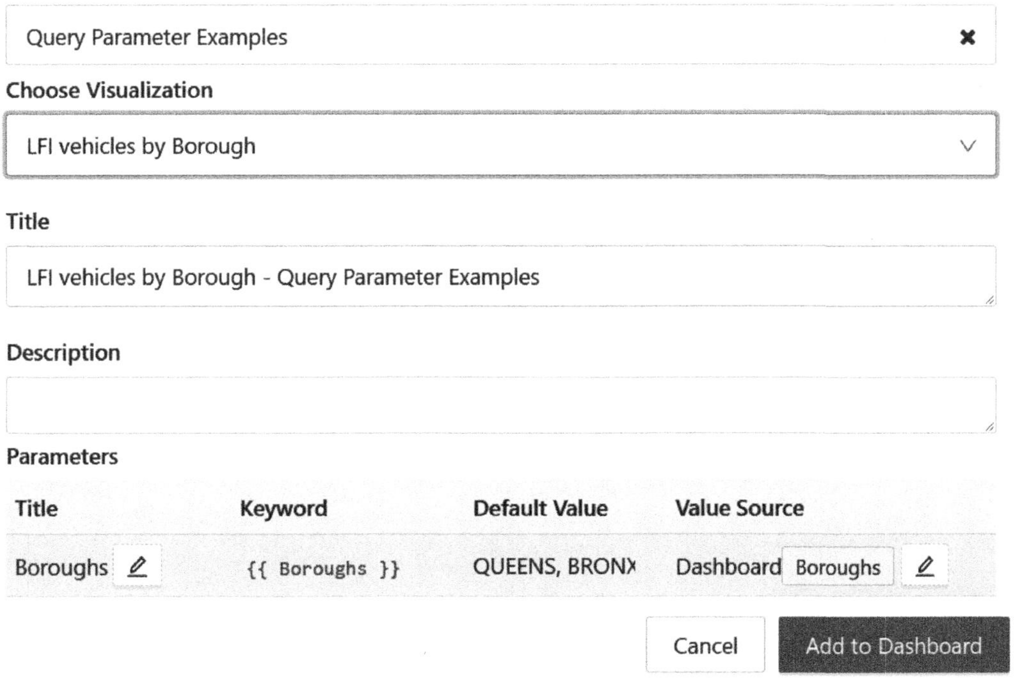

Query Parameter Examples	✖

Choose Visualization

LFI vehicles by Borough	⌄

Title

LFI vehicles by Borough - Query Parameter Examples

Description

Parameters

Title	Keyword	Default Value	Value Source		
Boroughs 🖉	{{ Boroughs }}	QUEENS, BRONX	Dashboard	Boroughs	🖉

Cancel   Add to Dashboard

Figure 8.34 – Add widget

The following is a screenshot after adding all the widgets (visuals) to the dashboard:

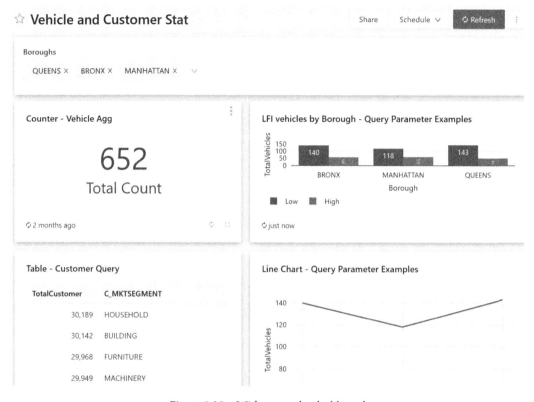

Figure 8.35 – Widgets on the dashboard

5. You can refresh the dashboard manually or schedule it to run at regular intervals as shown in the following screenshot:

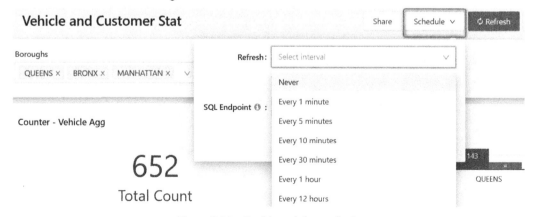

Figure 8.36 – Dashboard data refresh

A dashboard provides a great way to bring data from various queries and visualizations onto a single screen. You can further download a dashboard as a PDF and share it with an audience that doesn't have access to the dashboard and share meaningful insights from the data in a data lake.

How it works...

Creating dashboards in Databricks SQL is a quick way to create some interesting dashboards that can be shared with other users. While sharing a dashboard, you can specify whether the user can manage or just view the dashboard. You don't have to keep the SQL endpoint running to view the dashboard. You would need the SQL endpoint to be running only when you want to refresh the dashboard.

Connecting Power BI to Databricks SQL

Databricks SQL provides built-in connectors for Power BI users to connect to objects in Databricks SQL. Power BI users can now connect to a SQL endpoint to get a list of all tables and can connect using the import or direct query mode.

In this recipe, you will learn how to connect to a SQL endpoint from Power BI.

Getting ready

Before starting the recipe, ensure you have executed both of the following notebooks. The following notebook creates the required tables on which we can build our visualizations and dashboard. You need to ensure you download the latest version of Power BI Desktop:

- `https://github.com/PacktPublishing/Azure-Databricks-Cookbook/blob/main/Chapter07/7.1-End-to-End%20Data%20Pipeline.ipynb`

- `https://github.com/PacktPublishing/Azure-Databricks-Cookbook/blob/main/Chapter06/6_1.Reading%20Writing%20to%20Delta%20Tables.ipynb`

You can go through the following link which has the requirements for connecting Power BI to SQL Endpoints.

`https://docs.microsoft.com/en-in/azure/databricks/integrations/bi/index-dbsql`

How to do it...

Let's run through the following steps to connect to a SQL endpoint and create a basic dashboard:

1. Before connecting to Power BI, we need to get the connection details of the SQL endpoint. Go to the **Endpoints** page in the Databricks SQL workspace and copy the server hostname and HTTP path, which is required for connecting to the SQL endpoint from Power BI, as shown in the following screenshot:

Figure 8.37 – SQL endpoint connection details

2. We will be authenticating to the SQL endpoint from Power BI using a personal access token. Click on the **Create a personal access token** link you see in the preceding screenshot to generate a new token. Copy the token as soon as it is generated.

3. Open the Power BI app, click on **Get Data**, search for `Azure Databricks`, and click on **Connect**. Now provide the details for the server hostname and HTTP details that we captured in *Step 1*:

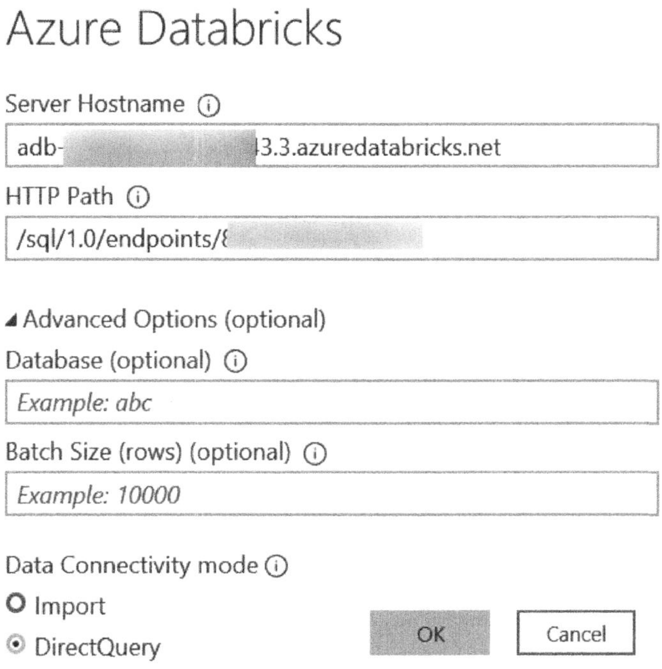

Azure Databricks

Server Hostname ⓘ

adb-   3.3.azuredatabricks.net

HTTP Path ⓘ

/sql/1.0/endpoints/8

◢ Advanced Options (optional)

Database (optional) ⓘ

Example: abc

Batch Size (rows) (optional) ⓘ

Example: 10000

Data Connectivity mode ⓘ

○ Import

◉ DirectQuery

OK   Cancel

Figure 8.38 – Power BI connecting to the SQL endpoint

4. For authentication, we are using the **Personal Access Token** option and provide the token value that you generated as part of *Step 2*:

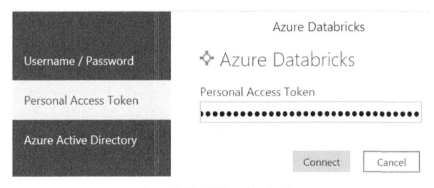

Figure 8.39 – PAT authentication

5. Run the following code to create a view that will be used in the Power BI report:

```
CREATE VIEW vehiclesensor.LFIVehicleDetails as
SELECT
  COUNT(*) AS   TotalVehicles,
  case
    when lfi = 0 then "Low"
    else "High"
  end as LowFuelIndicator,
  Borough
FROM
  vehiclesensor.vehicledelta_silver
  GROUP BY LowFuelIndicator,Borough
```

6. Now select the view from the list and click on the **Load** option as shown in the following screenshot:

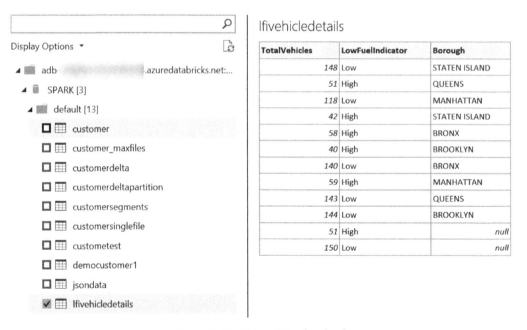

Figure 8.40 – Power BI – data load

7.   Now you can create any kind of dashboard in Power BI. The following screenshot is the Power BI report after adding a few visuals based on the data we have loaded:

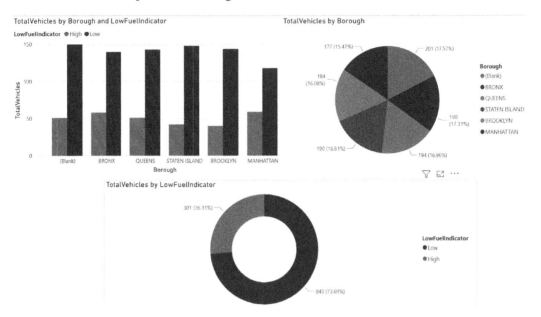

Figure 8.41 – Power BI report

In this recipe, we have learned how to use Azure Databricks Databricks SQL built-in connectors to connect to a SQL endpoint from Power BI.

9
DevOps Integrations and Implementing CI/CD for Azure Databricks

DevOps is the core of any project/organization these days. DevOps enables organizations to build and quickly deploy their applications and solutions to various environments by providing a framework that can be used for seamless deployment. In this chapter, you will learn how Azure DevOps is used for **Continuous Integration** and **Continuous Deployment** for **Azure Databricks** notebooks. Knowing how **Azure DevOps** works is helpful as it will help you to plan, develop, deliver, and operate your end-to-end business applications.

In this chapter, we're going to cover the following main topics:

- How to integrate Azure DevOps with an Azure Databricks notebook
- Using GitHub for Azure Databricks notebook version control
- Understanding the CI/CD process for Azure Databricks

- How to set up an Azure DevOps pipeline for deploying notebooks
- Deploying notebooks to multiple environments
- Enabling CI/CD in an Azure DevOps build and release pipeline
- Deploying an Azure Databricks service using an Azure DevOps release pipeline

Technical requirements

To follow along with the examples shown in the recipes, you will need to have the following:

- An Azure subscription and the required permissions on the subscription that was mentioned in the *Technical requirements* section of *Chapter 1, Creating Azure Databricks Service.*
- We will be using an Azure Databricks premium workspace for this chapter. There is no need to spin up a cluster in the workspace as we are not running any notebooks.
- An Azure DevOps repo should be created, and you need to ensure the Azure DevOps Services organization is linked to the same Azure AD tenant as Databricks. You can follow along with the steps mentioned at the following link to create a repository if you don't have one already created: `https://docs.microsoft.com/en-in/azure/devops/repos/git/create-new-repo?view=azure-devops`.

Once you have the repository created, you can get started with this chapter.

How to integrate Azure DevOps with an Azure Databricks notebook

Nowadays, DevOps is an integral part of any project and is heavily used for deploying the resources and artifacts to various environments apart from other services and features that Azure DevOps provides. Integrating Azure DevOps with Azure Databricks helps teams and organizations to source control the notebooks that can be used for collaborations and this enables the enterprise practice of Continuous Integration and Continuous Deployment for Azure Databricks resources and notebooks. In this recipe, you will learn how to integrate Azure DevOps with Azure Databricks.

Getting ready

Before starting with this recipe, you need to ensure that you have the resources created as mentioned in the *Technical requirements* section of the current chapter.

The Azure DevOps Services organization must be linked to the same Azure AD tenant that the Azure Databricks resource is part of. You need to set the Gitprovider to Azure DevOps in your Databricks workspace to integrate Azure DevOps with the Azure Databricks workspace. The user who is performing the following steps should be a workspace admin. Let's go through the following steps to set the Git provider for the workspace as Azure DevOps:

1. On the Databricks workspace home page, click the **User** icon and select **User Settings**.

Figure 9.1 – User Settings

2. Go to the **Git Integration** tab and select **Azure DevOps Services** for **Git provider** as shown in the following screenshot:

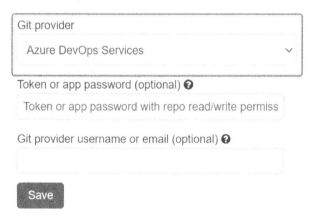

Figure 9.2 – Git integration

3. If your repository is not initialized, then you need to initialize it first. For this chapter, we will be using a repository named CookbookRepo and the name of the project is CookbookProj:

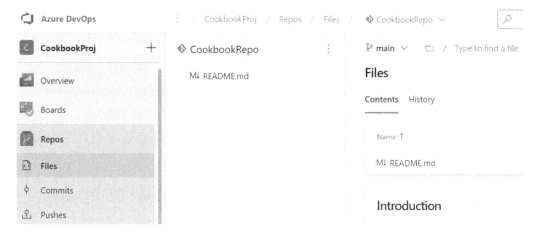

Figure 9.3 – Azure DevOps repos

4. As you can see from the preceding screenshot, an Azure DevOps repo is created with just a readme file. Once we integrate Azure DevOps with Azure Databricks and start committing changes, you will see files and folders getting created in CookbookRepo. You will have created a new Dev branch where all your changes will be committed.

You will be using the notebook from *Chapter 6, Exploring Delta Lake in Azure Databricks*, which will be synced with Azure DevOps. You can get the notebook from https://github.com/PacktPublishing/Azure-Databricks-Cookbook/blob/main/Chapter06/6_1.Reading%20Writing%20to%20Delta%20Tables.ipynb.

How to do it...

In this recipe, you will learn how to integrate Azure DevOps and how to commit changes to source control. Let's go through the following steps to learn and understand how it is done:

1. Go to your Databricks workspace and select the notebook that you have created and click on **Revision history**. You will see all the changes that were made to the notebook and the status of Git as Not linked Here we are using the notebook 6.1- Reading Writing to Delta Tables:

Figure 9.4 – Git status

2. From the preceding screenshot, you can see that by default, without any integration with Git, all the changes that happen to the notebook are saved and different versions are created. To version control the changes to an Azure DevOps repo, you need to link the notebook to Azure DevOps.

3. Click on the **Git: Not linked** option and provide the link for your repo. To get the URL for the Azure DevOps repo, go to the **Azure DevOps** page, click on **Repos**, and copy the URL as shown in the following screenshot.

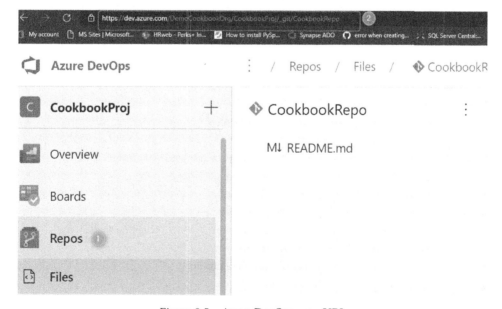

Figure 9.5 – Azure DevOps repo URL

4. Switch back to the **Databricks** page and provide the URL copied in the preceding step as shown in the following screenshot. Let's select Dev as the branch and commit all our changes in the Dev branch. Provide the value for **Path in Git Repo** as notebooks/6.1-Reading Writing to Delta Tables.py. A folder with the name notebooks will be created in CookbookRepo and all your notebooks will be saved as .py file. Click on **Save** after providing all the details:

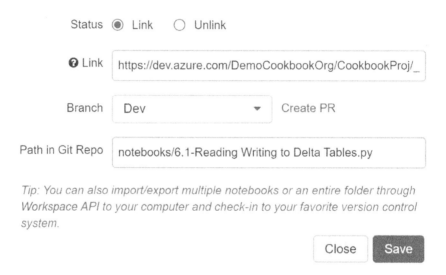

Figure 9.6 – Git Preferences

5. Once the Git is linked and synced, it will ask you to commit and save the current version.

Figure 9.7 – Git commit

6. You will see the status of the Git shown as synced, as shown in the following screenshot:

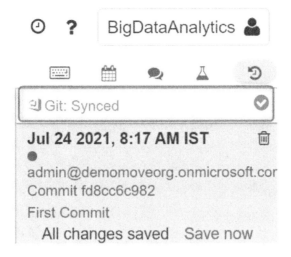

Figure 9.8 – Git Synced status

7. After changes are saved and committed, a **pull request** (**PR**) is created in the Dev branch. Go to **Azure DevOps Pull Request** to check for the PR. You can click on the commit number you see in the preceding screenshot, which will take you to the Azure DevOps PR page:

Figure 9.9 – PR page

8. Once you complete the PR, you will find all the changes from the Dev branch merged to the main branch. Details about pull requests are outside the scope of this chapter.

9. Go to the Azure DevOps repo page and you will see the `notebooks` folder created, which includes the Databricks notebook that you checked in. The notebook is saved as a Python file in the Azure DevOps repo:

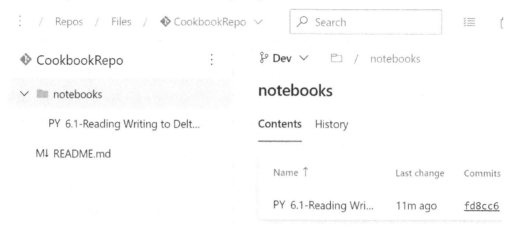

Figure 9.10 – Pull request page

10. Let's add one comment to simulate another change that needs to be committed, as shown in the following screenshot:

```
# Adding new comment
storageAccount="cookbookadlsgen2storage"
mountpoint = "/mnt/Gen2Source"
storageEndPoint ="abfss://rawdata@{}.dfs.cor
print ('Mount Point ='+mountpoint)
```

Figure 9.11 – Adding a comment

11. After adding the comment, click on **Save** under **Revision history**, which will push the comment to the Git repo by checking the **Also Commit to Git** option. You will find the new changes ID for the new commit:

Figure 9.12 – Commit details

12. Once you have committed the changes, go to Azure DevOps repo and you will find the new PR for the recent commit:

Figure 9.13 – Changes in the repo

By following the preceding steps mentioned in this recipe, you can integrate Azure DevOps with Azure Databricks and check your notebook into an Azure DevOps repo.

Using GitHub for Azure Databricks notebook version control

Apart from using Azure DevOps for version control of your Azure Databricks notebooks, you can also use GitHub. Using a specific type of version control depends upon the organizational, project, and business needs. In this recipe, you will learn how to integrate a GitHub repository with Azure Databricks to version control your notebooks.

Getting ready

Before starting with this recipe, you need to ensure that you have generated a *personal access token*, which is used for authentication to GitHub. To generate a *personal access token*, go through the steps mentioned at the following link: https://docs.github.com/en/github/authenticating-to-github/keeping-your-account-and-data-secure/creating-a-personal-access-token.

You need to only select the **repo** scope as shown in the following screenshot; other scopes are not required before generating the token:

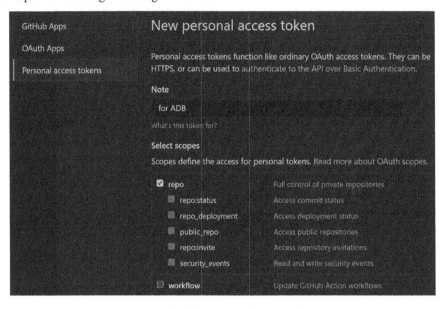

Figure 9.14 – GitHub Personal access tokens page

Once the personal access token is generated, you can integrate GitHub for version control as shown in the next section of this recipe. An Azure Databricks workspace can be integrated with only one version control at a time. For this recipe, we have created a new workspace with the name `GitHub-BigDataWorkspace` and imported the following notebook: `https://github.com/PacktPublishing/Azure-Databricks-Cookbook/blob/main/Chapter06/6_1.Reading%20Writing%20to%20Delta%20Tables.ipynb`.

If you have completed the preceding recipe, then you can also unlink Azure DevOps from the Azure Databricks workspace and link it with GitHub by following the steps mentioned in the next section without the need to create a new workspace.

How to do it...

Let's go through the following steps to set up version control for the notebooks using GitHub:

1. From the Azure Databricks home page, go to the **User settings**.

2. On the **User Settings** page, click on the **Git Integration** tab, set **Git Provider** as `GitHub`, as shown in the following screenshot, and paste the personal access token you generated in GitHub along with it provide your Git username or email:

Generating tokens

To generate a GitHub personal access token, follow the GitHub permission.

To generate a Bitbucket Cloud app password, follow the Bitbuck must have "read" and "write" permission under repository.

To generate a GitLab personal access token, follow the GitLab "write_repository" permission.

To generate a Azure DevOps personal access token, follow the have "Full access" scope.

Git provider

| GitHub | ∨ |

Token or app password

| •••••••••••••••••••••••••••••••••••••• |

Git provider username or email ❓

| |

Save

Figure 9.15 – Git provider

3.   Go to the notebook and click on **Revision history** and click on **Git: Not linked**:

Figure 9.16 – Git sync update

4. Copy the GitHub repo URL, for example, `https://github.com/YourOrgName/YourRepoName`, provide the URL for linking GitHub, and select **main** for **Branch** or any branch you want the changes to get committed in. When you select from the drop-down list for **Branch**, you will find all the branches to which you have access. In this recipe, we are using **main** for **Branch** as shown in the following screenshot.

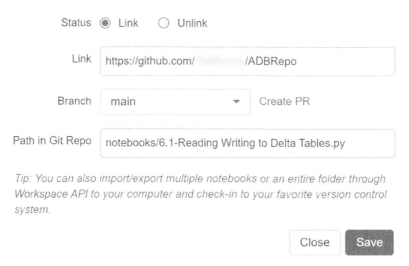

Figure 9.17 – Git preferences for GitHub link

5. You can provide any location for **Path in Git Repo** and click on **Save**. As soon the Git is linked, it will prompt you to make your first commit.

6. After you commit, you will find the `notebooks` folder created in your GitHub repository with the notebook saved as `.py file`:

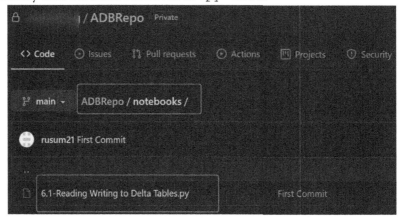

Figure 9.18 – GitHub code repo page

7. Let's go ahead and add a few comments and check whether the changes are getting committed. Go to the notebook and add a comment:

```
#Adding comment for GitHub
display(dbutils.fs.ls("/mnt/Gen2Source/Customer/
parquetFiles"))
```

8. Now let's commit the changes by clicking on **Save Now** and it will prompt you to commit the changes to GitHub.

9. You will find the comment added in your GitHub repository, as shown in the following screenshot:

```
#Adding comment for GitHub
display(dbutils.fs.ls("/mnt/Gen2Source/Customer/parquetFiles"))
```

Figure 9.19 – Changes added in the GitHub repository

By following the steps mentioned in this section, you can integrate GitHub with Azure Databricks for version controlling notebooks. You need to link every notebook you create in the workspace. New notebooks are not linked automatically to the repo.

How it works...

If you are working on a non-main branch such as a Dev branch, then after making the required changes and committing the changes, you can raise a PR by going to **Git Preferences** and clicking on **Create PR**:

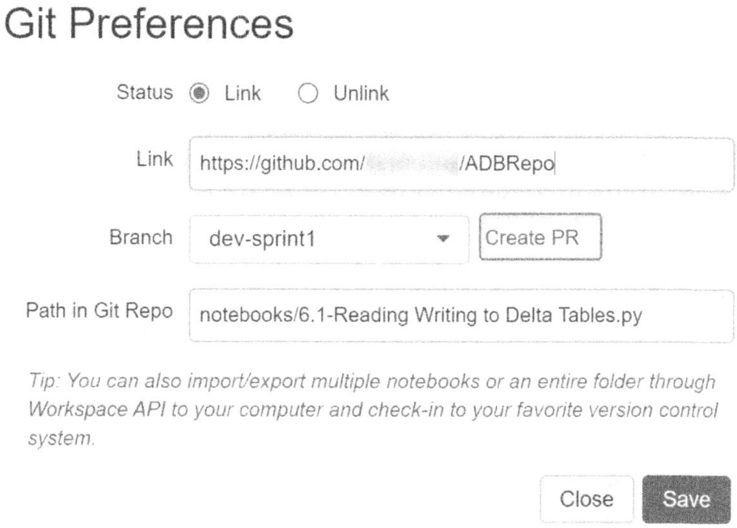

Git Preferences

Status ◉ Link   ○ Unlink

Link   `https://github.com/          /ADBRepo`

Branch   dev-sprint1   ▼   Create PR

Path in Git Repo   `notebooks/6.1-Reading Writing to Delta Tables.py`

Tip: You can also import/export multiple notebooks or an entire folder through Workspace API to your computer and check-in to your favorite version control system.

Close   Save

Figure 9.20 – Creating a PR

Clicking on **Create PR** will take you to the GitHub pull request page and you can view the changes and click on **Create pull request** to merge the changes with the main branch.

Apart from Azure DevOps and GitHub, you can use Bitbucket Cloud and GitLab to version control your notebooks.

Understanding the CI/CD process for Azure Databricks

In this recipe, we will learn what the advantage is of using the **Continuous Integration and Continuous Delivery (CI/CD)** process while working with Azure Databricks.

CI/CD is a method to frequently integrate code changes with a repository and deploy them to other environments. It offers an automated way of integrating, testing, and deploying code changes. CI in Azure Databricks enables developers to regularly build, test, and merge code changes to a shared repository. It's a solution for the very common problem of having multiple developers working on the same code or having multiple branches that could cause a conflict with each other in the software development life cycle.

CD refers to continuous delivery and/or continuous deployment. Continuous delivery means developers' changes are automatically tested and merged or uploaded to a repository such as Azure DevOps or Git. From there, changes can be deployed to other environments, such as Production. It reduces the efforts required to deploy changes to other environments, thus avoiding overloading operations teams that used to deploy code changes manually.

Getting ready

In this recipe, we are learning how CI/CD can be used with Azure Databricks to maintain source code in the repository and to automate deployment in different environments using a continuous deployment approach. You are expected to be aware of the CI/CD process, Azure DevOps, and a source code repository such as GitHub.

How to do it...

We will learn how to check in an Azure Databricks notebook and set up a build and release pipeline in the upcoming recipes.

How it works...

When you work on projects with multiple team members, it's not easy to integrate code changes made by each team member and there will always be the chance of conflicts when the code is merged. But when the CI/CD process is followed in a project, it becomes convenient to track each team member's code changes and resolve conflicts if there are any. The flow is very simple. When a developer develops any module, they check the code into the source control. Then the checked-in code is merged into the master branch. Using the release pipeline, the updated version of the code from the master branch is deployed to different environments such as test, **User Acceptance Testing (UAT)**, and production.

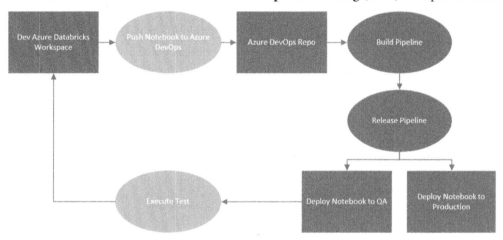

Figure 9.21 – Azure DevOps CI/CD process

The preceding diagram illustrates how an Azure Databricks notebook is integrated with the CI/CD process.

How to set up an Azure DevOps pipeline for deploying notebooks

An Azure DevOps release pipeline provides users with an option to automate the process of deploying various Azure resources such as Azure Databricks and Azure SQL Database to different environments such as dev, test, UAT, and production. It helps project teams to streamline the process of deployment and have a consistent deployment framework created for all their deployments to Azure. We can use Azure DevOps release pipelines to deploy Azure Databricks artifacts such as notebooks and libraries to various environments.

Setting up the DevOps build and release pipeline will enable you to implement CI/CD for Azure Databricks notebooks.

Getting ready

Before getting started on this recipe, you should have completed the first recipe of this chapter where you integrated Azure DevOps with an Azure Databricks workspace. After you check in all your notebooks, you can move ahead with the next section of this recipe.

You need to have two Databricks workspaces. One workspace will be integrated with Azure DevOps and all required notebooks will be checked in, and the other workspace (the production workspace) will be used to deploy the artifacts from Azure DevOps using the release pipeline.

How to do it...

In this section, you will learn how to create an Azure build pipeline for Azure Databricks notebooks and later create an Azure release pipeline to deploy the notebooks to a different Azure Databricks workspace.

a) The following are the steps for creating a build pipeline (Continuous Integration – CI):

1. From the Azure DevOps pipeline, select **Pipelines** under the **Pipelines** section and select **Use the classic editor** as shown in the following screenshot:

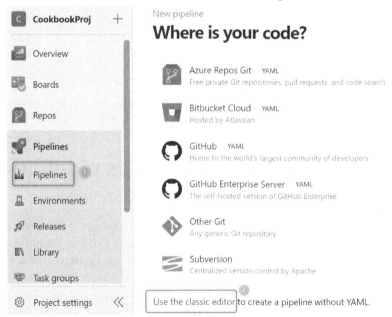

Figure 9.22 – Azure DevOps build pipeline

2. After selecting the classic editor, you will be prompted for the **Repository** and branch details. Provide the required details as per your environment:

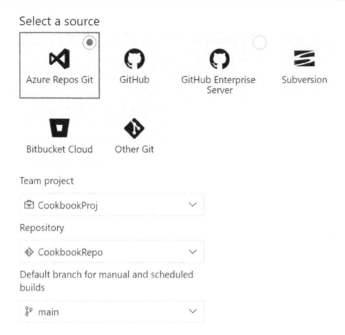

Figure 9.23 – Azure DevOps build pipeline – contd

3.   When you click on **Continue**, you will be asked to select the template. For our build pipeline, we will be selecting **Empty job** as shown in the following screenshot:

Figure 9.24 – Azure DevOps build pipeline template

4. In this step, you will be adding tasks for **Agent job**. Click on the + symbol, search for **Publish build artifacts** as shown in the following screenshot, and click on **Add**:

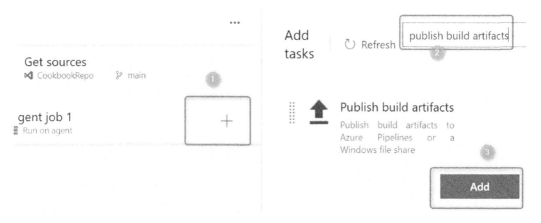

Figure 9.25 – Azure DevOps build pipeline – contd

5. For **Path to publish**, you will provide the location of your notebooks, which are saved as .py files in the repository. We are selecting the entire notebooks folder, which has two notebooks that will be deployed to the production Databricks workspace. Provide the artifact name as adfnotebooks_drop. This artifact name will be the source build location for the release pipeline that you will be creating in this recipe:

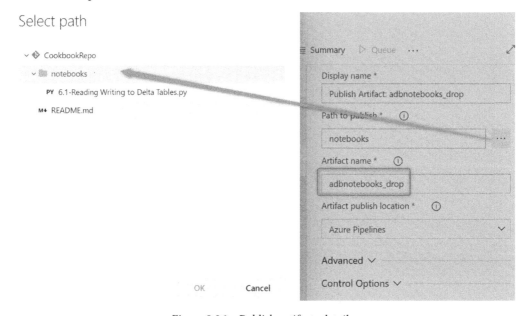

Figure 9.26 – Publish artifacts details

6. After you have provided the folder for the notebooks, click on **Save & queue**, which will build the pipeline you have created, and the following is the output after the build pipeline run completes You can click on the **Agent job 1** under **Jobs** to find the artifact which is created.

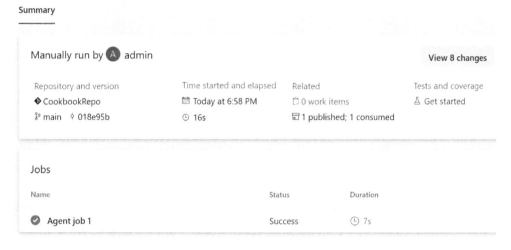

Figure 9.27 – Build run status

After following the preceding steps, you have created and executed the build pipeline successfully.

b) The following are the steps for creating a release pipeline (Continuous Deployment – CD):

1. From the Azure DevOps pipeline, select the **Release** option under **Pipelines**. Click on **+ New release pipeline** and select the **Empty job** template as shown in the following screenshot:

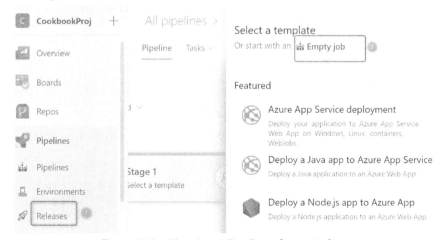

Figure 9.28 – New Azure DevOps release pipeline

2. Rename the pipeline to **Deploy Notebooks** and click on **1 job, 0 task,** as shown in the following screenshot.

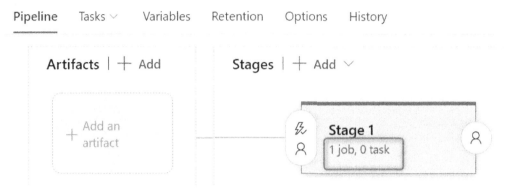

Figure 9.29 – Adding a task to the release pipeline

3. For Azure Databricks DevOps operations, we are using the extension **DevOps for Azure Databricks** by Microsoft DevLabs from the marketplace. You can choose any other extension that is approved by your security team. Under **Tasks**, search for Azure Databricks and click on **Get it free**.

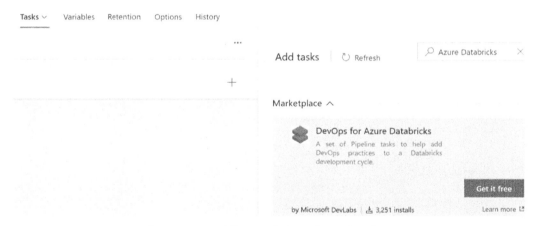

Figure 9.30 – Adding a task from the marketplace

4. When you click on **Get it free**, you will be taken to a different page where you will send a request to install the extension.

5. Provide the details about the DevOps organization where you will be installing the extension. This request goes to the admin of the Azure DevOps team in your organization, and they must approve the request. If you are the admin, then the request will be auto-approved:

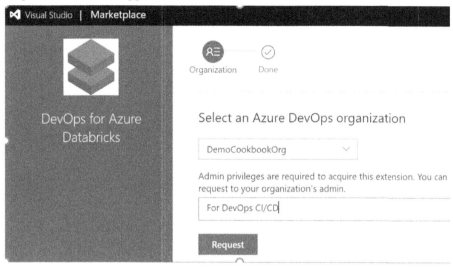

Figure 9.31 – Send a request to add an extension from the marketplace

6. After the extension is added, go back to the release pipeline and click on **Add an artifact** and **Source (build pipeline)** will be the build pipeline name that we created earlier in this recipe, as shown in the following screenshot:

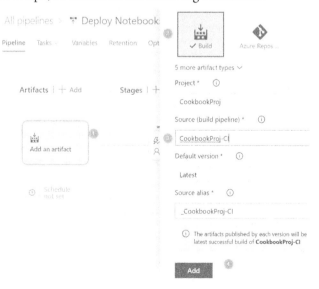

Figure 9.32 – Adding artifacts

7. Now click on **1 job, 0 task**, search for the task **Databricks** and add the **Configure Databricks** tasks:

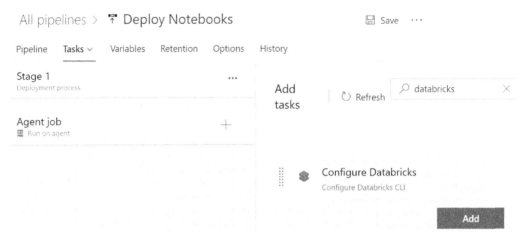

Figure 9.33 – Adding release pipeline tasks

8. In this task, you will provide the production Databricks workspace URL and the access token where the notebooks will be deployed:

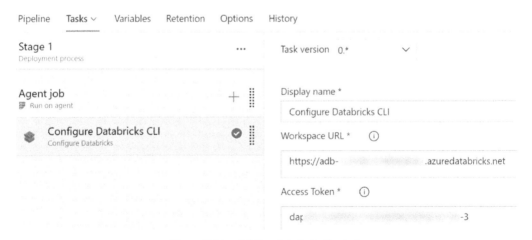

Figure 9.34 – Adding details to the task

9. In this step, you will be adding one more task, which will be the **Deploy Databricks Notebooks** task, as shown in the following screenshot:

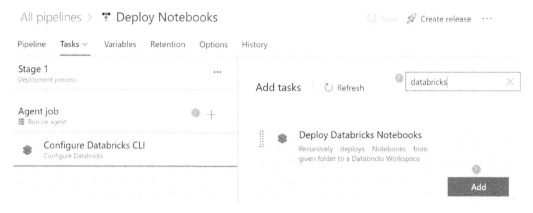

Figure 9.35 – Adding another task to the release pipeline

10. In the **Deploy Databricks Notebooks** task, provide the `notebooks` folder path and the workspace name will be `/Shared`. All our notebooks will be deployed under the shared folder path in the production workspace:

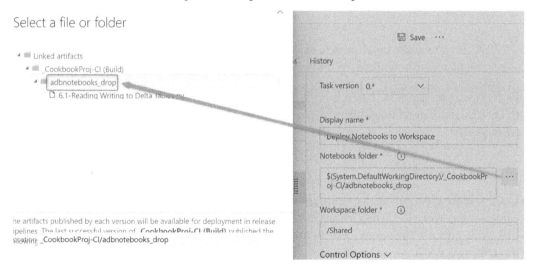

Figure 9.36 – Adding details to the task

11. After providing the details for the **Deploy Databricks Notebooks** task, click on **Save and Create release**, which will start executing the release pipeline and the following will be the output after the release pipeline gets executed successfully:

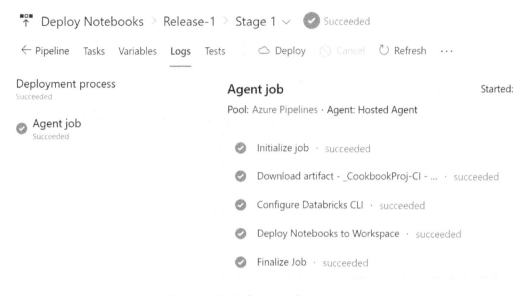

Figure 9.37 – Release pipeline run status

12. After the release pipeline gets executed, you will find the two notebooks deployed to the production workspace under the shared folder path.

By following the steps in the recipe, you have implemented a build and release pipeline to deploy Azure notebooks from an Azure DevOps repo to a production Databricks workspace.

How it works...

In the release pipeline for the **Configure Databricks CLI** task, we have exposed the token value so that every user who has access to the release pipeline can get the value. To avoid that, you can store the token value in an Azure Key Vault secret and read the secret value by creating an Azure Key Vault task in the release pipeline. Later, use the variable that stores the secret value in the Databricks CLI task.

Deploying notebooks to multiple environments

The Azure DevOps CI/CD process can be used to deploy Azure resources and artifacts to various environments from the same release pipelines. Also, we can set the deployment sequence specifically to the needs of a project or application. For example, you can deploy notebooks to the test environment first. If the deployment to the test environment succeeds, then deploy them to UAT, and later, upon approval of the changes, they can be deployed to the production environment. In this recipe, you will learn how to use variable groups and mapping groups in a specific environment and use the values in variables at runtime to deploy Azure Databricks notebooks to different environments.

In **variable groups**, we create a set of variables that hold values that can be used in the release pipeline for all the stages or scope it to one specific stage. For example, if we have two stages in the release pipeline that are deploying to different environments (UAT and Production), then we can scope each variable group having the same variable name to a specific stage. This way, we are using the same variable names in both stages, but variable groups are different for each stage. You can learn more about variable groups from the following link: `https://docs.microsoft.com/en-us/azure/devops/pipelines/library/variable-groups?view=azure-devops&tabs=yaml`.

In the next section, you will learn about the pre-requisites to get started on this recipe.

Getting ready

Before starting, you need to ensure you have set up an Azure DevOps repo and integrated that with an Azure Databricks workspace. To test deployment to a different Databricks workspace, create the following three workspaces.

The following are the workspace details for this recipe. All the workspaces are of the premium tier.

Environment	Resource Group	Workspace Name
Dev	CookbookRG	BigDataAnalytics
UAT	UATCookbookRG	UATBigDataAnalytics
Production	ProdCookbookRG	ProdBigDataAnalytics

The Dev workspace will be integrated with Azure DevOps, which users will commit their changes to. The Azure DevOps Release pipeline will deploy changes to different environments in sequence. If the deployment to one environment fails, then changes will not be deployed to the next environment defined in the sequence. You will learn how to create variable groups in the next section.

How to do it...

In this section, you will learn how to create variable groups and use them in the release pipeline that you created in the preceding recipe, which deploys notebooks to the UAT and Production environments.

Let's run through the following steps to create and use variable groups in the release pipelines:

1. Go to the **Variables** tab as shown in the following screenshot and click on **Manage variable groups**:

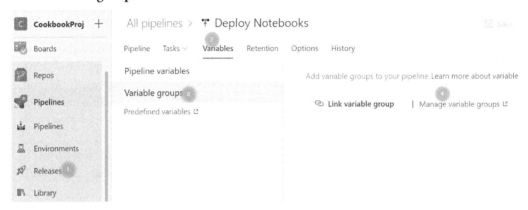

Figure 9.38 – Variable group creation

2. Once you are on the variable groups page, click on **+Variable group** to create variable groups.

3. You will be creating two variable groups, one for the UAT stage and one for the Prod stage in the release pipeline. Each variable group will have two variables created:

    a) **Token** – This will hold the Azure Databricks token value for the workspace.

    b) **URL** – This variable will hold the value for the Azure Databricks workspace URL:

Library > 🔲 UAT Variable Group*

Variable group   💾 Save   📋 Clone   ♡ Security   ⟳ Pipeline permissions   🗐 Approvals

Variable group name

UAT Variable Group

Description

(●) Link secrets from an Azure key vault as variables ⓘ

Variables

Name ↑	Value
Token	********
URL	https://adb-... .azuredatabrick

+ Add

Figure 9.39 – Adding variables to a variable group

4. The following are the two variable groups you should see on the **Variable groups** page:

Library

Variable groups   Secure files

▽ Search variable groups

Name ↓↑

fx Prod Variable Group

fx UAT Variable Group

Figure 9.40 – Variable groups

5. After creating the variable groups, go to the release pipeline and you should create two stages: one will deploy notebooks to the UAT workspace, and the **Prod** stage will deploy notebooks to the Prod workspace. Each stage will have the same tasks that you created in the recipe *How to set up an Azure DevOps pipeline for deploying notebooks* from the source repo to various environments:

Figure 9.41 – Stages in the release pipeline

6. After creating the two stages, you need to link the variable groups to the release pipeline. Click on the Variables tab in the release pipeline you have created, click **Link variable group**, and link both of the variable groups you have created:

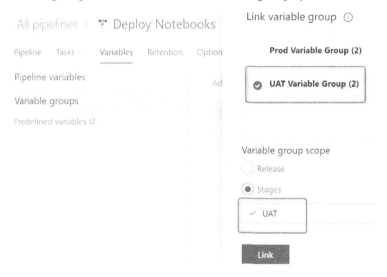

Figure 9.42 – Linking variable groups to the release pipeline

7. You need to make sure the scope of the variable groups is set correctly. The **UAT Variable Group** scope should be mapped to the **UAT** stage and the scope of **Prod Variable Group** should be mapped to the **Prod** stage, as shown in the following screenshot:

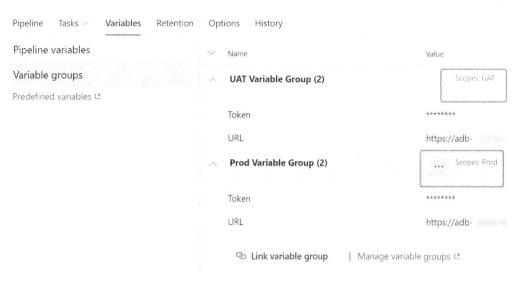

Figure 9.43– Variable group scope

8. Assign the variables created in the variable groups to the release pipeline tasks. In the UAT stage for the **Configure Databricks CLI** task, provide the value as $ (URL) for **Workspace URL**, which is the Databricks workspace URL. For **Access Token**, set the value as $ (Token), as shown in the following screenshot:

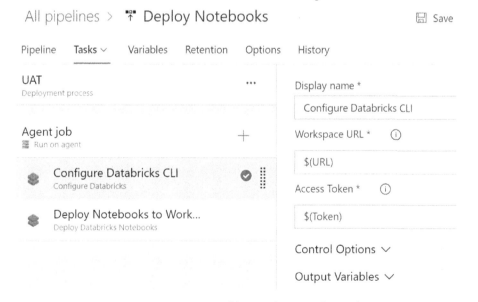

Figure 9.44 – Using variables in release pipeline tasks

9. You must follow the same steps for the Prod stage of the **Configure Databricks CLI** task.

10. After assigning the variables to both stages, trigger the release pipeline and you will find the notebooks are deployed to both the UAT and Prod workspaces. The following is the screenshot after the release pipeline is executed:

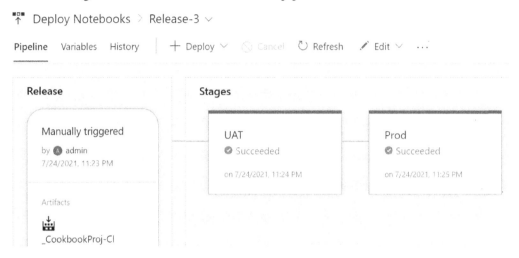

Figure 9.45 – Release pipeline run status

In this recipe, you have learned how to deploy Azure Databricks notebooks to multiple environments from an Azure DevOps release pipeline using variable groups.

How it works...

Instead of creating variables manually in variable groups, you can import secrets from Azure Key Vault and use them as variables in the release pipeline as shown in the following screenshot. In the following screenshot, we are getting the access token secret for the Databricks workspace from a key vault:

Library > 🛡 Prod Variable Group*

Variable group   🖫 Save   ⌧ Clone   ◇ Security   ◇ Pipeline permissions

Prod Variable Group

Description

⬤◯ Link secrets from an Azure key vault as variables   ⓘ

Azure subscription * · | Manage ⬈

⌄   ↻

ⓘ Scoped to subscription 'Visual Studio Enterprise'

Key vault name *   Manage ⬈

CookbookKeyVault   ⌄   ↻

Variables   Last refreshed: 6 hours ago

Delete	Secret name	Content type	Status	Expiration date
	ADBToken		Enabled	Never

Figure 9.46 – Using secrets in variable groups

You can also control how the deployment of notebooks or resources to production can happen. You can have approvers added to a stage who can **Approve** or **Reject** the deployment to production based on certain conditions. You can add pre-deployment conditions to a stage in the release pipeline, as shown in the following screenshot:

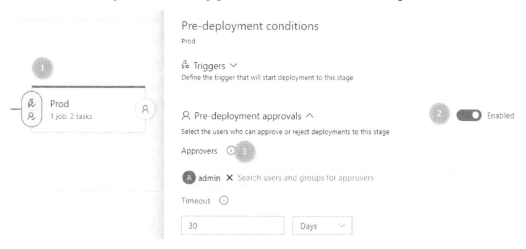

Figure 9.47 – Adding pre-deployment conditions

Once you assign a user to approval for a specific stage, then before deploying the resources or notebooks, it will prompt the owner to approve the deployment. Once approved, only then will the deployment proceed, as shown in the following screenshot:

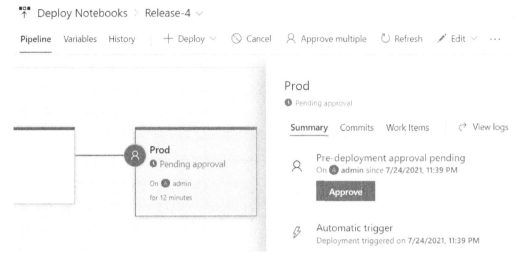

Figure 9.48 – Approval for the Prod deployment

In the next recipe, you will learn how to automate the triggering of build and release pipelines after changes are checked in.

Enabling CI/CD in an Azure DevOps build and release pipeline

As you have learned in the preceding recipes how to create DevOps pipelines and the concepts around the CI/CD process for Azure Databricks notebooks, in this recipe you will implement CI/CD for the Azure DevOps pipeline that you created in the *How to set up an Azure DevOps pipeline for deploying notebooks recipe.*

In this recipe, you will learn the entire process of how to enable a build to be triggered automatically when changes are merged to the main branch. Later, you will learn how to trigger the release pipeline automatically when the build succeeds, which will deploy the artifacts (notebooks) to the different Databricks workspaces.

Getting ready

Before getting started, you need to complete the following two recipes of this chapter:

- *How to set up an Azure DevOps pipeline for deploying notebooks*
- *Deploying notebooks to multiple environments*

The following is the flow for the automated CI/CD process for deploying Azure Databricks notebooks to UAT and production workspaces:

1. Users commit their changes to the Dev branch and create a PR to merge the changes from the Dev branch to the master branch.

2. When the merge completes, the build pipeline is triggered automatically, and it copies the artifacts to the drop folder we specified in the build definition.

3. When the build succeeds, then the release pipeline is triggered without any manual intervention and deploys the notebooks to the UAT and production workspace that is mentioned in the release pipeline.

In the next section, you will implement the steps mentioned in the preceding points.

How to do it...

Let's go through the following steps to enable CI/CD for the build and release pipeline:

1. To enable CI on the build pipeline, go to the build pipeline you created and, on the **Triggers** tab, enable the **Enable continuous integration** option. Select **main** for **Branch specification**, as shown in the following screenshot:

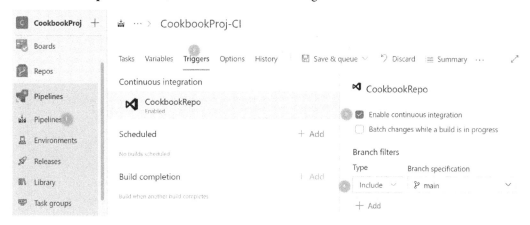

Figure 9.49 – Enable triggers for CI

2.   To enable Continuous Deployment on the release pipeline, go to the release pipeline you created, and under **Artifacts**, you have an option to enable Continuous Deployment, as shown in the following screenshot. Once you select the CI trigger, you will get an option to enable it and select **main** for **Build branch**:

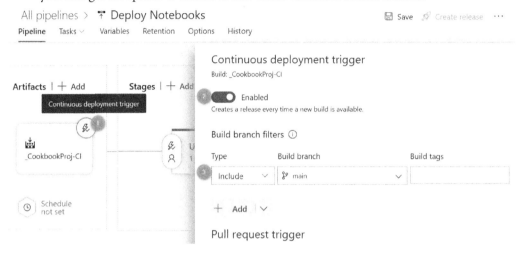

Figure 9.50 – Enable triggers for CD

3.   To test the end-to-end CI/CD process, start by adding a comment in the notebook and commit the changes to the Dev branch. Once the changes are committed to the Dev branch, raise a PR and merge the Dev changes to the master branch.

4.   As soon the changes are merged in the master branch, the build pipeline is triggered as shown in the following screenshot. The build pipeline run number is **#18**:

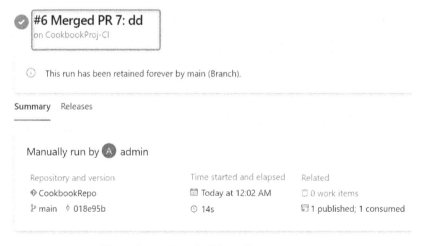

Figure 9.51 – Auto build pipeline run status

5. After the build pipeline run completes, the release pipeline is triggered, which succeeds in deploying the changes to both the UAT and Prod Azure Databricks workspaces.

6. To identify which build triggered the release pipeline, go to the **History** tab of the latest release and you will find the comment stating it was triggered by **build CookbookProj-CI 6** which is by build 6.

7. You can also identify which release pipelines are triggered by a build pipeline run by going to the CI build and checking the **Release** tab, and you will find the release pipeline execution details.

In this recipe, you have learned how to implement the CI/CD process for Azure Databricks notebooks and how to identify the details about which build run triggered a release pipeline execution. In the following recipe, you will learn how to deploy an Azure Databricks service from an Azure DevOps release pipeline.

Deploying an Azure Databricks service using an Azure DevOps release pipeline

Azure DevOps release pipelines can be used to automate the process of Azure resource deployment to different environments. In this recipe, you will learn how to deploy Azure Databricks to a specific resource group in a subscription. Knowing this process will not only help you to deploy Azure Databricks services but can also be used to deploy other Azure resources as well.

Getting ready

In this recipe, we will be using ARM templates to deploy Azure Databricks resources from Azure DevOps pipelines. To use the ARM templates in the Azure DevOps release pipeline, you will have to check in the ARM JSON files. You can download the JSON files from the following link: `https://github.com/Azure/azure-quickstart-templates/tree/master/quickstarts/microsoft.databricks/databricks-workspace`.

The following is a screenshot of the folder in the Azure DevOps repo where we have checked in the JSON files:

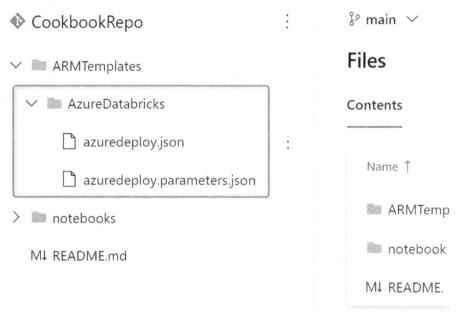

Figure 9.52 – ARM templates in the Azure DevOps repo

In the next section, you will learn how to use the template files from the Azure DevOps repo and deploy an Azure Databricks service to any resource group or environment.

How to do it...

Let's learn how to create an Azure DevOps pipeline to deploy an Azure Databricks service by going through the following steps:

1. Create a new Azure DevOps release pipeline and use **Azure Repo** as the source type for the artifacts, as shown in the following screenshot. The name of the release pipeline is **DeployAzureDatbricksService**:

Figure 9.53 – Release pipeline source type

2.   Click on **1 job, 0 task** to add a task to the DevOps pipeline, search for **ARM template deployment** to deploy ARM templates, and click on **Add**.

3.   After adding the **ARM template deployment** task, provide the details for the task as shown in the following screenshot. Click on the ellipsis for **Override template parameters** and provide the value for the Databricks workspace – you can provide **Standard** or **Premium** for **PricingTier**:

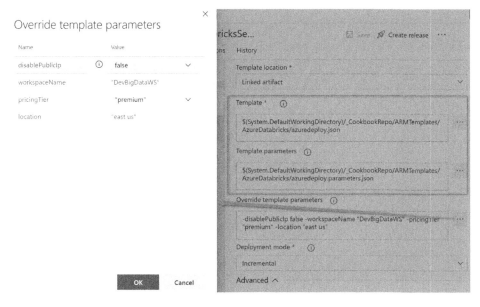

Figure 9.54 – ARM template deployment task details

4. Trigger the pipeline after providing all the details for the preceding task and you should see the status of the pipeline as **Succeeded**:

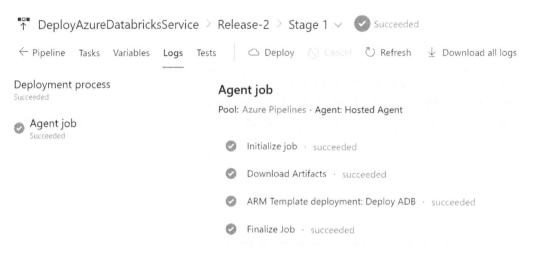

Figure 9.55 – Release pipeline run status

You can further make the pipeline more dynamic by adding variables to the pipeline and deploying the Azure Databricks service to different resource groups. You can also create a different release pipeline for each of the different subscriptions/environments.

10
Understanding Security and Monitoring in Azure Databricks

When organizations start their digital transformation journey, security plays a very important role in any digital transformation and its operations. Security defines how the network infrastructure and customer data should be secured. Data security defines who has access to what kind of data and at what grain. These concepts are no different for the Azure Databricks service. Azure Databricks provides various options and tools for securing the network infrastructure and enhancing data security.

In this chapter, you will learn how to secure the Azure Databricks service by deploying it to your own virtual network. You will also learn how to define fine-grained access control on the data, as well as enable users to access the storage without the need to mount a Storage Account using an **Account Key** or **Service Principal**. Knowing these tools and methods will help you secure your Azure Databricks service and control the permissions users have regarding the data.

In this chapter, we're going to cover the following recipes:

- Understanding and creating RBAC in Azure for ADLS Gen2
- Creating ACLs using Storage Explorer and PowerShell
- How to configure credential passthrough
- How to restrict data access to users using RBAC
- How to restrict data access to users using ACLs
- Deploying Azure Databricks in a VNet and accessing a secure storage account
- Using Ganglia reports for cluster health
- Cluster access control

Let's check out the prerequisites for this chapter.

Technical requirements

To follow along with the examples shown in this chapter, you will need to have the following:

- An Azure subscription and the required permissions for that subscription, as mentioned in the *Technical requirements* section of *Chapter 1*, *Creating an Azure Databricks Service*.
- An Azure Databricks premium workspace, since most of the access control features are available only in a premium workspace. All notebooks were executed on Spark 3.0 clusters with the Databricks 7.5 runtime.

Let's get started by understanding what RBAC and ACLs are in Azure.

Understanding and creating RBAC in Azure for ADLS Gen-2

In this chapter, you will be learning how to allow AAD users to securely access the files and directories in an ADLS Gen-2 storage account using AAD authentication from Azure Databricks. ADLS Gen-2 supports two methods for securing access to the data lake via security principals:

- **Role-Based Access Control (RBAC)**: Used to restrict access to the Storage Account and to individual containers in theStorage Account.

- POSIX-like **Access Control Lists (ACLs)**: Used to restrict access to individual folders and files.

In this recipe, you will learn how to use RBAC to control access at the container level in an ADLS Gen-2 Storage Account.

Getting ready

RBAC uses role assignments to apply sets of permissions to a user, group, service principal, or managed identity that is present in **Azure Active Directory (AAD)** and is requesting access to Azure resources.

With RBAC, Azure resources are constrained as top-level resources. In the case of Azure Data Lake Storage Gen2, RBAC can be used to grant permissions at the Storage Account level, which can be extended to the container (filesystem) resource.

Azure role assignments for ADLS Gen-2 are used to control access permissions. The smallest granularity that a permission can be assigned is at the container level, and not to individual directories inside a container.

To demonstrate access permissions using RBAC and ACLs, we will work with two AAD users (SQLUser and Appuser).

To do this, you will need to install individual modules such as `Az.Storage`, `Az.Resources`, and `Az.Accounts` or install entire Azure PowerShell cmdlets by running the following command:

```
Install-Module -Name Az
```

You can find more details about installing Azure PowerShell cmdlets at `https://github.com/Azure/azure-powershell`.

You can get the PowerShell code from `https://github.com/PacktPublishing/Azure-Databricks-Cookbook/tree/main/Chapter10/Code`.

How to do it...

Let's learn how to assign RBAC permissions to the users/groups of an ADLS Gen-2 account from the Azure portal and PowerShell:

1. From the Azure portal go to the Storage Account for which you want to grant Azure Storage Blob Data roles to the AAD user:

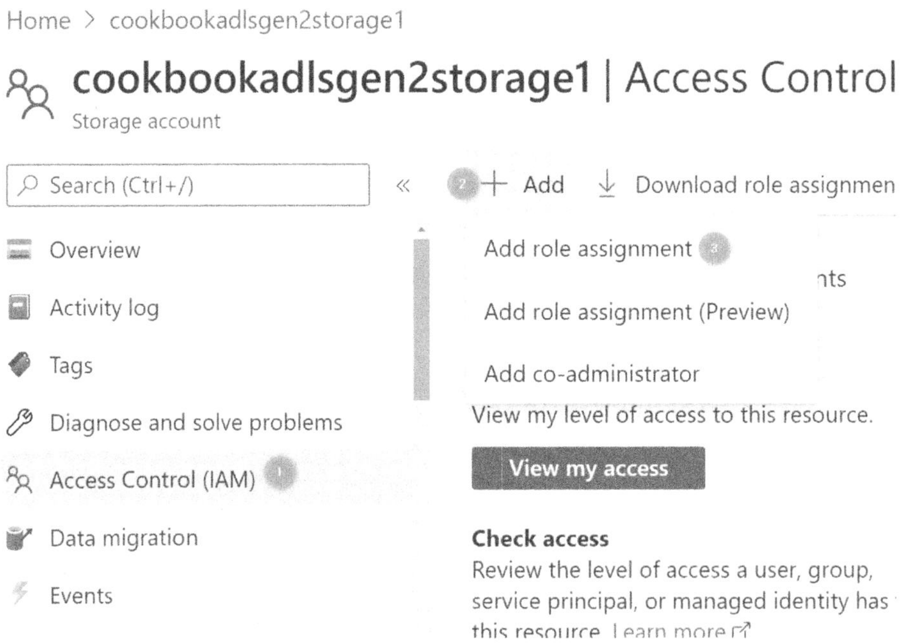

Figure 10.1 – Role assignment

2. On the **Add role assignment** screen, select **Storage Blob Data Owner** for the role, as shown in the following screenshot:

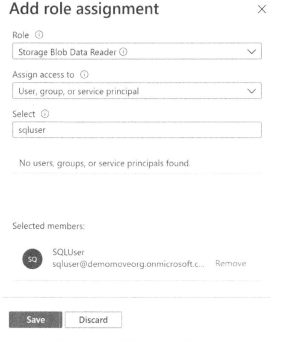

Add role assignment

e1 | Access Control (IA

Download role assignments

ccess   Role assignments   Roles

ss
level of access to this resource.

my access

ccess
he level of access a user, group,
rincipal, or managed identity has to
urce. Learn more

roup, or service principal

by name or email address

Role

Select a role

Select a role

Storage Account Backup Contributor Role

Storage Account Contributor

Storage Account Key Operator Service Role

Storage Blob Data Contributor

Storage Blob Data Owner

Storage Blob Data Reader

Storage Blob Delegator

Storage File Data SMB Share Contributor

Storage File Data SMB Share Elevated Contributor

Figure 10.2 – Role assignment – Selecting Storage Blob Data Owner

3. After selecting a role, select the SQLUser AAD user that you want to grant permissions on the Storage Account to:

Add role assignment   ×

Role

Storage Blob Data Reader

Assign access to

User, group, or service principal

Select

sqluser

No users, groups, or service principals found.

Selected members:

SQ   SQLUser
       sqluser@demomoveorg.onmicrosoft.c...   Remove

Save   Discard

Figure 10.3 – Selecting AAD user

So far, you have learned how to assign RBAC to an AAD user on ADLS Gen-2 from the Azure portal. Now, let's learn how to grant the Storage Blob Data Reader role to Appuser on ADLS Gen-2 using a PowerShell script:

1. Connect to your subscription by running the following code:

    ```
    $Tenantid="xxxxxx"
    $subscriptionId="xxxxxx"
    Connect-AzAccount -Tenant $Tenantid -Subscription
    $subscriptionId


    Connect-AzureAD -TenantId $Tenantid
    Select-AzSubscription -SubscriptionId $subscriptionId
    -Tenant $Tenantid |select *
    ```

2. The following code will list all the available roles for Azure Blob storage:

    ```
    Get-AzRoleDefinition | Where-Object -Property Name -match
    "Blob" | FT Name, IsCustom, Id
    ```

3. We need to get the principal ID for the AAD user/group. Run the following code to get the AppUser Principal ID:

    ```
    $principalId = (Get-AzADUser  | Where-Object -Property
    UserPrincipalName -Match "appuser").Id
    ```

4. Next, we need to get the scope, which is the resource ID of the ADLS Gen-2 Storage Account where we will grant Storage Blob Data Reader access to AppUser. Run the following code to get the resource ID for the Storage Account:

    ```
    $accountInfo = Get-AzStorageAccount -ResourceGroupName
    'CoookbookStorageRG' -Name 'cookbookadlsgen2storage1'
    $accountResourceId = $accountInfo.Id
    $blobResourceID = $accountResourceId + "/blobServices/
    default"
    ```

5. Run the following code to assign the Storage Blob Data Reader permissions of the cookbookadlsgen2storage1 Storage Account to AppUser (AAD user):

    ```
    New-AzRoleAssignment -ObjectId $principalId `
    -RoleDefinitionName "Storage Blob Data Reader" `
    -Scope $accountResourceId
    ```

6. Run the following code to check the role assignments for AppUser:

```
Get-AzRoleAssignment -ObjectId $principalId -Scope
$accountResourceId
```

7. You can also verify the role's assignment from the Azure portal. On the **Storage Account** page, click on **Access Control (IAM)** and go the **Role assignments** tab; you will see AppUser with the Azure Storage Blob Reader role granted:

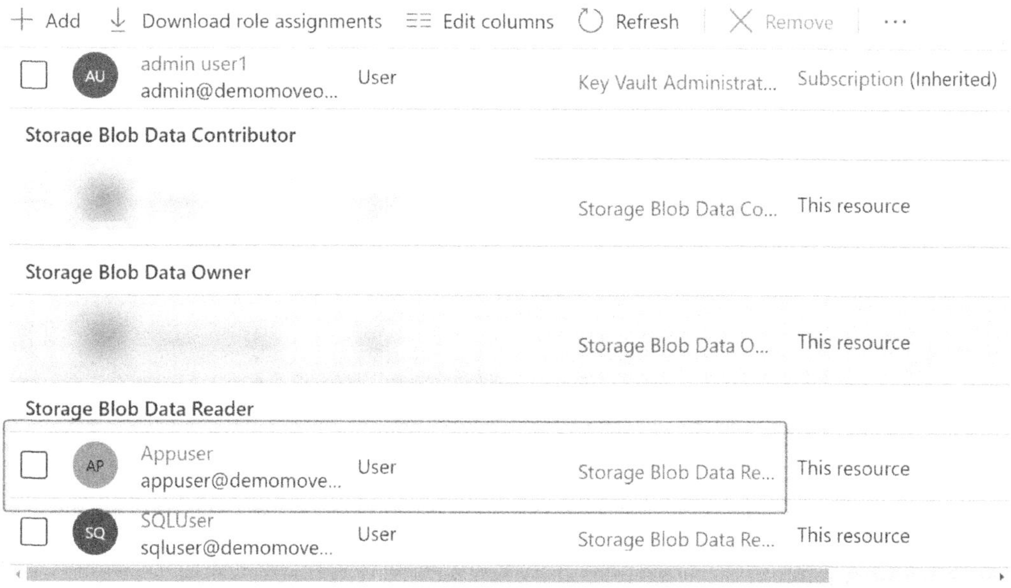

+ Add	↓ Download role assignments	☰ Edit columns	↻ Refresh	✕ Remove	⋯
☐ **AU**	admin user1 admin@demomoveo...	User		Key Vault Administrat...	Subscription (Inherited)

Storage Blob Data Contributor

			Storage Blob Data Co...	This resource

Storage Blob Data Owner

			Storage Blob Data O...	This resource

Storage Blob Data Reader

☐ **AP**	Appuser appuser@demomove...	User		Storage Blob Data Re...	This resource
☐ **SQ**	SQLUser sqluser@demomove...	User		Storage Blob Data Re...	This resource

Figure 10.4 – Checking the assigned role

8. The preceding PowerShell code granted access at the Storage Account level. We can also assign RBAC roles at the container level for ADLS Gen-2 storage. Run the following command to delete the existing assignment for AppUser:

```
Remove-AzRoleAssignment -ObjectId $principalId
-RoleDefinitionName "Storage Blob Data Reader" -Scope
$accountResourceId
```

9. At this point, AppUser doesn't have access to the Storage Account, as shown in the following screenshot:

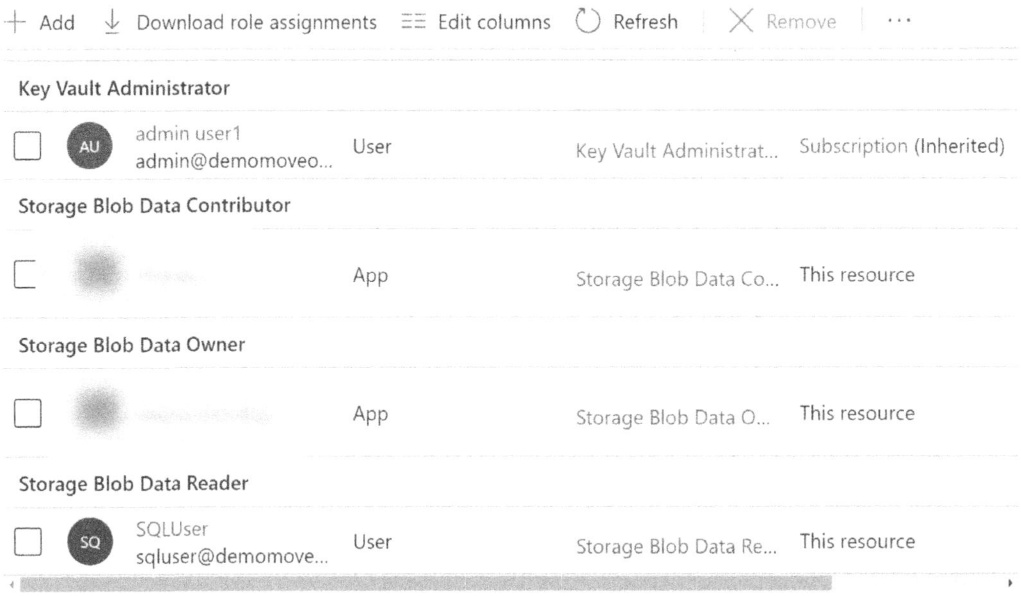

+ Add   ↓ Download role assignments   ☰ Edit columns   ↻ Refresh   ✕ Remove   ···

Key Vault Administrator

☐	AU	admin user1 admin@demomoveo...	User	Key Vault Administrat...	Subscription (Inherited)

Storage Blob Data Contributor

| ☐ | | | App | Storage Blob Data Co... | This resource |

Storage Blob Data Owner

| ☐ | | | App | Storage Blob Data O... | This resource |

Storage Blob Data Reader

| ☐ | SQ | SQLUser
sqluser@demomove... | User | Storage Blob Data Re... | This resource |

Figure 10.5 – Checking the assigned role

10. Run the following code to find the resource ID of the Storage Account. It will also assign a role to the container (sourcedata) that was created in the ADLS Gen-2 account:

```
$accountInfo = Get-AzStorageAccount -ResourceGroupName
'CoookbookStorageRG' -Name 'cookbookadlsgen2storage1'
$accountResourceId = $accountInfo.Id
#Getting resource id for container sourcedata in
cookbookadlsgen2storage1 account
$containerBlobResourceID = $accountResourceId + "/
blobServices/default/containers/sourcedata"

New-AzRoleAssignment -ObjectId $principalId `
-RoleDefinitionName "Storage Blob Data Reader" `
-Scope $containerBlobResourceID
```

11. Using the Azure portal, you can check that this access to Appuser is at the container (`sourcedata`) but not the entire Storage Account, as shown in the following screenshot. Appuser does not have access at Storage Account level:

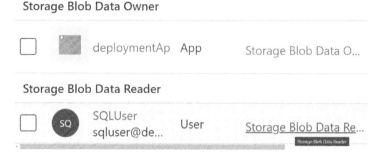

Figure 10.6 – Granting the Storage Blob Data Reader role

12. As we can see, no access has been given at the Storage Account level. Now, let's check the access at the container level from the Azure portal:

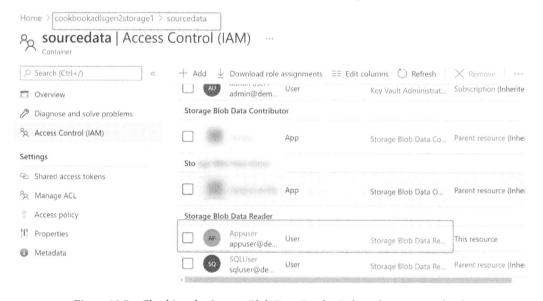

Figure 10.7 – Checking the Storage Blob Data Reader Role at the container level

13. You can also run the following code to check the role assignments for an AAD user:

```
Get-AzRoleAssignment -ObjectId $principalId -Scope
$containerBlobResourceID
```

By following the preceding steps, you provided fine-grained access to the AAD users at both the Storage Account and container level. In the next recipe, you will learn how to grant access to folders and files in the container of the ADLS Gen-2 storage account.

Creating ACLs using Storage Explorer and PowerShell

We use ACLs when we want to selectively give access to a set of directories and files to AAD users and groups in an ADLS Gen-2 storage account. Neither Azure built-in roles nor custom roles can't be used to restrict access at the directory/file level. Using ACL, we can provide access to specific directories and files in a container. Each file and directory in a Storage Account has an ACL.

Sets of permissions such as reading and writing can be granted to a security group in AAD, to an individual user on directories and files in an ADLS Gen-2 Storage Account, or to a container to restrict the access to the data that a user can see. You can't use an ACL to provide a level of access that is lower than a level granted by an Azure built-in role assignment (RBAC).

Getting ready

Before getting started, make sure you are the owner of the Storage Account or have Storage Blob Data Owner access to the storage account.

There are two kinds of ACLs:

- **Access ACLs**: These control access to an object. Files and directories both have access ACLs, and you can grant and revoke access to individual directories and files.

- **Default ACLs**: These are the templates of ACLs and they are associated with a directory. This directory determines the access ACLs for the child items that are created in that directory. Only directories have default ACLs, not files.

Learning about ACLs in detail is outside the scope of this chapter. Please refer to the following link to learn more about ACLs for ADLS Gen-2:

```
https://docs.microsoft.com/en-gb/azure/storage/blobs/data-
lake-storage-access-control#about-acls
```

It is important to know about the different permission levels – **Read**, **Write**, and **Execute** – and how they are used on directories and files to control access to them. The following link provides details about this:

```
https://docs.microsoft.com/en-gb/azure/storage/blobs/data-
lake-storage-access-control#levels-of-permission
```

> **Note**
>
> You can download Azure Storage Explorer from the following link: `https://azure.microsoft.com/en-in/features/storage-explorer/`.
>
> You can get the PowerShell code from `https://github.com/PacktPublishing/Azure-Databricks-Cookbook/blob/main/Chapter10/Code/10.5-ACL.ipynb`.

In the next section, we will learn how to add ACLs to directories and files using Azure Storage Explorer and PowerShell.

How to do it...

Let's go through the following steps to create ACLs for directories and files:

1. From Azure Storage Explorer, click on the Storage Account that you want to create ACLs for, as shown in the following screenshot:

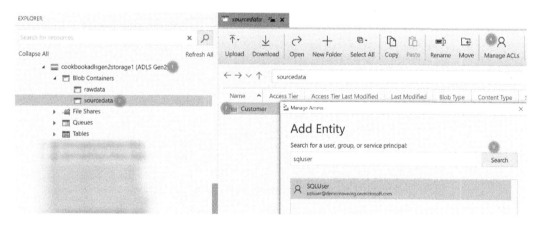

Figure 10.8 – Assigning ACLs to the user

2. After following the sequence of steps mentioned in the preceding screenshot, you will be taken to the **Manage Access** section, where you must provide the required ACLs for the AAD user you have added. In this example, we are providing **Read**, **Write**, and **Execute** permissions to SQLUser on the `Customer` directory in the `sourcedata` container:

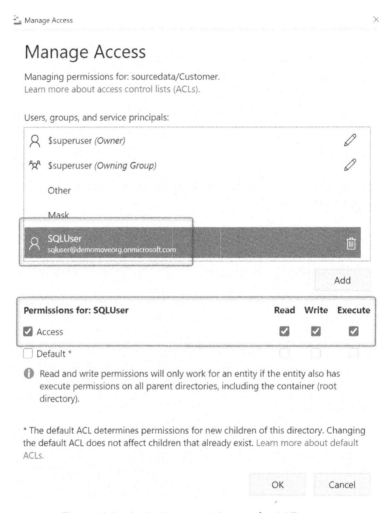

Figure 10.9 – Assigning permissions to the AAD user

3. At this point, we have only granted permissions to the `Customer` directory; permissions are not applied to the files and directories under `Customer`. You can verify this by checking the ACLs in the `parquetFiles` directory, as shown in the following screenshot. SQLUser does not have permissions for the `parquetFiles` directory:

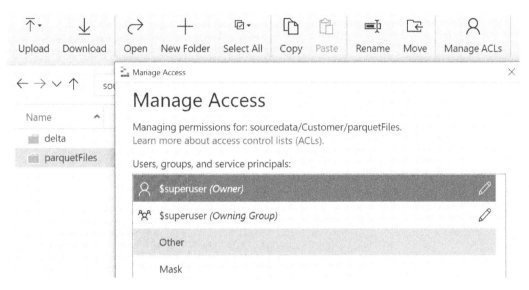

Figure 10.10 – Verifying ACLs for the AAD user

4. To grant access to all files and directories under `Customer`, right-click the **Customer** directory and select the **Propagate Access Control Lists...** option, as shown in the following screenshot. This will propagate all ACLs granted to `Customer` to all the files and directories under it:

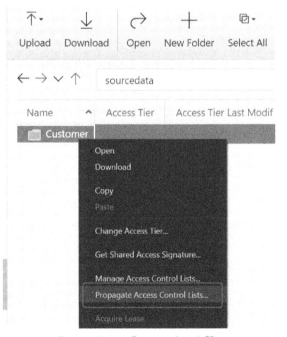

Figure 10.11 – Propagating ACLs

5. After completing the preceding step, you can verify the permissions on the `parquetFile` directory. You will see that SQLUser has the same **Read**, **Write**, and **Execute** permissions:

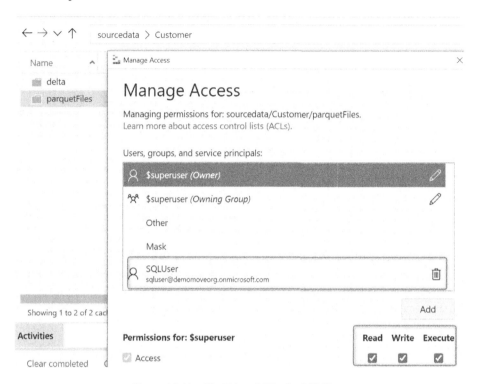

Figure 10.12 – Verifying ACLs for SQLUser

Now, let's learn how to grant ACLs to the AAD user (AppsUser) in the `Customer` directory in the `sourcedata` container using PowerShell:

1. From a PowerShell terminal, connect to the subscription that contains the ADLS Gen-2 Storage Account (used in the previous steps) by running the following code:

```
$Tenantid="xxx-xxxx-xxxx-xxxxx"

$subscriptionId="xxxx-xxxxx-xxxx-xxxx-xxxx"

Connect-AzAccount -Tenant $Tenantid -Subscription
$subscriptionId

Connect-AzureAD -TenantId $Tenantid

Select-AzSubscription -SubscriptionId $subscriptionId
-Tenant $Tenantid |select *
```

2. Run the following code to get the `principalId` parameter of the AAD user (AppUser):

```
$principalId = (Get-AzADUser   | Where-Object -Property
UserPrincipalName -Match "appuser").Id
```

```
$principalsqlId = (Get-AzADUser   | Where-Object -Property
UserPrincipalName -Match "sqluser").Id
```

3. To perform operations on this Storage Account such as adding and removing ACLs, you need to obtain authorization. You can use AAD or a storage account key to obtain this. In this example, we are using AAD to obtain authorization. Run the following code to obtain authorization using AAD:

```
#Obtaining authorization by using Azure Active Directory
(AD)
```

```
$ctx = New-AzStorageContext -StorageAccountName
'cookbookadlsgen2storage1' -UseConnectedAccount
```

4. To list the ACLs in the directories and files in the `sourcedata` container, run the following code:

```
$containerName = "sourcedata"
```

```
$filesystem = Get-AzDataLakeGen2Item -Context $ctx
-FileSystem $containerName -Path "Customer/parquetFiles"
```

```
$filesystem.ACL
```

5. Now, let's grant read and execute permissions to AppUser's `principalId` on all directories and files under `Customer/parquetFiles` recursively by running the following code. This code will preserve all the existing ACLs and add `Read` and `Execute` permissions to AppUser in all the directories and files under the `Customer/parquetFiles` folder in the `sourcedata` container:

```
$filesystemName = "sourcedata"
```

```
$dirname = "Customer/parquetFiles"
```

```
$acl = (Get-AzDataLakeGen2Item -Context $ctx -FileSystem
$filesystemName -Path $dirname).ACL
```

```
$acl = set-AzDataLakeGen2ItemAclObject -AccessControlType
user -EntityID $principalId -Permission r-x -InputObject
$acl
```

```
Update-AzDataLakeGen2AclRecursive -Context $ctx
-FileSystem $filesystemName -Path $dirname -Acl $acl
```

6. To overwrite any existing ACLs and add a new set of ACLs to directories and files recursively under `Customer/parquetFiles`, run the following code. Please note that the code will erase all the existing ACLs in `Customer/parquetFiles` and add new ACLs for the superuser, group, other, and to the AAD user. SQLUser does not have permissions anymore for `Customer/parquetFiles`:

```
$filesystemName = "sourcedata"
$dirname = "Customer/parquetFiles"

$acl = Set-AzDataLakeGen2ItemAclObject -AccessControlType
user -Permission rw-
$acl = Set-AzDataLakeGen2ItemAclObject -AccessControlType
group -Permission r-x -InputObject $acl
$acl = Set-AzDataLakeGen2ItemAclObject -AccessControlType
other -Permission "---" -InputObject $acl
$acl = Set-AzDataLakeGen2ItemAclObject -AccessControlType
user -EntityId $principalId -Permission r-x -InputObject
$acl
Set-AzDataLakeGen2AclRecursive -Context $ctx -FileSystem
$filesystemName -Path $dirname -Acl $acl
```

7. To update only one file permission, run the following code. This code updates the permissions to `Read`, `Write`, and `Execute` for only one file, `part-00001-tid-7877307066025976411-3a62bd06-bc9c-467f-ae7b-d5db8ca40833-57-1-c000.snappy.parquet`, in the `Customer/parquetFiles` directory:

```
$filesystemName = "sourcedata"
$dirname = "Customer/parquetFiles/part-00000-tid-
7877307066025976411-3a62bd06-bc9c-467f-ae7b-d5db8ca40833-
56-1-c000.snappy.parquet"
$acl = (Get-AzDataLakeGen2Item -Context $ctx -FileSystem
$filesystemName -Path $dirname).ACL
$acl = set-AzDataLakeGen2ItemAclObject -AccessControlType
user -EntityID $principalId -Permission rwx -InputObject
$acl
Update-AzDataLakeGen2Item -Context $ctx -FileSystem
$filesystemName -Path $dirname -Acl $acl
```

8. You can check the permissions for the preceding file by running the following code:

```
$filesystemName = "sourcedata"
$dirname = "Customer/parquetFiles/part-00000-tid-
7877307066025976411-3a62bd06-bc9c-467f-ae7b-d5db8ca40833-
56-1-c000.snappy.parquet"
$dir = Get-AzDataLakeGen2Item -Context $ctx -FileSystem
$filesystemName -Path $dirname
$dir.ACL
```

9. You will find that the permissions have only changed for a single file. For the others, the permissions are still Read and Execute.

With that, you have learned how to add ACLs to directories and files using Azure Storage Explorer and PowerShell.

How it works...

While authorizing security principals, role-based assignments are evaluated first and then ACL permissions. If a service principal such as an AAD user has been granted the Blob Data Reader role on a container, then the ACLs aren't evaluated if the service principal is requesting read access on a directory in a container.

Let's start with a hypothetical scenario where you have four AAD groups and you want to grant access to their files and folders using RBAC and ACLs. There are two containers or filesystems, **structured** and **curated**, in the ADLS Gen-2 storage account. The structured container contains two directories called Folder1 and Folder2, while the curated container contains three directories called Folder1, Folder2, and Folder3. Let's take a look at them:

- **Super Admin**: Users of this group need to have access to all containers, folders, and files. They will not add or delete files.

- **Data Engineering**: Members of this group will be doing various data engineering tasks. They will need access to a few of the folders from the container but not all folders. Users will add and delete files.

- **Data Scientist**: These users have access to specific folders from both containers. Members of this group will be using specific data to build machine learning models. They will need access to a few of the folders from the container but not all folders. They will only be reading files.

- **IT Admin**: These users need some data for ad hoc reporting. They only need access to one folder in a structured container. The users will only be reading files:

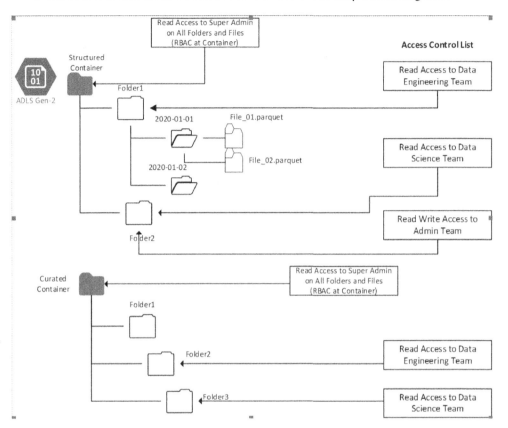

Figure 10.13 – Data access permission requirements

The permissions for this use case will be as follows:

- Grant the **Azure Storage Blob Data Reader** role for both containers to the **Super Admin** AAD group.

- Grant **Read**, **Write**, and **Execute** ACL permissions to `Folder1` and execute them on the root folder in a structured container. Then, grant **Read**, **Write**, and **Execute** to `Folder2` and execute this on the root folder in a curated container for the Data Engineering AAD group. There's no need for any RBAC on the storage account.

- Grant the **Read** and **Execute** ACLs permissions to `Folder2` and execute them on the root folder in a structured container; then, grant **Read** and **Execute** to `Folder3` and execute this on the root folder in a curated container for the Data Science AAD group. There's no need for any RBAC on the storage account.

- Grant **Read** and **Execute** ACL permissions to `Folder2` and Execute ACL permissions on the root folder in a structured container for the IT Admin AAD group. There's no need for any RBAC on the storage account.

You can learn more about ACLs at `https://docs.microsoft.com/en-gb/azure/storage/blobs/data-lake-storage-access-control`.

This and the preceding recipe helped you understand how to grant different types of access based on the business requirements. In the next recipe, you will learn how to configure credential passthrough to access ADLS Gen-2 storage using AAD credentials.

How to configure credential passthrough

Credential passthrough will allow you to authenticate ADLS Gen1 and ADLS Gen-2 using the same AAD login that is used to log into the Azure Databricks workspace. Credential passthrough helps you control what users can see in a container with the use of RBAC and ACLs. Credential passthrough removes the overhead of using multiple workspaces with different service principals that have different access to control the data that a user can see. It provides end-to-end security for the AAD users from Azure Databricks to ADLS Gen-2. If you want to control access to the AAD user based on the RBAC and ACL permissions that have been granted on ADLS, then you need to enable credential passthrough for the Azure Databricks cluster.

Getting ready

You must ensure you have the Azure Databricks premium plan to be able to use credential passthrough. For this recipe, we will be using ADLS Gen-2 with a hierarchical namespace.

We will also be using an AAD user who has Azure Storage Blob Data Owner permissions on the ADLS Gen-2 storage account.

You can configure credential passthrough for standard and high concurrency Databricks clusters. A standard cluster with credential passthrough is limited to only a single user. To support multiple users, you need to spin up credential passthrough so that it's enabled for a high concurrency cluster. Credential passthrough is supported from Databricks runtime 6.0 onward. In this recipe, we are using Databricks runtime 8.0 with Spark 3.1.1.

You can find the steps for this recipe in the following notebook:

`https://github.com/PacktPublishing/Azure-Databricks-Cookbook/blob/main/Chapter10/Code/10.3-Reading%20Writing%20using%20Credential%20passthrough.ipynb`

In the next section, you will learn how to create a standard cluster with the credential passthrough option enabled, as well as how to read data from an ADLS Gen-2 account using AAD credentials.

How to do it...

Let's learn how to create a standard cluster with credential passthrough and read and write directly from and to ADLS Gen-2 using AAD credentials while using a storage key or service principal. We will learn how to mount the ADLS Gen-2 Storage Account and read and write from the mount point using AAD credentials:

1. From the Azure Databricks workspace home page, click on **Compute**, then **+Create Cluster**, and provide the required values for **Databricks Runtime Version**, as well as other details mentioned in the following screenshot. Ensure you check the **Enable credential passthrough for user-level data access** option. Also, for **Single User Access**, provide the AAD user who has been granted the Storage Blob Data Owner role on the ADLS Gen-2 storage account:

Figure 10.14 – Enabling credential passthrough

2. When you create a **High Concurrency** cluster, you won't be asked for any user access details when you enable credential passthrough:

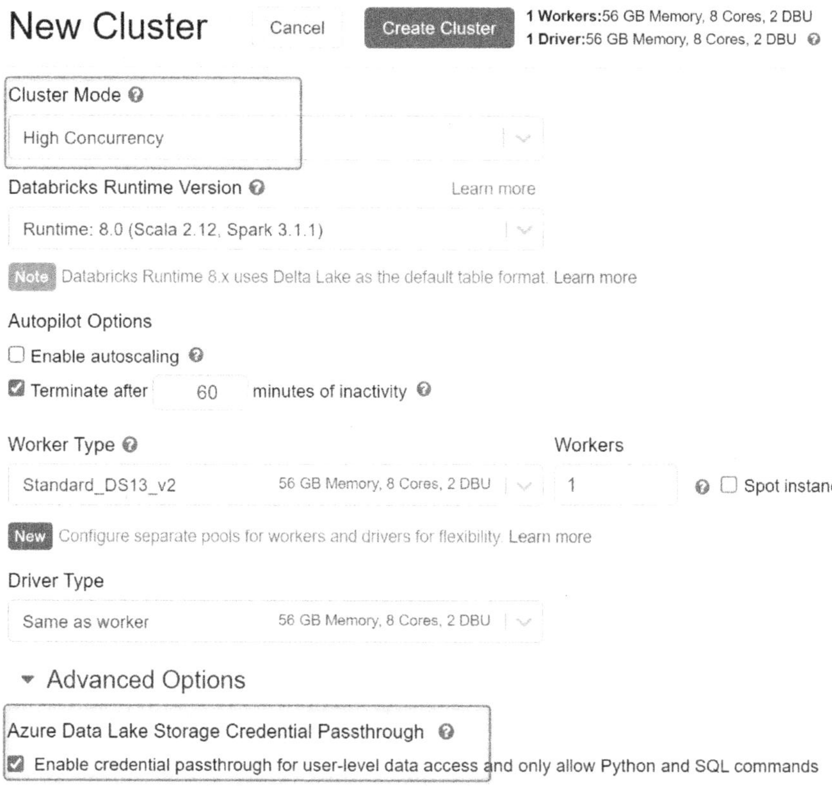

Figure 10.15 – High concurrency cluster with credential passthrough

3. To read the data directly from the absolute path for the ADLS Gen-2 Storage Account, run the following code. As you can see, we are not using a **storage account key** or **service principal** to access the ADLS Gen-2. Instead, we are using the Databricks workspace AAD user to read the files in the sourcedata container:

```
#Reading the files from ADLS Gen-2 using AAD
authentication of the user.
display(dbutils.fs.ls("abfss://sourcedata@
cookbookadlsgen2storage1.dfs.core.windows.net/Customer/
parquetFiles"))
```

4. Run the following code to create a database in Spark and import the required libraries:

```
db = "tpchdb"

spark.sql(f"CREATE DATABASE IF NOT EXISTS {db}")
spark.sql(f"USE {db}")
import random
from datetime import datetime
from pyspark.sql.functions import *
from pyspark.sql.types import *
from delta.tables import *
```

5. Let's create a DataFrame by reading `parquteFiles` from the `sourcedata` container by running the following code:

```
cust_path = "abfss://sourcedata@cookbookadlsgen2storage1.
dfs.core.windows.net/Customer/parquetFiles"

df_cust = (spark.read.format("parquet").load(cust_path)
        .withColumn("timestamp", current_timestamp()))
```

6. So far, we have been reading files from the absolute path of the files in the ADLS Gen-2 storage account. Run the following code to learn how to mount the ADLS Gen-2 Storage Account using the user AAD and read and write files from and to the mount path:

```
configs = {
    "fs.azure.account.auth.type": "CustomAccessToken",
    "fs.azure.account.custom.token.provider.class": spark.
conf.get("spark.databricks.passthrough.adls.gen2.
tokenProviderClassName")
}

dbutils.fs.mount(
    source = "abfss://sourcedata@cookbookadlsgen2storage1.
dfs.core.windows.net",
    mount_point = "/mnt/Gen2Source",
    extra_configs = configs)
```

7. Let's create a DataFrame by reading the Parquet files from the mount path and saving them in delta format by running the following code:

```
#Reading parquet files and adding a new column to the
dataframe and writing to delta table
cust_path = "/mnt/Gen2Source/Customer/parquetFiles"

df_cust = (spark.read.format("parquet").load(cust_path)
        .withColumn("timestamp", current_timestamp()))

df_cust.write.format("delta").mode("overwrite").save("/
mnt/Gen2Source/Customer/delta")
```

8. You can list the Delta files that were created in the mount path by running the following code:

```
display(dbutils.fs.ls("/mnt/Gen2Source/Customer/delta"))
```

9. You can also create an external Delta table pointing to the files that were created in the preceding step by running the following code:

```
%sql
-- Creating Delta table
DROP TABLE IF EXISTS Customer;
CREATE TABLE Customer
USING delta
location "/mnt/Gen2Source/Customer/delta"

select * from Customer limit 10;
```

In this recipe, you learned how to access files and directories in ADLS Gen-2 using AAD authentication via credential passthrough. We have given full rights to the AAD user on the ADLS Gen-2 account in this recipe, which means the AAD user can read and write data to ADLS Gen-2. In the next recipe, you will learn how to restrict access to the AAD user by changing the RBAC permissions on the ADLS Gen-2 account for an AAD user, as well as how to control which containers' data the user can read.

How to restrict data access to users using RBAC

In this recipe, you will learn how to grant access to the data on an ADLS Gen-2 container to an AAD user while using Storage Blob Data-related roles. We will assign minimal permissions to the AAD user on the workspace. We will start by assigning read access to a storage container called sourcedata. Then, we will grant read and write access by assigning Storage Blob Data Contributor access to the AAD user (Appuser), which will allow Appuser to write the data in the same container.

Getting ready

Before getting started, you should have an ADLS Gen-2 Storage Account and an Azure Databricks premium workspace.

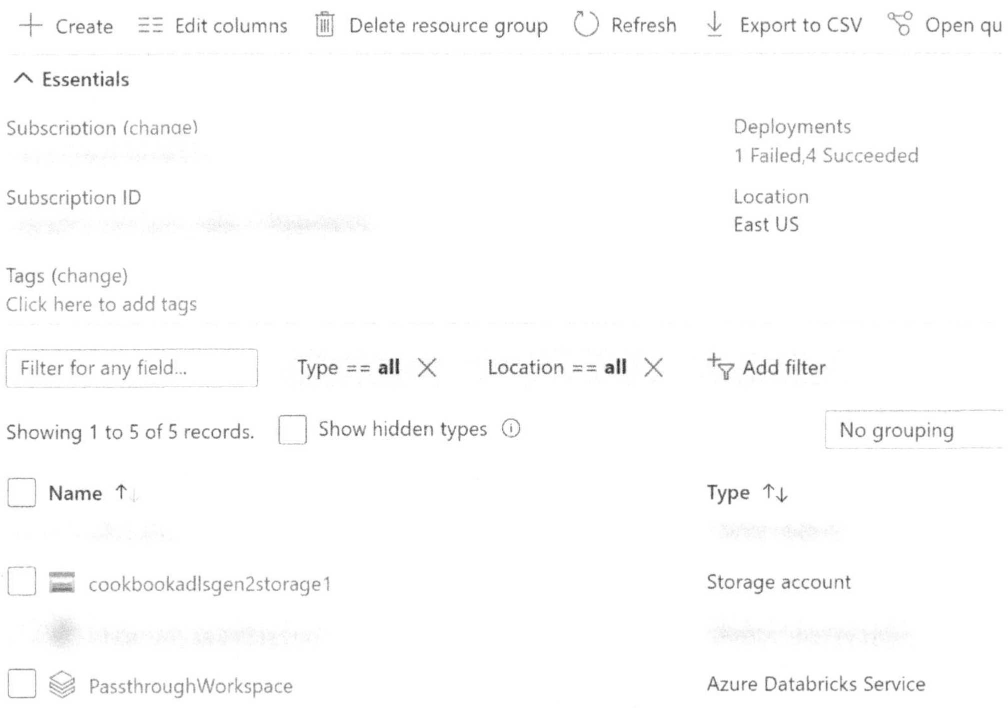

Figure 10.16 – Resources used in this recipe

Copy the Customer parquet files from the following location:

```
https://github.com/PacktPublishing/Azure-Databricks-Cookbook/
tree/main/Common/Customer/parquetFiles
```

You can get the Notebook used int the recipe from the following link:

```
https://github.com/PacktPublishing/Azure-Databricks-Cookbook/
blob/main/Chapter10/Code/10.3-Reading%20Writing%20using%20
Credential%20passthrough.ipynb
```

We need to create two containers and copy the `Customer` parquet files to both:

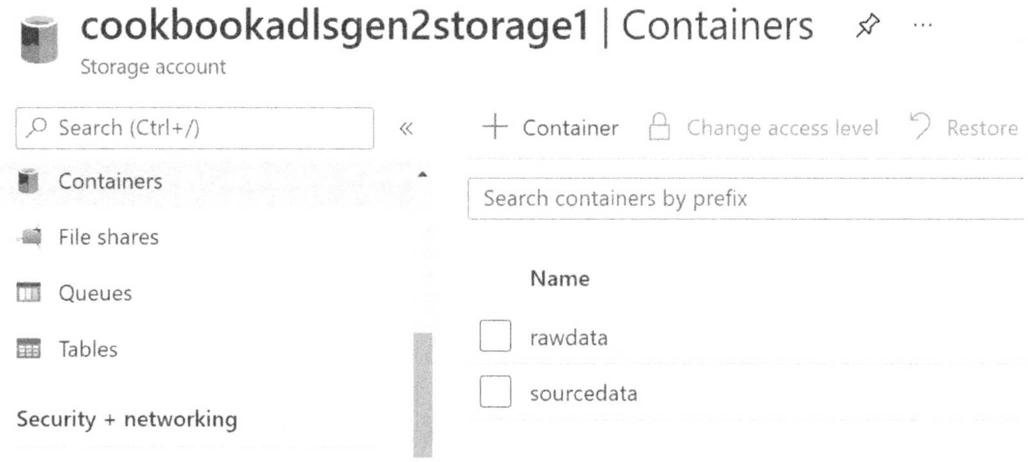

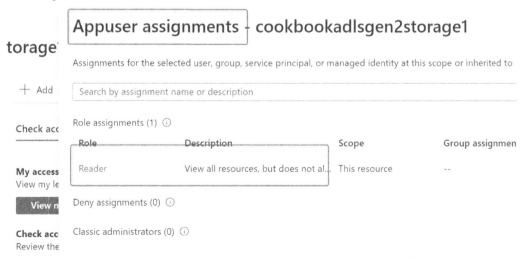

Figure 10.17 – Containers in the ADLS Gen-2

We will use an AAD user (Appuser) who will be assigned Azure Storage Data roles on the storage account. This AAD user has **Reader** access on the resource group, as shown in the following screenshot:

Figure 10.18 – Appuser permissions on the resource group

The Appuser AAD account is a regular user, not a workspace admin, as shown in the following screenshot:

Figure 10.19 – User permissions in the Databricks workspace

Here, we are using a high concurrency cluster. The AAD Appuser has permission to attach the cluster that has already been created. In the following screenshot, you can see that Appuser is being granted permissions to attach the cluster:

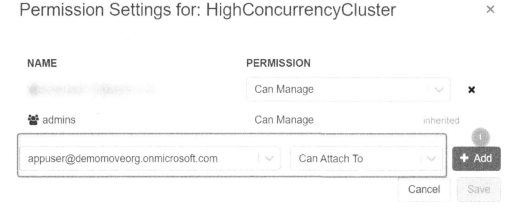

Figure 10.20 – Granting Can Attach To permissions to Appuser

In the next section, you will assign an Azure Storage Data-related permission to Appuser on the container and learn what operations can be performed based on the RBAC permissions that have been assigned.

How to do it...

Let's learn how to assign different Storage Blob Data roles to Appuser on an ADLS Gen-2 Storage Account and perform operations such as loading the parquet files to a DataFrame, as well as writing it in delta format based on the permissions that have been assigned to Appuser:

1. Run the following code to read the files from the `sourcedata` container. At this point, Appuser only has **Reader** access to all the resources in the Resource Group:

    ```
    #Reading the files from ADLS Gen-2 using AAD
    authentication of the user.
    display(dbutils.fs.ls("abfss://sourcedata@cookbookadlsgen
    2storage1.dfs.core.windows.net/"))
    ```

2. Since Appuser doesn't have a Storage Blob-related RBAC role assigned, you will get the following error. We will see a 403 error on `HTTP GET`, which means the user is not authorized to read the data:

    ```
    Operation failed:
    This request is not authorized to perform this operation
    using this pernission.is34;, 403, GET
    https://cookbookadlsgen2$toragel.dfs.core.windows.net/
    sourcedata?upn:fal$«iaip;r$ource:iilesystefltep;nai
    Results:5&0&anp;ti»*out:904aflp;recursive:faIse,
    AuthorizationPernissionMismatch,&#34;This request is not
    authorized to perform this operation using this
    permission.
    ```

3. Let's go ahead and assign **Storage Blob Data Reader** to the `sourcedata` container for Appuser. We are only granting access to one container, not an entire storage account. In the following screenshot, you can see that we have assigned the **Storage Blob Data Reader** role to `Appuser`:

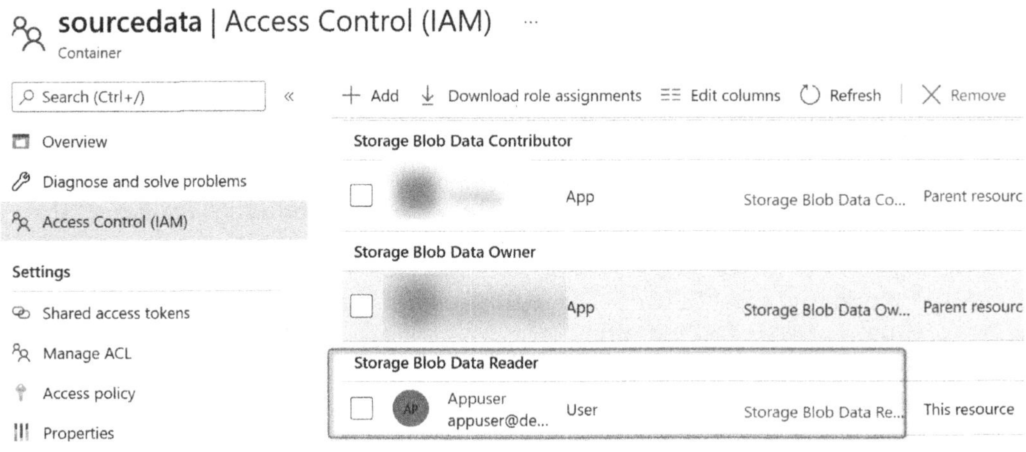

Figure 10.21– Permissions for AAD Appuser

> **Note**
> After granting Azure Storage Blob-related roles to an AAD user or group, it might take anywhere between 1-5 mins for the permissions to come into effect. You must wait a few minutes before reexecuting the code.

4. After assigning the role, execute the following code again. This will list all the files and folders in the container:

```
display(dbutils.fs.ls("abfss://sourcedata@
cookbookadlsgen2storage1.dfs.core.windows.net/"))
```

5. Execute the code shown in the following screenshot to list all the parquet files in a specific directory. Since RBAC was given at the container level, you can list all the files without the need for ACLs on the directories inside the container:

```
1   #Reading the files from ADLS Gen-2 using AAD authentication of the user.
2   display(dbutils.fs.ls("abfss://sourcedata@cookbookadlsgen2storage1.dfs.core.windows.net/Customer/parquetFiles"))
```

▸ (3) Spark Jobs

	path	name
1	abfss://sourcedata@cookbookadlsgen2storage1.dfs.core.windows.net/Customer/parquetFiles/part-00000-tid-7877307066025976411-3a62bd06-bc9c-467f-ae7b-d5db8ca40833-56-1-c000.snappy.parquet	part-00000-tid-78773
2	abfss://sourcedata@cookbookadlsgen2storage1.dfs.core.windows.net/Customer/parquetFiles/part-00001-tid-7877307066025976411-3a62bd06-bc9c-467f-ae7b-d5db8ca40833-57-1-c000.snappy.parquet	part-00001-tid-78773
3	abfss://sourcedata@cookbookadlsgen2storage1.dfs.core.windows.net/Customer/parquetFiles/part-00002-tid-7877307066025976411-3a62bd06-bc9c-467f-ae7b-d5db8ca40833-58-1-c000.snappy.parquet	part-00002-tid-78773
4	abfss://sourcedata@cookbookadlsgen2storage1.dfs.core.windows.net/Customer/parquetFiles/part-00003-tid-7877307066025976411-3a62bd06-bc9c-467f-ae7b-d5db8ca40833-59-1-c000.snappy.parquet	part-00003-tid-78773

Figure 10.22– Listing parquet files in the directory

6. Now, let's run the following code to read from another container that has no Storage Blob-related Azure roles assigned to Appuser:

```
display(dbutils.fs.ls("abfss://rawdata@
cookbookadlsgen2storage1.dfs.core.windows.net/"))
```

7. You will get the same 403 error if you are reading data from a container where Appuser does not have any Storage Blob roles assigned:

```
Operation failed: &#34;This request is not authorized to perform this operation using this permission.&#34;, 403, GET, https://cookbookadlsgen2storage1.dfs.core.windows.net/rawdata?upn=false&amp;resource=filesystem&amp;maxResults=500&amp;timeout=90&amp;recursive=false, AuthorizationPermissionMismatch, &#34;This request is not authorized to perform this operation using this permission. RequestId:3bc110f1-001f-008c-32a1-6c2309000000 Time:2021-06-29T04:45:08.9110582Z&#34;
Command took 0.68 seconds -- by appuser@demomoveorg.onmicrosoft.com at 6/29/2021,                                   uster
```

Figure 10.23 – HTTP GET error

8. So far, we have been accessing the files using the absolute path. Instead of using the absolute path, we can mount the ADLS Gen-2 Storage Account to a mount point in Azure Databricks using AAD credentials, similar to using a **Service Principal** to mount a storage account. Run the following code to mount the Storage Account using the AAD credentials of Appuser to /mnt/Gen2Source:

```
import random
from datetime import datetime
from pyspark.sql.functions import *
from pyspark.sql.types import *
from delta.tables import *
```

```
configs = {
    "fs.azure.account.auth.type": "CustomAccessToken",
    "fs.azure.account.custom.token.provider.class": spark.
conf.get("spark.databricks.passthrough.adls.gen2.
tokenProviderClassName")
}
```

```
dbutils.fs.mount(
    source = "abfss://sourcedata@cookbookadlsgen2storage1.
dfs.core.windows.net",
    mount_point = "/mnt/Gen2Source",
    extra_configs = configs)
```

9. Let's load the parquet files in the DataFrame by running the following code. Here, we are reading from the parquet files and writing to another folder in the same container in delta format:

```
#Reading parquet files and adding a new column to the
dataframe and writing to delta table
cust_path = "/mnt/Gen2Source/Customer/parquetFiles"

df_cust = (spark.read.format("parquet").load(cust_path)
        .withColumn("timestamp", current_timestamp()))

df_cust.write.format("delta").mode("overwrite").save("/
mnt/Gen2Source/Customer/delta")
```

10. Writing in delta format will fail with the following error. This is happening because Appuser does not have write access on the container:

```
Caused by: org.apache.spark.SparkException: Job aborted due to stage failure: Task 0 in stage 15.0 failed 4 times, most recent failure
Lost task 0.3 in stage 15.0 (TID 26) (10.139.64.5 executor 0): Operation failed: "This request is not authorized to perform this opera
ion using this permission.", 403, PUT, https://cookbookadlsgen2storage1.dfs.core.windows.net/sourcedata/Customer/delta/part-00000-54a9
3d8-1f28-48b2-8a33-a5b9282b3863-c000.snappy.parquet?resource=file&timeout=90, AuthorizationPermissionMismatch, "This request is not au
horized to perform this operation using this permission. RequestId:23f003f7-601f-0033-462b-8914ac000000 Time:2021-08-04T12:22:50.65749
4Z"
```

Figure 10.24– HTTP PUT error while writing

11. Now, let's assign **Storage Blob Data Contributor** access to Appuser in the sourcedata container.

12. Execute the following code again after assigning the **Storage Blob Data contributor** role. It will succeed, without throwing an error:

```
#Reading parquet files and adding a new column to the
dataframe and writing to delta table
cust_path = "/mnt/Gen2Source/Customer/parquetFiles"

df_cust = (spark.read.format("parquet").load(cust_path)
        .withColumn("timestamp", current_timestamp()))

df_cust.write.format("delta").mode("overwrite").save("/
mnt/Gen2Source/Customer/delta")
```

13. Run the following code to list the files that were created in the delta folder:

```
display(dbutils.fs.ls("/mnt/Gen2Source/Customer/delta"))
```

By following the steps in this recipe, you have learned how Azure Storage Blob Data roles can be used to restrict read or write access to data in the container to an AAD user from Azure Databricks users.

How to restrict data access to users using ACLs

In this recipe, you will learn how to use ACLs to restrict access to data for individual files and directories, without assigning Azure Storage Blob-related roles to the AAD user/group in an ADLS Gen-2 Storage Account.

In the next section, you will learn about the prerequisites for getting started with this recipe.

Getting ready

Before starting, you need to ensure you have completed the *Creating ACLs using Storage Explorer and PowerShell* recipe.

We haven't assigned any Azure Storage Blob-related roles to Appuser yet, as shown in the following screenshot:

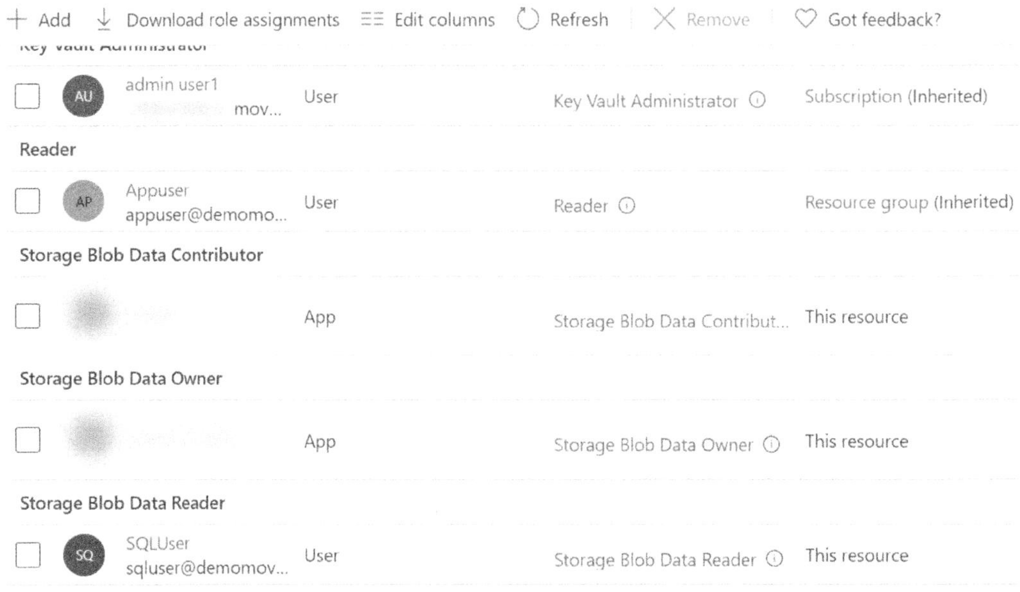

+ Add ↓ Download role assignments ≡≡ Edit columns ⟳ Refresh ✕ Remove ♡ Got feedback?				
Key Vault Administrator				
☐ **AU**	admin user1 .... mov...	User	Key Vault Administrator ⓘ	Subscription (Inherited)
Reader				
☐ **AP**	Appuser appuser@demomo...	User	Reader ⓘ	Resource group (Inherited)
Storage Blob Data Contributor				
☐		App	Storage Blob Data Contribut...	This resource
Storage Blob Data Owner				
☐		App	Storage Blob Data Owner ⓘ	This resource
Storage Blob Data Reader				
☐ **SQ**	SQLUser sqluser@demomov...	User	Storage Blob Data Reader ⓘ	This resource

Figure 10.25 – Role assignments to Appuser

You can find the Notebook that was used for this recipe at the following link:

```
https://github.com/PacktPublishing/Azure-Databricks-Cookbook/
blob/main/Chapter10/Code/10.5-ACL.ipynb
```

In this recipe, we will create a container called `rawdata` in an ADLS Gen-2 Storage account and copy the `Customer` parquet file from the following link into the `rawdata` container:

```
https://github.com/PacktPublishing/Azure-Databricks-Cookbook/
tree/main/Common/Customer/parquetFiles
```

You should copy the parquet files into a sub-directory called `Customer/parquetFiles` in the `rawdata` container.

How to do it...

In this section, you will learn how to assign permission using ACLs to files and directories for Appuser and grant read access for the AAD user, which will allow them to only read the data into a DataFrame, and later will assign write access. This will allow the AAD user to write the DataFrame to another location in delta format.

Let's run through the following steps to assign permission using ACLs for files and directories in the `rawdata` container and process data in Azure Databricks:

1. From Storage Explorer, assign the **Read** and **Execute** permissions to the `parquetFiles` subdirectory of the `Customer` directory, which is part of the `rawdata` container:

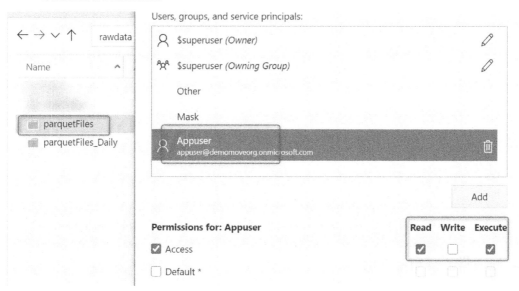

Figure 10.26 – Granting the Read and Execute permissions to AppUser

2. To read the parquet files in the `parquetFiles` sub-directory, you need to assign execute permissions starting from the root folder, which is the `rawdata` container, all the way until the `parquetFiles` subdirectory. In the following screenshot, we are assigning **Execute** permissions to Appuser on the `Customer` directory:

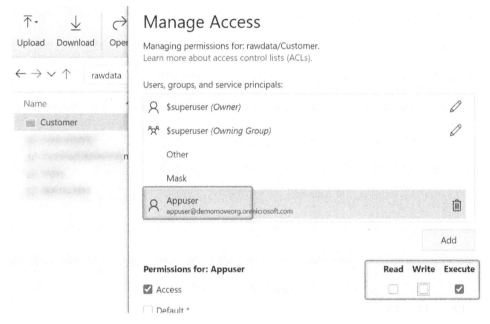

Figure 10.27 – Granting Execute permissions for the Customer folder

3. After assigning **Execute** permissions to the `Customer` directory, go ahead and assign **Execute** permissions to the `rawdata` container, as shown in the following screenshot:

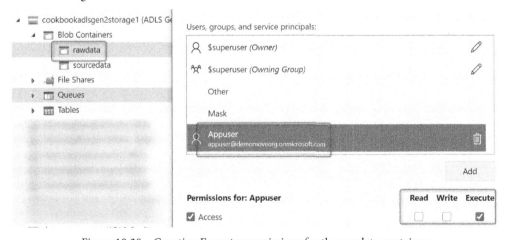

Figure 10.28 – Granting Execute permissions for the rawdata container

4. Once the required permissions have been assigned using ACLs to all the directories and sub-directories, you can execute the following code, which reads all the parquet files from the `parquetFiles` sub-directory:

```
display(dbutils.fs.ls("abfss://rawdata@
cookbookadlsgen2storage1.dfs.core.windows.net/Customer/
parquetFiles"))
```

5. Since Appuser had read permissions on the `parquetFiles` sub-directory, all the files in that sub-directory will be listed when we execute the preceding code. This can be seen in the following screenshot:

```
1    #Reading the files from ADLS Gen-2 using AAD authentication of the user with ACLs granted to folders
2    display(dbutils.fs.ls("abfss://rawdata@cookbookadlsgen2storage1.dfs.core.windows.net/Customer/parquetFiles"))
```

▸ (2) Spark Jobs

	path		name
1	abfss://rawdata@cookbookadlsgen2storage1.dfs.core.windows.net/Customer/parquetFiles/part-00000-tid-7877307066025976411-3a62bd06-bc9c-467f-ae7b-d5db8ca40833-56-1-c000.snappy.parquet		part-00000-tid-7877307C
2	abfss://rawdata@cookbookadlsgen2storage1.dfs.core.windows.net/Customer/parquetFiles/part-00001-tid-7877307066025976411-3a62bd06-bc9c-467f-ae7b-d5db8ca40833-57-1-c000.snappy.parquet		part-00001-tid-7877307C
3	abfss://rawdata@cookbookadlsgen2storage1.dfs.core.windows.net/Customer/parquetFiles/part-00002-tid-7877307066025976411-3a62bd06-bc9c-467f-ae7b-d5db8ca40833-58-1-c000.snappy.parquet		part-00002-tid-7877307C
4	abfss://rawdata@cookbookadlsgen2storage1.dfs.core.windows.net/Customer/parquetFiles/part-00003-tid-7877307066025976411-3a62bd06-bc9c-467f-ae7b-d5db8ca40833-59-1-c000.snappy.parquet		part-00003-tid-7877307C
5	abfss://rawdata@cookbookadlsgen2storage1.dfs.core.windows.net/Customer/parquetFiles/part-00004-tid-7877307066025976411-3a62bd06-bc9c-467f-ae7b-d5db8ca40833-60-1-c000.snappy.parquet		part-00004-tid-7877307C

Figure 10.29 – Listing all files in the parquetFiles sub-directory

6. When you run the following code on any other sub-directory in the `Customer` folder, you will get a 403 authorization error. The following code is reading from another sub-directory in the `Customer` directory:

```
display(dbutils.fs.ls("abfss://rawdata@
cookbookadlsgen2storage1.dfs.core.windows.net/Customer/
parquetFiles_Daily"))
```

7. You will get the following error when you execute the preceding code:

```
Operation failed: &#34;This request is not authorized to perform this operation using this permission.&#34;, 403, GET, https://cookbook
adlsgen2storage1.dfs.core.windows.net/rawdata?upn=false&amp;resource=filesystem&amp;maxResults=500&amp;directory=Customer/parquetFiles_
Daily&amp;timeout=90&amp;recursive=false, AuthorizationPermissionMismatch, &#34;This request is not authorized to perform this operatio
n using this permission. RequestId:6afba26f-801f-006c-29a8-6c0427800000 Time:2021-06-29T05:35:43.8238029Z&#34;
```

Figure 10.30 – Error while reading data from another sub-directory

8. Now, let's go ahead and assign **Read**, **Write**, and **Execute** permissions to the Customer directory by creating any new directory or file under the Customer directory:

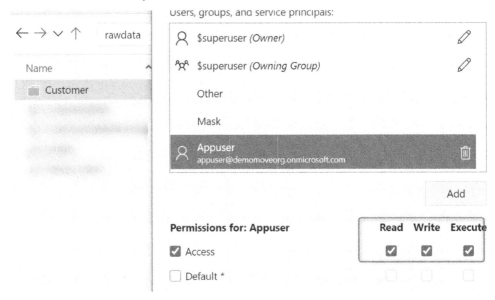

Figure 10.31 – Granting Read, Write, and Execute permissions for the Customer directory

9. To list all the directories and files in the Customer directory, run the following code:

```
display(dbutils.fs.ls("abfss://rawdata@
cookbookadlsgen2storage1.dfs.core.windows.net/
Customer/"))
```

10. Run the following code to add a new sub-directory called newFolder to the Customer directory:

```
dbutils.fs.mkdirs("abfss://rawdata@
cookbookadlsgen2storage1.dfs.core.windows.net/Customer/
newFolder")
```

11. Execute the following code to list all the directories and files under the Customer directory, including newFolder, which was created in *Step 9*:

```
display(dbutils.fs.ls("abfss://rawdata@
cookbookadlsgen2storage1.dfs.core.windows.net/
Customer/"))
```

12. Running the following code will mount the `Customer` directory to a mount point called /mnt/Customer using AAD authentication:

```
#Reading parquet files and adding a new column to the
dataframe and writing to delta table
configs = {
    "fs.azure.account.auth.type": "CustomAccessToken",
    "fs.azure.account.custom.token.provider.class": spark.
conf.get("spark.databricks.passthrough.adls.gen2.
tokenProviderClassName")
}


# Optionally, you can add <directory-name> to the source
URI of your mount point.
dbutils.fs.mount(
    source = "abfss://rawdata@cookbookadlsgen2storage1.dfs.
core.windows.net/Customer/",
    mount_point = "/mnt/Customer",
    extra_configs = configs)
```

13. Once the Storage Account has been mounted, you can load the parquet files into a DataFrame by running the following code:

```
cust_path = "/mnt/Customer/parquetFiles"
df_cust = (spark.read.format("parquet").load(cust_path))
```

14. Since we haven't assigned read permissions to the parquet files in the `parquetFiles` sub-directory, we will get a 403 error, as shown in the following screenshot:

```
Caused by: Operation failed: "This request is not authorized to perform this operation using this permissio
n.", 403, GET, https://cookbookadlsgen2storage1.dfs.core.windows.net/rawdata/Customer/parquetFiles/part-00000-
tid-7877307066025976411-3a62bd06-bc9c-467f-ae7b-d5db8ca40833-56-1-c000.snappy.parquet?timeout=90, Authorizatio
nPermissionMismatch, "This request is not authorized to perform this operation using this permission. RequestI
d:d5024788-701f-0096-55aa-6c42d6000000 Time:2021-06-29T05:51:03.3595431Z"
```

Figure 10.32 – Unauthorized access while reading Parquet files

15. We need to assign **Read** permissions to all the files in the `parquetFiles` sub-directory to load the parquet files into a DataFrame. To propagate these permissions to all the parquet files, right-click the `parquetFiles` sub-directory and click on the **Propagate Access Control Lists...** option:

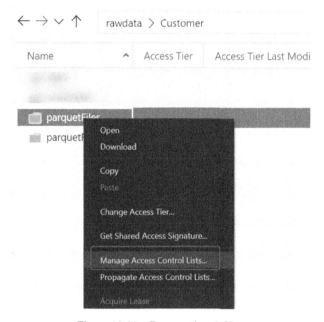

Figure 10.33 – Propagating ACLs

16. Run the following code to load the parquet files into a DataFrame. Later, this will write the DataFrame into another `newFolder` sub-directory in delta format. Since we have **Read**, **Write**, and **Execute** permissions in the `newFolder` sub-directory, executing the following code will ensure that no authorization errors are thrown:

```
cust_path = "/mnt/Customer/parquetFiles"
df_cust = (spark.read.format("parquet").load(cust_path))


df_cust.write.format("delta").mode("overwrite").
save("abfss://rawdata@cookbookadlsgen2storage1.dfs.core.
windows.net/Customer/newFolder/delta")
```

17. Run the following code to list all the files in the `newFolder/delta` sub-directory that were created when the preceding code was executed:

```
display(dbutils.fs.ls("abfss://rawdata@
cookbookadlsgen2storage1.dfs.core.windows.net/Customer/
newFolder/delta"))
```

In this recipe, you learned how to use ACLs to control access to individual directories in a container. This ensures that AAD users can only load data that they have access to into a DataFrame. They cannot load or perform any kind of transformation on any directories or files that they don't have access to.

Deploying Azure Databricks in a VNet and accessing a secure storage account

In this recipe, you will learn how to deploy an Azure Databrick service in your own **Virtual Network (VNet)**. Deploying Azure Databricks in a VNet enables you to connect to services such as Azure Storage over private endpoints. It also allows you to connect to on-premises data sources and restrict outgoing traffic. Control plane resources will be deployed to a Microsoft-managed VNet. Only data plane resources can be deployed in your own VNet.

Getting ready

Before you start this recipe, you need to create a VNet. To do so, follow the steps mentioned in the following article:

`https://docs.microsoft.com/en-us/azure/virtual-network/quick-create-portal`

Ensure you have created two subnets, including the IP range, with the names shown in the following screenshot in the VNet you have created. Provide CIDR ranges in a block up to `/26` in size (for this recipe, since we are creating a small cluster) while providing the IP address for the subnet:

| + Subnet   + Gateway subnet   ⟳ Refresh   ⣿ Manage users |

Name ↑↓	IPv4 ↑↓	IPv6 ↑↓
default	10.0.0.0/24	-
private-subnet	10.0.2.0/24	-
public-subnet	10.0.1.0/24	-

Figure 10.34 – Required subnets

In the next section, you will deploy Azure Databricks to the VNet that you created in this section. You will also learn how to securely access an ADLS Gen-2 account from the Azure Databricks workspace that you've deployed to your own VNet.

How to do it...

Let's deploy Azure Databricks to a VNet by going through the following steps:

1. On the Azure Databricks service creation page, choose **Standard** for the **Pricing Tier** option while creating the workspace:

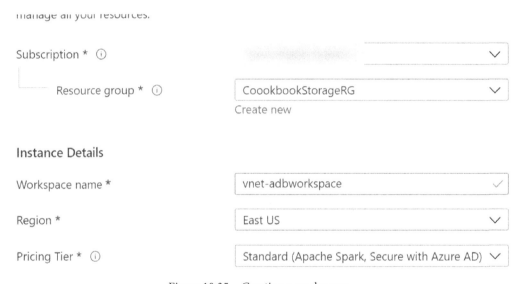

Figure 10.35 – Creating a workspace

2. In the **Networking** tab, ensure you specify the subnet names you created in the *Getting ready* section of this recipe. The subnet names must be the exact names that you created earlier. If you didn't create the subnets in the VNet previously, then you can specify the names of the private and public subnets. However, ensure that the subnet names do not already exist in that VNet. Provide CIDR ranges in a block up to /26 in size when providing the IP address for the subnet:

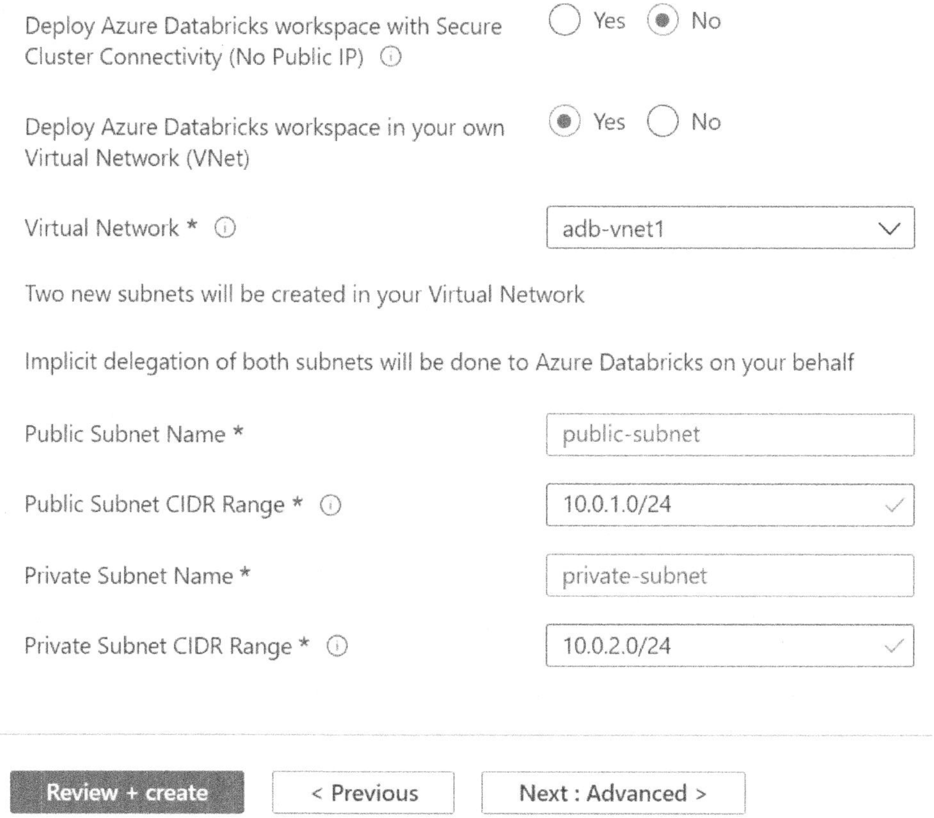

Deploy Azure Databricks workspace with Secure Cluster Connectivity (No Public IP) ⓘ   ○ Yes ◉ No

Deploy Azure Databricks workspace in your own Virtual Network (VNet)   ◉ Yes ○ No

Virtual Network * ⓘ   adb-vnet1 ⌄

Two new subnets will be created in your Virtual Network

Implicit delegation of both subnets will be done to Azure Databricks on your behalf

Public Subnet Name *   public-subnet

Public Subnet CIDR Range * ⓘ   10.0.1.0/24 ✓

Private Subnet Name *   private-subnet

Private Subnet CIDR Range * ⓘ   10.0.2.0/24 ✓

Review + create   < Previous   Next : Advanced >

Figure 10.36 – Deploying a workspace in a virtual network

3. Click on **Review + create** after providing all the details in the preceding step.

4. Once the workspace has been created, you will find the **Virtual Network** and **Private Subnet Name** information on the Azure Databricks Service home page:

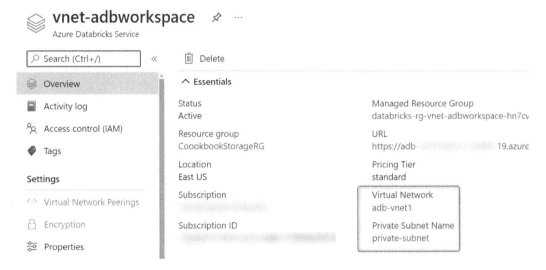

Figure 10.37 – Private subnet details for the workspace

Now that Azure Databricks has been deployed in your own network, let's learn how to access the ADLS Gen-2 account securely. Copy the `Customer` parquet files from the following link to your ADLS Gen-2 Storage Account: `https://github.com/PacktPublishing/Azure-Databricks-Cookbook/tree/main/Common/Customer/parquetFiles`.

You can follow along by running the code in the following Notebook: `https://github.com/PacktPublishing/Azure-Databricks-Cookbook/blob/main/Chapter10/Code/10.7-Reading%20from%20Secure%20Storage.ipynb`.

Let's restrict access to the ADLS Gen-2 Storage Account that we used in the preceding recipe. Here, we will restrict access to the Storage Account from the selected VNet:

1. Go to the **Storage Account** page, click on **Networking**, and select the **Firewalls and virtual networks** tab. Click on **+ Add existing virtual network** and select the VNet name you created from the drop-down list. Select `public-subnet` and any other subnet that was created in the *Getting ready* section. To use `public-subnet`, the **Microsoft.Storage** service endpoint needs to be enabled. Click on **Enable**. It will take a few seconds to enable the service endpoint for **Microsoft.Storage**. Click **Save** once you've finished:

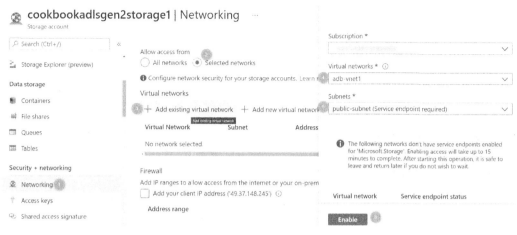

Figure 10.38 – Adding a virtual network to the storage firewall

2. Once you have added the Virtual Network, you will see that **Endpoint Status** is **Enabled**, as shown in the following screenshot:

○ All networks ⦿ Selected networks

ⓘ Configure network security for your storage accounts. Learn more ☑

Virtual networks

+ Add existing virtual network   + Add new virtual network

Virtual Network	Subnet	Address range	Endpoint Status
∨ adb-vnet1	1		
	public-subnet	10.0.1.0/24	✓ Enabled

Figure 10.39 – Configuring network security for the storage account

3. You need to grant **Storage Blob Contributor** access to both the **Storage Account** and **Service Principal** entities that you will be using in the Notebook. After granting the Azure Storage Blob data-related roles, it will take around 1 to 5 minutes for the permissions to kick in for the AAD user or service principal.

4. Execute the following code to mount the Storage Account to DBFS:

```
storageAccount="cookbookadlsgen2storage1"
mountpoint = "/mnt/Gen2Source"
storageEndPoint ="abfss://rawdata@{}.dfs.core.windows.
net/".format(storageAccount)
```

```
print ('Mount Point ='+mountpoint)

#ClientId, TenantId and Secret is for the
Application(ADLSGen2App) was have created as part of this
recipe
clientID ="xxxx-xxxx-xxxxx"
tenantID ="xxxx-xxxx-xxxx-xxxx"
clientSecret ="xxxx-xxx-xxx-xxx-xxxxx "
oauth2Endpoint = "https://login.microsoftonline.com/{}/
oauth2/token".format(tenantID)
configs = {"fs.azure.account.auth.type": "OAuth",
          "fs.azure.account.oauth.provider.
type": "org.apache.hadoop.fs.azurebfs.oauth2.
ClientCredsTokenProvider",
          "fs.azure.account.oauth2.client.id": clientID,
          "fs.azure.account.oauth2.client.secret":
clientSecret,
          "fs.azure.account.oauth2.client.endpoint":
oauth2Endpoint}
dbutils.fs.mount(
source = storageEndPoint,
mount_point = mountpoint,
extra_configs = configs)
```

5. You can query the files under the parquetFiles folder by running the
    following code:

    ```
    display(dbutils.fs.ls("/mnt/Gen2Source/Customer/
    parquetFiles"))
    ```

6. Load the required libraries by executing the following code:

    ```
    import random
    from datetime import datetime
    from pyspark.sql.functions import *
    from pyspark.sql.types import *
    from delta.tables import *
    ```

7. Run the following code to read the parquet files and write them in delta format:

```
cust_path = "/mnt/Gen2Source/Customer/parquetFiles"


df_cust = (spark.read.format("parquet").load(cust_path)
        .withColumn("timestamp", current_timestamp()))


df_cust.write.format("delta").mode("overwrite").save("/
mnt/Gen2Source/Customer/delta")
```

8. Run the following code to create a Delta table:

```
%sql
-- Creating Delta table
DROP TABLE IF EXISTS Customer;
CREATE TABLE Customer
USING delta
location "/mnt/Gen2Source/Customer/delta"
```

9. To confirm that we can read from the table, run the following code:

```
%sql
select * from Customer limit 10;
```

In this recipe, you learned how to deploy Azure Databricks to your own VNet, as well as how to securely access a Storage Account from Azure Databricks once it has been deployed to your own VNet.

There's more…

Apart from using the Azure portal UI experience to deploy the Azure Databricks workspace in a VNet, you can also use ARM templates.

Follow the steps mentioned in the following links to use an ARM template with PowerShell or the CLI to deploy Azure Databricks in your own VNet:

*   https://azure.microsoft.com/en-us/resources/templates/
    databricks-vnet-for-vnet-injection/
*   https://azure.microsoft.com/en-in/resources/templates/
    databricks-all-in-one-template-for-vnet-injection/

Using Ganglia reports for cluster health

Ganglia is one of the most popular cluster monitoring tools available. An Azure Databricks cluster's performance and health can be monitored using Ganglia. It is a scalable distributed monitoring system. Azure Databricks uses many clusters for operating in the backend, as well as for performing tasks, so it's very important to monitor the performance and health of the clusters for troubleshooting reasons, as well as to capture live metrics.

Getting ready

Before getting started, ensure you have completed *Chapter 3, Understanding Spark Query Execution*, where you learned how to create Azure Databricks jobs. In this recipe, we will run the Notebook and monitor the cluster utilization percentage (%) using the Ganglia UI.

How to do it...

Let's learn how to use the Ganglia UI to monitor Azure Databricks clusters by going through the following steps:

1. Before checking the Ganglia UI, let's get the worker and driver node's IPs from the **Cluster details** page. These IPs are required when specific node metrics need to be checked. You can get the driver and worker node's IPs by going to the **Spark Cluster UI - Master** tab:

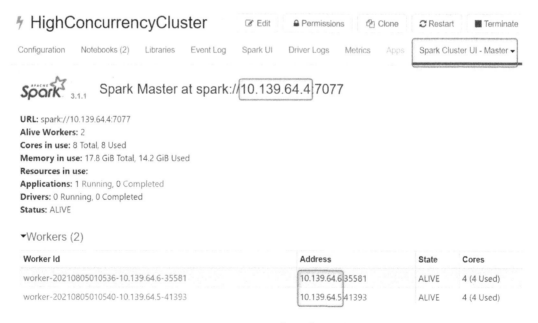

Figure 10.40 – Driver and Worker node IPs

2. The Ganglia UI can be accessed by navigating to the **Metrics** tab on the **Cluster details** page:

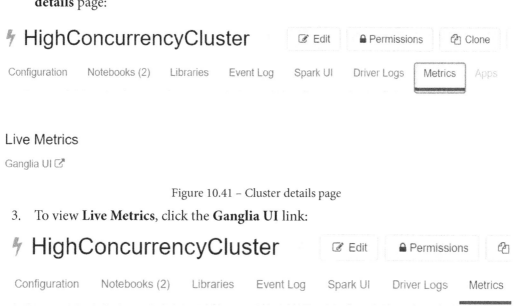

Figure 10.41 – Cluster details page

3. To view **Live Metrics**, click the **Ganglia UI** link:

Figure 10.42 – Ganglia UI link

4. The CPU metrics for all the Databricks runtimes are available in the Ganglia UI. GPU metrics are available for GPU-enabled clusters.

5. Historical metrics can be seen by clicking the necessary snapshot file. This snapshot contains an hour's worth of aggregated metrics, preceding the selected time:

Figure 10.43 – Historical metrics

6. By default, this report shows the metrics for all the clusters. However, you can also select a specific node based on the IP of the driver and worker nodes that you selected in *Step 1* of this recipe:

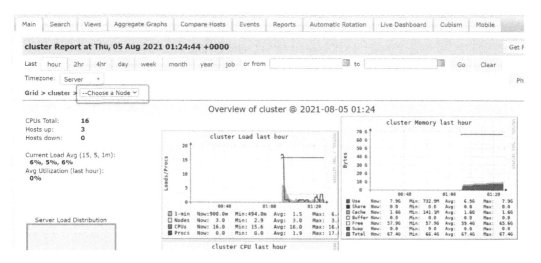

Figure 10.44 – Historical metrics

7. You will be able to see the **CPU**, **Load**, **Memory**, **Network**, and **Disk space** details in the report:

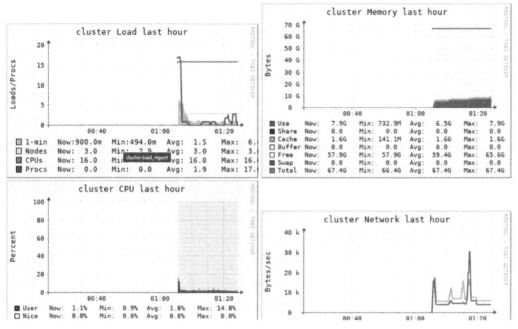

Figure 10.45 – Ganglia report

8.   You can also click on a specific section, such as **CPU**, **Memory**, **Load**, or **Network**, to get details about a specific node or cluster. Once you've done this, you will get a report for **Last hour**, **Last 2 hours**, **Last 4 hours**, **Last day**, **Last week**, **Last month**, and **Last year**:

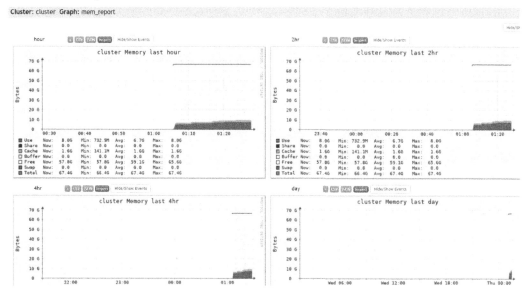

Figure 10.46 – Ganglia report intervals

Databricks collects Ganglia metrics every 15 minutes and uses less than 10 GB of data for storing metrics. In the next recipe, we will learn how to grant cluster access to AAD users.

Cluster access control

Administrators can enable cluster access control to provide the required rights for Azure Databricks users. By default, users have the right to create and modify clusters unless cluster access control is enabled.

There are two types of cluster permissions:

- The **Allow Cluster Creation** permission allows us to create clusters.
- The **Cluster-level** permission controls how we use and modify clusters.

The following permissions can be controlled by enabling **Cluster access control**:

- The administrator can control whether a user has rights for cluster creation.

- A user with the `Can Manage` permission for a cluster can provide rights that state whether a user can manage that cluster.

> **Note**
> **Cluster access control** is only available in the Azure Databricks premium plan.

Getting ready

Before getting started, ensure you have completed *Chapter 1, Creating an Azure Databricks Service*, where you learned how to create an Azure Databricks workspace and add users and groups to it.

How to do it...

Let's learn how to configure **cluster access control** in the Azure Databricks workspace.

Configuring cluster access control

Follow these steps:

1. Go to the **Admin Console** area of the Azure Databricks workspace:

Figure 10.47 – Admin Console

2.   Click on the **Workspace Settings** tab:

Access Control

Figure 10.48 – Workspace Settings

3.   Enable **Workspace Access Control**, if not enabled,via the **Workspace Access Control** toggle:

Access Control

Figure 10.49 – Workspace Access Control

4.   Click on the **Confirm** button to apply the configuration change. This will enable **Cluster Access Control** at the workspace level.

Restricting users on clusters

By default, clusters are visible to all users, even when those users don't have permission. To prevent users from seeing them, follow these steps:

1.   Go to the **Admin Console** area of your Azure Databricks workspace.

2.   Click on the **Workspace Settings** tab.

3.   Enable **Cluster Visibility Control** in the **Cluster Visibility Control** section:

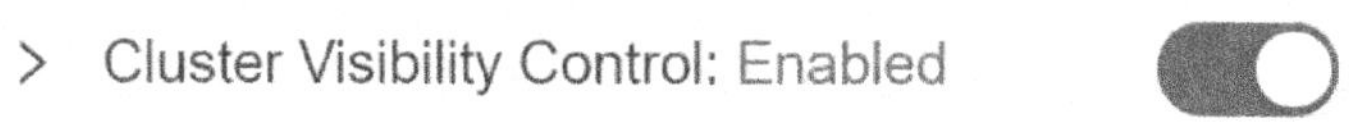

>   Cluster Visibility Control: Enabled

Figure 10.50 – Cluster Visibility Control

4. Click on the **Confirm** button to apply the configuration change. This will enable **Cluster Visibility Control** at the workspace level.

5. Users can be restricted from viewing the cluster from the **Cluster details** tab in the workspace. Click on the **Compute** tab and select the cluster where you want to deny permissions for to a user or group. Click on **Edit** and expand **Advanced Options** and go to the **Permissions** tab. Here, you can select the **No Permissions** option for the user or group to apply restrictions. You can grant other permissions like **Can Restart** and **Can Managed** based on user profile and the requirements:

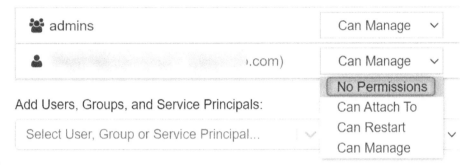

Figure 10.51 – Managing cluster permissions for a user

> **Note**
> Cluster Visibility Control is enabled by default for workspaces created after the release of Azure Databricks platform version 3.34. Workspaces created in earlier versions require an admin to enable this feature.

6. You can learn more about what kind of operations can be performed by granting the required cluster permissions to users and groups by going through the following link.

    ```
    https://docs.microsoft.com/en-us/azure/databricks/security/
    access-control/cluster-acl#cluster-level-permissions
    ```

    By the end of this recipe, you have learned how to grant and restrict permissions on the cluster to users or groups.

Packt.com

Subscribe to our online digital library for full access to over 7,000 books and videos, as well as industry leading tools to help you plan your personal development and advance your career. For more information, please visit our website.

Why subscribe?

- Spend less time learning and more time coding with practical eBooks and Videos from over 4,000 industry professionals

- Improve your learning with Skill Plans built especially for you

- Get a free eBook or video every month

- Fully searchable for easy access to vital information

- Copy and paste, print, and bookmark content

Did you know that Packt offers eBook versions of every book published, with PDF and ePub files available? You can upgrade to the eBook version at packt.com and as a print book customer, you are entitled to a discount on the eBook copy. Get in touch with us at customercare@packtpub.com for more details.

At www.packt.com, you can also read a collection of free technical articles, sign up for a range of free newsletters, and receive exclusive discounts and offers on Packt books and eBooks.

Other Books You May Enjoy

If you enjoyed this book, you may be interested in these other books by Packt:

Azure Data Factory Cookbook

Dmitry Anoshin, Dmitry Foshin, Roman Storchak, Xenia Ireton

ISBN: 978-1-80056-529-6

- Create an orchestration and transformation job in ADF
- Develop, execute, and monitor data flows using Azure Synapse
- Create big data pipelines using Azure Data Lake and ADF
- Build a machine learning app with Apache Spark and ADF
- Migrate on-premises SSIS jobs to ADF

- Integrate ADF with commonly used Azure services such as Azure ML, Azure Logic Apps, and Azure Functions

- Run big data compute jobs within HDInsight and Azure Databricks

- Copy data from AWS S3 and Google Cloud Storage to Azure Storage using ADF's built-in connectors

ETL with Azure Cookbook

Christian Cote, Matija Lah, Madina Saitakhmetova

ISBN: 978-1-80020-331-0

- Explore ETL and how it is different from ELT

- Move and transform various data sources with Azure ETL and ELT services

- Use SSIS 2019 with Azure HDInsight clusters

- Discover how to query SQL Server 2019 Big Data Clusters hosted in Azure

- Migrate SSIS solutions to Azure and solve key challenges associated with it

- Understand why data profiling is crucial and how to implement it in Azure Databricks

- Get to grips with BIML and learn how it applies to SSIS and Azure Data Factory solutions

Packt is searching for authors like you

If you're interested in becoming an author for Packt, please visit authors. packtpub.com and apply today. We have worked with thousands of developers and tech professionals, just like you, to help them share their insight with the global tech community. You can make a general application, apply for a specific hot topic that we are recruiting an author for, or submit your own idea.

Share Your Thoughts

Now you've finished *Azure Databricks Cookbook*, we'd love to hear your thoughts! Scan the QR code below to go straight to the Amazon review page for this book and share your feedback or leave a review on the site that you purchased it from.

https://packt.link/r/1-789-80971-1

Your review is important to us and the tech community and will help us make sure we're delivering excellent quality content.

Index

F

file types
   storage benefits 126-129
filters
   using 306-315

G

Ganglia reports
   using, for cluster health 412-416
GitHub
   for Azure Databricks notebook
      version control 337-341
   PR, creating 341, 342

I

input partitions
   learning 118-120

J

JavaScript Database Connectivity
   (JDBC) 252
JavaScript Object Notation (JSON) 247
JSON, including nested JSON
   data, reading from 88-92
   data, writing to 88-92

K

Kafka-enabled Event Hubs
   data, reading from 145-151
Kusto Query Language (KQL) 195

L

Log Analytics workspace
   creating 195-199
   integrating, with Azure
      Databricks 199-203
log files
   data, streaming from 151-155
lookup tables (LUTs) 263

M

massively parallel processing (MPP) 69
MetadataChangedException 225

N

native connectors
   used, for reading data from Azure
      SQL database 61-68
   used, for reading data from
      Azure Synapse SQL 69-76
   used, for writing data to Azure
      SQL database 61-68
   used, for writing data to Azure
      Synapse SQL 69-76
near-real-time analytics
   visualization and dashboard, creating
      in notebook for 277-282
   visualization, creating in
      Power BI for 282-286
notebook
   dashboard, creating for
      near-real-time analytics 277-282
   visualization, creating for
      near-real-time analytics 277-282

U

Uniform Resource Identifier (URI) 268
Uniform Resource Locator (URL) 39
user
  access to object, granting 298-300
  creating, in SQL Analytics 293-295
user interface (UI)
  cluster, creating from 19-22
  used, for creating Azure Key Vault
      to store secrets 177-181

V

VACUUM command 231
Virtual Network (VNet)
  Azure Databricks, deploying in 405-411
visualizations
  in SQL Analytics 315-318

W

Window aggregation
  on streaming data 162-167

Z

Z order 231

Made in United States
North Haven, CT
10 May 2023